PRAISE FOR
COMMON SENSE ON MUTUAL FUNDS

From Money Managers

"Cogent, honest and hard-hitting—a must read for every investor. Bogle does the American investor a real service by carrying on his crusade. Absolutely terrific, particularly Part IV, 'On Fund Management,' I hope some journalists and the SEC get energized after reading it."

Warren E. Buffett

"Jack Bogle is one of the great pioneer/visionaries of the investment business. In this book he shares his knowledge, experience, and judgment to enable us to become better investors. The final philosophical chapters provide some insights that may help some of us become better people."

Byron R. Wien
Chief U.S. Investment Strategist,
Morgan Stanley Dean Witter

"My good friend Jack Bogle has done it again by providing investors a road map for success. His message is clear, concise, and, most importantly, rational. In essence, he rightfully advocates, with supporting documentation, that investors should develop a plan based on a few simple principles, and then develop the necessary discipline to stick to it, and not be distracted by temporary transitory events. As we all know, the first part is easier than the second. To help in this regard, Jack puts in proper perspective some prevailing trends and attitudes likely to prove detrimental to the investor's well being. All of us should pay attention."

Arthur Zeikel
Chairman, Merrill Lynch Asset Management

"Written in his characteristic forthright and visionary style, Bogle penetrates the myths and jargon to shed a powerful light on the central issues that confront every investor, no matter what their level of experience or sophistication."

Martin L. Leibowitz
Vice Chairman and Chief Investment Officer,
TIAA-CREF

"Common sense at a fair price has always been Bogle's product and this book is no exception. Chapter 2, 'On the Nature of Returns: Occam's Razor' is worth the price of admission alone."

> William H. Gross
> Managing Director, Pacific Investment Management Co.

From Academia

"Buffett cannot teach you or me how to become a Warren Buffett. Bogle's reasoned precepts can enable a few million of us savers to become in twenty years the envy of our suburban neighbors—while at the same time we have slept well in these eventful times."

> Paul A. Samuelson
> Massachusetts Institute of Technology,
> Department of Economics

"Bogle's new book keeps the reader focused on what returns are possible in the long run by rightly confirming that recent stock trends cannot be sustained. And when markets return to normal, excessive fees will cost the investor dearly. Bogle's insights are truly the ingredients of successful investing. This book is marvelous—even better than *Bogle on Mutual Funds.*"

> Jeremy J. Siegel
> Author, *Stocks for the Long Run*
> The Wharton School, University of Pennsylvania
> Department of Finance

"The man who brought index funds and a universe of low-cost, consumer-oriented mutual funds to the American public now brings the wisdom and judgment of his half century of experience to the issues of investment management. *Common Sense on Mutual Funds* is a must read for all investors from the beginner to the portfolio manager."

> Burton G. Malkiel
> Author, *A Random Walk Down Wall Street*
> Princeton University,
> Department of Economics

"*Common Sense on Mutual Funds* offers an instructive collection of insightful and sometimes controversial essays on the nature of financial markets, investment returns, and mutual funds. When considered collectively, they present a simple consistent low cost investment philosophy for today's investors."

> Professor Jay O. Light
> Harvard Business School

From the Financial Community

"Superior in intellect, character, and performance, Jack Bogle is the quintessential model for money managers, and ranks among the best of his generation. He is an investment genius who defied conventional wisdom and proved his critics wrong. In *Common Sense on Mutual Funds*, Jack Bogle gives readers a glimpse of his genius. This is a book filled with a wealth of practical advice gleaned from the long-term investment strategy he perfected in creating the highly successful Vanguard Funds. This book is a must read for everyone interested in the world of investment."

> Hon. William E. Simon
> Former Secretary of the Treasury

"*Common Sense on Mutual Funds* marks the culmination of one of Wall Street's most inspired careers. Invoking both Thomas Paine and Benjamin Graham, Jack Bogle outlines a supremely logical plan not only to better investors' returns, but to improve the whole fund industry. This isn't just the best book yet by Bogle, it may well be the best book ever on mutual funds. Required reading for every fund investor, executive, or director. Bravo, Jack!"

> Don Phillips
> President & CEO, Morningstar, Inc.

"Jack Bogle still believes candor with investors, integrity in investing, and low cost are important. Thank goodness. Thank you, Jack. You are so right!"

> Charles D. Ellis
> Author, *Winning the Loser's Game*

"A book no investor—individual or professional—should miss. Jack Bogle guides us through the landmine that the investment world has become and reminds us just what investing is all about and shows how we can best succeed—as investors, as professionals. Thoughtful and provocative, *Common Sense on Mutual Funds* will open many eyes to the perils (and safe havens) of stock, bond, and global funds."

> Frank J. Fabozzi
> President, Frank J. Fabozzi Associates

"*Common Sense on Mutual Funds* explains how you can improve your returns for maximum results over the long term. Bogle gives practical advice on taxes, costs, and other mutual fund matters. This is a must read for the mutual fund investor."

> Michael Bloomberg
> Founder & CEO of Bloomberg, LP

From the Media

"I date my success as an investor from the day I met Jack Bogle and learned about index mutual funds. If you want to do better in the market, and really understand what you're doing, read this book."

Jane Bryant Quinn
Newsweek columnist and author,
Making the Most of Your Money

"After a lifetime of picking stocks, I have to admit that Bogle's arguments in favor of the index fund have me thinking of joining him rather than trying to beat him. Bogle's wisdom and his commonsense way of explaining things make this book indispensable reading for anyone trying to figure out how to invest in this crazy stock market."

James J. Cramer
Money manager and senior columnist for *TheStreet.com*

"With his customary clarity and candor, Bogle delivers a sophisticated book that will make you a smarter, richer, and perhaps most welcome of all, far calmer investor. Memorize his eight rules for fund investing right away. They will make and save you money."

Tyler Mathisen
Financial journalist

"A must read for anyone who invests in mutual funds. Bogle not only offers simple, strong advice that proves that common sense and mutual funds are not 'mutually' exclusive, he also tells us what's wrong with the industry and how to fix it. As usual, the man who invented the index fund as we know it (while other investment executives laughed) is ahead of his time."

Brenda L. Buttner
Contributing editor, *TheStreet.com*

"Jack Bogle has championed and served individual investors since before the popular concept of 'individual investor' existed."

David Gardner
Co-founder, The Motley Fool

COMMON SENSE

ON

MUTUAL FUNDS

COMMON SENSE
—— ON ——
MUTUAL FUNDS

New Imperatives for the Intelligent Investor

JOHN C. BOGLE

JOHN WILEY & SONS, INC.

New York ▪ Chichester ▪ Weinheim ▪ Brisbane ▪ Singapore ▪ Toronto

This book is printed on acid-free paper. ∞

Copyright © 1999 by John C. Bogle. All rights reserved.

Published by John Wiley & Sons, Inc.

Published simultaneously in Canada.

No part of this publication may be reproduced, stored in a retrieval system or transmitted in any form or by any means, electronic, mechanical, photocopying, recording, scanning or otherwise, except as permitted under Section 107 or 108 of the 1976 United States Copyright Act, without either the prior written permission of the Publisher, or authorization through payment of the appropriate per-copy fee to the Copyright Clearance Center, 222 Rosewood Drive, Danvers, MA 01923, (978) 750-8400, fax (978) 750-4744. Requests to the Publisher for permission should be addressed to the Permissions Department, John Wiley & Sons, Inc., 605 Third Avenue, New York, NY 10158-0012, (212) 850-6011, fax (212) 850-6008, E-Mail: PERMREQ @WILEY.COM.

This publication is designed to provide accurate and authoritative information in regard to the subject matter covered. It is sold with the understanding that the publisher is not engaged in rendering professional services. If professional advice or other expert assistance is required, the services of a competent professional person should be sought.

Library of Congress Cataloging-in-Publication Data:

Bogle, John C.

    Common sense on mutual finds : new imperatives for the intelligent investor / John C. Bogle.
        p.   cm.
    ISBN 0-471-29543-4 (cloth : alk. paper)
    1. Mutual funds. 2. Investments. I. Title.
HG4530.B633 1999
332.63'27—dc21   98-55377

Printed in the United States of America.

10 9 8 7 6 5 4 3

Dedicated to Walter L. Morgan
1898–1998

Founder of Wellington Fund, dean of the mutual fund industry,
fellow Princetonian, mentor, friend.

He gave me my first break. He remained loyal through thick and thin.
He gives me strength to carry on.

Foreword

Why This Book Is Unique

Jack Bogle has written a book on investing unlike any investment book that I have ever encountered because he discusses sensitive matters that other authors ignore. I hesitate to speculate on why these topics receive such short shrift elsewhere, but I suspect that other experts have horizons that are more limited than Bogle's, or they have less concern for their readers' best interests.

People often forget that Bogle is much more than an investment professional who is deadly serious about how individual investors should manage their hard-earned wealth. He is first and foremost a fabulously successful businessman who has built one of the great mutual fund empires with skill and determination, always driving it in the direction of the vision that inspired him when he launched forth on this adventure many years ago. Readers of this book are therefore treated to a unique and unvarnished exposure of the nature of the mutual fund world and how it affects their pocketbooks.

Despite all the high-minded talk we hear from the corporate spinmasters, conflict of interest between seller and buyer is inherent in our economic system. Jack Bogle's goal was to build a business whose primary objective was to make money for his customers by minimizing the elements of that conflict of interest, but at the same time to be so successful that it would be able to continue to grow and sustain itself. That has been no easy task. The complexity of the job that Bogle set out for himself, however, has enabled him to look at the competition with a very special kind of eye. One of the loud and clear messages in this book is that he is less than pleased with what that eye sees.

We must look at the investment management industry (yes, it is an industry even more than it is a profession) as a *business* and within the framework of the economic system as a whole. The investment management business is extraordinarily profitable. As such, it responds to the iron law of capitalism that capital will flow to those areas where the expected return is the highest. Over the past ten years, the number of mutual funds has increased from 2,710 to 6,870, and the number of investment managers has exploded from 1,260 to 5,810. On the other hand, investment management defies the rest of the iron law of capitalism, which is that the very process by which high returns attract new capital inevitably brings down the rate of return as new competitors strive to take market share away from the old. Joseph Schumpeter, in a famous aphorism, referred to this process as "creative destruction." It is the essence of why our economic system has been so successful and why, despite its many glaring flaws, it continues to command such wide public acceptance.

Investment management firms never heard of such a thing. The growth in the number of managers far exceeds the rate of growth in the number of customers they serve. Willy-nilly, more and more people enter the field without in any way diminishing the profitability of those who have established themselves. Occasionally a startup will fail to make it or an established firm goofs up in some horrible fashion and disappears from the scene, but the great mass of investment managers go right on earning a return on their own capital that most other industries can only envy.

Bogle's skill in dispensing uncommon wisdom about how to invest and how to understand the capital markets would be reason enough to read these pages. But the big message in this book is that what happens to the wealth of individual investors cannot be separated from the structure of the industry that manages those assets. Bogle's insight into what that structure means to the fortunes of the individuals whose welfare concerns him so deeply is what makes this book most rewarding. It is not only fun to read: It has a big payoff as well.

PETER L. BERNSTEIN

Preface

In writing this book, my objective is to accomplish two goals: first, to help readers become more successful investors, and second, to chart a course for change in the mutual fund industry. My first objective is familiar terrain. In *Bogle on Mutual Funds*, published in 1993, I set forth a commonsense approach to developing a sound investment program through mutual funds. Similarly, this book focuses exclusively on mutual funds, for I believe that a widely diversified portfolio of stocks and bonds is essential to long-term investing. For nearly all investors, the most sensible and efficient way to diversify is through mutual funds. *Common Sense on Mutual Funds*, however, even as it covers some of the same ideas as my previous book, addresses the significant changes in the investment landscape that have since taken place.

My second objective marks new literary, if not professional, terrain for me. In the past decade, as strong financial markets have made mutual funds the investment of choice for millions of shareholders, the industry has embraced practices that threaten to diminish seriously their chances of successful long-term investing. Amid the mutual fund industry's disorienting promotional din, *Common Sense on Mutual Funds* identifies these practices and presents simple principles for implementing a sound investment program. These investment principles also form the basis for my call for industry change. If mutual funds are to remain the investment of choice for America's families, change is imperative.

It is time for investors to examine these issues. Mutual fund shareholders are now 50 million strong, and their ranks are growing rapidly. Industry assets exceed $5 trillion, compared with $1 trillion when the 1990s began. Mutual funds have assumed an increasingly central role in our financial lives; for most investors, they represent the best hope of reaching important goals such as a secure retirement. It is imperative that we consider the issues that will determine the success of fund shareholders and the fund industry in the coming century.

This is a book with a strong point of view. Its point of view is increasingly endorsed by mutual fund investors, but only rarely endorsed by other fund industry leaders, at least in their public pronouncements. Indeed, my position more likely receives negative responses: grudging acceptance, marked skepticism, downright opposition, and even bitter denunciation.

Because my position is a minority view in this industry—perhaps even a minority-of-one among industry leaders—I can rely only on common sense and sound reason as I seek its acceptance. I have relied heavily on a careful analysis of the facts as they appear in the historical record. History is only history, so I have explained not only *how* my investment philosophy has worked in the past, but *why* it has worked. The investment theories set forth in this book have worked in practice simply because both common sense and elementary logic dictate that they *must* work. Indeed, intelligent investing turns out to be little more than common sense and sound reason. The sooner investors realize that elemental principle, the better will be their ability to accumulate the maximum possible amount of capital for their financial security. Indeed, I chose the subtitle of my book to convey the timeliness of the principles I shall express: *New Imperatives for the Intelligent Investor.* Time is indeed money for fund shareholders.

"Common Sense" Defined

The Second Edition of the *Oxford English Dictionary* (OED II) captures the essence of these principles in its definition of common sense: "The endowment of natural intelligence possessed by rational beings . . . the plain wisdom which is every man's inheritance . . . good sound practical sense." Throughout this book, I try to honor these qualities, confident that plain-spoken reason makes not only a powerful case for common sense in mutual fund investing, but a persuasive argument for change in the mutual fund industry as well. The OED II also offers this fitting citation, published by *The Times* of London in 1888: "The general demand was for intelligence, sagacity, soundness of judgment, clearness of perception, and that sanity of thinking called common sense." I believe that mutual fund investors will eventually make this same demand, and that it will become increasingly imperative as the ranks of fund shareholders, and the level of assets invested in mutual funds, continue to grow.

I chose the title *Common Sense on Mutual Funds* not only to emphasize the importance of common sense as it is defined by the foregoing words, but also because "Common Sense" is the title of a remarkable tract written in 1776. The author, Thomas Paine, a Philadelphian and one of America's Founding Fathers, was eager to end the governance of the American colonies by George III of Great Britain. Perhaps more than any other man, this author set the stage for the American Revolution. In the opening paragraph of the first of four pamphlets that were to constitute "Common Sense," Thomas Paine acknowledged the challenge he was facing:

> *Perhaps the sentiments contained in the following pages are not yet sufficiently fashionable to procure them general favor; a long habit of not thinking a thing wrong, gives it a superficial appearance of being right, and raises at first a formidable outcry in defense of custom. But the tumult soon subsides. Time makes more converts than reason.*

My sentiments about this industry, too, "are not yet sufficiently fashionable to procure them general favor." Nonetheless, I believe that the formidable consensus that exists today in accepting without question the status quo of the mutual fund industry will soon subside. But I expect that it will take both time *and* reason to make converts, and that common sense will eventually prompt the conversion.

And so I ask you, dear reader, to bear with me as you explore new and important ways both of investing successfully in mutual funds, and of thinking about the mutual fund industry. I offer these ideas in the same sense that Thomas Paine offered his ideas:

> *In the following pages, I offer nothing more than simple facts, plain arguments, and common sense; and have no other preliminaries to settle with the reader, than that he will divest himself of prejudice and prepossession, and suffer his reason and his feelings to determine for themselves; that he will put on, or rather that he will not put off, the true character of a man, and generously enlarge his views beyond the present day.*

A FIVE-PART APPROACH

The book is divided into five distinct parts. The first three are devoted to the examination of commonsense principles in the three prime areas that should most concern investors in the establishment of their mutual fund portfolios: investment strategy, investment selection, and investment performance. Part I, "On Investment Strategy," emphasizes the need for a long-term focus, an understanding of the nature of the returns earned in the stock and bond markets, and the important role of asset allocation in investors' portfolios. Each chapter in this section leads to the conclusion that common sense and simplicity are the keys to financial success. The same conclusion holds in Part II, "On Investment Choices," in which I first cover index mutual funds and then describe choices among individual stock and bond funds and among various investment styles in each category. I also explore global investing in some depth, emphasizing the additional risks entailed in that strategy, but again finding that common sense carries the day. I reach the same finding when I discuss the search for the "Holy Grail"—mutual funds that provide predictably superior returns. Part III, "On Investment Performance," includes some sobering reminders of challenging investment realities, including the profound—but rarely discussed—tendency of past fund returns and past financial market returns, whether high or low, to revert to long-term norms in the future. I also discuss the current, but dubious, focus on short-term relative (rather than long-term absolute) returns, the surprisingly negative implications of fund asset growth, and the extraordinary tax-inefficiency of most mutual funds. Part III concludes with a study of the vital role played by time: it enhances returns, reduces risks, and magnifies the baneful impact of investment costs as well.

Many readers will find the content of the final two parts surprising in a book about successful investing in mutual funds. Were it not for the fact that the issues discussed in Part IV, "On Fund Management," are a major cause of the generally inadequate fund returns discussed in earlier chapters, they would indeed be inappropriate here. But this industry has moved away from its traditional principles. Its focus today is on marketing rather than management, and it often uses today's wondrous information technology in ways that are detrimental to investors. All told, the interests of fund shareholders are not being well served. The root of the problem, I suggest, lies with mutual fund governance and the industry's peculiar operating structure, in which fund directors delegate all of a fund's operations to an external management company. Again, I point to common sense and simplicity as the solutions to these problems; one option would be a restructuring of the industry so that it could far better serve mutual fund investors. Recognizing, however, that even the best corporate structures inevitably reflect the values of the individuals who constitute the corporation, in Part V, "On Spirit," I take the liberty of discussing my personal experience in the entrepreneurship and leadership involved in the establishment of a major, but uniquely structured, mutual fund firm. I then conclude the book with a presentation of some reactions from some of those human beings who have served in that unique environment, and those who have been served by it.

Before we proceed further, a few words about this book. Although I have organized the chapters to be read consecutively, with the later material building on principles established earlier in the book, my goal has been to make each chapter a free-standing and independent essay on a particular issue. Thus, it was sometimes necessary to reiterate certain themes and statistics. This reinforcement, I hope, will be more than compensated for by the convenience of enabling the reader to focus on particular issues as interest and time dictate. Portions of these chapters may be familiar to some readers, for some of these themes, first tested in speeches or in journals or magazines, have been more fully developed here. However, much of the material appears here for the first time in any form.

COMMON SENSE REDUX

Despite the fact that the commonsense investment principles and the commonsense principles of industry structure that I express in the coming pages are, like the arguments expressed by Thomas Paine, "not yet sufficiently fashionable to procure them general favor," I hope that readers will not fall back on a "formidable outcry in defense of custom." Paine's impassioned arguments—backed by little more than common sense—finally met with the favor of the citizens of the colonies, and the American Revolution ensued, even as I hope that my commonsense arguments will soon meet with the favor of mutual fund investors.

Common Sense on Mutual Funds will demonstrate that the ills and injustices suffered by mutual fund investors are not dissimilar to those our forebears suffered under English tyranny. The mutual fund industry is rife with "taxation without representation" in the form of the high fees charged by fund managers, facilitated by boards of directors that acquiesce to counter-productive management policies and excessive fees, with inadequate consideration of their powerful negative impact on the returns earned by fund shareholders. Fund shareholders, like the citizens of the American colonies, should be responsible for their own governance.

As Thomas Paine pointed out, "The king is not to be trusted without being looked after . . . a thirst for absolute power is the natural disease of monarchy." Mutual fund management companies seem to have gained the power of kings in ruling the investments of the fund shareholders. If the English aristocracy in the eighteenth century was acceding to the king's every whim, cannot the same be said of fund boards of directors? I have no quarrel with management companies' focusing on their own profits. But the trade-off between the profits that accrue to fund shareholders and the profits that accrue to the fund management companies seems subject to no effective independent watchdog or balance wheel, despite the fact that the shareholders actually *own* the mutual funds. As in every other corporation in America, they ought to control them too.

PRINCIPLES AND PRACTICES

Mutual fund investors should return—and insist that the funds that they own return—to the sound investment principles and practices that are described in the first three parts of this book. And because the corporate structure of the industry has given rise to the abandonment of those investment principles and practices, fund investors should insist that mutual funds alter their organizational structures to mend the rift between ownership and control that exists today. In a commonsense manner, I have tried to reason through these issues with you, in the hope that the returns you earn on the assets you have entrusted to mutual funds will be meaningfully enhanced.

You haven't quite heard the last word from Thomas Paine. As you reflect on the critical issues discussed in this book, without doubt you will think some of them strange to contemplate and difficult of accomplishment. So it was, too, in 1776, when Paine concluded the fourth pamphlet of "Common Sense" with these words:

> *These proceedings may at first appear strange and difficult; but, like all other steps which we have already passed over, will in a little time become familiar and agreeable; and, until an independence is declared, the Continent will feel itself like a man who continues putting off some unpleasant business from day to day, yet knows it must be done, hates to set about it, wishes it over, and is continually haunted with the thoughts of its necessity.*

I am under no illusions. It won't be easy, and surely won't be fully accomplished in my lifetime. But I hardly need to remind you, using Thomas

Paine's most famous words, written one year before General George Washington's battered army bivouacked in Valley Forge, enduring the bitter winter of 1777–1778: "These are the times that try men's souls . . . 'Tis the business of little minds to shrink; but he whose heart is firm, and whose conscience approves his conduct, will pursue his principles unto death . . . Tyranny, like hell, is not easily conquered, yet the harder the conflict, the more glorious the triumph."

JOHN C. BOGLE

Valley Forge, Pennsylvania
February 1999

Acknowledgments

To acknowledge all of those who contributed to this book is no mean task. I begin by recognizing some of the writers whose intellects have helped to nourish my thinking about investing, beginning with Dr. Paul Samuelson, whose textbook I read at Princeton University in 1948, followed by (in the approximate order of my readings) Adam Smith, John Maynard Keynes, Charles Ellis, Dr. William Sharpe, Peter Bernstein, Warren Buffett, Arthur Zeikel, Byron Wien, and Jeremy Siegel.

If the minds of these men helped me to develop the intellectual framework for the book (though they may not agree with all I've written), several more fine minds helped turn my first draft into what I hope is a well-finished final manuscript. Princeton Professor Burton G. Malkiel, *Money* magazine associate editor Jason Zweig, and Vanguard principals Craig Stock and James M. Norris were generous with their time and unsparing with their comments, although I accept full responsibility for the book in its final form.

The most important role of all, however, was played by Andrew S. Clarke, assistant to the senior chairman of Vanguard (forgive the third-person formulation), who provided consistent and timely support in developing the myriad statistics and graphs, helped to edit portions of the book, and translated my own scribbled editorial changes into a text that the printers could follow. Andy came to Vanguard from Morningstar less than two years ago, and has served with me but a year. Now he has experienced his baptism by fire and has exceeded my highest expectations.

Andy picked up the cudgels from Walter H. Lenhard, my previous aide, who had already invested considerable effort on the data in many of the chapters, and I remain deeply in his debt. I'm also indebted to others at Vanguard who provided commentary and assistance along the way, including John S. Woerth, Mortimer J. Buckley, Gus Sauter (especially on the index fund chapter), and Mary Lowe Kennedy; and at John Wiley & Sons, Pamela van Giessen, who played the key role as we worked through the book's development, editing, and publication. Finally, Emily A. Snyder, my long-time assistant and good right arm, and a paragon of patience and loyalty, did far more than her fair share as the book developed from an idea into what you now have before you.

Outside of the world of mutual funds, I also acknowledge the incredible support of my guardian angels at Philadelphia's Hahnemann Hospital, led by Susan C. Brozena, M.D., F.A.C.C. Receiving a heart transplant just three years ago was truly a miracle, one without which this book would never have come into existence. My highest hope is that the human beings who own mutual fund shares in America will be well served by the continuation of my career made possible by my second chance at life.

Finally, my deepest appreciation to my beloved wife, Eve, who stoically endured the countless hours I've spent in bringing this task to completion, all the while hoping that I would, finally, after a near half-century career in the mutual fund industry, slow down a bit. While that time has not yet come, I promise her that no deadlines will be set for my next book.

JOHN C. BOGLE

Contents

PART V

On Spirit

PART I

ON INVESTMENT STRATEGY

Investment strategy is the first issue that investors should consider. At the outset, investing is an act of faith, a willingness to postpone present consumption and save for the future. Investing for the long term is central to the achievement of optimal returns by investors. Unfortunately, the principle of investing for the long term—eschewing funds with high turnover portfolios and holding shares in soundly managed funds as investments for a lifetime—is honored more in the breach than in the observance by most mutual fund managers and shareholders.

To bring the advantages of long-term investing into focus, I examine here the historical returns, and *risks*, that have characterized the U.S. stock and bond markets, as well as the sources of those returns: (1) fundamentals represented by earnings and dividends, and (2) speculation, represented by wide swings in the market's valuation of these fundamentals. The first factor tends to be reliable and sustainable over the long pull; the second is both episodic and spasmodic. These lessons of history are central to the understanding of investing.

This discussion of returns and risks serves as a background for a discussion of asset allocation, now conceded by virtually all thoughtful observers to be by far the most important single decision in shaping the long-term returns earned by investors. Finally, I deal with the paradox that, more than ever in these days of complexity, simplicity underlies the best investment strategies.

CHAPTER 1

ON LONG-TERM INVESTING
CHANCE AND THE GARDEN

*I*nvesting is an act of faith. We entrust our capital to corporate stewards in the faith—at least with the hope—that their efforts will generate high rates of return on our investments. When we purchase corporate America's stocks and bonds, we are professing our faith that the long-term success of the U.S. economy and the nation's financial markets will continue in the future.

When we invest in a mutual fund, we are expressing our faith that the professional managers of the fund will be vigilant stewards of the assets we entrust to them. We are also recognizing the value of diversification by spreading our investments over a large number of stocks and bonds. A diversified portfolio minimizes the risk inherent in owning any individual security by shifting that risk to the level of the stock and bond markets.

Americans' faith in investing has waxed and waned, kindled by bull markets and chilled by bear markets, but it has remained intact. It has survived the Great Depression, two world wars, the rise and fall of communism, and a barrage of unnerving changes: booms and bankruptcies, inflation and deflation, shocks in commodity prices, the revolution in information technology, and the globalization of financial markets. In recent years, our faith has been enhanced—perhaps excessively so—by the bull market in stocks that began in 1982 and has accelerated, without significant interruption, toward the century's end. As we approach the millennium, confidence in equities is at an all-time high.

Chance, the Garden, and Long-Term Investing

Might some unforeseeable economic shock trigger another depression so severe that it would destroy our faith in the promise of investing? Perhaps. Excessive confidence in smooth seas can blind us to the risk of storms. History is replete with episodes in which the enthusiasm of investors has driven equity prices to—and even beyond—the point at which they are swept into a whirlwind of speculation, leading to unexpected losses. There is little certainty in investing. As long-term investors, however, we cannot afford to let the apocalyptic possibilities frighten us away from the markets. For without risk there is no return.

Another word for "risk" is "chance." And in today's high-flying, fast-changing, complex world, the story of Chance the gardener contains an inspirational message for long-term investors. The seasons of his garden find a parallel in the cycles of the economy and the financial markets, and we can emulate his faith that their patterns of the past will define their course in the future.

Chance is a man who has grown to middle age living in a solitary room in a rich man's mansion, bereft of contact with other human beings. He has two all-consuming interests: watching television and tending the garden outside his room. When the mansion's owner dies, Chance wanders out on his first foray into the world. He is hit by the limousine of a powerful industrialist who is an adviser to the President. When he is rushed to the industrialist's estate for medical care, he identifies himself only as "Chance the gardener." In the confusion, his name quickly becomes "Chauncey Gardiner."

When the President visits the industrialist, the recuperating Chance sits in on the meeting. The economy is slumping; America's blue-chip corporations are under stress; the stock market is crashing. Unexpectedly, Chance is asked for his advice:

> *Chance shrank. He felt the roots of his thoughts had been suddenly yanked out of their wet earth and thrust, tangled, into the unfriendly air. He stared at the carpet. Finally, he spoke: "In a garden," he said, "growth has its season. There are spring and summer, but there are also fall and winter. And then spring and summer again. As long as the roots are not severed, all is well and all will be well."*

He slowly raises his eyes, and sees that the President seems quietly pleased—indeed, delighted—by his response.

> *"I must admit, Mr. Gardiner, that is one of the most refreshing and optimistic statements I've heard in a very, very long time. Many of us forget that nature and society are one. Like nature, our economic system remains, in the long run, stable and rational, and that's why we must not fear to be at its mercy. . . . We welcome the inevitable seasons of nature, yet we are upset by the seasons of our economy! How foolish of us."[1]*

This story is not of my making. It is a brief summary of the early chapters of Jerzy Kosinski's novel *Being There*, which was made into a memorable film starring the late Peter Sellers. Like Chance, I am basically an optimist. I see our economy as healthy and stable. It is still marked by seasons of growth and seasons of decline, but its roots have remained strong. Despite the changing seasons, our economy has persisted in an upward course, rebounding from the blackest calamities.

Figure 1.1 chronicles our economy's growth in the twentieth century. Even in the darkest days of the Great Depression, faith in the future has been rewarded. From 1929 to 1933, the nation's economic output declined by a cumulative 27 percent. Recovery followed, however, and our economy expanded by a cumulative 50 percent through the rest of the 1930s. From

FIGURE 1.1

Real Gross National Product, 1992 Dollars (1900–1998)

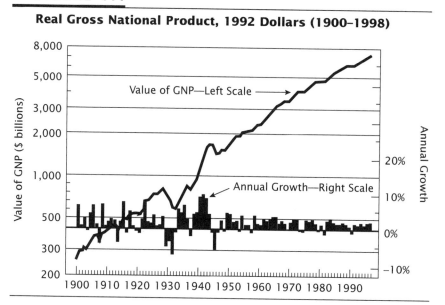

1944 to 1947, when the economic infrastructure designed for the Second World War had to be adapted to the peacetime production of goods and services, the U.S. economy tumbled into a short but sharp period of contraction, with output shrinking by 13 percent. But we then entered a season of growth, and within four years had recovered all of the lost output. In the past five decades, our economy has evolved from a capital-intensive industrial economy, keenly sensitive to the rhythms of the business cycle, to an enormous service economy, less susceptible to extremes of boom and bust.

Long-term growth, at least in the United States, seems to have defined the course of economic events. Our real gross national product (GNP) has risen, on average, 3½ percent annually during the twentieth century, and 2.9 percent annually in the half-century following the end of World War II—what might be called the modern economic era. We will inevitably continue to experience seasons of decline, but we can be confident that they will be succeeded by the reappearance of the long-term pattern of growth.

Within the repeated cycle of colorful autumns, barren winters, verdant springs, and warm summers, the stock market has also traced a rising secular trajectory. In this chapter, I review the long-term returns and risks of the most important investment assets: stocks and bonds. The historical record contains lessons that form the basis of successful investment strategy. I hope to show that the historical data support one conclusion with unusual force: *To invest with success, you must be a long-term investor.* The stock and bond markets are unpredictable on a short-term basis, but their long-term patterns of risk and return have proved durable enough to serve as the basis for a long-term strategy that leads to investment success. Although there is no guarantee that these patterns of the past, no matter how deeply ingrained in the historical record, will prevail in the future, a study of the past, accompanied by a self-administered dose of common sense, is the intelligent investor's best recourse.

The alternative to long-term investing is a short-term approach to the stock and bond markets. Countless examples from the financial media and the actual practices of professional and individual investors demonstrate that short-term investment strategies are inherently dangerous. In these current ebullient times, large numbers of investors are subordinating the principles of sound long-term investing to the frenetic short-term action that pervades our financial markets. Their counterproductive attempts to trade stocks and funds for short-term advantage, and to time the market (jumping aboard when the market is expected to rise, bailing out in anticipation of a decline), are resulting in the rapid turnover of investment portfolios that ought to be designed to seek long-term goals. We are not able to control our investment returns, but a long-term investment program, fortified by faith in the future, benefits from careful attention to those elements of investing that *are* within our power to control: risk, cost, and time.

HOW HAS OUR GARDEN GROWN?

In reviewing the long-term history of stock and bond returns, I rely heavily on the work of Professor Jeremy J. Siegel, of the Wharton School of the University of Pennsylvania. This material is somewhat detailed, but it deserves careful study, for it provides a powerful case for long-term investing. As Chance might say, the garden represented by our financial markets offers many opportunities for investments to flower. Figure 1.2, created by Professor Siegel for his fine book *Stocks for the Long Run*,[2] demonstrates that stocks have provided the highest rate of return among

FIGURE 1.2

Total Real Return on $10,000 Initial Investment (1802–1997)

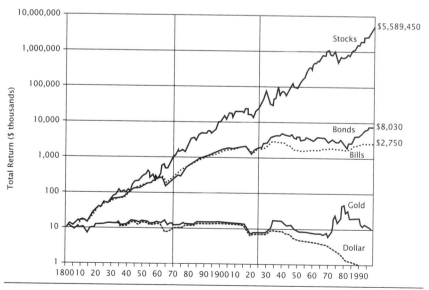

the major categories of financial assets: stocks, bonds, U.S. Treasury bills, and gold. This graph covers the entire history of the American stock market, from 1802 to 1997. An initial investment of $10,000 in stocks, from 1802 on, with all dividends reinvested (and ignoring taxes) would have resulted in a terminal value of $5.6 *billion* in real dollars (after adjustment for inflation). The same initial investment in long-term U.S. government bonds, again reinvesting all interest income, would have yielded a little more than $8 *million*. Stocks grew at a real rate of 7 percent annually; bonds, at a rate of 3.5 percent. The significant advantage in annual return (compounded over the entire period) exhibited by stocks results in an extraordinary difference in terminal value, at least for an investor with a time horizon of 196 years—long-term investing approaching Methuselan proportions.*

Since the early days of our securities markets, returns on stocks have proved to be consistent in each of three extended periods studied by Professor Siegel. The first period was from 1802 to 1870 when, Siegel notes, "the U.S. made a transition from an agrarian to an industrialized economy."[3] In the second period, from 1871 to 1925, the United States became an important global economic and political power. And the third period, from 1926 to the present, is generally regarded as the history of the modern stock market.†

These long-term data cover solely the financial markets of the United States. (Most studies show that stocks in other nations have provided lower returns and far higher risks.) In the early years, the data are based on fragmentary evidence of returns, subject to considerable bias through their focus on large corporations that survived, and derived from equity markets that were far different from today's in character and size (with, for example, no solid evidence of corporate earnings comparable to those reported under today's rigorous and transparent accounting standards). The returns reported for the early 1800s were based largely on bank stocks; for the post-Civil War era, on railroad stocks; and, as recently as the beginning of the twentieth century, on commodity stocks, including several major firms in the rope, twine, and leather business. Of the twelve stocks originally listed in the Dow Jones Industrial Average, General Electric

---

*Methuselah, a biblical forebear of Noah, reputedly lived for 969 years—time enough, no doubt, to develop a unique perspective on the seasons and cycles of the economy and its financial markets.

†The data for the first period are somewhat anecdotal. For the second period, they are based on a 1938 study by the Cowles Commission, a respected independent study group. The third period covers the entire history of the highly respected Standard & Poor's indexes.

alone has survived. But equity markets do have certain persistent characteristics. In each of the three periods examined by Professor Siegel, the
U.S. stock market demonstrated a tendency to provide real (after-inflation)
returns that surrounded a norm of about 7 percent, somewhat lower from
1871 to 1925, and somewhat higher in the modern era.

In the bond market, Professor Siegel examined the returns of long-
term U.S. government bonds, which still serve as a benchmark for the performance of fixed-income investments. The long-term real return on
bonds averaged 3.5 percent. But, in contrast with the remarkably stable
long-term real returns provided by the stock market, bond market real
returns were quite variable from period to period, averaging 4.8 percent
during the first two periods, but falling to 2.0 percent during the third.
Bond returns were especially volatile and unpredictable during the latter
half of the twentieth century.

STOCK MARKET RETURNS

Let's look first at the stock market. Table 1.1 contains two columns of
stock market returns: nominal returns and real returns. The higher figures are nominal returns. Nominal returns are unadjusted for inflation.
Real returns are corrected for inflation and are thus a more accurate reflection of the growth in an investor's purchasing power. Because the goal
of investing is to accumulate real wealth—an enhanced ability to pay for
goods and services—the ultimate focus of the long-term investor must be
on real, not nominal, returns.

In the stock market's early years, there was little difference between
nominal returns and real returns. In the first period (with its more dubious

TABLE 1.1

Average Annual Stock Market Returns (1802–1997)

	Total Nominal Return %	Consumer Price Inflation	Total Real Return %
1802–1870	7.1	0.1	7.0
1871–1925	7.2	0.6	6.6
1926–1997	10.6	3.1	7.2
1802–1997	8.4	1.3	7.0
1982–1997	16.7	3.4	12.8

provenance), from 1802 to 1870, inflation appears to have been 0.1 percent annually, so the real return was only one-tenth of a percentage point lower than the nominal stock market return of 7.1 percent.

Inflation remained at an extremely low level through most of the nineteenth century. In the stock market's second major period, 1871 to 1925, returns were almost identical to those in the first period, although the rate of inflation accelerated sharply in the later years. Nominal stock market returns compounded at an annual rate of 7.2 percent, while the real rate of return was 6.6 percent. The difference was accounted for by annual inflation averaging 0.6 percent.

In the modern era, the rate of inflation has accelerated dramatically, averaging 3.1 percent annually, and the gap between real and nominal returns has widened accordingly. Since 1926, the stock market has provided a nominal annual return of 10.6 percent and an inflation-adjusted return of 7.2 percent. Since the Second World War, inflation has been especially high. From 1966 to 1981, for example, inflation surged to an annual rate of 7.0 percent. Nominal stock market returns of 6.6 percent annually were in fact negative real returns of –0.4 percent. More recently, inflation has subsided. From 1982 to 1997, during substantially all of the long-running bull market, real returns averaged 12.8 percent, approaching the highest return for any period of comparable length in U.S. history (14.2 percent in 1865–1880).

The high rate of inflation in our modern era is in large part the result of our nation's switch from a gold-based monetary system to a paper-based system. Under the gold standard, each dollar in circulation was convertible into a fixed amount of gold. Under our modern paper-based system, in which the dollar is backed by nothing more (or less) than the public's collective confidence in its value, there are far fewer constraints on the U.S. government's ability to create new dollars. On occasion, rapid growth in the money supply has unleashed bouts of rapid price inflation. The effect on real long-term stock returns has nonetheless proved neutral. Even as nominal returns have risen in line with inflation, the rate of real return has remained steady at about 7.0 percent, much as it did through the nineteenth century.

Stock Market Risk

Although the stock market's real rate of return has apparently been remarkably steady over long periods, the rate has been subject to considerable variation from year to year. To measure the volatility of these returns, we use the standard deviation of annual returns. Table 1.2 presents the year-to-year volatility of returns in each of the three major periods of stock market history and since 1982. It also presents the all-time high and low annual returns in each period. From 1802 to 1870, returns varied from the 7 percent average by a standard deviation of 16.9 percent; in other words, real returns fell within a range of −9.9 percent to +23.9 percent about two-thirds of the time. From 1871 to 1925, the standard deviation of returns was 16.8 percent, almost unchanged from the first period. In the modern era, 1926 to the present, the standard deviation of returns has risen to 20.4 percent. As Table 1.2 indicates, annual stock returns can, of course, fall beyond the ranges described by their standard deviations. The stock market's all-time high, reached in 1862, was a real return of 66.6 percent. The all-time low, recorded in 1931, was a real return of −38.6 percent. Plainly, the tidy patterns that are evident in a sweeping history of the stock market's real returns tell little about the return an investor can expect to earn in any given year.

Nonetheless, these wide variations tend to decline sharply over time. Figure 1.3 shows that the one-year standard deviation of 18.1 percent *drops by more than half*, to 7.5 percent, over just five years. It is cut nearly in half *again*, to 4.4 percent, over 10 years. Though most of the sting of volatility has been eliminated after a decade, it continues to decline as the period lengthens, until it reaches just 1.0 percent over an investment lifetime of 50 years, with an upper range of return of 7.7 percent and a lower range of

TABLE 1.2

Annual Stock Market Volatility (1802–1997)

	Standard Deviation of Real Annual Return	Highest Annual Real Return %	Lowest Annual Real Return %
1802–1870	16.9	66.6	−29.9
1871–1925	16.8	56.1	−31.2
1926–1997	20.4	57.1	−38.6
1802–1997	18.1	66.6	−38.6
1982–1997	13.2	31.0	−11.5

STANDARD DEVIATION: WHAT IS IT?

Standard deviation is the accepted academic measure of variability; it expresses the range of an investment's returns over a given time period. For example, if an investment has earned an average annual return of 10 percent, and two-thirds of its annual returns have ranged between –5 percent and +25 percent—a range of 15 percentage points in either direction—one standard deviation is defined as 15. Two standard deviations is defined as the range that would include 95 percent of the annual returns.

FIGURE 1.3

Range of Stock Market Annual Returns

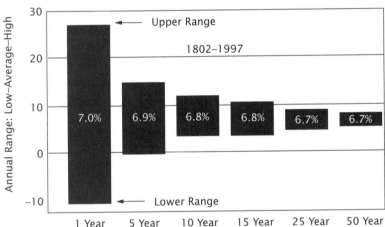

Standard Deviation of Returns (%)					
	1 Year	5 Year	10 Year	15 Year	25 Year	50 Year
Upper Range	25.1	14.4	11.2	10.3	8.7	7.7
Lower Range	–11.1	–0.6	2.4	3.4	4.7	5.7
Standard Deviation	18.1	7.5	4.4	3.3	2.0	1.0

5.7 percent. *The longer the time horizon, the less the variability in average annual returns.* Investors should not underestimate their time horizons. An investor who begins contributing to a retirement plan at age 25, and then, in retirement, draws on the accumulated capital until age 75 and beyond, would have an investment lifetime of 50 years or more. Our colleges, universities, and many other durable institutions have essentially unlimited time horizons.

BOND MARKET RETURNS

In the bond market, perhaps surprisingly, historical returns are far less consistent than stock returns. Since 1802, U.S. Treasury long-term bonds have generated real returns of 3.5 percent per year. During that time, however, as shown in Table 1.3, returns have been subject to considerable variability. From 1802 to 1870, average annual real returns on long-term U.S. Treasury bonds amounted to 4.8 percent. From 1871 to 1925, the average was 3.7 percent. But from 1926 forward, long-term Treasury bonds earned a real return of only 2.0 percent. In the shorter periods that make up the post-World War II era, real bond returns have been especially inconsistent. From 1966 to 1981, annual real returns were negative: −4.2 percent. The picture was then completely reversed from 1982 to 1997, when the bond market generated annual real returns of 9.6 percent, an exceptionally generous return, albeit one that pales somewhat in comparison to the stock market's powerful real return of 12.8 percent during the same period.

TABLE 1.3

Average Annual Bond Market Returns—Long-Term Government Bonds (1802–1997)

	Total Nominal Return %	Consumer Price Inflation	Total Real Return %
1802–1870	4.9	0.1	4.8
1871–1925	4.3	0.6	3.7
1926–1997	5.2	3.1	2.0
1802–1997	4.8	1.3	3.5
1982–1997	13.4	3.4	9.6

A CAUTION ABOUT LONG-TERM HISTORICAL RETURNS

This discussion about long-term investing relies heavily on the *average* long-term returns achieved by stocks and bonds. But investors should be mindful that the use of averages tends to minimize the wide variations that have inevitably existed throughout history. As Stephen Jay Gould put it in *Full House: The Spread of Excellence from Plato to Darwin:* "Variation stands as the fundamental reality and calculated averages become abstractions." Gould's quotation was cited in a recent report by economist–author Peter Bernstein,[4] who added this marvelous reminder:

> Long-run averages gleam like beacons, or perhaps like sirens, continually luring the investor to a long-run future that is expected to resemble these average returns, more or less. [The wide variations in returns that take place in the interim] tend to diminish over the long run, and so average returns define our expectations.
>
> But these variations are not a pool of inconsequential happenstances, nor are the individual episodes a set of accidents. Each episode is equally telling and significant in helping us understand how markets function. Each episode is also the consequence of the preceding episode—and you can define "episode" as everything from what happened yesterday to what happened last quarter to what happened seventy or a hundred years ago.

Bernstein then cites these blunt comments from an article in *The Journal of Portfolio Management* by Laurence Siegel, treasurer of the Ford Foundation:

> Risk is not short-term volatility, for the long-term investor can afford to ignore that. Rather, because there is no predestined rate of return, only an expected one that may not be realized, *the risk is the possibility that, in the long run, stock returns will be terrible.*

These comments provide a healthy reminder of the uncertainty of future returns in the financial markets. But they hardly vitiate my central message: Focusing on the long term is far superior to focusing on the short term. It is a lesson too few investors have learned.

Bond Market Risk

Hand in hand with their lower returns, bonds have generally come with less risk than stocks. Table 1.4 presents the standard deviation of bond returns and the annual high and low returns in the three major investment periods and in the long-term market since 1982. Since 1802, the average annual standard deviation of bond returns has been 8.8 percent—less than half the standard deviation for stocks. From 1802 to 1870, the standard deviation of bond returns was a modest 8.3 percent. In the second major period, 1871 to 1925, volatility declined slightly; the annual standard deviation was 6.4 percent. Since 1926, by contrast, the annual standard deviation of returns on bonds has risen to 10.6 percent. And from 1982 to 1997, it reached 13.6 percent, and in contrast to the historical pattern, surpassed the 13.2 percent standard deviation for returns on stocks during the same period. This departure from the historical pattern might be the result of rapid and dramatic changes in the inflation rate in the years that preceded and then punctuated this period.

Although changes in the rate of inflation from period to period have done little to alter the real rate of returns in the stock market, they have had a profound impact on the real returns provided by bonds. A bond's interest payment is fixed for the number of years specified until it matures and is repaid. In times of rapidly rising prices, the real value of this fixed interest payment declines sharply, diminishing the real return provided by the bond. If investors expect rapid inflation, they demand that the bond

TABLE 1.4

Annual Bond Market Volatility—Long-Term Government Bonds (1802–1997)

	Standard Deviation of Real Annual Return	Highest Annual Real Return %	Lowest Annual Real Return %
1802–1870	8.3	29.8	−21.9
1871–1925	6.4	17.8	−16.9
1926–1997	10.6	35.1	−15.5
1802–1997	8.8	35.1	−21.9
1982–1997	13.6	35.1	−10.0

issuer pay a commensurately higher rate of interest, compensating for the anticipated inflation and securing an acceptable rate of real return. But the historical record indicates that investors have often failed to anticipate rapid inflation. For example, they were willing to ignore inflation during the 35 years following the Second World War, only then demanding compensation for it in the early 1980s. But by 1982 it had been substantially conquered. ("Generals fighting the last war" come to mind.) Real bond returns have varied widely. As a basis for future expectations, in any realistic time frame, past returns on bonds have been of little assistance in looking ahead.

That said, recent years have witnessed the introduction of new types of U.S. Treasury bonds that obviate two of the traditional risks of bonds. Zero coupon bonds guarantee a fixed rate of compound return over periods as long as 25 years or more, enabling investors to lock in a specific long-term return (typically, at the current interest rate for regular coupon-bearing bonds of the same maturity). Also available are inflation-hedge bonds, which offer a lower interest rate but guarantee full protection against the risk of increases in the Consumer Price Index (CPI). In neither case, however, is there any guarantee that the nominal or real returns of these instruments will exceed the returns of the traditional bond structure—only that their returns will be more predictable.

PLANTING SEEDS FOR GROWTH

The long-term risks and returns of stocks and bonds suggest the outlines of a commonsense investment strategy for the long-term investor. First, the long-term investor should make a significant commitment to stocks. Since 1802, and in each of the extended periods examined by Professor Siegel, stocks have earned higher returns than bonds, providing the best long-term opportunity for growth, as well as for protection against the threat of inflation. The data make clear that, if risk is the chance of failing to earn a real return over the long term, bonds have carried a higher risk than stocks. If you have faith that our economic garden is basically healthy and fertile, the best way to reap long-term rewards is to plant seeds with prospects for growth, as investing in common stocks clearly allows. But you must also be well provisioned for the onset of unexpectedly cold winters, and that is where bonds play a vital role.

During the long sweep of U.S. history since 1802, the variability of stock returns has been greater than that of bonds. In the short run, stocks are riskier than bonds. Even in the longer run, stocks can—and do—underperform bonds. Indeed, in the 187 rolling 10-year periods since the establishment of our securities markets, bonds have outperformed stocks in 38 periods—one out of every five. In still longer holding periods, however, the instances of bond market outperformance shrink to a statistical anomaly. In the 172 rolling 25-year periods since 1802, bonds have outperformed stocks in eight periods—only one out of every 21. As insurance against the possibility of short-term, or even extended, weakness in stocks, then, long-term investors should also include bonds in their portfolios. The result is a balanced investing program, a strategy discussed at length in Chapter 3. Select a sensible balance of stocks and bonds, hold that portfolio through the market's inevitable seasons of growth and decline, and you will be well positioned both to accumulate profit *and* to withstand adversity.

THE FINANCIAL MARKETS ARE NOT FOR SALE

The market returns presented here, however useful as a benchmark for determining a long-term investment strategy, have an important drawback. These returns reflect the entirely *theoretical* possibility of cost-free investing. As a group, investors earn less because the market return is inevitably reduced by the costs of investing. In the mutual fund industry, the range of investment costs is extremely wide. In an aggressively managed small-cap equity fund, total asset-related charges, including operating expenses and transaction costs, might be as high as 3 percent. The lowest range is set by a market index fund, a passively managed fund that simply buys and holds the stocks in a particular index. Because it entails no advisory fees or transaction costs and only minimal operating expenses, costs can be held to 0.20 percent of assets, or even less. On average, a common stock mutual fund, managed by a professional adviser who buys and sells securities in an effort to outperform the market, incurs annual operating expenses equal to about 1.5 percent of assets (known as the expense ratio). With portfolio transaction costs conservatively estimated at 0.5 percent, total costs reduce gross returns by at least 2.0 percentage points each year.

When estimating expected levels of future returns, the long-term investor must be aware of the portion of investment return that will be consumed by these expenses. Cost lops the same number of percentage points off both nominal and real returns, but, given persistent inflation, it nearly always consumes a proportionally larger share of real returns. Here is one example, assuming a nominal annual return of 10 percent on stocks. An equity mutual fund incurring annual expenses at the industry average would lop off some two percentage points—fully *one-fifth* of the market's annual return. Now let's say that inflation is 3 percent; then the market's real return is 7 percent, and costs would consume nearly *one-third* of the market's reward. And taxes must be paid—sooner or later—by the investor. Fair or not, taxes are assessed, not on real returns, but on the (higher) nominal returns. If taxes on fund income and capital gains distributions are assumed to reduce pretax returns by, say, another 2 percent to 5 percent (a rather modest assumption), that 2 percent all-in cost of a mutual fund could consume fully *four-tenths* of the market's net real return after taxes. To state the obvious, the long-term investor who pays *least* has the greatest opportunity to earn *most* of the real return provided by the stock market.

The Pie Theory

Let's now consider the real-world effect of costs. Assume that the stock market as a whole provides the nominal rate of return of about 11 percent enjoyed by investors during the modern era of the stock market that began in 1926. (This figure is unadjusted for inflation and includes the truly extraordinary 17 percent annual return from 1982 to 1997.) If you visualize that return as a flat circular surface—a pie, for example—11 percent is, by definition, the entire pie that market participants in the aggregate can divide among themselves. If we aggregate the returns of all investors who do better, those returns *must* be offset by the aggregate returns earned by all of those who do worse, and by precisely the same amount. That is the *gross* pie, if you will, before costs. Thus, the successful investors' gain—say, a return of 2 percent—will be offset by the returns of their unsuccessful colleagues who fall short by the same 2 percent. One group earns 13 percent; the other earns 9 percent.

Now assume that, for all participants in the market, the costs of investing are 2 percent. The gross pie of 11 percent has shrunk to a net pie of 9 percent to be divided among market participants. It truly is as simple as that. Our winners earn a net return of 11 percent *(the same as the gross return of the market)*, and our losers earn a net return of 7 percent *(a 4 percent shortfall)*. The fact that our winners, after expenses, merely match the market and our losers lose by four percentage points suggests why garnering market returns is so difficult. The odds against victory are long.

The pie analogy is hardly revolutionary. It entails nothing more than simple second-grade arithmetic:

Gross market return – Cost = Net market return

This syllogism then becomes obvious:

1. All investors own the entire stock market, so both active investors (as a group) and passive investors—holding all stocks at all times—must match the gross return of the stock market.
2. The management fees and transaction costs incurred by active investors in the aggregate are substantially higher than those incurred by passive investors.
3. Therefore, because active and passive investments together must, by definition, earn equal gross returns, passive investors must earn the higher net return. QED.

If there was ever an elementary, self-evident certainty in a financial world permeated by uncertainties, surely this is it. It establishes the principle underlying the growing use of passive investment techniques—most notably, the unmanaged index fund, of which I'll have much more to say during the course of this book. So, while we should applaud the extensive equations and elegant proofs of efficient market theory developed by such Nobel prize-winning economists and finance specialists as Samuelson, Tobin, Modigliani, Sharpe, Markowitz, and Miller, we should recognize that one need not drive to the farthest reaches of the efficient frontier—the market return that provides the optimal utility relative to the risk incurred—to find simple solutions to complex problems. And as you'll learn in Chapter 4, in the serious game of accumulating financial assets, simplicity trumps complexity.

PRACTICE DEPARTS FROM PRINCIPLE

The odds against beating the market, so clearly established by the pie theory, have some rather extreme implications. If the long-term investing ideal is a sensible balance in a diversified portfolio of stocks and bonds, held through the market's changing seasons, and with costs kept to a minimum, then that principle should be honored in practice by mutual fund managers and mutual fund investors alike. But, in both groups, it is honored more in the breach than in the observance. The challenge of the chase for market-beating returns seems to have obscured the simple lessons we should have learned. To paraphrase the late Charles Dudley Warner, editor of the *Hartford Courant,* on the subject of weather: Everybody talks about long-term investing, but nobody does anything about it.

Investors, professional and individual, are not ignorant of the lessons of history; rather, they are unwilling to heed them. Too many portfolio managers, investment advisers, and securities brokers, and too many mavens of the financial press and television (perhaps for obvious reasons) thrive on short-term forecasts, expected market trends, and hot (and, with less frequency, cold) stocks. Thus, today's overheated investment climate seems to demand urgent action, as in, "Act now, before it is too late."

To demonstrate the deficiencies of a short-term approach to long-term investment, I will examine two pervasive short-term strategies and show how mutual fund investors have followed them—to their detriment. The first is market timing—the attempt to shift assets from stocks to bonds or cash in hopes of escaping a stock market dip, then shift the assets from bonds or cash back to stocks in an attempt to ride the next stock market wave. For most practitioners, market timing is apt to bring the opposite result: they are in the market for the dips, but out of the market for the rallies.

The idea that a bell rings to signal when investors should get into or out of the stock market is simply not credible. After nearly fifty years in this business, I do not know of anybody who has done it successfully and consistently. I don't even know anybody who *knows* anybody who has done it successfully and consistently. Yet market timing appears to be increasingly embraced by mutual fund investors and the professional managers of fund portfolios alike.

The second short-term strategy is the rapid turnover of long-term investment portfolios. It too is evident in the actions of both mutual fund investors and fund managers. It is a costly practice, predicated, much like market timing, on the belief that investors can invest in a particularly attractive stock or mutual fund, watch it grow, and then eject the investment from their portfolio as it crests. As with market timing, the record provides no evidence that rapid turnover enhances the returns earned by fund investors or by fund managers.

Market Timing in the Press—"The Death of Equities"

The financial media provide a good place to begin our review of the eternal search for market-beating returns, whether through market timing or other means. The media reflect the actions of the financial markets, which are determined by the investment decisions made by all investors. The media also magnify the impact of market actions by highlighting—and, in some respects, sensationalizing—them.

Consider two covers from *Business Week*, one of our nation's most respected business periodicals. On August 13, 1979, *Business Week* ran a cover story called "The Death of Equities." As Figure 1.4 reveals, the story's timing could hardly have been more unfortunate. The Dow Jones Industrial Average of stock prices was at 840 when the article was written. It rose to 960 by the end of 1980. In the next two years, the index declined. It scraped 800 in July 1982, but then rebounded to 1200 by May 1983. *Business Week* then ran another cover story, called "The Rebirth of Equities," on May 9, 1983, *after* the near-50 percent market rise that had ensued since the August 1979 article. After the publication of the 1983

FIGURE 1.4

Investing with the Press—*Business Week* and *TIME*

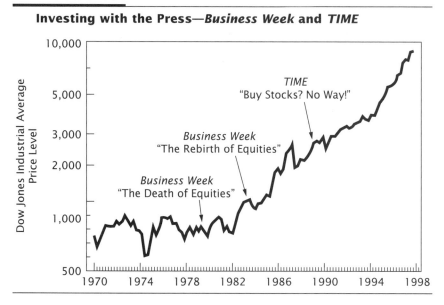

article, I said to one of my colleagues, "Watch out, the fun is over." And the equity market fun *was* sidetracked, if only for a while. *Business Week* said "Sell" when the Dow Jones Industrial Average was at 840, and "Buy" after it had climbed to 1200. Yet two years after the buy recommendation, in May 1985, the Dow still languished at about 1200.

It may be unfair to single out these *Business Week* classics. *TIME* gave us an equally poignant example of the hazards of taking strong and unequivocal stands on the future course of the stock market. In its September 26, 1988, issue, *TIME* ran a cover story titled "Buy Stocks? No Way." The cover pictured an enormous bear. The article included these pearls of wisdom about the stock market: "It's a dangerous game . . . it's a vote of confidence that things are getting worse . . . the market has become a crapshoot . . . the small investor has become an endangered species . . . the stock market is one of the sleaziest enterprises in the world." When those words were published, the Dow Jones Industrial Average was at the 2000 level, down from the peak of 2700 reached just before the market crash of October 1987. Since then, the Dow has topped 9000—greater than a fourfold increase. Investors who acted on *TIME*'s conclusion would have sat mournfully on the sidelines through one of history's most powerful bull markets.

I intend neither to slam *Business Week* and *TIME* nor to offer them up as the perfect contrary indicators—those wonderful sources whose advice is so consistently wrong that we can count on profits simply by doing the opposite. My point is: The market is simply unpredictable on any short-term month-to-month or even year-to-year basis. We should not expect it to be predictable, nor should we base our investment decisions on impulses inspired by the conventional wisdom of the day. Whether they come in large headlines in respected publications or arise from our own daily hopes and fears, these calls to action generally have a short-term focus that muddles our view of the long pull.

Market Timing by Mutual Fund Investors

Unfortunately, the available data suggest that, rather than ignoring the impulses engendered by the press or by emotional responses to market swings, the individual mutual fund shareholder responds to them with alacrity and follows the crowd. Mutual fund investing has proved to be extremely "market sensitive," as fund shareholders overreact to fluctuations in stock prices. Consider Figure 1.5, with its jagged peaks and valleys charting cash flows into and out of equity mutual funds as a percentage of

FIGURE 1.5

Equity Fund Cash Flows (1970–1997)

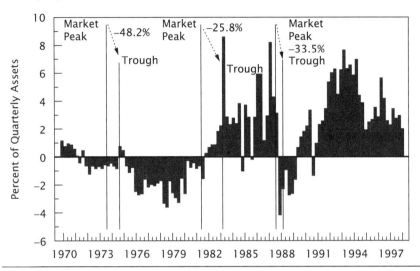

fund assets. Following the −48 percent market decline in 1973–1974, investors made withdrawals from their holdings of equity mutual funds during 24 consecutive quarters, from the second quarter of 1975 through the first quarter of 1981. The cumulative total withdrawn was $14 billion, fully 44 percent of the value of the initial holdings. Then, just before the market began its long-running bull charge in the third quarter of 1982, fund investors finally turned positive again. Fund cash flow totaled $80 billion (122 percent of the initial fund assets) through the third quarter of 1987.

Investors made particularly heavy investments in funds during the first nine months of 1987 ($28 billion of the $80 billion cumulative inflow). For the most part, they bought at what proved to be inflated prices. Then came the October 1987 stock market crash, and out went the investors' dollars. During each quarter over the next year and a half, soaring equity fund redemptions exceeded declining new share purchases, and nearly 5 percent of equity fund assets were liquidated. By then, stocks were at more realistic valuations. Sadly, these exiting investors had given up their market participation just before the market rebound that was soon to come.

The stock market crash of October 1987 caused many otherwise rational investors to abandon the stock market. But as soon as the bull market resumed its rampage, these same investors changed their course again. Cash flows into equity funds resumed in full force and remained positive in each quarter through mid-1998. What began as a tiny trickle became a roaring river. Net purchases of $1 billion in 1983, the first full year of the bull market, multiplied more than 200 times and reached $219 billion in 1997. If massive mutual fund inflows and outflows from investors remain contrary indicators, the industry's recent cash inflows may not be good news. But whatever the future may hold, these figures are one more manifestation of one of the great paradoxes of the stock market: When stock prices are high, investors want to jump on the bandwagon; when stocks are on the bargain counter, it is difficult to give them away.

Fund Shareholders Become Short-Term Investors . . .

It is not only in their love–hate relationship with equity funds that investors reflect their short-term orientation. They have come to adopt another short-term strategy: rapid turnover of their equity fund holdings. The tendency of investors to follow high-turnover policies in their own mutual fund portfolios has reached staggering proportions. As Figure 1.6 shows, during the 1960s and most of the 1970s, annual turnover rates ran in the 8 percent range, suggesting a 12½-year holding period by fund owners. (The estimated holding period is simply the inverse of the turnover ratio.) Currently, turnover of fund shareholdings is running at an annual rate of 31 percent, suggesting that the typical investors in an equity fund hold their shares for barely three years. (This 31 percent rate includes the rate of redemptions of equity funds, averaging about 17 percent of assets per year, plus exchanges out of equity funds—either into other equity funds or into bond or money market funds—of another 14 percent.) This 75 percent reduction in the holding period for mutual funds is counterproductive to a fault, for a holding period of that brevity impinges on the implementation of an intelligent long-term investment strategy.

Of particular note in the chart is the violent upward thrust in share turnover in 1987, not coincidentally the time of the last major market decline. Then, the turnover rate soared to 62 percent (a holding period of only 1.6 years!). It makes one wonder what may be in store for mutual funds if shareholders follow a similar redemption pattern the next time the market turns sharply lower.

FIGURE 1.6

Annual Investor Turnover of Equity Fund Shares (1961–1997)

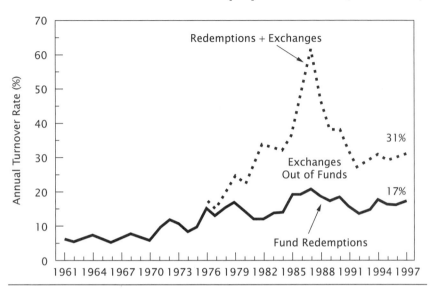

... *Following the Example of Fund Managers*

No doubt fund investors came by this short-term philosophy honestly—
they learned it from the portfolio managers who run the funds they own.
From the 1940s to the mid-1960s, annual portfolio turnover of the typical
general equity fund averaged a modest 17 percent. In 1997, average
turnover of U.S. equity funds stood at 85 percent, an amazing fivefold increase. Portfolio managers, on average, were holding the stocks in their
portfolios for only slightly longer than one year! It was odd behavior for
investment advisers, who are entrusted with a fiduciary responsibility to
manage clients' assets prudently. Instead, they were shuffling through
their portfolios like short-term speculators. During the past few decades,
abetted by the proliferation of sophisticated communications technologies,
portfolio managers of other people's money have adopted a new method to
try to beat the market: rapid-fire trading, a practice that can burden investors with enormous portfolio transaction costs, as well as staggering tax
costs. As Columbia Law School Professor Louis Lowenstein expressed it
in a 1998 article, mutual fund managers "exhibit a persistent emphasis on

momentary stock prices. The subtleties and nuances of a particular business utterly escape them." Despite the example set by some of what I describe as the "best practice" mutual funds (those that follow relatively steady low-turnover policies), the mutual fund industry pursues a far less productive path. The astonishing rise in fund portfolio turnover is charted in Figure 1.7.

Fund managers also ignore the lesson of long-term investing set by Warren Buffett, without doubt America's most successful investment manager. The turnover in his huge portfolio (limited to a relative handful of stocks) is not only low, it is virtually nonexistent. Here is his philosophy, as described in the 1996 Annual Report of Berkshire Hathaway, the investment holding company he controls:

> *Inactivity strikes us as intelligent behavior. Neither we nor most business managers would dream of feverishly trading highly-profitable subsidiaries because a small move in the Federal Reserve's discount rate was predicted or because some Wall Street pundit had reversed his view on the market. Why, then, should we behave differently with our minority positions in wonderful businesses?*

FIGURE 1.7

Mutual Fund Portfolio Turnover (1946–1997)

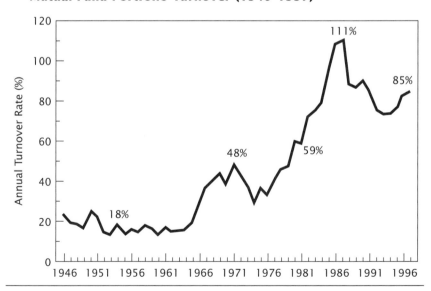

One might well ask: Why should any fiduciary behave differently from the Buffett principles? Mr. Buffett describes his extraordinarily productive investment approach as keeping "most of our major holdings regardless of how they are priced relative to (current) intrinsic business value . . . a 'til death do us part attitude. . . . We are searching for operations that we believe are virtually certain to possess enormous strengths *ten or twenty years from now.* [Italics added.] As investors, our reaction to a fermenting industry is much like our attitude toward space exploration. We applaud the endeavor but prefer to skip the ride."

Mr. Buffett doesn't cotton to the high turnover that characterizes mutual funds. "Investment managers are even more kinetic: their behavior makes whirling dervishes appear sedated by comparison. Indeed the term 'institutional investor' is becoming one of those self-contradictions called an oxymoron, comparable to 'jumbo shrimp,' 'lady mud-wrestler,' and 'inexpensive lawyer.'"

Given this situation as it exists in the modern mutual fund industry, Mr. Buffett quickly comes to the correct conclusion. "An investor who does not understand the economics of specific companies but wishes to be a long-term owner of American industry," he says, should "periodically invest in an index fund." In this way, "the know-nothing investor can actually outperform most investment professionals. Paradoxically, when 'dumb' money acknowledges its limitations, it ceases to be dumb." Money invested for the long term, like the proverbial plodding tortoise, wins the race over speculative money, analogous to the fits and starts of the hare. The mutual fund industry is ignoring this truism.

Let's consider whether the fund industry's rapid turnover might possibly be the side effect of well-executed plans for earning superior investment returns. The obvious answer is: *For the industry as a whole,* it cannot be. Now controlling one-third of all stocks, fund managers are largely trading, not with other investors, but with one another. Thus, each trade balances out for fund shareholders as a group. It is a zero-sum game. But, importantly, money is left on the table for the dealers executing the trades, meaning that the activity becomes a negative-sum game. The evidence confirms this conclusion. A recent study by Morningstar found that few managers were able to improve returns significantly through portfolio turnover, but that on balance, the tiny increases in return that turnover may have engendered were gained only by buying riskier stocks. The study hardly serves as an encouraging defense of the industry's high-turnover policies.

SHORT-TERM SPECULATION DISPLACES LONG-TERM INVESTMENT

When I wrote my Princeton senior thesis on mutual funds in 1951, I expressed what I fear was callow optimism about the role of mutual fund portfolio transactions in the financial markets. I concluded that the professional analytical capability of fund managers, along with their focus on investment valuation rather than on forecasting swings in a stock's price, would bring to the marketplace "a demand for securities that is steady, sophisticated, enlightened, and analytic, a demand based essentially on the performance of a corporation rather than the public's appraisal of the share prices."

In taking this approach, I was responding to John Maynard Keynes's argument that because the powerful role of speculation in the markets was based on increasing ownership of stocks "by persons who have no special knowledge of their investments . . . and the conventional valuation of stocks based on the mass psychology of a large number of ignorant individuals," professional investors and experts in the securities business would be unable to offset the mass opinion, so they would try to foresee changes in the public valuation.

I based my contrary opinion on the expectation that mutual funds and other financial institutions would grow in importance. I argued that they would rely on their specialized knowledge of investments and value stocks accurately, based on the prospective long-term merits of the stocks, not on the psychology of ignorant individuals (or, in Lord Keynes's words, not "in discovering what average opinion expects average opinion [of a share's worth] to be"). With fund portfolio turnover then running well below 20 percent per year, I concluded that continued mutual fund growth "will mean that enterprise in investment will cease to be (using Keynes's words) 'a mere bubble in a whirlpool of speculation.'"

Sadly, as the figures on fund portfolio turnover show, my youthful optimism was misplaced. Industry practice today is as close to short-term speculation—and as far from long-term investment—as the law allows.

Further, my own (admittedly anecdotal) studies over the years suggest that the Morningstar results may be too optimistic. The evidence that I have seen shows that the overwhelming majority of funds would earn higher returns each year if they simply held their portfolios static at the beginning of the year and took no action whatsoever during the ensuing twelve months. Whatever the cause, professional managers have fallen further behind the market averages with today's high-turnover practices than with the low-turnover practices that were long an industry hallmark. I suggest that the high costs imposed by their manic trading are in part responsible for this growing gap.

In this exceedingly creative industry, we will no doubt witness the development of countless new short-term strategies, each with an alluring but ultimately vacant promise that hyperactive short-term management of a long-term investment portfolio can generate better results than a sensible buy-and-hold approach. Market timing has thus far been a singular failure, and the rapid turnover of investment portfolios has been no more effective. As costly and tax-inefficient turnover accelerates—for funds and fund investors alike—this practice seems destined to become ever more damaging.

Understanding the Economics of Investing

In my view, market timing and rapid turnover—both by and for mutual fund investors—betray both a lack of understanding of the *economics* of investing and an infatuation with the *process* of investing. As I shall make clear in Chapter 2, the source of long-term financial market returns is easily explained: for the stock market, corporate earnings and dividends; for the bond market, interest payments. Market returns, however, are calculated *before* the deduction of the costs of investing, and are most assuredly *not* based on speculation and rapid trading, which do nothing but shift returns from one investor to another. For the long-term investor, returns have everything to do with the underlying economics of corporate America and very little to do with the mechanical process of buying and selling pieces of paper. The art of investing in mutual funds, I would argue, rests on simplicity and common sense.

If individual stocks derive their value from the businesses that issue them, then the broad stock market obviously represents not a mere collection of paper stock certificates but the tangible and intangible net assets of American business in the aggregate. Before taking costs into account, investors will inevitably earn long-term returns that approximate the earnings and dividends produced by corporate America. Rapid turnover can ultimately produce no value for investors as a group, for it does nothing to increase the level of corporate earnings and dividends. Nor can market timing have any effect on the intrinsic value of corporate America. The ideal for the long-term investor remains a sensible balance of stocks and bonds held through the market's seasons of growth and decline.

SIMPLE PRINCIPLES FOR LONG-TERM SUCCESS

Although most investors have yet to embrace the ideal of long-term investing, it is surprisingly easy to achieve. In the real world of mutual funds, intelligent investors must pay attention to the elements of long-term investing that are within their power to control. No matter how difficult or how much easier said than done, they must focus not on the market's short-term direction, nor on finding the next hot fund, but on intelligent fund selection. The key to fund selection is to focus, not on future return—which the investor cannot control—but on risk, cost, and time—all of which the investor *can* control.

Just as the garden's fledgling shoots develop slowly and blossom over the course of a season, with their roots strengthening over years, investment success takes time. Give yourself all the time you can. Begin to invest in your 20s, even if you invest only a small amount. Nourished by the miracle of compound interest, your portfolio should flourish with the market's passing cycles. Over a 10-year period, for example, if market returns average a nominal 10 percent annually, an initial investment of $10,000 will grow to almost $26,000, more than 2½ times the initial investment. (Assuming a real return of 7 percent, the terminal value would represent a near doubling of your initial purchasing power.) In 50 years, assuming the same 10 percent return, $10,000 would grow to almost $1.2 million, or 120 times the initial investment.

To exploit the full power of compounding in real markets, pay particular attention to the negative implications of cost—the cost of investment advice, portfolio management and administration, buying and selling investments, and taxes. By the end of the period over which you accumulate your retirement nest egg, the returns earned in individual diversified portfolios are almost sure to lag behind those of the markets in which they invest in direct proportion to the expenses and taxes they incur. Superficially small differences in annual returns, extended over long periods of time, will make a dramatic difference in how much capital you finally accumulate. Give your portfolio plenty of time to benefit from the magic of compounding, and minimize the costs you incur. Never forget that costs, like weeds, impede the garden's growth.

These simple principles are the basis of a long-term investment strategy that should reward investors' faith in the promise of investing. Most mutual fund investors who deviate from the long-term investing ideal are rewarded only with dashed expectations. The relentless pursuit of unrealistic performance, practiced through costly short-term strategies, distracts them from one of the most important secrets of investment success: *simplicity.* As they complicate the process, they increase the likelihood of stumbling down an ill-lit path to disappointment. Follow a simple plan, and let the cycles of the market take their course. *The secret of investing is, finally, that there is no secret.*

So I return to the wisdom of Chance the gardener. We have had a long spring and summer—the longest sustained equity bull market in history. But "there are also fall and winter." Don't be surprised when the season changes, for change it will. Indeed, that time may be now in prospect. In the long run, however, your investments will survive and prosper if you rely on a few simple rules:

- **Invest you *must*.** The biggest risk is the long-term risk of not putting your money to work at a generous return, not the short-term—but nonetheless real—risk of price volatility.

- **Time is your friend.** Give yourself all the time you can. Begin to invest in your 20s, even if it's only a small amount, and never stop. Even modest investments in tough times will help you sustain the pace and will become a habit. Compound interest is a miracle.

- **Impulse is your enemy.** Eliminate emotion from your investment program. Have rational expectations about future returns, and avoid changing those expectations as the seasons change. Cold, dark winters will give way to bright, bountiful springs.

- **Basic arithmetic works.** Keep your investment expenses under control. Your net return is simply the gross return of your investment portfolio, less the costs you incur (sales commissions, advisory fees, transaction costs). Low costs make your task easier.

- **Stick to simplicity.** Don't complicate the process. Basic investing is simple—a sensible asset allocation to stocks, bonds, and cash reserves; a selection of middle-of-the-road funds that emphasize high-grade securities; a careful balancing of risk, return, and (lest we forget) cost.

- **Stay the course.** No matter what happens, stick to your program. I've said "Stay the course" a thousand times, and I meant it every time. It is the most important single piece of investment wisdom I can give to you.

Let the brief and uncertain years roll by, and face the future with faith. Perhaps a future winter will be longer and colder than usual, or a summer will be drier and hotter. In the long run, however, our economy and our financial markets are stable and rational. Don't let short-run fluctuations, market psychology, false hope, fear, and greed get in the way of good investment judgment. Success will be yours if you remember Chance's lesson:

> *I know the garden very well. I have worked in it all of my life . . . .*
> *Everything in it will grow strong in due course. And there is plenty of*
> *room in it for new trees and new flowers of all kinds. If you love your*
> *garden, you don't mind working in it, and waiting. Then in the proper*
> *season you will surely see it flourish.*[5]

CHAPTER 2

ON THE NATURE OF RETURNS

Occam's Razor

he preacher Ecclesiastes said, "There is no remembrance of things past; neither shall there be remembrance of things to come." That philosophy is doubtless sound for investors concerned about the erratic, unpredictable, short-term volatility in the U.S. financial markets. But in developing a long-term investment strategy, remembering the past is essential, because it can help us to understand the forces that drive security prices. When we subject financial realities to reasoned analysis, we gain insights into the sources and patterns of the long-term returns produced by stocks and bonds in the past. Those insights can provide a sound basis for determining the nature of future returns. What is more, they can form the basis for rational discourse about investing in the years ahead.

Sir William of Occam, a fourteenth-century British philosopher, is responsible for the insight that the simpler the explanation, the more likely it is to be correct. This postulate has come to be known as "Occam's Razor," and I have used it in the analytical methodology with which I approach the financial markets. Wielding Sir William's razor, I have shorn my methodology of all complication, paring the sources of investment return down to three essential components. This analysis takes into account

my conviction both that the performance of *individual* securities is unpredictable, and that the performance of *portfolios* of securities is unpredictable on any short-term basis. While the long-term performance of
portfolios is also unpredictable, a careful examination of the past returns
can help establish some probabilities about the prospective parameters of
return, offering intelligent investors a basis for rational expectations
about future returns.

The application of Occam's Razor to the financial markets is most appropriate for investors who select broadly diversified mutual funds run at
modest cost, and who hold them for the long term. The full market returns presented in this chapter reflect *gross* returns, but investors as a
group inevitably earn less. (Recall the discussion of investment costs in
Chapter 1.) So, whatever market returns we expect, we must reduce them
by up to two percentage points (or more) to account for those costs.

Because long-term investment returns are conventionally measured by
market indexes tracking the broad U.S. stock and bond markets, my analysis has the greatest direct relevance to index funds that follow these same
benchmarks. (Index funds are discussed in Chapter 5.) Diversified stock
funds that emphasize corporations with large market capitalizations, along
with funds investing in high-grade bonds, also fit nicely into this analysis.
In both cases, the gap between fund returns and market returns is mini-
mized by those funds that have the lowest costs.

OCCAM'S RAZOR AND THE STOCK MARKET

Our discourse begins with a journey of nearly 200 years' duration. As we
learned in Chapter 1, since 1802, annual real (after-inflation) returns on
stocks have settled near an average of 7 percent, though with awesome interim variation—a high of 67 percent in 1862 and a low of –39 percent in
1931. Huge though it may be, that range of 106 percentage points can
serve as a powerful reminder of short-term risk in the stock market, even
as 7 percent has proved a remarkably consistent standard for the market's
long-term return.

Figure 1.2 showed the returns earned by stocks during this period of
nearly two centuries. An investment of $10,000 in stocks early in 1802,
growing at an average real rate of 7 percent, would now be worth a cool
$5.6 billion in real (inflation-adjusted) dollars. Let's now consider Profes-
sor Siegel's data over a somewhat shorter time frame, breaking the returns
down into 25-year increments.

The huge 106-percentage-point range of stock returns from high to low over 196 individual years contracts to a very much narrower range when viewed in increments over 172 overlapping 25-year periods, as Figure 2.1 shows. In each of those periods, real annual returns on stocks fell within a positive range of 2 percent to 12 percent. (In no 25-year period were the returns negative.) In two-thirds of the cases, annual returns fell within a range of 4.7 percent to 8.7 percent, two percentage points on either side of the norm, establishing the standard deviation of real annual returns at 2 percent.

What explains these returns? Where did they come from? What is their nature? Why do the variations shrink with the passage of time? As it turns out, equity markets have certain seemingly eternal characteristics. As the time frame increases from a single year to a 25-year period, the powerful short-term influence of speculation recedes, and investment returns conform much more closely, if not precisely, to the investment fundamentals: dividend yields and earnings growth. Together, these two elements constitute the driving force for stock returns, and, from 1871

FIGURE 2.1

Rolling 25-Year Real Stock Returns (1826–1997)

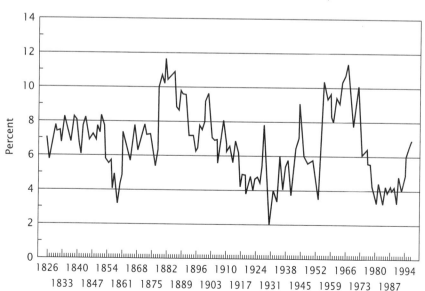

on, the first year of a careful study conducted by the Cowles Commission during the 1930s, we can trace the impact of those two fundamentals with some considerable accuracy.

We can use the historical data to answer a simple question: *Why* have stocks provided long-term real returns of 7 percent? Answer: Almost entirely because of the rising earnings and dividends of U.S. corporations.*
The sum of real dividend yields and earnings growth generated during 1871–1997, adjusted for inflation, equals 6.7 percent in real terms. In other words, the total long-term real return on stocks derived from dividend yields and earnings is virtually identical to the 7 percent real return actually provided by the stock market itself. All other factors combined have almost inconsequential impact on the returns provided by these two fundamental factors alone.

There were, to be sure, significant variations around this norm. They were caused by the fluctuations in the valuations that investors were willing to pay for $1 of earnings—the price–earnings ratio. This speculative factor has often proven powerful enough to add as much as 4 percentage points annually to the fundamental return, or to reduce it by an equal amount. Over a 25-year period, for example, an increase in the price–earnings ratio from 8 to 20 times will add 4 percentage points to return; a drop from 20 times to 7 times will do the reverse. The difference between the *fundamental* and the *actual* return on stocks, then, is accounted for by the element of speculation—the changing valuation that investors place on common stocks, measured by the relationship between the stock prices and corporate earnings per share.

Figure 2.2 makes crystal clear the overpowering role of fundamental returns in determining the actual returns earned on stocks over the long run. In this chart, comparing the cumulative returns generated by the fundamentals and the returns of the stock market during the 1871–1997 period, the lines diverge over and over again, only to return to convergence. These divergences to and fro are explained by changes in the price–earnings ratio, but the fundamentals clearly dominate the relationship.

---

*These data are based on 1871–1997 historical dividend yields and earnings growth. Only total return data—not its components—are available for the 1802–1870 period. However, real stock returns of 7 percent prevailed during both eras, giving us two centuries of data that establish the consistency of real stock returns—surely a full test of time for us mere mortals with rather shorter expected lifetimes.

FIGURE 2.2

Fundamental Return versus Market Return (1872–1997)

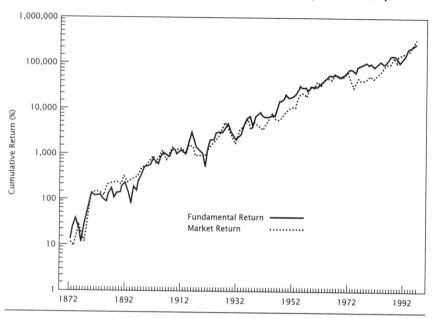

Enter Occam's Razor

So, courtesy of Occam's Razor, I advance a simple theory. These variables determine stock market returns over the long term:

- The dividend yield at the time of initial investment.
- The subsequent rate of growth in earnings.
- The change in the price–earnings ratio during the period of investment.

The total of these three components explains nearly all of the stock market's returns over extended holding periods. By analyzing the contribution to total return of the three factors, reasoned consideration of future returns can take place. The initial dividend yield is a known quantity. The rate of earnings growth has usually been relatively predictable within fairly narrow parameters. And the change in the price–earnings ratio has proven highly speculative. Total return is simply the sum of these three factors. For example, an initial dividend yield of, say, 3 percent plus a forecasted earnings growth of 7 percent annually over the next 10 years would bring the return to 10 percent. A change in the price–earnings ratio—from, say, 15 times at the beginning of the period to a forecasted 18 times at the end—would add 2 percentage points to that total, bringing the return on stocks to 12 percent. This simple arithmetic is the basis for the historical analysis presented in Table 2.1.

As I mentioned in Chapter 1, the long-term investor's main objective is to earn high rates of real returns. Because real returns have been adjusted for inflation, they represent the true growth in the purchasing power of investment dollars. In this analysis, however, I rely on nominal returns. I do so because the most accurate data on dividend yields, earnings growth, and price–earnings ratios are stated in nominal terms. While we know the impact that inflation has had on the total market return, there is no method of apportioning its impact among the three components of return. The spread between the actual returns and the returns calculated with the Occam's Razor methodology is, of course, the same for both nominal returns and real returns.

TABLE 2.1

Ten-Year Nominal Stock Market Returns (1927–1997)

| Periods | | 1 | 2 | 3 | | 1 + 2 + 3 | | |
Start 1-Jan.	End 31-Dec.	Initial Yield	10-Year AEG*	Closing P/E Ratio**	P/E Effect***	Calculated Return	Actual Return	Difference
1927	1936	5.1%	–1.9%	16.8	4.5%	7.7%	7.8%	–0.1%
1930	1939	4.5	–5.7	13.9	0.4	–0.8	–0.1	–0.7
1940	1949	5.0	9.9	7.2	–6.3	8.6	9.2	–0.6
1950	1959	6.8	3.9	17.7	9.4	20.1	19.4	+0.7
1960	1969	3.1	5.5	15.9	–1.0	7.6	7.8	–0.2
1970	1979	3.4	9.9	7.3	–7.6	5.7	5.9	–0.2
1980	1989	5.2	4.4	15.5	7.8	17.4	17.5	–0.1
1990	1997	3.1	7.3	24.1	5.7	16.1	16.6	–0.5
Average		4.5%	4.2%	14.8	1.6%	10.3%	10.5%	–0.2%

Note: Data based on Standard & Poor's Composite Stock Price Index.
*Average earnings growth.
**Initial price–earnings ratio: 10.9 times.
***10-year return generated by change in P/E ratio.

The analysis covers the modern stock market era, beginning in 1926. I use the Occam's Razor model to examine 10-year, rather than 25-year, stock market returns, since I suspect that few investors—however unwisely—expect to demonstrate the patience to think of investing in the quarter-century intervals shown in Figure 2.1. But even a decade allows us to ignore the wild and often inexplicable short-term factors that drive markets on a daily—and even a yearly—basis.

As Table 2.1 indicates, the sum of the initial dividend yield, the earnings growth rate, and the change in the price–earnings ratio yields a remarkably accurate approximation of the actual nominal returns provided by stocks in the six full decades and two partial decades from 1926 to the present. *In no case does the variation reach even a single percentage point.* From January 1960 to December 1969, for example, the sum of the initial dividend yield (3.1 percent), the decade's average annual earnings growth (5.5 percent), and the annualized change in the price–earnings ratio (–1.0 percent) came to 7.6 percent, just 0.2 percent shy of the 7.8 percent actually provided by stocks during the decade. For the full period, the calculated stock return of 10.3 percent per year is virtually identical to the actual return of 10.5 percent. The parallelism is crystal-clear.

Investment and Speculation

The Occam's Razor approach to the components of return echoes the philosophy of John Maynard Keynes, perhaps the most influential economist of the twentieth century. Keynes posited these sources of financial returns:

- Investment (which he called "enterprise"): "the activity of forecasting the prospective yield on the asset over its whole life . . . assuming that the existing state of affairs will continue indefinitely."

- Speculation: "the activity of forecasting the psychology of the market . . . attaching hopes to a favorable change in the conventional basis of valuation."

In our Occam's Razor model, the combination of initial dividend yield and prospective 10-year earnings growth—the two investment fundamentals—is the analog for the Keynesian concept of enterprise—the estimated yield of the asset over its lifetime. The change in price–earnings ratios is the analog for speculation—a change in the basis of valuation, or a barometer of investor sentiment. Investors pay more for earnings when their expectations are high, and less when they lose faith in the future. When stocks are priced at a multiple of 21 times earnings (or higher), the mood is exuberance. At 7 times earnings, the mood approaches despair. After all, the price–earnings ratio simply represents the price paid for a dollar of earnings. But, as the valuation falls from 21 to 7 times earnings, prices fall by 67 percent. If the reverse occurs, prices increase by 200 percent. If there is no change in the price–earnings ratio, the total return on stocks depends almost entirely on the initial dividend yield and the rate of earnings growth.

As Table 2.1 demonstrates, investment, or enterprise, has prevailed over speculation in the long run. In the eight virtually consecutive decades from 1926 through 1997, the nominal initial dividend yield has averaged 4.5 percent, and earnings growth has averaged 4.2 percent. The sum of these two components is a fundamental stock return of 8.7 percent, slightly less than the 10.5 percent nominal return actually provided by stocks over the same rolling periods. We can chalk up the remaining 1.8 percent to speculation (or, more likely, to the imprecise nature of our analysis).* In short, the fundamentals of investment—dividends and earnings growth—are the *right* things to remember about things past. In the very long run, the role of speculation has proven to be a neutral factor in the shaping of returns. Speculation cannot feed on itself forever. Periods in which speculation has enhanced returns have been followed by periods in which speculation has diminished returns. No matter how compelling—or even predominant—the impact of speculation on return is in the short run, expecting it to repeat itself leads our expectations down the wrong road. Speculation is the *wrong* thing to remember as we peer into the future to consider things yet to come.

The Fruits of Knowledge

The point of this analytical exercise is pragmatic. If there are favorable odds of making reasonably accurate *long-term* projections of investment returns, and if fundamental returns—earnings and dividends—are the dominant force in shaping the long-term returns that actually transpire, would not a strategy focused on those fundamental factors be more likely

---

*If we look at all 61 "rolling" decades during the 1926–1997 period, the results are virtually identical.

to be successful than a strategy of speculation for the investor with a long-term time horizon?

Short-term investment strategies—which effectively ignore dividend yield and earnings growth, both of which are virtually inconsequential in a period of weeks or months—have almost nothing to do with investment. But they have a lot to do with speculation; that is, simply guessing at the price that other investors might be willing to pay for a diversified portfolio of stocks or bonds at some future time when we are willing to sell.

Speculation is typically the *only* reason for the sometimes astonishing daily, weekly, or monthly swings we witness. But speculation can also play a major role in longer-term periods. In the 1980s, for example, stocks delivered a truly remarkable annual total return of 17.5 percent, virtually all of which was derived from an initial yield of 5.2 percent; earnings growth of 4.4 percent; and an annual valuation *increase* of 7.8 percent, as the price–earnings multiple more than doubled, from 7.3 to 15.5 times. The speculative element outweighed, by a wide margin, each of the fundamental elements, and came close to matching their *combined* contribution.

Speculative mania can also take a depressing turn. In the 1970s, stocks produced an average return of 5.9 percent, explained almost entirely by the initial yield of 3.4 percent, earnings growth of 9.9 percent, and a valuation *decrease* at an annual rate of –7.6 percent, as the price–earnings ratio dropped from 15.9 to 7.3 times. The market's loss of confidence exacted a heavy toll on the bounty generated by investment fundamentals.

If the former extreme was a "Golden Decade," the latter could be called a "Tin Decade" (see Table 2.2). It may not be entirely by accident

TABLE 2.2

The Tin Decade and the Golden Decade

Components of Stock Returns	1970s	1980s
Investment component		
Dividend yield	3.4%	5.2%
Earnings growth	9.9	4.4
Total fundamental return	13.3	9.6
Speculative component	–7.6	7.8
Calculated return	5.7%	17.4%
Actual market return	5.9%	17.5%

that the total combined return for the two decades came to 11.5 percent. That figure is remarkably close to the fundamental return of 11.4 percent (an average 4.3 percent dividend yield plus average earnings growth of 7.1 percent); the price–earnings ratio fell slightly, from 15.9 percent to 15.5 percent, reducing return by just 0.1 percent annually. Together, the combined returns surely represent the "back to normalcy" nature that financial markets tend to exhibit.*

From the Past to the Future

As the 1990s began, I reasoned that these long-term data could help provide a framework of expectations for the coming decade. I knew that the initial dividend yield on stocks on January 1, 1990, was 3.1 percent. I needed only to project the other two variables: earnings growth and the change in the price–earnings ratio for the decade. For help in thinking through these forecasts, I relied on a matrix similar to the one shown in Table 2.3. For example:

- If the future earnings growth rate were 8 percent, and the price–earnings ratio were to ease downward from 15.5 times to a more traditional 14 times, the total return on stocks would approximate 10.3 percent per year. At the time this matrix was constructed, this earnings growth rate, relative to its past historical rate of 5.8 percent, was aggressive. The price–earnings ratio, while below the then-existing level, was above the historical norm.

- "Too low," one might say. "The 1990s will be just like the 1980s." However, to get the remarkable 17 percent return achieved during the 1980s, given the initial dividend yield of about 3.1 percent, would take, among other combinations, a 9 percent earnings growth rate and an increase in the price–earnings multiple to 24 times. This seemed both an aggressive earnings projection and a multiple that had often signaled substantial overvaluation that had ultimately been corrected by a market decline.

- "Too high," another might say. "I expect 6 percent earnings growth and an earnings multiple of 12 times." Net result: An annual

---

*This tendency is referred to as reversion to the mean. I call it the law of gravity in the financial markets. It is discussed at length in Chapter 10.

TABLE 2.3

Stock Market Total Return Matrix for the 1990s

Earnings Growth	Total Stock Market Return						
	0%	2%	4%	6%	8%	10%	12%
6	−5.1%	−3.4%	−1.7%	0.0%	1.8%	3.6%	5.3%
8	−2.6	−0.9	0.9	2.8	4.6	6.4	8.2
10	0.6	1.2	3.1	4.9	6.8	8.7	10.6
12	1.1	3.0	4.9	6.8	8.7	10.6	12.5
14	2.5	4.5	6.4	8.3	10.3	12.2	14.2
16	3.8	5.8	7.8	9.7	11.7	13.7	15.7
18	5.0	7.0	9.0	11.0	13.0	15.0	17.0
20	6.0	8.1	10.1	12.1	14.1	16.2	18.2
22	6.7	8.7	10.8	12.9	14.9	17.0	19.1
24	7.6	9.7	11.7	13.8	15.9	18.0	20.1
26	8.4	10.5	12.6	14.7	16.8	18.9	21.0
28	9.2	11.3	13.4	15.6	17.7	19.8	21.9

(Leftmost axis label: Terminal P/E)

Initial dividend yield = 3.1%; Initial P/E = 15.5.

return of 6.8 percent—about two-thirds of the historical 10.3 percent norm, on assumptions that were far short of catastrophic.

In an article for *The Journal of Portfolio Management*, published in 1991, I explained my reasoning:

> The point of these examples is that the model sets the framework for a rational discourse on the returns on stocks in the 1990s. It makes it clear that, unless we have unusually optimistic sentiment that results in high price–earnings ratios in 1999 (indeed, why not?), and earnings growth for the decade higher than that of any past decade (again, why not?), stocks will have their work cut out for themselves to exceed returns in the 8 percent to 12 percent range during the 1990s, perhaps averaging 10 percent annually.[1]

My "why nots?" now seem almost prophetic. Since the mid-1990s, we have experienced a combination of a remarkable boom in the U.S. economy, unusually robust growth of corporate earnings, and price–earnings ratios that have soared to record highs based on extreme investor optimism that approaches exuberance. Taken together, these factors have so far resulted in stock returns well beyond my initial base expectations, even exceeding my optimistic expectation of 13 percent.

Honing the Razor

Shortly after the 1991 article was published, I decided to put a finer point on my projections. Rather than using a matrix, with a range of different returns under different conditions, I developed a model that would endeavor to provide, in retrospect, the returns that might have been expected in past decades. I knew the dividend yield and the market's price–earnings ratio at the outset of each decade. Forecasting would be a matter of estimating, retrospectively, what rate of earnings growth might have been expected for each decade, and what final price–earnings ratio might have been expected at the end of each decade.

Creating, in advance, tailor-made forecasts for each variable and each prospective time period would have been an exercise in futility. How could one ever guess what rate of earnings growth might occur, and what value investors would place on earnings a decade hence? I chose to avoid these issues. Instead, I added back the (known) initial yield to the average earnings growth rate *that the market had experienced in the past*, and I assumed that the terminal price–earnings ratio would equal the market's past average price–earnings ratio.

To test this approach, I examined my results over the 53 10-year rolling periods, from 1926 to 1989. The results were striking. The general parallelism between the actual returns of the Standard & Poor's 500 Index and the returns forecast by my simple reliance on the past was, with some notable exceptions, quite accurate. Most of the exceptions occurred during the traumatic environment of the 1930s and the dislocation surrounding World War II. Figure 2.3, updated through 1997, compares the actual returns in each rolling decade with those forecast by the model since 1926. (As Figure 2.3 reveals, exceptions to the reliability of these forecasts have reappeared during the great bull market of the late 1990s.) In statistical argot, the coefficient of correlation of +0.54 between the projected and the actual results was, if far from perfect, impressive—infinitely better than the 0.00 correlation that would be predicted by mere chance, and indeed more than halfway to the perfect correlation that would be indicated by +1.00, under which each forecast would have hit the mark precisely.

Occam in Action

Backtesting, of course, should always be viewed with skepticism. ("Torture the data until they confess" is the customary way of viewing it.) The

FIGURE 2.3

Ten-Year Nominal Stock Market Returns

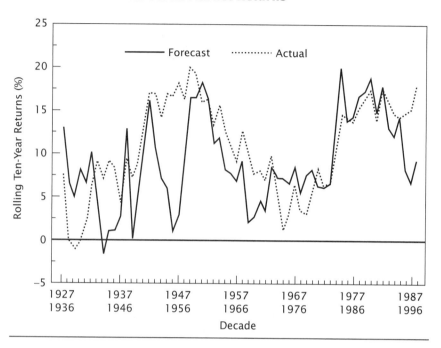

real test of my methodology was to be its performance as a forecasting tool. The results have been poor at worst, mixed at best.

In 1991, I had stated that stocks might reasonably be expected to provide an annual return in the range of 10 percent during the 1990s. Later, in a second article for *The Journal of Portfolio Management*,[2] I offered a more precise projection using history as my guide. Based on an initial dividend yield of 3.1 percent, plus assumed earnings growth of 6.6 percent per year (the average rate of the prior 30 years), the analysis called for an *investment* return of 9.7 percent per year during the 1990s. As to the *speculative* return, a decline in the price–earnings ratio from the then-current level of 15.5 times to its 30-year historical average of 14.1 times would reduce this return by −1.0 percent per year. The result: A stock market return of 8.7 percent, a bit below my earlier ballpark projection.

I presented my findings as variations on the theory of rational expectations that might be useful as a rudimentary forecasting tool. After careful examination of all 53 decade-long periods since 1926, the results of the model had been reasonably accurate in one-third of those periods, measurably better in one-third of the periods, and quite poor only in the remaining one-third of the periods. I described these variations as a healthy reminder that equity markets have exhibited wildly aberrant behavior from time to time. Ever mindful of the fallibility of forecasting, I then warned—prophetically, as it turned out—that "it would be unwise to apply this new forecasting tool without considering the possibility that precisely such wild aberrations lie directly before us. Surely stranger things have happened."

The Envelope, Please

My analysis of stock returns was right twice, but only in a most perverse sense. Halfway to the finish line, the forecast was exactly on the mark. My projection had called for a 10-year rate of total return on equities of 8.7 percent. Astonishing as it may seem, for the first half of the decade (1990–1994), the actual rate of return was 8.7 percent. The long-term investment fundamentals on which I based my thesis dominated the forces of speculation that have often had a major impact on short-term returns. Nonetheless, in a third article in *The Journal of Portfolio Management* in 1995,[3] when I reviewed that remarkably accurate forecast, I acknowledged that luck, pure and simple, played a role in the virtually exact correspondence of the forecast and actual returns.

Alas, my 1991 comment that strange things might happen was soon to be right on the mark, too. Wild aberrations *did* lie directly before us. In fact, they would strike the stock market during the second half of the decade. As proof that forecasting returns is a fallible and humbling profession, stocks took off as 1995 began, and, in an amazing sequence that lasted more than three years, returns averaged 31 percent *annually*. By the end of 1998, reality bore little relation to my earlier projection (in the 10 percent range). With only twelve months remaining in the decade, stocks had provided returns averaging 18.0 percent. Even if stocks were to decline by as much as 20 percent during the final year of the decade, the return would still average 13.5 percent, slightly higher than my optimistic forecast, early in the decade, of 13.0 percent (based on 9 percent earnings growth rate and a terminal price–earnings ratio of 17 times).

What Happened after 1994?

During the second half of the 1990s, the market's robust returns have reflected two extraordinary developments. First, two years after the decade began, earnings began to grow at a rate that was more than double the historical 6.9 percent earnings growth of stocks since 1926. From their depressed level in 1991, corporate earnings leaped upward, increasing at an annual rate of 16.6 percent through 1997. Interestingly, however, from the start of the decade in January 1990, the growth rate proved to be 7.3 percent, only a bit above my historically derived forecast of 6.6 percent. With the initial dividend yield of 3.1 percent, my forecast of investment—or fundamental—return was 9.7 percent, a fairly accurate initial projection compared to the actual figure of 10.4 percent.

Second, however, reflecting the extraordinary resurgence in corporate earnings, the speculative element of stock prices leaped to the fore. From the start of 1990 to mid-1998, the stock market's price–earnings ratio ballooned from 15.5 times earnings to 27 times earnings—a level that had been exceeded only once since 1926. This huge expansion in the multiple—in sharp contrast to the slight contraction of the historical norm of 14.1 times that I had calculated—accounted for almost the entire difference between my projection and the market's actual return so far. Such a multiple expansion, virtually impossible to forecast, added fully 6.7 percentage points annually to the fundamental return of 10.4 percent, bringing the total stock market return to 17.1 percent annually over the decade so far, just 0.7 percentage points shy of the stock market's actual 17.8 percent return.

With the clarity of hindsight, my initial forecast, based on a reversion of the price–earnings ratio to the historical norm, proved an exercise in humility. It also confirmed what I have so often said to investors about investing: Don't think you know more than the market. Nobody does. Put another way, in volatile and uncertain financial markets, rationality provides only a reasonable *range* of expectations, and only over a long time horizon at that. (Further, as I write this chapter, the decade has not yet reached its conclusion and may yet hold surprises for investors.) By definition, a rational model is powerless to forecast stock market bubbles built on "irrational exuberance"—if indeed a bubble is what we are experiencing in the late 1990s, and if Federal Reserve Board Chairman Alan Greenspan's 1996 warning about stock prices finally holds true. Only in retrospect will we learn the verdict of history.

OCCAM'S RAZOR AND THE BOND MARKET

Occam's Razor has proven more useful in setting a framework for future returns in the bond market than in the stock market, albeit in a very different fashion. My simple methodology is a far cry from the bond market models engineered by econometricians on Wall Street, but it seems at least equally useful in considering future bond returns.

My analysis of bond returns begins with an examination of the same post-1926 era we used for stock returns. The 62-year nominal return on the long-term U.S. Treasury bond has averaged 5.2 percent, an odd combination of returns averaging a puny 3.1 percent from 1926 through 1979, and an extraordinary 11.8 percent thereafter. However, past returns on bonds (unlike past returns on stocks) are devoid of meaning when forecasting future returns. Sadly, almost no lesson of past history is relevant, except the *wrong* lesson: Never buy bonds!

Fortunately, however, the simple explanation is the correct one, and it further reinforces the Occam's Razor concept. The initial interest rate at the start of a given decade is by far the preponderant force governing subsequent returns. According to Table 2.4, which shows the interest rate on

TABLE 2.4

Ten-Year Nominal Bond Market Returns—Long-Term U.S. Government Bonds (1927–1997)

Period		Initial Yield*	Actual Return	Difference
Start 1-Jan.	End 31-Dec.			
1927	1936	3.5%	4.9%	−1.4%
1930	1939	3.4	4.9	−1.5
1940	1949	2.3	3.2	−0.9
1950	1959	2.1	−0.1	2.2
1960	1969	4.5	1.4	3.1
1970	1979	6.9	5.5	1.4
1980	1989	10.1	12.6	−2.5
1990	1997	8.2	9.9	−1.7
Average		5.1%	5.3%	−0.2%

Note: Yield at end of 1997 was 5.9 percent.

long-term U.S. Government bonds at the start of each decade, it is a remarkably efficient, if imperfect, indicator of future returns. It is efficient because the entry yield is a known quantity, just as it is for stocks. However, the initial interest rate on long-term bonds far surpasses the other two factors that come into play: the reinvestment rate (that is, the rate at which the interest coupons compound) and the terminal (or end-of-period) bond yield.

These variables fit neatly into the Keynesian dual formulation of returns. I liken the current interest rate to Keynes's first element—investment, or enterprise—for the interest coupon on a long-term Treasury bond is surely a precise statement of the prospective yield on the asset over its whole life, assuming that the existing state of affairs (i.e., the interest coupon) will continue indefinitely. The average yield during the period, which establishes the reinvestment rate of the interest coupons, and the yield on the bond ten years later correspond to the second element, speculation, or attaching hopes to a favorable change in the conventional basis of valuation. That is, a change in the general level of interest rates will lead to an increase or decrease in the bond's market value during the interim period before it reaches maturity. (If a U.S. Treasury bond is held until maturity, however, it will be redeemed by the federal government for its face value.)

The reinvestment rate is highly important in forecasting bond returns, simply because interest comprises by far the dominant proportion of bond returns over the long run, when the rate at which interest is reinvested may rival the terminal yield in importance. However, changes in interest rates tend to have a countervailing effect on bond prices and bond reinvestment rates: a higher yield lowers interim values before maturity, but raises the rate at which the interest is reinvested. (A lower yield does the reverse.) As a result, the initial interest rate remains the critical variable in forecasting the subsequent 10-year returns on bonds. This single factor has a very strong correlation (+.93) with the returns subsequently earned by bonds. It is even stronger than the impressive +.54 correlation between the total of the dividend yield, past earnings growth, and the average price–earnings ratio used in the Occam's Razor model to forecast subsequent returns on stocks. (As noted in Chapter 1, zero-coupon U.S. Government bonds eliminate both maturity risk and reinvestment risk for investors holding them to maturity, although in the interim, their prices are extremely volatile.)

In the 1991 article in *The Journal of Portfolio Management*, in which I forecast bond returns, I relied not on history but on a simple matrix using all three factors: the initial yield of the long-term U.S. Treasury bond; a series of different reinvestment rate assumptions; and a series of terminal interest rates at the end of the decade. I used this matrix toward the same purpose as the stock return matrix: to create a framework of expectations for returns from bonds in the future. (See Table 2.5.)

Assuming an initial interest rate of 9 percent, the matrix showed that if the terminal interest rate soared to 11 percent a decade later, and if the average reinvestment rate were 7 percent, bonds would provide a return as low as 7.4 percent. On the other hand, the return would rise to 10.7 percent if the reverse were true: if terminal yield dropped to 7 percent and the reinvestment rate rose to 11 percent. Interestingly, even if these two almost self-contradictory scenarios were to ensue, the range of future returns—from 7.4 percent to 10.7 percent—would not be extraordinarily wide.

As the 1990s began, I relied on Occam's Razor to offer some guidance in projecting bond market returns over the coming decade. Looking at a long-term historical norm of 5.2 percent for annual bond returns and a return of 12.6 percent during the 1980s, I opined that performance comparable to that of the 1980s was probably unrealistic; a repeat of the long-term norm seemed almost inconceivable. Perhaps the best central reference point for the Treasury bond would be its current yield to maturity of 8.2 percent, with annual returns possibly ranging between the highs reached in the 1980s and the midrange (5.5 percent) levels of the 1970s.

TABLE 2.5

Bond Market Total Return Matrix for the 1990s

Terminal Yield	Reinvestment Rate % (10 Years)	Total Bond Market Return*						
		6%	7%	8%	9%	10%	11%	12%
	12	6.6%	7.0%	7.3%	7.7%	8.0%	8.4%	8.2%
	11	7.1	7.4	7.7	8.1	8.5	8.5	9.2
	10	7.5	7.8	8.2	8.5	8.7	9.3	9.7
	9	8.0	8.3	8.6	9.0	9.4	9.9	10.1
	8	8.5	8.8	9.3	9.5	9.9	10.2	10.6
	7	9.0	9.6	9.6	10.0	10.4	10.7	11.1
	6	10.0	9.8	10.2	10.5	10.9	11.3	11.7

*20-year bond with 9% initial yield.

In the spirit of Occam, I considered only the *initial* interest rate, making no attempt to estimate the reinvestment rate or the terminal yield. By 1994, with half the decade on the books, bonds had returned 8.3 percent, closely in line with my 8.2 percent forecast. Indeed, the forecasted bond return coincided with the actual return almost as closely as the stock return. During the first half of the 1990s, Occam's Razor had led to two remarkably accurate forecasts.

Then, during 1995, interest rates tumbled and bonds took off. The annual rate of return rose to 10.4 percent, slightly better than my optimistic forecast. Given the lower reinvestment rate engendered by the sharp drop in interest rates through mid-1998, however, the rate of return has already fallen to 9.9 percent and, with the reinvestment rate now at 5¼ percent, will likely continue to fall during the remainder of the decade. Assuming that interest rates remain near current levels, the decade-long return should come in at about 9 percent—close to the 8.3 percent projected, and well within the expected range.

PRECISION AND PERVERSITY

As to the first half of the 1990s, after giving luck, pure and simple, credit for the precision of my forecasts of stock and bond returns, my 1995 article in *The Journal of Portfolio Management* noted that the luck was that the returns happened to represent solely investment fundamentals, without apparent speculation, perhaps a rare coincidence. I added that it remained to be seen whether the decade would reaffirm my findings. As it now appears, the decade will come very close to my bond forecast, but do precisely the reverse for my stock forecast, largely because the market, perversely enough, raised stock valuations to unprecedented levels.

Whether the powerful 1992–1998 recovery of corporate America from its abysmal earnings performance during the previous five years will continue—or whether it has been magnified in the stock market by a bout of speculative mania—remains to be seen. But some commentators, including the London-based editors of *The Economist*, argue that "America is experiencing a serious asset-bubble." Speculative mania, *The Economist* noted in April 1998, had coincided with rapid growth in the money supply, fueling an inflation in asset prices—stock prices, in particular.

The mere use of the word *bubble* by a distinguished publication was sufficient to set the financial community on edge. A *New York Times* editorial, headlined "The Economic Bubble Theory," denied that any bubble existed, except the one created by the economists, "who, try as they might, cannot seem to find a bubble worth worrying about." *The Wall Street Journal* then chimed in with "Let's Burst the Bubble Theory," describing it as "extreme paranoia about imaginary future disasters."

Later in the year, however, the idea that we were in fact experiencing a market bubble spread further. Morgan Stanley Dean Witter headlined its *Economics* bulletin: "The Great American Bubble," and a *New Yorker* article entitled "Pricking the Bubble" quoted Nobel economist and monetary historian Milton Friedman as agreeing: "Both the market of 1929 and the market today are bubbles . . . I suspect there is even more of a bubble today." Whatever the case, surely no one can disagree that, as *The Economist* reported, "there is no room for doubt that on standard time-tested measures, prices are way out of line." This is a difficult time to peer into the future.

Stock Returns in the Coming Decade

Despite the considerable challenge of doing so, let's see what Occam's Razor might suggest from 1999 forward. Given what we know of stocks in the past, the relative consistency of the fundamental elements of return— dividend yields and earnings growth—and the volatility of the speculative element—the ratio of stock prices to earnings—the Occam's Razor methodology suggests that we're at a high level of stock prices at the end of 1998. Here are the key elements:

- Dividend yields are at an all-time low of 1.4 percent, compared to a post-1926 average of 4.3 percent.
- Earnings growth is slowing from its heady 1992–1997 run (16.6 percent per year).
- Earnings growth in 1998 is expected to be around 5 percent, below the norm of 6.6 percent since the end of World War II.
- Stocks are priced at an all-time high of 27 times earnings, unarguably far removed from their historical norm of 14 times earnings.

Against this stock market backdrop, we are enjoying an economy operating at full employment and with little excess capacity, suggesting that the economic growth that brought us here may be difficult to repeat. But, looking toward the decade ahead, even if we suppose that earnings will increase at their historical rate of 6.6 percent or will even go as high as 10 percent (hardly bearish scenarios), stocks would provide a fundamental return of between 8.0 percent and 11.4 percent. If the price–earnings ratio were to hold at 27, that pure investment return would be equal to the market's *actual* return in the next 10 years—a far cry from the past few years of 30-percent-plus annual gains.

It is worth noting, however, that a sustained price–earnings ratio of 27 would demand a wholesale revision of our traditional approach to risk in the stock market. Even if the new norm were as high as 20 times earnings, nominal stock returns in the first decade of the new century would be reduced by three percentage points below the fundamental range of 8 percent to 11 percent, to a range of 5 percent to 8 percent. (There is, of course, always the possibility that a new, higher mean for both earnings growth and price–earnings ratios is now being established, a possibility that I discuss in Chapter 10.)

On the other hand, some vocal market mavens believe that we have thrown off the old shackles on the profitability of corporate America. These true believers are convinced that, having been liberated by a painful restructuring during the 1990s, the information technology revolution, and the boom in global trade, U.S. corporations will rule the world. In this brave new era, a price–earnings ratio of 20 or more, supported by robust profit growth, will be the norm, not a euphoric exception.

My innate sense of caution argues otherwise, but it is possible that we are beginning to enjoy the benefits of at least some increase in the sustained rate of long-term corporate earnings growth. (Again, I recall my own frequent advice to investors: Never forget that *anything* can happen in the stock market.) If, in fact, the modern norm of 6.6 percent earnings growth has moved upward to a new and higher norm of, say, 8 percent, then a higher price–earnings ratio could be justified—say, up to 20 times earnings versus the historic norm of 14 times earnings. However, even these increases, hardly of trivial dimension, would not be sufficient to create future returns that would support the current level of stock prices at a price–earnings ratio of 27 times earnings.*

Bond Returns in the Coming Decade

There is much optimism in the bond market, too, though it is less pronounced than in the stock market. With the long-term U.S. Treasury

---

*Given the wide range of professional opinion about the stock market outlook, I have added Appendix I, "Some Thoughts about the Current Stock Market as 1999 Begins."

bond yielding about 5¼ percent, interest rates have fallen to levels not seen since the early 1970s. Because inflation seems subdued, however, bonds still offer, by historical standards, a relatively generous real return. Based on the recent bond yield, the Occam's Razor methodology suggests a fairly narrow range of future returns:

- With "normal" assumptions (that is, interest rates in a yield range of 5 percent to 9 percent), bonds should provide a return of 5-plus percent, give or take a percentage point or so, during the coming decade.

- Under extreme conditions (rates of 4 percent to 10 percent), the best case, an 8.6 percent total return, would contrast with a worst case of 3.1 percent.

- In these extreme cases, the sensitivity of total return to the terminal yield would be about double its sensitivity to the reinvestment rate. Thus, the tricky question of what the bond yield will be a decade hence makes traditional forecasting especially challenging.

It is not my intent to argue that interest rates may not go to 4 percent and remain there (although it does seem unlikely), nor that rates may not go to 10 percent (perhaps even less likely) and remain there, at least for a time. Rather, I want to make the elemental point that, when we know the current interest coupon, we know *most* of what we need to know to forecast bond returns over the coming decade. Then, we can engage in rational discourse about our other assumptions: At what rates will the coupons be reinvested? What will be the terminal yield?

Back to the Future

I make no apology for Occam's Razor nor for the simplicity of my three-step concept of evaluating returns, even as I realize, quoting Renoir: "Nothing is as disconcerting as simplicity." To which I might add: nothing is as futile as expecting past returns to be slavishly translated into future returns on a linear basis. Too many of the complex academic investment strategies and forecasting methodologies appearing in the financial journals are entirely retrospective and, often, entirely dependent on the particular period chosen. Some of them approach witchcraft. The simplicity postulated by Occam's Razor can help cut through much of the confusion that clutters investment theory. It presents a simple and rational picture of future possibilities, based largely on the lessons we can learn from the study of past returns and our view of the elements of future returns. *Occam's Razor will not tell us what future returns will be, but it will tell us what the elements of stock and bond returns must be to provide us with any rate of return we wish to assume.*

You are free to disagree with my conclusions, particularly because, to reiterate, we *know* that anything can happen in the financial markets. And it usually does! There is no reason for slavish adherence to even a rational forecasting methodology, for markets are not always rational. Judgment is not only permitted, but encouraged. But the thrust of the theoretical exercise we have now completed is that disagreement must be fact-founded and data-based, not merely intuitive. Going through the Occam's Razor exercise should help investors make intelligent decisions about where to invest their assets. If we focus on the fundamentals of investment and ignore the dross of speculation, we come to the same conclusion reached by Warren Buffett:

> "In the short run, the stock market is a voting machine; in the long run, it is a weighing machine."[4]

HOW IMPORTANT IS IT TO FORECAST FUTURE RETURNS?

There is no way for investors to avoid thinking about the future course of the financial markets. In this chapter, I have tried, above all, to put into perspective the forces that drive market returns. They are worth knowing and understanding. But we must face the reality that, even if rational analysis of the relationship between investment fundamentals and speculation in investing gives us favorable odds (and no more than that) of accurately forecasting market returns, *the game may not be worth the candle for the long-term investor.* After all, we would be foolish to take our investment portfolios to the betting window and wager everything on a single race, even if the odds were 8 out of 10, to say nothing of $5\frac{1}{2}$ out of 10, in our favor.

Peter Bernstein and Robert Arnott reflected on this question in a recent article in *The Journal of Portfolio Management:* "Bull Market? Bear Market? Should You Really Care?" They concluded that, "for most long-term investors, bull markets are not nearly as beneficial, and bear markets not nearly as damaging as most investors seem to think." They noted, correctly, that, "a bull market raises the asset value, but delivers a proportionate *reduction* in the prospective real yields that the portfolio can deliver from that point forward, while a bear market does the reverse, reducing portfolio value, which is largely offset by an *increase* in prospective yields, other things being equal."[5] This being the case, what we would ideally like to see is a bull market late in the lives of our portfolios, and a bear market during the early years of accumulating them. But that's a bit of timing beyond our control.

Those who believe that the market's incredible momentum will be sustained, that the huge sustained purchases of stocks by individual investors will not slacken, and that we are indeed in a new era of global growth will hold the line in their equity allocation—or perhaps even increase it. But those who believe—as I do—that fundamentals such as earnings and dividends matter, and that, in the fullness of time, some semblance of historic norms will prevail, should consider at least some modest leaning against the powerful wind that is driving the high returns in this great bull market. And those who believe that another Great Crash lies around the corner must consider an even larger reduction of their equity exposures. Irrespective of what the future holds, however, it seems to me that equities should remain the investment of choice for the long-term investor—the dominant component of a well-balanced asset allocation program.

So, invest with intelligence and common sense; engage in an enlightened and rational discourse when considering the future; always have some significant portion of your assets both in stocks and in bonds; be sparing about precipitate and extreme changes in these proportions. And be skeptical about every prognostication you are given, including mine. If you have set an intelligent route toward capital accumulation, stay the course—no matter what.

With a bow to Occam's Razor and the role of simple concepts, I hope I have given you a better understanding of what is fundamental and what is transitory—what is investment and what is speculation—to help you come to a rational expectation of the range of returns that both stocks and bonds can provide over the long term. Now, we can get down to the most basic element of long-term investment strategy: the allocation of our investments between stocks and bonds.

CHAPTER 3

ON ASSET ALLOCATION
THE RIDDLE OF
PERFORMANCE ATTRIBUTION

*A*sset allocation is no more complicated than Chance's lessons about the garden. We invest with faith in the financial markets, dividing our portfolios among distinct asset classes that blossom and wither in different seasons of the economic cycle. Following the simple logic of diversification, we seek to maximize our participation in the market's seasons of plenty, while ensuring that we survive its seasons of want.

For nearly all investors, the principal asset classes of choice boil down to common stocks (for maximum total return), bonds (for reasonable income), and cash reserves (for stability of principal). Each differs in risk: stocks are the most volatile, bonds are less so, and the nominal value of cash reserves is inviolable.

FROM THE TALMUD TO MODERN PORTFOLIO THEORY

In the past 25 years, we have come to frame the simple logic of diversification in terms of a rigorous statistical model developed by finance academics: Modern Portfolio Theory. Investors almost universally accept this theory, which is based on developing investment portfolios that seek returns that optimize the investor's willingness to assume risk. Risk, in turn, is defined in terms of short-term fluctuations in expected value.

57

In its most comprehensive form, modern portfolio theory dictates that portfolio composition should include *all* liquid asset classes—not only U.S. stocks, bonds, and cash reserves, but international investments, short positions, foreign exchange, and various curios (gold, for example) from the financial marketplace. Such a range may be theoretically attractive, but the basic concept need not be so complex. Indeed, more than fourteen centuries ago, the Talmud prescribed this simple asset-allocation strategy: "A man should always keep his wealth in three forms: one third in real estate, another in merchandise, and the remainder in liquid assets."[1] My advice is not much different from what is recommended in that ancient body of Jewish tradition and law.

Rather than real estate and merchandise, however, my focus is on the marketable securities for an investment portfolio: stocks and bonds. For simplicity's sake, I omit cash reserves such as money market funds from the equation. Because they tend to deliver very modest returns, such reserves should be considered as *savings* for short-term and emergency needs, not as *investment* for long-term capital accumulation. For *investors*, short-term bonds are a superior alternative to money market funds. Short-term bonds are relatively insensitive to interest rate fluctuations; long-term bonds are hugely sensitive. Most of the examples presented in this book are based on intermediate-term and long-term bonds.

Like the Talmud's asset allocation advice, my guidelines are simple: as a crude starting point, two-thirds in stocks, one-third in bonds. From the day I began my career in this business, I was imbued by my mentor, the late Walter L. Morgan, an industry pioneer and the founder of the Wellington Fund, with the philosophy of portfolio balance. Balance optimizes returns from the stock market in order to reach investment goals such as the accumulation of assets for retirement, but it holds the risk of loss to tolerable levels by ownership of some bonds, too. Despite (or perhaps because of) the long bull market in stocks that has made balanced investing seem old-fashioned and stodgy to some advisers, I continue to advocate a balanced policy today—with more enthusiasm than ever.

My guidelines also respect what I call the four dimensions of investing: (1) return, (2) risk, (3) cost, and (4) time. When you select your portfolio's long-term allocation to stocks and bonds, you must make a decision about the real returns you can expect to earn and the risks to which your portfolio will be exposed. You must also consider the costs of investing that you will incur. Costs will tend to reduce your return and/or increase the risks you must take. Think of return, risk, and cost as the three spatial dimensions—the length, breadth, and width—of a cube. Then think of time as the temporal fourth dimension that interplays with each of the other three. For instance, if your time horizon is long, you can afford to take more risk than if your horizon is short, and vice versa.

RISK TO THE FORE

So far, I've described risk mostly in academic terms: standard deviation, or the volatility of monthly or annual returns (described in Chapter 1). In truth, however, risk is something far more difficult to quantify. It relates to how much you can afford to lose without excessive damage to your pocketbook or your psyche. Table 3.1 offers some historical perspective on the frequency and severity of loss that investors with various allocations to stocks and bonds have suffered since 1926, the first year in which the definitive statistics on our modern stock market became available. During this period, the stock market has provided a negative return about once every three-and-a-half years. The average loss in these years of decline has been 12 percent. The table also shows the extent to which this average decline has been muted by various holdings of bonds, ranging from 20 percent to 80 percent. For example, with a typical conservative balance of 60 percent stocks and 40 percent bonds, there would have been, not 20 loss years, but 16—one every four years—and the decline would have averaged some 8 percent, or fully one-third less.

Perhaps the three-year market decline from 1929 through 1932 can give us a "worst case" scenario. Then, an all-stock portfolio tumbled a

TABLE 3.1

Risk and Allocation (1926–1997)

Stock/Bond Allocation (%)*	Number of Years with a Loss	Average One-Year Loss (%)	Three-Year Loss (%) 1930–1932	Two-Year Loss (%) 1973–1974
100/0	20	−12.3	−60.9	−37.3
80/20	19	−9.8	−45.6	−29.2
60/40	16	−8.2	−30.2	−21.1
40/60	15	−5.5	−14.9	−13.0
20/80	14	−3.7	+0.5	−4.9

*Allocations are not rebalanced annually.

staggering −61 percent. However, bonds actually rose by 16 percent, and an allocation of 40 percent bonds and 60 percent stocks, left untouched in the three years of collapse, lost 30 percent—only half as much. Forty years later, during 1973–1974, we experienced the second most calamitous market of the past 67 years. (Interestingly enough, this two-year period is the stock market's most recent major market decline—a full quarter-century ago.) In that comparatively brief span, a portfolio invested only in equities, much like the allocations advocated by the current bull market's most ebullient cheerleaders, would have shed −37 percent of its value (including dividends). Again, a 40 percent bond position would have moderated the decline. While a 21 percent short-term loss of capital is hardly inconsequential, it was only slightly more than one-half of the 37 percent loss reflected in the all-stock portfolio.

Risk through the Seasons

Could these examples suggest that bonds are a better investment than stocks? Some investors, chastened by the stock market's 1973–1974 collapse, might well have reached that conclusion. For the long-term investor, however, it would have been tragic to do so. For in the 23 years that followed, stocks provided an annual return of 16.6 percent, compared to just 10 percent for bonds. A portfolio that began with a 40 percent bond/60 percent stock allocation and was left untouched would have enjoyed a return of 14.6 percent. (At the end of the period, its stock allocation would have grown to 86 percent.)

Bonds are best used as a source of regular income and as a moderating influence on a stock portfolio, not as an alternative to stocks. Remember, the goal of the long-term investor is not to preserve capital in the short run, but to earn real, inflation-adjusted, long-term returns. The stock market can dole out extremely heavy short-term losses, but, as we saw in Chapter 1, stocks have provided higher long-term real returns than bonds nearly all of the time—indeed, in 95 percent of all 25-year periods and 80 percent of all 10-year periods since 1802.

Real bond returns have been variable, but they have settled near a long-term average of 3.5 percent—half the 7 percent real return generated by stocks. In other words, stocks have delivered more than twice as much growth in purchasing power as bonds. As shown earlier, compounding that superficially small margin over the years makes a world of difference. Although stocks are extremely volatile in the short run, the long-term investor cannot afford *not* to take those risks.

And do not forget that even as return grows dramatically over time, so risk diminishes dramatically over time. As Figure 1.3 (p. 12) illustrated, the volatility of stock returns quickly falls as the holding period lengthens. The one-year standard deviation on stocks drops from 18.1 percent to 2.0 percent over 25 years, but most of that drop had taken place by the end of just 10 years, when the standard deviation reached 4.4 percent.

BENEFITING FROM BALANCE

The greatest benefit of a balanced investment program is that it makes risk more palatable. An allocation to bonds moderates the short-term volatility of stocks, giving the risk-averse long-term investor the courage and confidence to sustain a heavy allocation to equities. Choose a balance of stocks and bonds according to your unique circumstances—your investment objectives, your time horizon, your level of comfort with risk, and your financial resources.

Table 3.2 shows the returns you would have earned under the various allocations shown above had you (a) held your stocks for the two years *before* and during the 1973–1974 decline; (b) held your stocks for the two years during and *after*; and (c) held your stocks for all *six* years, including the span of the decline. (The figures assume that at the end of each year in the periods displayed, after divergent stock and bond market performances had altered the initial allocation, the portfolios were rebalanced to their original proportions.)

Here is Chance writ large: even without summer, the prior spring and ensuing autumn were enough to provide positive returns in almost all of

TABLE 3.2

Risk, Time, and Allocation (1971–1976)

Stock/Bond Allocation (%)*	Annualized Total Return			
	1971–1974	1973–1976	1971–1976	1971–1997
100/0	−3.9%	1.7%	6.4%	13.3%
80/20	−1.8	3.1	7.0	12.7
60/40	0.2	4.4	7.4	12.0
40/60	2.1	5.5	7.7	11.2
20/80	3.8	6.4	7.8	10.4
0/100	5.4	7.1	7.9	9.2

*Allocations are rebalanced annually.

the portfolio allocations. Only the two most aggressive portfolios, with stock allocations equal to 100 percent and 80 percent of assets respectively, sustained losses, but only in the 1971–1974 period. Because the periods examined surround a ferocious bear market, the portfolios with the largest allocations to bonds did best in each of the three periods. In fact, a portfolio invested only in bonds would have done best of all.

Look at the same allocations over time, however, and the data make a strong argument for heavy long-term investment in stocks. In the 27 years after 1970, return increased in direct proportion to a portfolio's stock allocation. As shown in Table 3.2, a portfolio with 80 percent of its assets in stocks and 20 percent in bonds earned an annual return of 12.7 percent. A portfolio with the opposite proportion—20 percent stocks, 80 percent bonds—returned 10.4 percent. Over the entire period, a $10,000 investment in the stock-heavy portfolio would have grown to $252,300, or $107,700 more than the $144,600 of capital accumulated in the bond-heavy portfolio. The greater the allocation to stocks, the greater the average long-term returns. Despite punishing winters, as in the early 1970s, the market's seasons eventually change; spring comes, and then summer. A well-balanced portfolio is best positioned to benefit.

Striking Your Own Balance

How can you determine an appropriate balance for your own needs? I continue to advocate the simple model represented in Figure 3.1: a four-quadrant matrix with suggested allocations for older and younger investors who are in different stages of their investment life cycles. The model assumes that, over long time periods, stocks will outperform bonds, as they have since 1802. It also assumes that stock returns will be less predictable, as demonstrated by a higher standard deviation of returns. These assumptions are consistent with the historical record.

The main points of the matrix are based on common sense. During the *accumulation* phase of your personal investment cycle, when you are building assets, you are putting aside money that you would otherwise spend. (It's never easy, but always essential.) You invest your capital, and you reinvest your dividends and your capital gains distributions. Because you have no immediate need for these assets, you can put your capital at greater risk in pursuit of higher return. As a younger investor, you might allocate as much as 80 percent or more of your portfolio to stocks, with the remainder in bonds. As the later years of your accumulation phase begin,

FIGURE 3.1

Basic Asset Allocation Model (Stocks/Bonds)

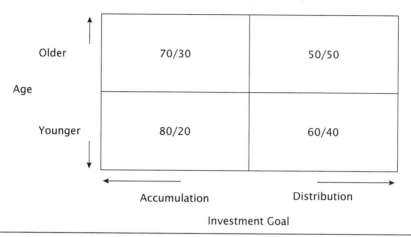

you are older and you have less time to recoup any decline in the value of your portfolio. At that point, you might limit your stock exposure to no more than 70 percent.

During the *distribution* phase of your investment cycle—when you enjoy the fruits of the accumulation phase—you depend on a relatively fixed pool of capital to generate income for your needs. You are withdrawing the income generated by your investments, and you cannot afford substantial short-term loss. At the start of the distribution phase, you might reduce your stock allocation to 60 percent or so. As you age, you might want to cut it to 50 percent. Even then, earning adequate income presents a challenge. In the latter part of 1998, with blue-chip stocks yielding about 1.4 percent and U.S. Treasury bonds yielding about 5.4 percent, a 50/50 balanced *market* portfolio was providing a yield of 3.3 percent. Given the average operating costs of the typical stock and bond fund, a similar mutual fund portfolio would yield only 2.0 percent—a reduction of almost 40 percent in your income. This simple calculation reinforces the giant impact of fund costs. The selection of funds in your asset allocation underlines why I repeatedly stress the vital role of fund costs in your investment decision-making process.

As you develop your strategic asset allocation, modify the model's broad guidelines to account for your own financial circumstances, your

AGE, ASSETS, AND ASSET ALLOCATION— MIXED REVIEWS

That the combination of age and asset level provides a sensible proxy for risk level seems almost self-evident. A young person who is just beginning to accumulate capital, with a small amount at stake, is able to: take considerable risk, seek maximum advantage from equity returns, and rely on time to iron out volatile short-term returns. An older person who has accumulated large assets has less time to recover possible losses and thus should seek greater certainty, lower risk, and sustained income return even at the expense of a lower capital return.

There are countervailing arguments. If you are young and scraping along, why take *any* equity risk? If you are old and have adequate retirement income, why not continue to emphasize equities and bequeath the largest possible estate to your heirs? Does not the younger investor, then, have a short-term time horizon and the older investor a time horizon that is almost infinite?

There are other facts of life, too. How much debt do you have? Is your cash flow positive or negative? Is your income rising or falling? What about college education for your children? How much can you expect from fixed-dollar pension benefits (including Social Security)? Are you an aggressive risk taker or a cautious conservator?

Academics raise the issue of human capital versus financial capital, too. The present value of the future labor of the young wage earner dwarfs the importance of investing. "*I* am the biggest asset in my portfolio," as it were. Would not individuals do better to manage their own lives in a way that maximizes their huge human capital potential rather than to focus on the relatively smaller amount of financial capital they will likely accumulate? Aren't the value of human capital and the value of the stock market both heavily influenced by the growth of the U.S. economy and thus apt to be highly correlated?

Tough questions all, and worthy of your careful consideration. But using age and asset level as a rule of thumb in establishing an asset allocation baseline seems to me a wise starting point for most— granted, not all—investors, whose infinite variety of circumstances belies pat solutions. Asset allocation is not a panacea. It is a reasoned—if imperfect—approach to the inevitable uncertainty of the financial markets.

age, your objectives, and your appetite for risk. It would not be imprudent for a highly risk-tolerant young investor (25 years old or so), who is just beginning to invest for retirement, to allocate everything to stocks, provided that the investor had confidence that regular investments could be made through thick and thin. In the distribution phase, a highly risk-averse older investor who has substantial means could cut the stock allocation to as low as 30 percent. A key factor in that decision is the relationship between the dollars to be invested and the capital already accumulated. A young investor just beginning with, say, a $150 monthly contribution to an IRA (or corporate-defined contribution pension or thrift plan) has time as an ally and has very little to risk at the outset. An older investor, on the other hand, must consider both the opportunity for return and the hazard of risk on a far larger and more crucial amount of capital. The time is already upon us when a $1,000,000-plus accumulation in a tax-deferred plan is the standard for an investor who has enjoyed a reasonably rewarding career during 40 years in the workforce.

Fine-Tuning Your Balance

Once you have determined a strategic long-term asset allocation, you must decide whether this balance will be relatively fixed or dynamic. There are two principal options. You can (1) keep your strategic ratio fixed, periodically buying and selling stocks and bonds to restore your portfolio to its original allocation; or (2) set an initial allocation and then let your investment profits ride. In the latter case, your initial allocation will gradually evolve to reflect the relative performance of stocks and bonds.

With the first option—the fixed allocation ratio—you will need to rebalance your portfolio from time to time. If strong stock markets transform your original allocation of 60 percent stocks and 40 percent bonds to a mix of 70 percent stocks and 30 percent bonds, you may need to sell stocks and invest the proceeds in bonds. This is easily done in a tax-deferred retirement account, where portfolio adjustments entail no tax liability. For taxable accounts, however, a sale of securities today is all too likely to trigger adverse tax consequences. If your holdings are primarily in a taxable account, a wiser course of action would be to redirect future contributions to bonds and gradually restore your portfolio to its original proportions. The advantage of a fixed-ratio strategy is that you automatically lock in your gains and reduce your equity exposure as equity prices increase. Correspondingly, you would increase your equity holdings (with the proceeds of bond sales, or by redirecting new investments) as stocks decline in value, reducing your equity exposure, and keeping your original balance between risk and reward relatively constant. Many investors will find greater peace of mind with a stable balance of stocks and bonds—a strategy that is counterintuitive but may prove productive—than with taking no action and allowing risk exposure to rise in tandem with the stock market—a strategy that is intuitive but may prove counterproductive.

If you choose to let your original asset allocation ride, you will, in effect, be following a policy of benign neglect. After you have determined an initial allocation, your risk and reward balance will dance to the rhythms of the financial markets. What started as 60 percent stocks and 40 percent bonds might eventually become 75 percent or more in stocks and 25 percent or less in bonds. As a recent example, an investor in a 50/50 stock/bond program before the current bull market began in 1982 would, 16-plus years later, be 76 percent invested in stocks and 24 percent in bonds.

There is a third option, but only for bold and self-confident investors. It does not abandon the "stay the course" principle, but it allows for a midcourse correction if stormy weather threatens on the horizon. If rational forecasts indicate that one asset class offers a considerably better investment opportunity than another, you might shift a modest percentage of your assets from the class judged less attractive to the class judged more attractive. This policy is referred to as *tactical asset allocation*. It is an opportunistic, transitory, aggressive policy that—*if skill, insight, and luck are with you*—may result in marginally better long-term returns than either a fixed-ratio approach or benign neglect.

It's grand to possess skill and insight, though all of us tend to overrate our abilities in both areas. But luck, too, plays a role. Many investors are right, but at the wrong time. It does no good to be too early or too late. Tactical asset allocation, if the strategy is used at all, should therefore be used only at the margin. That is, if your optimal strategic allocation is 65 percent stocks, limit any change to no more than 15 percentage points (50 to 80 percent stocks), and implement the change gradually. The prospect of having the skill, insight, *and* luck to eliminate your stock position overnight and restore it "when the time is right" is, in my view, patently absurd. Cautious tactical allocation may have a lure for the bold. Full-blown tactical allocation lures only the fool.

What might dictate moderate shifts in tactical asset allocation? One example: concern that stocks are substantially overvalued relative to bonds. Then, investors with conviction, courage, and discipline might benefit from a bow toward caution. I say "bow," not "capitulation." In an inevitably uncertain world, the reduction should not exceed 15 percentage points in your equity position. If you have 65 percent of your portfolio in equities, retain at least 50 percent; if 50 percent, at least 35 percent, and so on. A little caution may represent simple prudence, and, if you are relatively risk-averse, may enable you to sleep better, a blessing that is hardly trivial. One doesn't have to have investment experience to recognize the wisdom in this saying, from a remarkably parallel field: "There are old pilots and there are bold pilots, but there are no old bold pilots."

A Third Dimension

An ideal asset allocation incorporates the two most obvious dimensions of investing: risk and return. Investment costs represent a more subtle but equally critical third dimension of investing. The idea that cost rivals asset allocation in importance is not widely shared in the mutual fund industry. After all, with stocks having earned nearly 20 percent annually in the long bull market, and 30 percent annually in recent years, and with bonds yielding only about 5½ percent currently, asset allocation has dwarfed cost in importance. Costs rarely amount to much more than a few percentage points per year. So, industry lore has it that asset allocation must be given the highest priority. By ignoring the impact of costs, the industry implicitly argues that cost doesn't matter. Industry lore is wrong.

A rigorous academic study, published in 1986, seemed to confirm the lore, however. In the *Financial Analysts Journal*, authors Brinson, Hood, and Beebower reported: "Investment *policy* (the allocation of assets) dominates investment *strategy* (market timing and security selection), explaining on average 93.6 percent of the variation in total [pension] plan returns."[2] This statement may well be the seminal citation on the subject of asset allocation. It is surely the most quoted.

The authors went on to say: "Although investment strategy can result in significant returns, these are dwarfed by the return contribution from investment policy—the selection of asset classes and their normal weights." In other words, the return contribution from asset allocation dwarfs the other elements.

This finding for the ten years through 1983 was reaffirmed for the ten years through 1987 by the same authors in 1991, in a follow-up article published in the *Financial Analysts Journal*.[3] In the period ending in 1987, the impact of asset allocation was calculated at 91.5 percent, an inconsequential change.

Financial Scripture

When properly understood, the conclusion is, I think, beyond challenge. Unfortunately, however, it has been subject to considerable misunderstanding. It is often cited as meaning that asset allocation accounts for the differences in the *annual rates of return* earned by pension funds, rather than the *quarterly variations of returns*. I must confess that, at the outset, I made that same error by stating that the allocation of assets among stocks, bonds, and cash "has accounted for an astonishing 94 percent of the differences in total returns achieved by institutionally managed pension funds." Happily, I qualified that shorthand summary by coming up with what is surely the correct conclusion: "Long-term fund investors might profit by concentrating more on the allocation of investments between stock and bond funds, and less on the question of what particular stock and bond funds to hold." Although I stand by that conclusion today, I would surely add: ". . . as long as cost is held constant and low." In other words, make your selections from among the lower-cost funds.

William Jahnke, a 1997 winner of the Graham & Dodd award for an outstanding article published in the *Financial Analysts Journal,* exposed this widespread misinterpretation.[4] He noted that although asset allocation may explain 93.6 percent of the variation in quarterly portfolio returns, modest variations in short-term returns mean almost nothing to most investors. Using the original study's data, Jahnke concluded that investment policy—a pension plan's normal allocation to stocks, bonds, and reserves—explained only 14.6 percent of the differences in long-term total returns. Jahnke then offered his powerful conclusion: "For many individual investors, cost is the most important determinant of portfolio performance, not asset allocation policy, market timing, or security selection."[5]

I find myself, perhaps uncharacteristically, with both feet planted firmly on the middle ground. Asset allocation *is* critically important; but cost is critically important, too. When compared to these two issues, all the other factors that go into investing in a diversified portfolio of high-grade stocks and bonds pale into insignificance.

How Costs Change the Perspective

The Brinson/Hood/Beebower study (hereinafter, BHB) did not account for advisory fees and administrative and custody costs. In fairness, there was probably no need to do so. Given the nature of the study—its focus was primarily on quarterly variations rather than on cumulative annualized re-turns—and the nature of institutional pension plans in which there are fairly moderate variations in advisory fees (fees are set at competitive levels within narrow ranges—probably from 0.40 percent to 0.80 percent of assets annually), cost would likely have had little impact on the conclusions.

Costs in the mutual fund industry are a different matter. They vary widely and are generally much higher than those paid by pension funds. Equity fund expense ratios average 1.5 percent annually and range from 0.2 percent to 2.2 percent or more. Balanced funds today carry average ex-penses of 1.4 percent, and range from 0.2 percent to 1.8 percent or more. Bond funds range from 0.2 percent to 1.5 percent or more. (See Fig-ure 3.2.) These wide variations in costs among mutual funds only margin-ally affect their quarterly returns, but they have a great impact on the dif-ferences in long-term returns. Mountains of data strongly affirm that the

FIGURE 3.2

Portfolio Expense Ratios

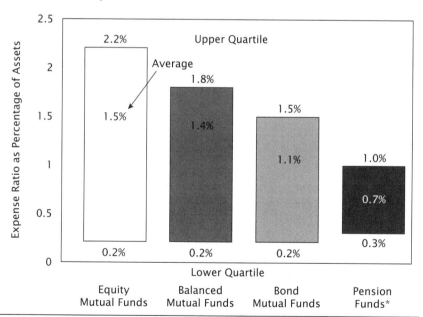

* Estimated.

cost of investing goes hand in hand with asset allocation as the key determinant of long-term returns. The bottom line: *Costs matter.*

In analyzing the role of costs, I chose balanced mutual funds because their asset allocation patterns are similar to those of the pension funds studied by BHB—usually, about 60 percent to 65 percent in common stocks. The results, based on the ten years ended December 31, 1997, clearly reaffirmed the basic finding of BHB: the impact of asset allocation dwarfs the impact of market timing and stock selection. In fact, 84.9 percent of the variation in the quarterly returns of the balanced funds was explained by asset allocation, a figure closely akin to the pension fund result. The similarity was striking, as the comparison of results in Table 3.3 reveals.

Turning from *variations* in return to *total* return, both the pension plans and the mutual funds displayed returns *before expenses* that fell slightly short of the returns of the market index benchmarks. For the pension study, BHB used a market benchmark comprising the Standard & Poor's 500 Index for stocks, the Lehman Government/Corporate Bond Index for bonds in the first study and then the Salomon Broad Investment Grade Bond Index for bonds in the second study, and U.S. Treasury Bills for cash. For the balanced Mutual Fund study, we used similar benchmarks: the Standard & Poor's 500 Index for stocks, the Lehman Intermediate-Term Corporate Bond Index for bonds, and U.S. Treasury Bills for cash. (In neither the BHB study nor our study did the results vary significantly if the all-market Wilshire 5000 Equity Index was used instead of the S&P 500.)

What we are witnessing (as has been reaffirmed over what seems like time immemorial) is the failure of active managers, *on average*, to outperform

TABLE 3.3

Source of Variations in Return*

Factor	BHB Study	Mutual Fund Study
Allocation policy	92.5%	84.9%
Allocation changes and security selection	7.5	15.1
Total	100.0%	100.0%

*Average of BHB's 1986 and 1991 studies; Mutual Fund study based on ten years ended December 31, 1997.

TABLE 3.4

Performance of Managers of Mutual Funds and Pension Funds

Managers' Returns before Costs	Pension Fund Study	Mutual Fund Study
Index composite return	11.8%	14.2%
Fund return (before costs)	11.2	14.1
Difference before costs	−0.6%	−0.1%
Managers' Returns after Costs		
Average expense ratio	−0.6	−1.1
Fund return (after costs)*	10.6%	13.0%
Difference after costs	−1.2%	−1.2%

*Excluding sales charges.

appropriate market indexes, even before costs are deducted. It didn't matter whether the managers were advising pension funds or mutual funds. In neither case were they particularly successful. (See Table 3.4.)

The failure of active managers to add value by outpacing passive market indexes largely reflects undistinguished individual stock selection (or, if you will, highly efficient markets). The actual subtraction of value is likely caused by portfolio transaction costs (which surely exist, although they can't be quantified with precision). Together, these two factors doubtless played a heavy role in the shortfalls experienced by both the pension funds and the mutual funds relative to the unmanaged index portfolios.

When we take operating expense ratios into account, however, the failure of the managers becomes self-evident.* Table 3.4 also presents the after-cost results of our study. Note that the total shortfall in return was 1.2 percent annually in both cases, a reduction of about 8 percent in the market index return. Expenses accounted for 92 percent of the mutual fund shortfall. What is more, since the decade covered by the study, the expense

---

*The mutual fund shortfall would have been even more apparent if we had also adjusted for fund sales charges. For load funds (those charging sales commissions), sales charges would have consumed about 0.6 percent of total annual returns. For load and no-load funds combined, the reduction in return would have been about 0.4 percent.

TABLE 3.5

Balanced Funds: Returns vs. Costs (1987–1997)

Cost Quartile	Net Return	Expense Ratio*	Gross Return
First (lowest costs)	14.0%	0.6%	14.6%
Second	13.2	1.0	14.2
Third	12.6	1.2	13.8
Fourth (highest costs)	12.1	1.7	13.8
Average	13.0%	1.1%	14.1%

*In 1998, the costs in the four quartiles were: 0.7 percent (lowest), 1.0 percent, 1.2 percent, and 1.9 percent (highest).

ratio of the average balanced fund has risen from 1.1 percent to 1.4 percent, an ominous sign that future shortfalls are apt to be even larger.

As it turns out, there is a fairly systematic relationship between the costs and net returns of the balanced funds in our sample. Indeed, when costs are eliminated from consideration, the gross returns of the second, third, and fourth quartiles are virtually identical at about 14.0 percent. The results are illustrated in Table 3.5. Not surprisingly, *in each quartile, lower costs ineluctably lead to higher returns.*

The icing on the cake is that the lowest-cost group also achieved superior returns while taking no more risk than the balanced fund average. Differences in asset-allocation policy among these balanced funds (four of the funds carried significantly higher proportions of common stocks than the group average) accounted for some moderately significant differences in total return. But when risk (measured by standard deviation) was taken into account, only the low-quartile expense group distinguished itself with outstanding risk-adjusted returns. Specifically, the average risk-adjusted return (using the Sharpe ratio*) of the low-expense quartile was 15 percent *above* average while the risk-adjusted returns of the three quartiles with higher expenses were all 4 percent *below* the average of the group. (The average Sharpe ratio for the funds in the lower cost quartile was 0.94; each of the three higher-cost quartiles averaged

---

*The Sharpe ratio, developed by Nobel Laureate William F. Sharpe, is the customary basis for calculating risk-adjusted returns. The ratio is based on annual rate of return (in excess of the risk-free rate of return on U.S. Treasury Bills) per unit of risk—more accurately, volatility, as measured by standard deviation.

about 0.79.) This relationship drives home the "costs matter" thesis with powerful force.

The conclusion of this study of balanced mutual funds, then, demands the addition of this important *caveat* to the BHB phrase: "Although investment strategy can result in significant returns, these are dwarfed by the return contribution from investment policy, *and the total return is severely impacted by costs.*"

This conclusion is derived not only from the limited evidence provided by this study of balanced mutual funds, but also in an exhaustive study of the returns of all 741 domestic equity mutual funds in operation from 1991 to 1996. When fund investment styles (growth versus value) and market capitalization (large versus small) are taken into account, funds in the low-cost quartile outpaced funds in the high-cost quartile with remarkable consistency, as we'll show in Chapter 6. We see the same broad impact repeated in bond funds, discussed in detail in Chapter 7.

Low Costs Magnify Fund Returns

Further, for whatever reason, low costs systematically magnified the gross return advantage earned by the top-quartile funds, giving them an even larger edge. Randomness seems an unlikely explanation; perhaps the higher-cost funds reached for extra income yield or lower-grade securities to offset their excess expenses, but the implicit extra risk came home to roost. In any event, for the balanced funds, every 10 basis points of lower expenses accounted, on average, for 17 basis points of enhanced net return. Leverage, if such it were, almost doubled the negative impact of higher cost.

To give some context to what this mathematics means, consider this example: A 10 percent net return on a high-cost fund would translate, not merely into an 11.1 percent return for a balanced fund with a 1.1 percent expense ratio advantage (high-cost balanced funds with expense ratios averaging 1.7 percent; low-cost funds, 0.6 percent), but into an 11.9 percent total return. *That would be a 19 percent enhancement of the 10 percent annual return of the high-cost fund.* When compounded over 10 years, the advantage is huge; over 25 years, it soars; and over 50 years, the advantage is truly stratospheric—a 2½-fold increase in value, from $1.174 million to $2.764 million (see Table 3.6). As I have noted, 50 years is no more than an investment lifetime for investors who begin to invest in a 401(k) tax-deferred savings plan at age 25 and are living off the fruits of their accumulation at age 75. The figures in the table speak for themselves.

TABLE 3.6

Cumulative Impact of Costs on a $10,000 Investment

Years	High Cost 10.0% Return	Low Cost 11.9% Return
10	$ 25,900	$ 30,800
25	108,300	166,200
50	1,173,900	2,763,800

With the powerful impact of costs—and the favorable leverage that has accompanied it—we can now turn to the implications of costs for asset-allocation policy, focusing on the relationship of long-term stock returns and bond returns.

THREE PERSPECTIVES ON THE IMPACT OF COST

The customary perspective for investors is to consider fund expenses as a percentage of assets—in the mutual fund field, the stated expense ratio. These ratios range from 0.2 percent of assets annually for the lowest-cost equity funds (often, as it happens, market index funds) to 1.5 percent for the average equity fund and 2.2 percent for highest-cost equity funds (those in the top quartile in terms of expense ratio). Even the highest of these figures, however, tends to trivialize the impact of cost for the uninitiated. An investor might ask: "Does a percentage point or so really matter?"

A second perspective shows that it matters a great deal: Consider expenses as the percentage of an initial investment consumed over a 10-year holding period. Here, the range would be only 2.8 percent for the lowest-cost funds, 19.8 percent for the average fund, and a healthy (or unhealthy!) 28.1 percent for the highest-cost funds. Converting these percentages into dollars may lend even more impact to this perspective. An 0.2 percent annual cost on an initial investment of $10,000 (assuming that the investment appreciated at 5 percent annually) would cost the investor only $280 over 10 years. But at 2.2 percent, the 10-year cost would be $2,810. That's "real money." As you can imagine, the mutual fund industry is not particularly smitten by this perspective, for it brings the cost issue into sharp relief.

Costs can also be thought of from a third perspective—as a percentage of the expected annual return on equities. Using the same examples—expense ratios of 0.2 percent, 1.5 percent, and 2.2 percent—and assuming long-term market returns of 10 percent, costs would consume 2 percent, 15 percent, and 22 percent of annual return, reducing the net return earned by investors to 9.8 percent, 8.5 percent, and 7.8 percent, respectively. This drain is substantial, though it is seldom referenced by fund promoters. However, it is a stark fact of investment experience.

And a Fourth Perspective . . .

There is also yet a fourth perspective on cost: *cost as a percentage of the equity risk premium*. It provides the most striking perspective of all. To assess the impact of cost on the equity risk premium, let's take a simple example. Assume that the expected return on long-term U.S. Treasury bonds is 6 percent and the expected return on stocks is 8.5 percent. The risk premium would be 2.5 percent. Taking an extreme example, if equities carried a risk premium of 2.5 percent over long-term U.S. Treasury bonds, and if an equity fund carried a high total cost of 2.5 percent (say, an expense ratio of 2 percent and transaction costs of 0.5 percent), the investors would be indifferent in making the choice. Theory would say that the long-term returns of the two investments over time would be identical. There would be no premium for assuming the extra risk. *Cost would have consumed 100 percent of the equity risk premium.*

Viewed in this light, all of the costs in investing—advisory fees, other fund expenses, *and* transaction costs—bite into the risk premium. The difference is simply a matter of *degree*, although at the highest cost levels it is arguably a difference in *kind* because it changes the very character of the returns. Table 3.7 shows the percentage of the risk premium consumed by mutual fund expenses at various risk-premium levels. For simplicity, transaction costs, which could add another 0.1 percent to 1.0 percent to the cost

TABLE 3.7

Percentage of Equity Risk Premium Consumed by Expenses

Fund Group	Expense Ratio*	Equity Risk Premium			
		2%	3%	4%	5%
Lowest cost	0.2%	10%	7%	5%	4%
Average cost	1.5	75	50	38	30
Highest cost	2.2	110	73	55	44

* Excluding transaction costs.

THE EQUITY RISK PREMIUM

The equity risk premium is, simply stated, the extra return required by investors to compensate them for taking the extra risk of owning common stocks rather than risk-free U.S. Treasury bonds. The premium can be calculated either in retrospect (i.e., the spread between the two returns over a given past period) or prospectively (the difference between the expected future returns of each).

Judging from the levels of today's stock and bond market, a 2 to 3 percent risk premium might be a reasonably cautious guess for the coming decade. Indeed, many respected investment advisers (a few were noted in Appendix I) have placed the probable number at less than 2 percent.

impact of the expense ratios, are ignored in the table, giving the funds the benefit of a very large doubt.

Asset Allocation and Cost

The average equity risk premium over history (since 1802) has been 3.5 percent. As Figure 3.3 shows, this premium has ranged between zero and 5 percent in about 50 percent of all periods, consistently exceeding that upper bound *only* during the 10-year periods ending between 1947 and 1970. Since no one can be certain about future premiums, I will rely on this 3.5 percent average during the rest of my analysis. Let's imagine that you are an investor who is confronting the real world of mutual funds today, and you examine what happens when you come to make your asset allocation decision. For the purpose of argument, let's assume you expect to maintain a stock–bond ratio of 65 percent/35 percent, and you want to determine the implications of cost on your decision. Further, let's assume a long-term return of 10 percent on stocks and 6.5 percent on long-term Treasuries, and a risk premium of 3.5 percent. You decide to hold a Treasury bond for the bond allocation. For the equity allocation, your choice is between a fund in the lowest cost range (0.20 percent) and a fund in the highest cost quartile (an expense ratio of 2.2 percent). The low-cost program

FIGURE 3.3

Equity Risk Premium vs. Long-Term U.S. Treasury Bonds (1802–1997)

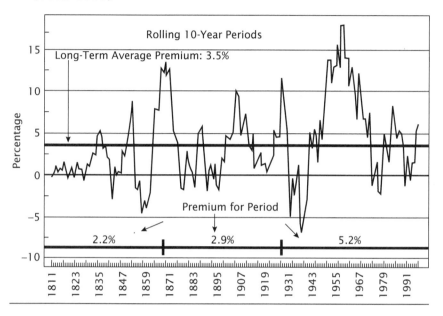

provides a return of 8.6 percent; the high-cost program, a return of 7.3 percent (see Table 3.8).

That 1.3 percent spread in assumed return—*with risk held constant*—is a meaningful difference. The low-cost program would build an assumed investment of $10,000 to $22,800 in 10 years and to $78,700 in 25 years (taxes excluded). The respective results for the high-cost program would be $20,200 and $58,200, with the latter figure representing a staggering $20,500 shortfall for the long-term investor over 25 years—more than twice the amount of the initial investment.

But now let's look at the situation slightly differently, from the standpoint of risk premium. Assume you accept the basic premises I've used—a 10 percent return on stocks and a 3.5 percent equity risk premium—and you are investing with the hope and the objective of receiving a long-term return of 7.5 percent. Question: What allocation would you make, given a choice between a low-cost equity fund and a high-cost equity fund? Answer: If you select the low-cost program, your required ratio would be 30

TABLE 3.8

Cost, Returns, and Asset Allocation

	Annualized Return	
	Low-Cost Fund	High-Cost Fund
Equity allocation	9.8%	7.8%
Bond allocation	6.5	6.5
65/35 Composite	8.6%	7.3%

percent stocks and 70 percent bonds. But if you select the high-cost program, your ratio would be 75 percent stocks and 25 percent bonds. To say the least, the difference in risk exposure is dramatic. In fact, you would have to raise your risk exposure by 2½ times to earn the same return in the high-cost portfolio.

Put another way, you could reduce your exposure to the risk of the stock market by 45 percentage points—a reduction of 60 percent—by the simple expedient of choosing the low-cost fund. This example obviously assumes that other factors are held constant—in effect, that costs make a systematic difference in long-term performances. It also assumes what we have learned from long years of experience: no *single* top-performing fund can be selected *in advance*. However, experience tells us that the top-performing *group* of funds can be selected in advance, simply by relying on low cost as the criterion.

We may know history's appraisal of the equity premium in the past, but we *never* can be certain of what equity premium will prevail in the future. Let's consider the implications of two future environments, one bearish and the other bullish: (1) an equity return of 7 percent and a bond return of 6 percent, resulting in a risk premium of 1 percent; and (2) an equity return of 12 percent and a bond return of 8 percent, resulting in a risk premium of 4 percent (Table 3.9). In case (1), the low-cost stock fund consumes 20 percent of the 1 percent risk premium, compared to 220 percent(!) for the high-cost fund. (Please recall that fully 25 percent of stock funds in the industry have costs averaging 2.2 percent.) In case (2), expenses of the low-cost fund would consume 5 percent of the 4 percent risk premium; the high-cost fund would consume 55 percent.

In sum, if you accept my premises and my forecast ranges, fairly obvious choices can be made, as reflected in Table 3.9, showing returns

TABLE 3.9

Cost, Returns, and Allocation

		(1) Bearish Environment			(2) Bullish Environment		
		Gross Annual Return: Stocks 7% Bonds 6% Equity Premium 1%			Gross Annual Return: Stocks 12% Bonds 8% Equity Premium 4%		
Allocation		Fund Return			Fund Return		
Stocks	Bonds	High Cost	Average Cost	Low Cost	High Cost	Average Cost	Low Cost
80%	20%	5.0%	5.6	6.6	9.4%	10.0	11.0
70	30	5.2	5.7	6.6	9.3	9.8	10.7
60	40	5.3	5.7	6.5	9.1	9.5	10.3
50	50	5.4	5.8	6.4	8.9	9.3	9.9
40	60	5.5	5.8	6.3	8.7	9.0	9.5
30	70	5.6	5.9	6.2	8.5	8.8	9.1
20	80	5.8	5.9	6.2	8.4	8.5	8.8

High-cost fund expense ratio: 2.2%.
Average-cost fund expense ratio: 1.5%.
Low-cost fund expense ratio: 0.2%.

achieved by high-, average-, and low-cost portfolios at various allocations. For example, in case (1), the bearish environment, an investor could choose an 80 percent *bond* portfolio and earn 6.2 percent, a higher return than the 5.0 percent net return on a portfolio 80 percent invested in higher-cost *stock* funds. In case (2), the bullish environment, an investor choosing a low-cost 40/60 stock/bond portfolio could expect a return of 9.5 percent, even larger than the 9.4 percent return on a portfolio with twice as much in stocks (high-cost 80/20). That is, the investor could earn a higher return despite a 50 percent reduction in equity exposure, simply by taking costs into account. Higher return *can* be earned hand in hand with the assumption of lower risk.

IS IT COST OR ASSET ALLOCATION?

Table 3.10 summarizes these four perspectives on the impact of costs on asset allocation. They clearly reaffirm our earlier amendment of the BHB

TABLE 3.10

Equity Fund Expenses

	Lowest Cost	Average Cost	Highest Cost
1. Annual percentage of assets	0.2%	1.5%	2.2%
2. Annual percentage of 10% return	2.0	15.0	22.0
3. Ten-year percentage of initial investment	2.8	19.8	28.1
4. Percentage of equity premium of 3.5%	5.7	42.9	62.9

conclusion: "Although investment strategy can result in significant returns, these are dwarfed by the return contribution from investment policy, and the total return is severely impacted by costs." They also illustrate that Jahnke makes a point worth considering when he goes even further: "Cost is the most important determinant of portfolio performance."

As you consider the issue of asset allocation and determine your own asset-allocation strategy, consider the choices that are available:

1. **Annual costs as a percentage of assets managed.** (The conventional measure.) You can pay an expense ratio of 0.2 percent of assets or one at 2.2 percent of assets. The choice is yours.

2. **Annual costs as a percentage of the total equity return.** You can relinquish from 2 percent to 22 percent of your annual return. The choice is yours.

3. **Cumulative costs as a percentage of the initial capital.** You can pay from 2.8 percent to 28.1 percent of initial capital over a period of a decade (from $280 to $2,810 on a $10,000 investment). The choice is yours.

4. **Annual costs as a percentage of the equity risk premium.** This is an important new concept. You can relinquish from 5.7 percent to 63 percent of the historical premium norm. Again, the choice is yours.

These key alternatives will heavily influence your asset allocation decisions and subsequent investment performance. You need only realize that *costs truly matter.* This concept must take its proper place as a high priority, not merely an afterthought, as investors decide on the proper strategic asset allocation for their investment portfolios. For there proves to be a simple solution to the riddle of performance attribution.

Is performance determined by asset allocation or by cost? Common sense gives us the answer to that question, and the data reaffirm it: Both.

CHAPTER 4

ON SIMPLICITY
How to Come Down to Where You Ought to Be

*W*e live in a world where a seemingly infinite amount of information is available to just about everyone. Financial facts, figures, and theories once available only to investment professionals are now at the fingertips of individual investors. No longer must the investor depend on the services of an investment professional. Buy and sell to your heart's content over the World Wide Web. The information age has truly transformed the world of investing.

Today, investors are bombarded on all sides by investment information—whether they want it or not. Complex quantitative analysis, real-time stock quotes, and the like are available at any local library, if not through a personal computer. Investors now ask their mutual fund managers about their "alpha"; they want to know a fund's "Sharpe ratio"; they read articles about "complexity theory" and "behavioral finance."

Yet this barrage of information has not necessarily translated into better returns. Instead, we focus on the quantity of data. We want more sophisticated and complex information. Presumably it will enhance our returns. Our world may or may not be any more complex than it has ever been, but we have certainly made the investment process more complicated. In today's environment of a mind-numbing information flow that is at once electrifying and terrifying, where is the intelligent investor to turn?

Turn to simplicity. The great paradox of this remarkable age is that the more complex the world around us becomes, the more simplicity we must seek in order to realize our financial goals. Never underrate either the majesty of simplicity or its proven effectiveness as a long-term strategy for productive investing. Simplicity, indeed, is the master key to financial success. The old Shaker hymn got it just right:

> 'Tis the gift to be simple;
> 'Tis the gift to be free;
> 'Tis the gift to come down
> Where we ought to be.

I'd like to offer some precepts to help you "come down where [you] ought to be" in your quest for investment success. Let me begin by describing what I regard as the realistic epitome of investment success. Here is my definition of the nature of the task: *The central task of investing is to realize the highest possible portion of the return earned in the financial asset class in which you invest—recognizing, and accepting, that that portion will be less than 100 percent.*

Why? Because of cost. As we have already seen, we must pay the costs of the intermediaries involved in making the investments in each financial asset class—cash reserves, bonds, stocks, and so on—available to us. To state the obvious, we know intuitively that our certificates of deposit and our money market funds will inevitably earn less than the going market rate for short-term commercial paper, simply because the costs of financial intermediaries—transaction costs, information costs, and the cost of convenience—are deducted from the interest rates paid by the government or by the corporate borrower.

Similarly, we do not—nor should we—expect our bond funds to provide us with higher yields than the average yield of the bonds held in a fund's portfolio. In fact, because of excessive fund fees in bond mutual funds as a group, the gap between 100 percent of the market return and the return that filters down to the investor after cost is often distressingly large—so large that *nearly* all bond funds are distinctly inferior investments.

The proposition applies even in the equity arena, the third major class of liquid financial assets. It is a mathematical impossibility—a definitional contradiction—for all investors *as a group* to outpace the returns that are earned in the total stock market. Indeed, given the high costs of equity fund ownership, it is a mathematical certainty that, over a lifetime of investing, only a handful of fund investors will succeed in doing so by any significant margin.

WHEN ALL ELSE FAILS, FALL BACK ON SIMPLICITY

I propose to challenge most of the conventional wisdom that you hear and read. A considerable amount of good common sense is available to investors. Pay attention to it. But a considerable amount of foolishness—investment wizardry, financial legerdemain, and tempting solutions—is also promoted, often by the apparently omniscient. Disregard it. No matter what you hear or read, do not forget that we live and invest today in an uncertain world of finance, of volatile and interrelated securities markets. You may have heard that we are living in a new era, but I strongly caution you that, in human history, many more "new eras" have been predicted than have ever come to pass.

Amid the cacophony of advice bombarding you, mine, I imagine, is the most basic: To earn the highest of returns that are *realistically* possible, you should invest with simplicity. Accepting this reality—that investors as a group will inevitably capture less than 100 percent of the rates of return provided in any asset class—is the first step toward simplifying investment decisions. What, then, is the optimal method of approaching the 100 percent target and accumulating a substantial investment account? Rely on the ordinary virtues that intelligent, balanced human beings have relied on for centuries: common sense, thrift, realistic expectations, patience, and perseverance. In investing, I assure you that those characteristics will, over the long run, be rewarded.

Where should you begin? Consider that the ultimate in simplicity comes with the additional virtue of low cost. The *simplest* of all approaches is to invest solely in a single balanced market index fund—just one fund. *And it works.* Such a fund offers a broadly diversified middle-of-the-road investment program for a typical conservative investor who is investing about 65 percent of assets in stocks and 35 percent in bonds. This portfolio is entirely "indexed"—that is, its stocks and bonds are not actively managed, but simply represent a broad cross-section of the entire U.S. stock market and bond market. (The next chapter explores this concept in considerable depth.) Over the past half-century, such a fund would have captured 98 percent of the rate of return of the combined stock and bond markets. Investing doesn't get much better than that.

Let me prove the point by evaluating the cumulative returns of balanced mutual funds—a group whose portfolios tend to be quite homogeneous, composed as they are of stocks with both value and growth characteristics, and good-quality bonds with intermediate-to-long maturities (usually including a small cash reserve). I'll compare the cumulative returns of the average balanced fund with a hypothetical no-load balanced index fund weighted 35 percent by the Lehman High-Grade Corporate Bond Index and 65 percent by the Standard & Poor's 500 Stock Index (rebalanced annually), with the annual return reduced by estimated costs of 0.2 percent. We'll take a half-century retrospective, in order to gain a broad view from the lessons of history. Figure 4.1 shows the results, based on an initial investment of $10,000 in 1947.

Note these three key observations:

1. At the end of the half-century, the initial $10,000 investment would have grown to $1,615,000 for the passively managed index fund, versus $1,080,000 for the actively managed traditional fund—a compound annual return of 10.7 percent, compared to 9.8 percent for the average balanced fund (and 10.9 percent for the composite index itself). When time and compounding join forces, this seemingly modest 0.9 percent advantage in annual return for

FIGURE 4.1

Owning a Single Balanced Fund, Half-Century Results, 1947 to 1997, $10,000 Investment

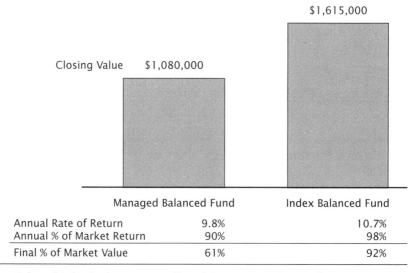

	Managed Balanced Fund	Index Balanced Fund
Annual Rate of Return	9.8%	10.7%
Annual % of Market Return	90%	98%
Final % of Market Value	61%	92%

Note: Balanced index fund returns are adjusted for expenses of 0.2% of assets per year.

the index fund over the average actively managed fund has created a profound difference in accumulated wealth—fully $535,000. *Little things mean a lot.*

2. The superiority of the index fund is not a matter of magic. The heavy costs of managed funds accounted for precisely 100 percent of the differential in rate of return. The average balanced fund incurred annual operating expenses of 0.9 percent, on average, during the period, and perhaps another 0.2 percent in portfolio turnover costs—a total handicap of 1.1 percent. The index fund cost was 0.2 percent, an advantage of 0.9 percent. That cost advantage is what made the difference.

3. While managed funds earned *annual* returns equal to 90 percent of the market returns for a 65/35 stock/bond portfolio, at the end of 50 years the final value was just 61 percent of the value of the market portfolio. For the balanced index fund, however, the final value was 92 percent of that of the market portfolio, more than half again as large as the managed funds.

Fifty years, to be sure, is a long time. The past 15 years may be more relevant for appraising today's fund industry, so let's look at the 35 balanced funds that have survived that period (Figure 4.2). As it turns out, you would have been wise not to waste your energy trying to find the best manager. *Only two funds outpaced the low-cost index fund for the full period.* During the past 15 years—including most of the bull market, with stock returns near historic highs—the average return of the actively managed balanced funds was 12.8 percent per year, compared with 14.7 percent for the balanced index fund, without a noticeable difference in risk. That 1.9 percent deficit may not matter to investors when they still earn 12.8 percent net, but when stock returns recede to more normal levels—as they are apt to—the deficit's significance will be more apparent.

This 1.9 percent relative advantage in recent times was more than double the 0.9 percent advantage over the half-century, and probably a better portent of things to come. The net results: $10,000 grew to $78,200 in the index fund versus $60,900 in the managed fund. The index fund advantage alone was $17,300—almost double the initial capital. And, this time, with the higher 14.9 percent return on the index itself, the index *fund*, with an annual cost of 0.2 percent, captured fully 99 percent of the market rate of return. Investing in a single balanced index

---

FIGURE 4.2

Owning a Single Balanced Fund, 15-Year Results, June 1983 to June 1998, $10,000 Investment

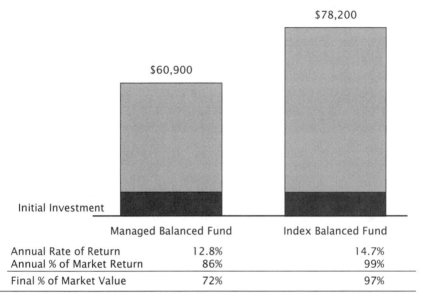

	Managed Balanced Fund	Index Balanced Fund
Annual Rate of Return	12.8%	14.7%
Annual % of Market Return	86%	99%
Final % of Market Value	72%	97%

Note: Balanced index fund returns are adjusted for expenses of 0.2% of assets per year.

fund represents not only the ultimate in simplicity, but a productive choice as well.

SIMPLICITY IN YOUR STOCK PORTFOLIO

Like most people, you may well be an investor who would like to control your own investment balance. Fair enough. I turn now to a second example of the value of simplicity—a single *equity* index fund for your stock port-folio. Again, during the past 15 years, the record of indexing has been truly remarkable. The total stock market index (Wilshire 5000) has outpaced the average diversified equity fund by 2.5 percentage points per year. Again, the index fund captured 99 percent of the annual market return of 16.0 per-cent. The cumulative result is really quite imposing, with an *added* return of more than $23,500—more than two times the value of the initial invest-ment (see Figure 4.3). This difference arises largely because *total* fund costs

FIGURE 4.3

Owning a Single Equity Fund, 15-Year Results, June 1983 to June 1998, $10,000 Investment

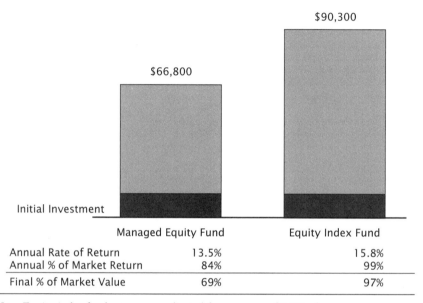

	Managed Equity Fund	Equity Index Fund
Annual Rate of Return	13.5%	15.8%
Annual % of Market Return	84%	99%
Final % of Market Value	69%	97%

Note: Equity index fund returns are adjusted for expenses of 0.2% of assets per year.

(expense ratios plus portfolio transaction costs) themselves ran to about two full percentage points.

As was the case with the balanced funds (only more so), this 15-year equity fund comparison amply justified a simple index approach to capturing the highest realistically possible portion of the market's returns—albeit slightly less than 100 percent.

What I have described here is the very essence of simplicity: owning the entire U.S. stock market (and, for a balanced index fund, the entire U.S. bond market as well); making no effort to select the best manager; holding the asset allocation constant and making no attempt at market timing; keeping transaction activity low (and minimizing taxes as well); and eliminating the excessive costs of investing that characterize managed mutual funds. *And it worked.* Even if future outcomes of this approach are less successful, it's hard to imagine that they could provide markedly inferior wealth accumulation relative to comparable managed funds. The success of the index fund reaffirms a basic piece of investment wisdom: When all else fails, fall back on simplicity.

Ever the realist, I recognize that few expect that "all else will fail." In the real world, lots of all-too-human traits get in the way of a simple, all-encompassing index fund approach:

"Hope springs eternal."

"I'm better than average."

"Even if the game is expensive, it's fun."

"That example is too good to be true."

"It can't be *that* simple."

These are common refrains in the words and thoughts of investors who choose to pursue the conventional strategy of relying entirely on actively managed funds to implement their investment strategies.

If You Decide Not *to Index* . . .

But if the beginning of simplicity is the index fund, it need not be the end. History suggests that, in the long run, only one of every five actively managed funds is apt to outpace the market index (after taxes, only one of seven). And some simple commonsense principles should help you to select them and to earn a generous portion of the market's return—again, all too likely, less than 100 percent. If there are long odds against outpacing the market, going about the task of fund selection intelligently can at least help to guard against a significant failure. Even master investor Warren Buffett, a strong proponent of the index approach, concedes that there may be other ways to construct an investment portfolio:

> Should you choose . . . to construct your own portfolio, there are a few thoughts worth remembering. Intelligent investing is not complex, though that is far from saying that it is easy. What an investor needs is the ability to correctly evaluate selected businesses. Note the word "selected": You don't have to be an expert on every company, or even many. You only have to be able to evaluate companies within your circle of competence. The size of that circle is not very important; knowing its boundaries, however, is vital.[1]

The Prussian General Karl von Clausewitz once said, "The greatest enemy of a good plan is the dream of a perfect plan." And, though I believe that an index strategy is a good strategy, you may want to seek a better plan, if not a perfect plan, no matter how great the challenge, no matter how overpowering the odds against implementing it with extraordinary success. So, much as I would urge you to commit your investments to an all-index-fund approach—or at least to follow an approach using index funds as the core of your portfolio—I'm going to offer you another simple approach: eight basic rules that should help you to capitalize on the advantages that have accounted for the historical ability of an index to provide superior returns. These eight rules are not complex. But they should help you to make intelligent fund selections for your investment program.

RULE 1: SELECT LOW-COST FUNDS

From much that I hear, I am known as a sort of fringe fanatic—an apostle of the message that costs play a crucial role in shaping long-term fund returns. I've said "Cost matters" for so long that one of my followers gave me a Plexiglas pillar inscribed with the Latin translation: *Pretium Refert.* But cost *does* matter. I've shown you the effect on returns and on asset allocation. I've been harping about costs for years, and it was with some delight that I read these words from Warren Buffett in the Berkshire-Hathaway Annual Report for 1996:

> Seriously, costs matter. For example, equity mutual funds incur corporate expenses—largely payments to the funds' managers—that average about 100 basis points,* a levy likely to cut the returns their investors earn by 10 percent or more over time.[2]

Sadly, Mr. Buffett was too conservative in his calculations. The average equity fund now charges not 100, but 155 basis points, and also incurs portfolio transaction costs of at least another 50 basis points. Together, they comprise expenses of 200 basis points or more. If I may revise his comment, then, fund costs are "a levy likely to cut the returns their investors earn by *20 percent* or more over time." Again, sadly—and unbelievably—bond fund fees also average more than 1 percent, a grossly unjustified levy on *any* gross interest yield, especially today's nominal yield of about 5¼ percent on the long U.S. Treasury bond, which would be cut by almost 20 percent. I regard such costs as unacceptable.

A low expense ratio is the single most important reason why a fund does well. Therefore, carefully consider the role of expense ratios in shaping

---

* 100 basis points equals 1 percent.

fund returns. If you select actively managed funds, emulate the index advantage by choosing low-cost funds. *The surest route to top-quartile returns is bottom-quartile expenses.* Using yet another period—the five years from 1991 to 1996 (detailed figures are given in Chapter 6)—Table 4.1 gives the record for funds owning stocks with large market capitalizations.

Note that both groups *earned* similar preexpense returns. But the 1.2 percent cost advantage was largely responsible for the 1.9 percent performance advantage for the low-cost funds. The link is hardly accidental. Lower costs are the handmaiden of higher returns.

The costs that actively managed funds incur in buying and selling portfolio securities are hidden, but nonetheless real. Fund portfolio turnover averages some 80 percent annually. It is expensive, perhaps adding as much as 0.5 to 1.0 percentage points (or more) to the more visible cost of fund expenses. So, favor low-turnover funds, but not only because these costs are lower. They also provide substantial tax advantages. The longer that actively managed funds hold portfolio securities, the greater the extraordinary value of deferral of capital gains becomes to their shareholders. Many high-turnover funds are expensive as well as tax-inefficient, so it behooves you to consider *after-tax* returns, along with present unrealized gains, which could lead to potentially massive future capital gains distributions and the burden of unnecessary taxes. The odds against active managers' outpacing the *after-tax* returns of index funds rise even higher. So if you own any funds outside of a tax-deferred retirement plan, *don't forget that taxes are costs too.*

Enough said, except that I would like to justify not only my appraisal of the importance of low-cost funds as a guideline for selecting funds, but also my selection of this warning as Rule 1. I rely on the support of William F. Sharpe, Nobel Laureate in Economics, who in a recent interview

TABLE 4.1

Large Capitalization Stock Funds: Returns vs. Expenses (1991 to 1996)

	Total Return before Expenses	Expense Ratio	Total Return after Expenses
Lowest-cost quartile	14.7%	0.5%	14.2%
Highest-cost quartile	14.0	1.7	12.3
Low-cost advantage	+0.7%	−1.2%	+1.9%

said: "The *first* thing to look at is the expense ratio" (italics added). You should follow his advice and recognize that selecting among low-cost managed funds should maximize the unlikely possibility that you will earn returns in excess of a low-cost index fund (20 basis points or less) simply because minimizing the cost differential gives a fund a far greater chance to compete successfully. After all, a low-cost fund with a 40-basis-point expense is fighting a 20-knot breeze in its efforts to win the sailing race, but a high-cost fund (150 basis points) is fighting a 130-knot typhoon.

RULE 2: CONSIDER CAREFULLY THE ADDED COSTS OF ADVICE

Tens of millions of investors need personal guidance in allocating their assets and selecting funds. Other tens of millions do not. For those in the latter category, some 3,000 no-load funds, without sales commissions, are available to choose from, and it is the essence of simplicity for self-reliant, intelligent, informed investors to purchase shares without resorting to an intermediary salesperson or financial adviser. Assuming the funds are properly selected, buying no-load funds is the least costly way to own mutual funds, and costs will consume the lowest possible proportion of future returns.

For the many investors who require guidance, there are registered advisers and brokerage account executives, many of whom serve their clients ably at a fair price. Good advisers give you their personal attention, help you avoid some of the pitfalls of investing, and provide worthwhile asset-allocation and fund-selection services. But, like any of us, they must earn their keep, providing you with valuable services that make it worth your while to invest through them. But I do not believe that they can identify, *in advance*, the top-performing managers—no one can!—and I'd avoid those who claim they can do so. The best advisers can help you develop a long-range investment strategy and an intelligent plan for its implementation.

You should know exactly how much the adviser's services will cost. Advice may be provided by registered "fee-only" investment advisers, who usually charge annual fees beginning at 1 percent of assets. It may also be provided by brokerage firm representatives who receive sales commissions. Commissions represent a significant drag on a mutual fund's performance, especially if the fund's shares are held for only a short period. It would be foolish to pay a 6 percent load if you expect to hold the shares for only a few years. Over 10 years, on the other hand, such a load would cut your return by a more modest 0.6 percent per year. In all, paying a reasonable price for guidance—especially when the adviser helps minimize your "all-in" cost (his or her cost, *plus* the costs of the funds) by focusing on low-cost funds—may well be acceptable in light of the services you receive.

Beware of the many *apparently* no-load funds that charge a hidden load—a special kind of sales charge, known as a 12b-1 fee, that is deducted from your returns each year. This fee may reduce your annual return by an additional one percentage point. If regular fund expenses are also 1.5 percentage points, the combined fee could consume one-fourth of a long-term 10 percent return on your portfolio, reducing it to 7.5 percent. Deductions may be even larger if you liquidate your fund shares within five or six years. Other funds use these 12b-1 fees, not to pay the salespeople, but to promote sales of the fund's shares through aggressive advertising and marketing programs. These fees provide no net benefit whatsoever to you, but they are paid out of your pocket. Be wary of funds that charge 12b-1 fees.

Most of all, beware of wrap accounts—packages of mutual funds assembled within a "wrapper" for which an additional fee is paid. They are usually expensive. Owning a package of managed funds may make sense under some circumstances, but paying 2 percent or more of assets per year for such a package defies reason. In my judgment, an investor who pays up to 4 percent a year in total costs (fund expenses plus the wrap fee) has destroyed any chance of approximating the total returns of the financial markets. Such a cost is simply too much dead weight—too great a handicap—on the return of *any* fund to enable it to be competitive. It cannot win the race.

RULE 3: DO NOT OVERRATE PAST FUND PERFORMANCE

My third rule has to do with the first element that catches the eye of most investors, whether experienced or novice: the fund's past track record. (The analogy to a horse race implied by the phrase "track record" is presumably unintentional!) But track records, helpful as they may be in appraising how thoroughbred horses will run (and they may not be very effective there either) are usually hopelessly misleading in appraising how money managers will perform. There is no way under the sun to forecast a fund's future absolute returns based on its past record. Even if someone could accurately forecast the future *absolute* returns the stock market will deliver—no mean task!—there is no way to forecast the future returns that an individual mutual fund will deliver *relative* to the market. The only exception would be the relative returns of index funds.

Now, I must contradict myself ever so slightly. Two highly probable, if not certain, forecasts *can* be made:

1. Funds with unusually high expenses are likely to underperform appropriate market indexes.

2. Funds with past relative returns that have been substantially superior to the returns of an appropriate market index will regress toward, and usually below, the market mean over time.

Reversion to the mean—the law of gravity in the financial markets that causes funds that are up to go down, and funds that are down to go up—is clear, quantifiable, and apparently almost inevitable. (I'll talk more about reversion to the mean, and the implications it holds for your portfolio selections, in Chapter 10.)

The two studies summarized in Table 4.2 show the deteriorating returns of top-quartile growth and growth and income funds relative to the market return over consecutive decades, as 99 percent of those funds reverted toward the mean. Note that only one fund was an exception to the rule. That fund—which ruled the world during both the 1970s and the 1980s and became the largest fund in the industry—reverted magnificently to the mean during the 1990s. Sometimes, reversion to the mean requires patience!

The mutual fund industry is well aware that nearly all top performers eventually lose their edge. Why fund sponsors persist in the vigorous,

TABLE 4.2

Reversion to the Mean

Period	Number of Funds in Top Quartile	Reversion Toward or Below Mean*	
		Number	Percentage
1970s to 1980s	34	33	97%
1987 to 1997	44	44	100
Total	78	77	99%

*Standard & Poor's 500 Index.

expensive, and finally misleading advertising and promotion of their most successful past performers defies all reason—except one. Promotion of funds with high past returns brings in lots of new money from investors, and lots of new fees to the adviser. Managers are highly rewarded for their transitory past success. Have you ever seen the promotion of a fund that has had either a low absolute return or a subpar relative return? (During the past 15 years, 95 percent of all equity funds have failed to beat the Standard & Poor's 500 Stock Index.) Promotions of funds based on past performance lead you in the wrong direction. Ignore them.

RULE 4: USE PAST PERFORMANCE TO DETERMINE CONSISTENCY AND RISK

Despite Rule 3, there *is* an important role that past performance can play in helping you to make your fund selections. While you should disregard a single aggregate number showing a fund's past long-term return, you can learn a great deal by studying the nature of its past returns. Above all, *look for consistency.* When I evaluate mutual funds (and I have looked carefully at many hundreds of them during my long career), I like to look at a fund's ranking among other funds with similar policies and objectives (i.e., I compare a large-cap value fund with other large-cap value funds, a small-cap growth fund with other comparable funds, and so on).

Morningstar Mutual Funds makes these comparisons easy. It shows, in a simple chart, whether a fund was in the first, second, third, or fourth quartile of its group during each of the preceding 12 years. The chart gives a fair reflection of *both* the consistency of a fund's policies *and* the relative success of its managers. For a fund to earn a top performance evaluation, it should have, in my opinion, at least six to nine years in the top two quartiles and no more than one or two years in the bottom quartile. I would normally reject funds with four or five years in the bottom quartile, even if offset by the same number in the top quartile. Figure 4.4 provides two examples of real-world funds that reflect the standards I've set forth.

The "good" fund was in the top half in 10 years, in the bottom quartile only once, and in the third quartile once. The "bad" fund was in the top half six times and in the bottom quartile four times, and it had two third-quartile appearances. I've taken the liberty of also showing in Figure 4.4 how an index fund stacks up. Remarkably—and I caution you not to expect the pattern to recur quite this favorably in the future—the S&P 500 index fund earned top-half ranking fully 11 times, without once finding

FIGURE 4.4

Morningstar Performance Profiles*: Consistency

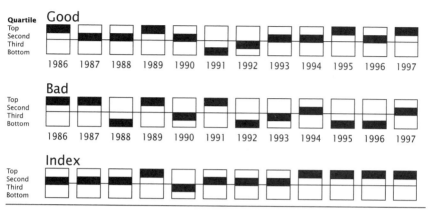

* Quartile within *Morningstar* style category.

its way into the bottom quartile. In any event, consistency is a virtue for a mutual fund. Intelligent investors will want to give it heavy weight in the fund selection process.

In using the word *performance*, I am not limiting my interest solely to return. *Risk is a crucial element in investing.* I especially like to know a fund's *Morningstar* risk rating—based on a fund's returns in the months in which it underperformed the risk-free U.S. Treasury bill—relative to its peers with similar objectives and policies, and relative to all equity funds. That rating serves as a rough guide to how much relative risk the fund typically assumes. There is a difference! Indeed, the risk of the average large-cap value fund (22 percent *below* average) has carried only half of the risk of its small-cap growth fund counterpart (93 percent above average). Table 4.3 compares the *Morningstar* risk ratings for the nine basic investment styles. Risk matters. For while future fund returns are utterly unpredictable, large differences in relative risk among funds have proven to be highly predictable.

Risk—however measured and however elusive a concept, except in retrospect—should be given the most careful consideration by the intelligent investor. Markets, no matter what you may have come to think, do not *always* rise!

TABLE 4.3

Risk Profile* (Average Fund = 100)

	Style		
Capitalization	Value	Blend	Growth
Large	78	84	114
Medium	85	105	156
Small	104	140	193

*This matrix places each fund into one of nine categories. The vertical columns represent the size of the companies in the portfolio. The horizontal rows represent the investment style, focusing on value stocks (those with below-average price–earnings ratios and above-average yields), growth stocks (the reverse), or a blend of both styles. The S&P 500 Index fund is categorized as large-cap blend, and carries a relative risk of 85.

RULE 5: BEWARE OF STARS

Here, I refer primarily to the recent emergence of fund portfolio managers as stars. Alas, the fact is that there are precious few, if any, mutual fund superstars who have had the staying power of Michael Jordan or Arnold Palmer or Robert Redford or Laurence Olivier. The few who may have fitted into this category were never, as far as I know, identified *in advance* of their accomplishments. Who had ever heard of Peter Lynch or John Neff or Michael Price in 1972, before they had achieved their splendid records?

Even though their light may shine brightly for a time, many superstars seem to limit their association with a given fund. The average portfolio manager lasts only five years at the helm of a fund, and, in one of the largest, most aggressive—and formerly hottest—fund organizations, the average stint has been only two and a half years. (Turnover in the fund portfolio, which inevitably accompanies a change of managers, results in truly onerous cost penalties.) These superstars are more like comets: they brighten the firmament for a moment in time, only to burn out and vanish into the dark universe. Seek good managers if you will, but rely on their professionalism, experience, and steadfastness rather than on their stardom.

Be careful, too, about star *systems* (as distinct from star *managers*). The best-known stars are, of course, those funds awarded top five-star billing by *Morningstar Mutual Funds*. (I call these funds "Morning-stars.") The fund world has embraced—and has encouraged investors to invest on the basis of—a system in which a fund with four or five stars is a success. (One or two stars—sometimes even three—mark a failure.) But, as the editors of *Morningstar Mutual Funds* candidly acknowledge, their star ratings have little predictive value. *The Hulbert Financial Digest* has demonstrated that buying five-star funds as they emerge, and redeeming them when they lose their top rating, produces below-market returns at above-market risk. Not a good combination! Based on the frequent fund switching implied by the Hulbert methodology, I accept that conclusion. But I would be more forgiving. I have little doubt that most of today's three-, four- and five-star funds, *if held over time*, will outpace their one-star peers. Even as you ignore star portfolio managers, then, be skeptical of funds with the lowest star ratings, and focus on funds with the higher star ratings. (But don't trade them!)

RULE 6: BEWARE OF ASSET SIZE

Funds can get too big for their britches. It is as simple as that. Avoid large fund organizations that (1) have no history of closing funds—that is, terminating the offering of their shares—to new investors, or (2) seem willing to let their funds grow, irrespective of their investment goals, to seemingly infinite size, beyond their power to differentiate their investment results from the crowd.

Just what constitutes "too big" is a complex issue. It relates to fund style, management philosophy, and portfolio strategy. A few examples: a fund investing primarily in large-cap stocks can surely be managed successfully—if not for truly exceptional returns—even at the $20 billion or $30 billion (or higher) level. (*None* of today's funds of that size has outpaced the Standard & Poor's 500 Index over the past five years.) For a fund investing aggressively in tiny microcap stocks (usually market capitalizations of less than $250 million), $300 million of assets might be too large.

Often, checking the fund's quartile rankings over time (mentioned in Rule 4) will reveal whether growing size has had an impact on relative return. Figure 4.5 shows the performance pattern of a once-popular midcap growth fund whose record deteriorated severely as it grew. In 1991–1995, it earned top-quartile ratings in four of the five years, and its assets grew from a tiny $12 million to the $1 billion range. But the three years since its assets moved to $2 billion, and then to $6 billion, were spent in the bottom quartile. Its failed "momentum" strategy (buying stocks with

FIGURE 4.5

Performance Profile: Problem Fund

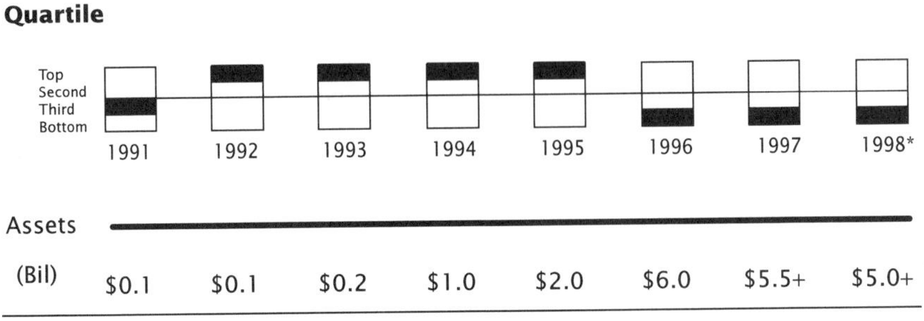

Quartile

	1991	1992	1993	1994	1995	1996	1997	1998*
Assets (Bil)	$0.1	$0.1	$0.2	$1.0	$2.0	$6.0	$5.5+	$5.0+

*June 1998.

powerful earnings thrust) may have accounted for part of the deterioration, but the clear message is that size has impeded return. It is not a positive message for investors considering the fund today.

Optimal fund size depends on many factors. A broad-based market index fund, for example, should be able to grow without size limits. A giant fund with very low portfolio turnover and relatively stable cash inflows from investors can be managed more easily than one with aggressive investment policies and volatile cash flows—in and out—that not only reflect, but are magnified by, its short-term performance. A multimanager fund—especially if it uses managers who are unaffiliated with one another—can be successful at larger asset levels than a fund supervised by a single management organization. But do not underestimate the challenge a fund faces in selecting two or three, or even four, truly excellent managers. There are no easy answers.

Size—present and potential—is a highly important concern. Excessive size can, and probably will, kill any possibility of investment excellence. The record is clear that, for the overwhelming majority of funds, the best years come when they are small. Small *was* beautiful, but "nothing fails like success." When these funds caught the public fancy—or, more likely, were vigorously hawked to a public that was unaware of its potential exposure to the problems of size—their best years were behind them. As I'll explain in Chapter 12, unbridled asset growth in a fund should be a warning flag to intelligent investors.

RULE 7: DON'T OWN TOO MANY FUNDS

A single *ready-made* balanced index fund—holding 65 percent stocks and 35 percent bonds, as shown in my earlier example—can meet the needs of many investors. A pair of stock and bond index funds with a *tailor-made* balance—a higher or lower ratio of stocks—can meet the needs of many more. But what is the optimal number of funds for investors who elect to use actively managed funds? I truly believe that it is generally unnecessary to go much beyond four or five equity funds. Too large a number can easily result in overdiversification. The net result: a portfolio whose performance inevitably comes to resemble that of an index fund. However, because of the higher costs of the non-index-fund portfolio, as well as its broadened diversification, its return will almost inevitably fall short. What is more, even though it may be overdiversified, such a portfolio (for example, one with two large-cap blend funds and two small-cap growth funds) may exhibit much more short-term variation around the market return. Therefore, according to the common definition of risk, it will be riskier than the index. To what avail?

A recent study by *Morningstar Mutual Funds*—to its credit, one of the few publications that systematically tackles issues like this one—concluded essentially that owning more than four randomly chosen equity funds didn't reduce risk appreciably. Around that number, risk remains fairly constant, all the way out to 30 funds (an unbelievable number!), at which point *Morningstar* apparently stopped counting. Figure 4.6 shows the extent to which the standard deviation of the various fund portfolios declined as more funds were added.

Morningstar noted that owning only a *single* large blend fund could provide a lower risk than any of the multiple-fund portfolios. I've added such a fund to Figure 4.6. But *Morningstar* did not note, though it might have, that a single all-market index fund provided as low a risk as did the 30-fund portfolio. I've added that too. *Morningstar* also failed to mention, though perhaps it should have, that the assumed initial investment of some $50,000, which would have grown to final values ranging from $85,000 to $116,000 in various fund combinations, would have grown to $113,000 in a single all-market index fund—right at the top of the range. The alleged virtues of multifund diversification and risk control hardly appear compelling.

I would add that I am not persuaded that international funds are a necessary component of an investor's portfolio. Foreign funds may reduce a

FIGURE 4.6

Reducing Risk by Owning Multiple Funds

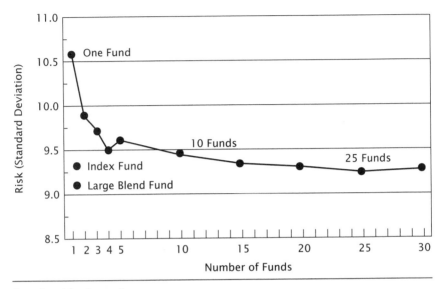

Data from Morningstar Investor.

portfolio's *volatility*, but their economic and currency risks may reduce *returns* by a still larger amount. The idea that a theoretically optimal portfolio must hold each geographical component at its market weight simply pushes me further than I would dream of being pushed. (I explore the pros and cons of global investing in Chapter 8.) My best judgment is that international holdings should comprise 20 percent of equities *at a maximum*, and that a zero weight is fully acceptable in most portfolios.

What is the point of having as many as 20 diversified funds in a portfolio (i.e., 5 percent of assets in each fund), and thus—given the inevitable overlap of their holdings—owning as many as 1,000 individual common stocks? I'm not at all sure. Perhaps a simple five-fund portfolio like the one shown in Table 4.4 would suit the needs of investors seeking active equity management.

This portfolio would be clearly different from an all-market index fund—and somewhat riskier—but it could provide an opportunity to add value, assuming that the five funds were well chosen. Each fund selected should have a significant impact on fully diversifying the portfolio.

TABLE 4.4

A Simple Five-Fund Portfolio

Fund	Percent of Investment
Large-cap	50%
Midcap	10
Small-cap	20
Specialty*	10
International	10
Total	100%

*Such as a health care, technology, or energy fund. Real estate funds might also be included, although my impression is that they are less apt to perform as a separate asset class than as a sector subject to the vagaries of the stock market.

RULE 8: BUY YOUR FUND PORTFOLIO—AND HOLD IT

When you have identified your long-term objectives, defined your tolerance for risk, and carefully selected an index fund or a small number of actively managed funds that meet your goals, *stay the course*. Hold tight. Complicating the investment process merely clutters the mind, too often bringing emotion into a financial plan that cries out for rationality. I am absolutely persuaded that investors' emotions, such as greed and fear, exuberance and hope—if translated into rash actions—can be every bit as destructive to investment performance as inferior market returns. To reiterate what the estimable Mr. Buffett said earlier: "Inactivity strikes us as intelligent behavior." Never forget it.

The key to holding tight is buying right. Buying right is *not* picking funds you don't fully understand; it is *not* picking funds on the basis of past performance; it is *not* picking funds because someone tells you they're hot or because they have managers who have been stars, or even because they have been awarded five *Morning-stars*; and it is most assuredly *not* picking high-cost funds. If you have avoided these fundamental errors, then simply keep an eye on how your fund performs. If you chose intelligently in the first place, an annual performance appraisal ought to be just fine. And patiently tolerate periodic nonextreme shortfalls relative to the fund's peers. A major event—an extended aberration in a fund's performance, a radical shift in its policy, a merger of its management company, a fee increase or the imposition of a 12b-1 fee—all should set off alarms.

SIMPLICITY . . . OR COMPLEXITY?

The opposite of simplicity is complexity. In recent years, according to Charles T. Munger, Warren Buffett's partner at Berkshire Hathaway, many large foundations and college endowment funds, have "tried to become better versions of Bernie Cornfield's 'Fund of Funds,' drifting toward more complexity, with not few but many investment counselors, chosen by an additional layer of consultants to decide which counselors are best, allocating funds to various categories, including foreign securities. . . . There is one thing sure about all of this complexity. The total costs can easily reach 3 percent of net worth per annum, paying the croupiers 3 percent of starting wealth. If the average gross real return from equities goes back, say, to 5 percent over some long future period, and the croupiers' take remains the same as it has always been, the average intelligent player will be in a prolonged, uncomfortable shrinking mode. For obvious reasons . . . I think indexing is a wiser choice for the average foundation than what it is now doing." Mr. Munger has clearly cast his lot with simplicity.

But, if I may modify the familiar phrase about investigating before you invest, I would urge: "Investigate before you divest."

Don't select funds as if they were simply individual common stocks, to be discarded and replaced as they face the inevitable ebb and flow of performance. Select a fund with the same thoughtful consideration you would give to appointing a trustee for your assets and establishing a lifetime relationship. That approach is the very essence of simplicity. Decades ago, many of America's wealthiest families chose a single trustee or investment adviser to look after their entire estates and to remain with them ever after. An investment account in a broadly diversified mutual fund is, in truth, neither more nor less than a diversified trust fund (except that the mutual fund is usually even *more* diversified). Suppress the temptation to add redundant layers of diversification. While you're at it, demand that the industry provide you with mutual funds that measure up to a high level of trusteeship responsibility. You deserve it.

THE PARADIGM OF SIMPLICITY

Simplicity will help you to come down to where you ought to be. Buy right and hold tight. Follow these eight basic rules for investing. In this complex world, stick with simplicity. To the extent you decide that indexing is not for you, these rules should still afford you considerable advantage in the quest for solid long-term returns. My approach to investing is simple in concept, but it is far from easy in implementation. You will find, I fear, a fairly small number of funds that filter through my screens. There ought to be lots more.

I would emphasize that each of the eight rules I have offered is designed to help you select a portfolio of funds that may give you the very advantages that have elevated the index fund—the paradigm of simplicity—to its present prominence and acceptance among individual and institutional investors alike. That parallelism is not an accident. So, as you consider your strategy, you cannot afford to ignore the low-cost index fund.

Don't forget that the central task of investing is to capture the maximum possible portion—even though it's almost certain to be less than 100 percent—of the market's rate of return. To an important degree, however, that comparison understates the importance of the task. Remember that because of the impact of compounding, the gap between the capital that is attainable and the capital that is actually created increases rapidly. For example, capturing even 90 percent of the market's annual return—9 percent versus 10 percent—produces only 86 percent of the capital increase over a decade and 76 percent of the increase over 25 years. Once again, little things mean a lot.

Indexing will probably never rule the *entire* world—only part of it! But indexing works so well only because most funds—burdened by excessive costs, promoted with claims of past performance success that is highly unlikely to be sustained, and managed with strategies that call for a short-term focus—*don't* work very well. For that reason, the index fund—which works very well indeed—has proved to be the optimal way to realize the highest possible portion of the return earned in the stock market. But it need not be the *only* way.

In this chapter, I have tried to present both the value of passively managed market index funds and the rudiments of how to select actively managed funds simply and successfully. Whichever route you decide to follow—and, happily, you have the ability to follow both routes—you will have acquired "the gift to be simple" from an investment standpoint, and "the gift to be free" of the cacophony of information that assaults us, seemingly without remission. I am confident that if you follow these basic standards, you will have acquired "the gift to come down to where you ought to be" in implementing your long-run financial plans.

The investment choices now offered by mutual funds are many and varied. Before we look at all the options, I first show how the now-proven principles of passively managed, low-cost market index funds have worked in actual experience. I then turn to an examination of equity fund investment styles in terms of their investment orientation toward value, growth, or a blend of the two, combined with their emphasis on stocks of corporations with large, medium, or small market capitalizations. Variations in equity fund returns and risks shrink drastically when compared, not with all types of funds, but with the returns of peers and market indexes following similar styles. The same conclusion holds true in my examination of the returns of bond funds following different styles, presented in the next chapter. All three of these chapters raise serious questions about the efficacy of active, often costly, management, and conclude that few fund portfolio managers have demonstrated the ability to earn excess returns sufficient to overcome high mutual fund costs.

The merits of global equity strategies are evaluated next. I present a skeptical view of the need for U.S. investors to put their money to work abroad, but for those who are unpersuaded, suggest optimal methods of doing so. Finally, I describe the futility of seeking to identify superior funds in advance, and of actively moving holdings from one fund to another. Here,

I rely on an examination of the major academic studies, the records of funds that have provided highly superior returns in the past, the records of advisory firms making fund selection recommendations, and the actual investment performance of professional advisers who select mutual funds. Each of these analyses suggests that the "Holy Grail" of superior performance is unlikely to be found by fund investors choosing actively managed funds. Rather, it is to be found in commonsense principles.

CHAPTER 5

ON INDEXING

THE TRIUMPH OF EXPERIENCE OVER HOPE

*W*ay back in 1978, in the third annual report of Vanguard Index Trust, the first index fund, I used a quotation from English lexicographer Samuel Johnson to make a point: "It was the triumph of hope over experience." With his inimitable wit, Dr. Johnson was speaking of a man who married for the second time; I was speaking of a poll of pension managers taken by *Institutional Investor*. Just 17 percent of these money management professionals, the magazine reported, had outpaced the Standard & Poor's 500 Index during the previous decade, but fully 95 percent *expected* to outpace the Index in the coming decade.

In the years that followed, what we witnessed was quite the reverse: "the triumph of experience over hope." The hope of beating the Index was dashed; the hard experience that had characterized so many professional managers before 1978 has repeated itself over and over. The Index has outpaced 79 percent of all managers of equity mutual funds that survived the 20 years since then. As 1995 began, I had the temerity to publish a booklet entitled *The Triumph of Indexing*, describing both the relative performance of the Standard & Poor's 500 Index and the growing acceptance of index mutual funds by the investing public, a trend that I had awaited for so long.

The timing of the booklet, as it turned out, was auspicious. Since its publication, the word "triumph" has hardly done justice to the colossal success that index funds have enjoyed. On the performance front, the Standard & Poor's 500 Index, given its bias toward stocks with large

INDEX CHOICES

The Standard & Poor's 500 Composite Stock Price Index includes 500 of the largest corporations in the United States. This index, which dates back to 1926, measures the returns of this group of stocks, weighted by the market value of each. In 1998, the $9 trillion value of these stocks was equal to approximately 75 percent of the $12.2 trillion of all U.S. stocks.

The entire U.S. stock market is measured by the Wilshire 5000 Index. (The name has remained the same, although the index is now composed of 7,400 stocks.) This index began in 1970. Because of its shorter history, it is less widely recognized, although it is clearly more comprehensive. Besides the large stocks represented by the Standard & Poor's 500, the index includes the small- and medium-size companies that make up the remainder of the U.S. stock market.

Other stock market indexes exist for growth stocks and value stocks in the large, medium, and small categories; for various industry sectors; for the markets of most nations and geographical regions, and indeed for the entire global stock market. In addition, indexes exist for the U.S. and world bond markets, and for a wide variety of subsets of the bond market.

In all, it's fair to say that there is no category of marketable financial assets for which a price index cannot be created. The choices of indexes are limited only by the creativity of the designers. *And where there is an index, there can be an index fund.* Index funds now track about 60 different indexes; the vast majority of index mutual fund assets are indexed to the Standard & Poor's 500.

market capitalizations, has outpaced a stunning 96 percent of all actively managed equity funds. The more representative all-market Wilshire 5000 Equity Index has outpaced 86 percent of those funds, also an imposing performance. On the acceptance front, assets of index mutual funds have risen more than sixfold, from $30 billion to some $200 billion.

Index mutual funds, which accounted for only 3 percent of equity fund assets in 1995, represented 6.4 percent just three years later. With estimated cash inflow of $50 billion in 1998, index fund flows were equal to 25 percent—fully one-fourth—of total equity fund cash flow. Index funds have become the fastest growing segment of the entire mutual fund industry.

The index fund is a most unlikely hero for the typical investor. It is no more (nor less) than a broadly diversified portfolio, typically run at rock-bottom costs, without the putative benefit of a brilliant, resourceful, and highly skilled portfolio manager. The index fund simply buys and holds the securities in a particular index, in proportion to their weight in the index. The concept is simplicity writ large.

But since the creation of the first index mutual fund in 1975, based on the Standard & Poor's 500 Stock Index, the concept has emerged triumphant. Because the index fund is the very essence of simplicity, and because it must be considered as the core investment in the fund-selection process—the baseline against which all other mutual funds must, finally, be measured—I begin Part II of this book with a discussion of its pros and cons. But, confession being good for the soul, I must acknowledge that I have often been described as the apostle of indexing, having started that first index fund nearly a quarter century ago. I am, if possible, a stronger believer in the concept today than I was when I created that fund.

After a slow start, the concept has not only steadily gained acceptance by investors but has come to play a dominant role in the evaluation of traditional, actively managed mutual funds. The index fund, arguably, is now the standard that dominates the debates about investment strategy, asset allocation, and fund selection. When I first looked at the record in 1975, the S&P 500 Index had outperformed the average actively managed mutual fund by about 1.6 percentage points per year during the prior 25 years. Updating the statistics today, its long-term record reflects an annual advantage of 1.3 percent, although in the past 15 years the margin has swelled to 4.0 percent annually. Table 5.1 shows the record of the passively managed index compared to the average actively managed equity fund over various periods.

I fully recognize that during the past 15 years the large-capitalization stocks that dominate the S&P 500 Index have led the overall market by a solid margin. I would emphasize that the accelerating advantage of the S&P 500 Index may well recede, and may even become a shortfall during interim future periods when stocks with smaller market caps return to favor. But its margins of superiority are nonetheless impressive, and surely undergird the powerful endorsement that index funds have received from

TABLE 5.1

S&P 500 Index vs. Equity Mutual Funds (Annual Returns for Periods Ended December 31, 1997)

Period (Years)	S&P 500 Index	Average Equity Mutual Fund	Index Advantage
50	13.1%	11.8%	1.3%
40	12.3	11.5	0.8
30	12.5	10.8	1.7
25	14.3	13.9	0.4
20	17.4	15.6	1.8
15	17.2	13.2	4.0
10	18.6	15.2	3.4
5	23.1	18.1	5.0

the academic community and the financial media, from many astute investment advisers, and from the investing public.

But even if the truly extraordinary 3.4 percent margin over the past decade fails to be matched in the future, the future would be bright. Even a sustained difference equal to half that of the past decade—or 1.7 percent annually—would result in dramatically different accumulations of capital. Assume a Standard & Poor's 500 Index return of 12.5 percent and a 10.8 percent return for the average mutual fund—the actual rates of return over the past 30 years. If those rates of return were to persist over the next 30 years, a $10,000 initial investment would grow to $342,400 in the Index and to $216,900 in the managed funds, a staggering $125,000 margin that would surely represent a continuing triumph. Figure 5.1 presents the results of each investment, compounded annually, over 30 years.

Whether such a margin will hold in the future, however, is mere speculation. What is not speculative is the fact that the lion's share of the margin is accounted for by the simple fact that market indexes incur no cost, whereas mutual funds incur heavy costs. Indeed, since total annual costs incurred by the average equity mutual fund have grown from as little as 1.0 percent of assets, or perhaps a bit more, during the 30 years prior to 1975 to at least 2.0 percent today, it becomes clear that mutual fund costs have been largely responsible for creating the industry's lag, and that the recent superior returns of the large-cap stocks that dominate the Standard & Poor's 500 Index have simply represented, as it were, the icing on the cake.

FIGURE 5.1

Growth of $10,000 over 30 Years: S&P 500 Index vs. Equity Funds*

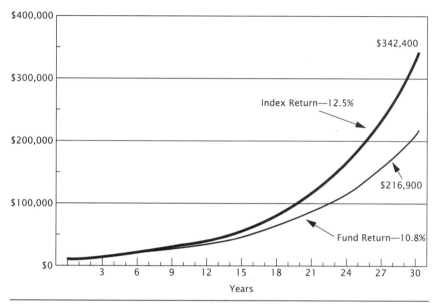

*Annual compounding based on average returns, 1967–1997, for the Standard & Poor's 500 Index and the average U.S. general equity fund.

The financial press in particular has begun to sing indexing's praises. In early 1997, index funds were recognized in major front-page articles in both *The New York Times* and *The Wall Street Journal.* At almost the same time, *TIME* and *Newsweek* ran solid indexing stories. The most enthusiastic endorsement came from *Money* magazine, which, in 1995, was generous enough to headline a lead editorial by Executive Editor Tyler Mathisen: "Bogle wins: Index funds should be the core of most portfolios today." Like Saul on the road to Damascus, *Money* had experienced an epiphany.

If we use the dictionary definition of *apostle*—"a messenger, specifically one who first advocates an important belief or system"—I suppose I might qualify as the apostle of the index mutual fund. Ever since 1951, when, in the course of my Princeton University thesis about the mutual fund industry, I expressed doubt about the ability of fund managers to outpace the stock market averages, the vague idea of a market index fund had

THE LESSONS OF HISTORY

I have long believed that it is important to have a sense of history. The history of the index fund serves as a good beginning to understanding its merits. I did not invent the concept of indexing, but I had been a long-time believer in the concept. I was confident that it could—against all odds—become a reality in the world of mutual funds. Not only did it make sense, but it dovetailed with my conviction that low costs truly make a difference—if not *the* difference—in emulating the returns available in financial markets. As I have noted, history tells us that doing so is hardly a modest goal for the long-term investor.

The pioneers of the indexing concept were William Fouse and John McQuown of Wells Fargo Bank. During 1969–1971, they had worked from academic models to develop the principles and techniques that led to index investing. Their efforts resulted in the construction of a $6 million index account for the pension fund of Samsonite Corporation, with a strategy based on an equal-weighted index of all equities listed on the New York Stock Exchange. Fouse described its execution as "a nightmare." The strategy was abandoned in 1976 and was replaced with a market-weighted strategy using the Standard & Poor's 500 Composite Stock Price Index. The first accounts run by Wells Fargo were components of its own pension fund and that of Illinois Bell Telephone Corporation.

Slightly later in 1971, Batterymarch Financial Management of Boston decided independently to pursue the idea of index investing. The developers were Jeremy Grantham and Dean LeBaron, two of the founders of the firm. Grantham described the idea at a Harvard Business School seminar in 1971, but found no takers until 1973. For its efforts, Batterymarch won the "Dubious Achievement Award" from *Pensions & Investments* magazine in 1972. Two years later, in December 1974, the firm finally attracted its first index client.

In 1974, the American National Bank in Chicago created a common trust fund modeled on the S&P 500 Index. A minimum investment of $100,000 was required. By that time, the idea had begun to spread from academia, and from three firms that were the first professional believers, to a public forum. Gradually, the press began to comment on index investing. A *cri de coeur* calling for the creation of index funds came from three remarkably intelligent and farsighted observers. I still treasure their articles, which inspired me nearly 25 years ago and read just as well today.

"Challenge to Judgment"

The first article was "Challenge to Judgment," by Paul A. Samuelson, Professor of Finance at the Massachusetts Institute of Technology, and a Nobel Laureate in economics. In *The Journal of Portfolio Management* (Fall 1974), he pleaded "that, at the least, some large foundation set up an in-house portfolio that tracks the S&P 500 Index—if only for the purpose of setting up a naïve model against which their in-house gunslingers can measure their prowess. . . . Perhaps CREF (College Retirement Equities Fund) can be induced to set-up a pilot-plant operation of an unmanaged diversified fund, but I would not bet on it . . . [or] the American Economic Association might contemplate setting-up for its members a no-load, no management fee, virtually no transaction-turnover fund." He noted, however, what might be an insurmountable difficulty: that "there may be less supernumerary wealth to be found among 20,000 economists [to provide capital for the fund] than among 20,000 chiropractors."

Dr. Samuelson concluded his challenge by calling on those who disagreed that a passive index would outperform most active managers to dispose of "that uncomfortable brute fact (that it is virtually impossible for academics with access to public records to identify any consistently excellent performers) in the only way that any fact is disposed of—by producing brute evidence to the contrary." There is no record that anyone tried to produce such evidence, nor is it likely that it could have been produced. But Dr. Samuelson had laid down an implicit challenge for *somebody, somewhere* to launch an index fund.

"The Loser's Game"

A year later, Charles D. Ellis, Managing Partner of Greenwich Associates, wrote a seminal article entitled "The Loser's Game" in the

(Continued)

Financial Analysts Journal (July/August 1975). Ellis proffered a provocative and bold statement: "The investment management business is built upon a simple and basic belief: professional managers can beat the market. That premise appears to be false." He pointed out that, over the preceding decade, 85 percent of institutional investors had underperformed the return of the S&P 500, largely because, in an environment in which institutional investors have become, and will continue to be, the dominant feature of their own environment, the costs of institutional investing have consumed 20 percent of the returns earned by the managers, "causing the transformation that took money management from a Winner's Game to a Loser's Game. The ultimate outcome is determined by who can lose the fewest points, not who can win them." He went on to note that "gambling in a casino where the house takes 20 percent of every pot is obviously a Loser's Game . . . so money management has become a Loser's Game."

Ellis did not call for the formation of an index fund, but he did ask: "Does the index necessarily lead to an entirely passive index portfolio?" He answered, "No, it doesn't necessarily lead in that direction. Not quite. But if you can't beat the market, you should certainly consider joining it. An index fund is one way." In the real world, of course, few managers indeed have consistently succeeded in achieving an annual return sufficient even to offset their costs and thereby match the index, let alone surpass it. Even those few have been exceptionally difficult to identify in advance.

Fortune Leads to a Flood Tide

"There is a tide in the affairs of men, which taken at the flood, leads to fortune." Shakespeare put those words in Brutus's mouth. Ironically, in the field of index funds, fortune, in a sense, helped turn the tide of investment affairs toward index funds. In July 1975, *Fortune* magazine published a third landmark article. "Some Kinds of Mutual Funds Make Sense," was written by Associate Editor A. F. Ehrbar. Ehrbar came to some conclusions that may seem obvious today, but were then hardly the accepted wisdom: "While funds cannot consistently outperform the market, they *can* consistently underperform it by generating excessive research (i.e., management fees) and trading costs . . . it is clear that prospective buyers of mutual funds should look over the costs before making any decisions." He concluded, "Funds actually do worse than the market."

Ehrbar despaired that an index mutual fund would be created very soon, noting that "there has not been much pioneering lately and the mutual-fund industry has not provided an index fund." But he described the best alternative for mutual fund investors: "A no-load mutual fund with low expenses and management fees, about the same degree of risk as the market as a whole, and a policy of always being fully invested." He could not have realized that he had described, with some accuracy, the first index mutual fund, which was soon to be formed. But that is what he had done.

Opportunity Is the Mother of Invention

Together, these three clarion calls for an index mutual fund were irresistible. I could no longer contain my enthusiasm for the opportunity to be in the vanguard, as it were, of the development of the index fund. Based on my research on past fund performance, well known in academia but acknowledged by few in the investing profession, I was confident it would work. Further, the firm I had founded in 1974 was focused on low cost, precisely the key to having an index fund that would emulate a cost-free index. It was the opportunity of a lifetime: to prove that the basic theory enunciated in these articles could be put into practice and made to work in a real-world framework. Alas, there was no demand for it by the investing public. So I relied on Say's Law (after French economist Jean Baptiste Say): "Supply creates its own demand." Before 1975 came to its close, Vanguard had created the first index mutual fund, modeled on the Standard & Poor's 500 Composite Stock Price Index.

lingered in my mind. And since the creation of the Vanguard Index Trust in 1975, I have been preaching the gospel of index investing with increasing fervor and conviction.

For a long time, my preaching fell on deaf ears. A brief review of the first index mutual fund's faltering start, in terms of both the relative performance of the Standard & Poor's 500 Index and the fund's labored cash inflow; its all-too-gradual acceptance by the investing public; and, finally, its extraordinary success in the late 1990s, will provide a good backdrop against which to examine some of the long-standing criticisms of indexing. The record should enable us to come to grips with the arguments crafted by critics who are skeptical that its extraordinary success can persist. In exploring the merits of indexing in greater detail, I hope to demonstrate that it is an extremely powerful strategy for the intelligent long-term investor.

INDEXING IS A LONG-TERM STRATEGY

The success that indexing has enjoyed in recent years has been based in part on recognition that acquiring and holding, at extremely low cost, a broadly diversified portfolio dominated by the large, high-grade stocks that dominate the capitalization weight of the market itself is an intelligent long-term strategy and a highly productive one as well. That success has also been engendered by the remarkable performance of the Standard & Poor's 500 Index over the past five years, during which its margin of advantage over the average U.S. equity mutual fund has been the highest in history.

But it is the long-term merits of the index fund—broad diversification, weightings paralleling those of the stocks that comprise the market, minimal portfolio turnover, and low cost—that commend it to wise investors. Consider these words from perhaps the wisest investor of all, Warren E. Buffett, from the 1996 Annual Report of Berkshire Hathaway Corporation:

> *Most investors, both institutional and individual, will find that the best way to own common stocks is through an index fund that charges minimal fees. Those following this path are sure to beat the net results (after fees and expenses) delivered by the great majority of investment professionals.*

No matter what the future holds, long-term investors who have chosen an index strategy because of its merits are unlikely to be disappointed. On the other hand, short-term investors who have chosen an index strategy simply because they expect a continuation of the highly superior returns demonstrated by the Standard & Poor's 500 Index in the recent past are likely to regret their choice. The historical record makes it clear that the S&P 500 Index has encountered intervals of significant shortfall relative to the average mutual fund. Figure 5.2 shows the percentage of mutual funds outperformed by the S&P 500 Index each year since 1963.

Despite its overall success, there were three periods in which the Index lagged, as reflected in Figure 5.2: 1965–1968, 1977–1980, and 1991–1993. Why? The first period included the "go-go" era of investing, when extremely risky small stocks provided extraordinary returns, and the mutual fund industry responded by creating large numbers of highly aggressive "go-go" funds. The conservative character of the industry changed during this period; funds accepted uncharacteristically high risks, and the S&P 500 Index's more modest short-term rewards made it look inadequate. The perception grew that mutual fund managers could easily outpace the market. However, when the go-go bubble burst in 1968, these newly formed funds collapsed, the returns of the average fund slumped, and the S&P 500 Index reclaimed its wide margin of superiority in 1969 through 1976.

FIGURE 5.2

General Equity Funds Outperformed by the Standard & Poor's 500 Index, 1963–June 30, 1998

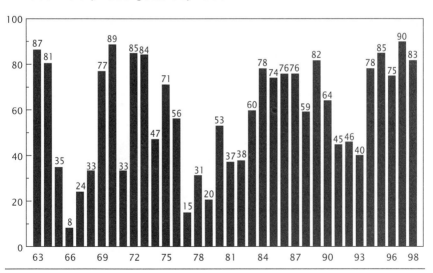

The second aberration occurred quickly thereafter. In 1977–1980, as the stock market continued to emerge from its decline in 1973 and 1974—an amazing 50 percent, from high to low—smaller stocks finally returned to the fore. Their recovery was rather later than that of their large-cap cousins. And three of the large stocks that then dominated the S&P 500 Index (IBM, 7.2 percent; AT&T, 6.4 percent; and General Motors, 2.6 percent), but were held in much smaller proportions by the highly diversified mutual funds, did particularly badly. On average, they turned in a four-year cumulative return of 7 percent, compared to a stunning 69 percent gain for the remaining stocks in the Index. (Overall, the Index cumulative gain was 55 percent.) As in the aftermath of the go-go era, the situation then began to return to normal, and the Index reasserted its strength for the next eight years.

Then came the most recent period of an S&P 500 Index shortfall. The primary reason was elemental. During 1991–1993, small and midsize stocks did better than large stocks. The S&P 500 gained a respectable 15.6 percent annually during this period, but the rest of the market rose at the rate of 22.5 percent.* As a result, the S&P 500 Index outpaced only (if that is the right word to describe what is in fact not so far from a parity of return) 44 percent of all actively managed funds—less (but not much less) than one-half. (The all-market Wilshire 5000 Equity Index, with a return of 17.7 percent, outpaced 53 percent of the equity funds.) That shortfall, however, was quickly followed by the largest sustained margin of superiority the S&P 500 Index has ever achieved. During 1994–1998, the S&P 500 Index outpaced 75 percent to 90 percent of managed funds over four consecutive years.

After such a sustained run, it would hardly seem surprising if the large-stock-dominated S&P 500 Index were to take a pause. It continues to be dominated by large companies that are global in reach, including General Electric at 3.1 percent of the weight of the Index capitalization; Microsoft, 2.4 percent; Coca-Cola, 2.2 percent; Exxon, 2 percent; and Merck, 1.6 percent. However, it is *less* concentrated. Today's five largest stocks account for 11 percent of the Index, only half the 22 percent weight of the five largest industrial giants of two decades ago. Those five former leaders, interestingly, now represent only 8 percent of the Index's weight. This large reduction in their importance underscores that the sheer force

---

*The rest of the market is measured by the Wilshire 4500 Equity Index, which includes all of the stocks in the all-market Wilshire 5000 Equity Index except those in the S&P 500.

of indexing has succeeded in overcoming this potential impediment. For new and growing companies have picked up the slack, enabling the Index to maintain its long-term performance leadership.

As the markets march on, times change and conditions change. And faith in an indexing strategy based on the widely celebrated success of the Standard & Poor's 500 Index will inevitably be tested from time to time in the years to come. Still, as a long-term strategy, it remains compelling.

THE S&P 500 INDEX IS NOT THE MARKET

The term *index fund* is all too often used interchangeably with one particular form of index fund: a fund modeled on the Standard & Poor's 500 Index. The first index mutual fund was structured in precisely that form, simply because the S&P 500 Index was: (1) the standard most widely followed by institutional investors in measuring their relative performance and assessing the results of their portfolio managers (mutual funds, in those days, generally didn't provide investors with comparative standards); (2) the more soundly structured of the two best-known indexes (stocks are weighted by market capitalization rather than, as in the case of the more familiar Dow Jones Industrial Average, by the price of one share of stock in each of only 30 companies); and (3) representative of 90 percent of the value of the entire stock market 25 years ago, and now represents about 75 percent of the value, and thus a solid proxy for the market. When the second index mutual fund appeared a full decade later, it too was S&P 500-based, as was a large majority of all the index funds that followed.

But the 75 percent of the market now represented by the large-cap stocks in the S&P 500 Index is *not* the market. Excluded are stocks with medium and small market capitalizations (and, typically, higher volatility). Nonetheless, the essential theory of indexing is based on owning *all* of the stocks in the market. Theoretically, the preferred standard for the basic index mutual fund would be the Wilshire 5000 Equity Index of all publicly held stocks in the United States.

With the large-cap stocks in the S&P 500 leading the way in the long bull market that began in 1982, the original 500 index funds have done especially well, and pragmatism has triumphed over dogma. But all-market index funds are slowly coming to the fore. Vanguard was the first of only a handful of firms to form mutual funds based on the Wilshire 5000 Equity Index. But the S&P 500 Index remains the principal measurement standard used by most mutual funds and pension accounts.

Does it matter which index is chosen? In the long run, no. Since 1970, when the Wilshire 5000 Equity Index began, the total returns of the two indexes have been identical: both have earned annual returns averaging 13.7 percent—a remarkably precise coincidence. It follows, then, that midcap and small-cap stocks, constituting 25 percent of the market's weighting measured by the Wilshire 4500 Equity Index, have also provided an average return of 13.7 percent. The 1970–1998 period is the longest period we have for comparison, although any period-dependent comparison is inevitably suspect. The precise parity of returns may overstate the case somewhat, but I am confident that we have learned something important when we observe that the returns of stocks with different investment characteristics converge so tightly over nearly three full decades.

But in the short run, yes: The difference *does* matter from one year to the next. As we look at comparisons that show the percentage of diversified U.S. equity mutual funds *of all types* that have been outpaced by the S&P 500 Index, its leadership in recent years has overstated its inherent strengths, even as its followership during 1976–1979 had overstated its weaknesses. For example, in that latter period, the S&P 500 Index outperformed 22 percent of all equity funds, but the Wilshire 5000 outperformed 44 percent. In 1995–1998, on the other hand, the S&P 500 outpaced 82 percent of all funds, while the Wilshire 5000 outpaced only (again, if that is the correct word) 72 percent. Figure 5.3 compares the relative standing of the two indexes over the past 28 years.

It is difficult to find a perfect standard against which to measure mutual fund returns. Although the total *assets* of U.S. equity funds are invested in proportions rather similar to those of the total value of the equity market among large-, medium-, and small-cap stocks, the total number of equity funds is divided differently, more heavily weighted toward medium- and small-cap funds. Figure 5.4 shows the comparisons.

Specifically, 75 percent of the aggregate value of all equities is represented by large-cap stocks, 15 percent by midcap stocks, and 10 percent by small-cap stocks. The distribution of equity fund *assets* is almost identical. But in terms of the *number* of funds, the current division is 52 percent large-cap, 26 percent midcap, and 22 percent small-cap, a significantly larger weighting in favor of these more volatile funds. The number of funds, however, is the basis of comparison when analysts count the percentage of funds outperformed by the Standard & Poor's 500 Index. So it follows that significant differences in annual returns will emerge as large-cap stocks lead or lag the overall market. When they lead, the success of the S&P 500 Index will be exaggerated; when they lag, the Index's failure will

FIGURE 5.3

General Equity Funds Outperformed by Market Indexes

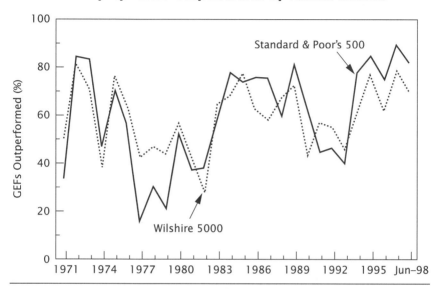

FIGURE 5.4

Equity Fund Composition vs. Indexes*

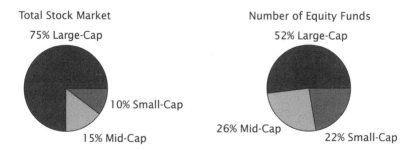

Total Stock Market
75% Large-Cap
10% Small-Cap
15% Mid-Cap

Number of Equity Funds
52% Large-Cap
26% Mid-Cap
22% Small-Cap

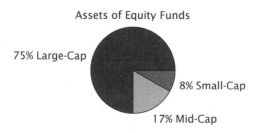

Assets of Equity Funds
75% Large-Cap
8% Small-Cap
17% Mid-Cap

* As of 9/30/98.

be exaggerated. In the long run, however, the differences haven't mattered. Always remember that simplistic, period-dependent comparisons—often selected to serve the interests of those making the comparisons—have the capacity to mislead unwary investors.

INDEXING WINS LARGELY BECAUSE OF COST

Given these variations between the composition of the capitalizations of the stock market (75 percent of the value of which is represented by large-cap stocks) and the number of funds in the equity fund universe (50 percent of which is represented by large-cap funds), how do we arrive at a fair basis for comparison? One simple, rudimentary way is to compare the results of the Wilshire 5000 (all-market) Equity Index with only those funds whose portfolios have weightings similar to the total market. As it turns out, mutual funds emphasizing stocks with large market capitalizations meet that standard.* Their performance can be approximated by combining all diversified growth funds and growth-and-income funds, and excluding small-cap and aggressive growth funds. The net result is about as fair as it can possibly be: funds emphasizing large-cap stocks, but not to the exclusion of all others, and an index that also emphasizes large-cap stocks, but, again, not to the exclusion of all others.

During the past 15 years, the average return of these large-cap-oriented funds, which I'll refer to as growth funds and value funds (rather than "growth and income" funds), has averaged 14.1 percent, compared to 16.0 percent for the Wilshire 5000 Equity Index. Cumulated over the period, this 1.9 percent difference, applied to an initial investment of $10,000, results in a final value of $72,600 for the average fund, a shortfall of more than $20,000 to the $92,700 that would have been accumulated in the Wilshire 5000 Index. (The return on the Standard & Poor's 500 Index, a much tougher standard during that time period, averaged 17.2 percent, for a final value of $107,800.)

Only 33 of the 200 growth and value funds that survived the 15-year period outpaced the Wilshire 5000 Index during this period; the remaining 167 funds fell short. The odds of fund superiority were thus one in six. Even more interesting and, I think, more significant, is the variation of fund returns around this average. We can get some sense of the significance of the

---

*The respective percentage weightings among giant-cap, large-cap, midcap, and small-cap stocks are: Wilshire 5000 Index: 48, 28, 15, 9; large-cap mutual funds: 47, 35, 16, 2.

differences among funds by arraying their fund returns around the returns of the Wilshire 5000 Index, as shown in Figure 5.5.

If we adjust our thinking and agree that a spread of less than one percentage point above or below the Index return is merely statistical noise, the odds shift: 15 funds topped the Index by more than that margin, compared to 125 funds that lost to it by the same margin. The odds of achieving that modest level of outperformance more than double: one in thirteen. Change the spread to three percentage points, a margin that has proven difficult for funds to achieve over the long run, and only one fund was a victor, with 43 funds among the vanquished. The odds of a given mutual fund's providing a three-point margin above the Index were just 1 in 200. These odds give you some idea of the Herculean challenge represented by the search to select the fund's big winners of tomorrow. (I explore this challenge more fully in Chapter 9.)

Another important lesson emerges here: The principal reason for the mutual fund shortfall is the heavy burden of fund expenses. The fund

FIGURE 5.5

Growth and Value Funds vs. Wilshire 5000 Index, 15 Years Ended June 30, 1998: Reported Net Returns (excluding sales charges)

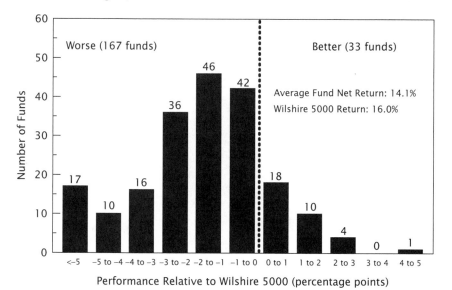

returns, relative to those of the Wilshire 5000 Equity Index shown above, are calculated in the basic manner—that is, after the deduction of all mutual fund operating expenses, which are explicit (they averaged about 1.4 percent per year during this period), and portfolio transaction costs, which are implicit (during the period, they appear to have averaged at least 0.5 percent per year for these growth and value funds). The Index was cost-free, incurring neither operating expenses nor transaction costs. If we adjust each fund's return for its approximate costs, we see a far different pattern of returns. Looking at fund returns on a gross (rather than a net) basis shifts the odds in a way that makes the industry profile look considerably better. (Fund shareholders, of course, earned only the net return.)

An examination of fund returns on a precost basis, presented in Figure 5.6, confirms the fundamental theory of indexing. Managers as a group must, by definition, provide *gross* returns equal to the market, just as a representative index does; therefore, the *net* returns earned by managers as a group will provide below-average returns once their investment costs are

FIGURE 5.6

Growth and Value Funds vs. Wilshire 5000 Index, 15 Years Ended June 30, 1998: Gross Return (net return + expenses + 50 basis points)

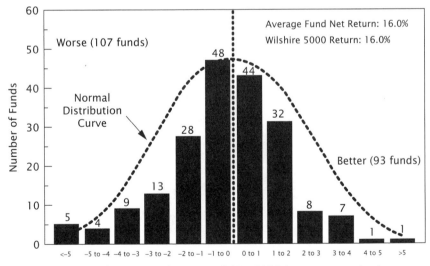

Performance Relative to Wilshire 5000 (percentage points)

deducted. That result is not astonishing, nor even counterintuitive. Indeed, over the past 15 years, the 16.0 percent return on the Wilshire 5000 Index exceeded the 14.1 percent net return on the average growth and value fund by 1.9 percentage points, precisely what we might have expected based on total estimated fund costs of 1.9 percent.*

In Figure 5.6, we present the returns of mutual funds *before expenses.* We simply redraw the previous chart and adjust for each fund's expense ratio and estimated transaction costs. In Figure 5.6, the fund distribution shifts to the right. Now, nearly half of the funds (93 of 200) outpace the Index, and 49 do so by one percentage point or more, compared to 107 that fail to match the Index. Still not great odds, but much improved over the after-cost pattern.

When we compare these gross returns with what would be a normal distribution of results—say, based on the random results of a coin-flipping contest—something interesting, or even astonishing, happens. When we fit the dotted line in the chart against the funds' gross returns, the result is almost perfect chance—similar to flipping a coin, albeit with the funds demonstrating a somewhat greater likelihood of falling in the middle of the distributions. Yes, one participant in 100 may flip heads ten times in a row, but 50 participants will flip five heads and five tails. The skill of portfolio managers, then, would appear to be largely a matter of luck, a game of chance. For, as Figure 5.6 shows, relative gross returns of mutual funds have followed a random pattern. For managers in the aggregate, the heavy handicap of cost is simply too heavy to overcome.

THE INDEX FUND IS *MUCH* BETTER THAN IT APPEARS

To illustrate that the benefits of a passively managed index fund (compared to an actively managed mutual fund) derive largely from the costs incurred by the traditional fund, I have based the above illustration on the results of a cost-free market index. An actual operating index fund, though it obviously need pay no advisory fees, must incur real-world operational expenses. In fact, the lowest-cost publicly available index funds operate at

---

*This simple equation ignores the fund disadvantage engendered by holdings of cash reserves, which probably accounted for an annual handicap of about 0.6 percent during this bull market period. (Index funds, by definition, hold no cash.) On the other hand, survivor bias likely accounted for an advantage of at least a similar dimension, roughly offsetting this handicap for growth and value funds. So the comparison remains valid.

annual expense ratios of less than 20/100 of 1 percent. Returns (at least for those that are operating most efficiently) should run about 0.20 percent per year behind those of the target index. These efficiently managed funds have, in fact, trailed the index by some 0.20 percent annually, implying that very low portfolio turnover, combined with minimal brokerage commissions, has held transaction costs to nominal levels. To account for costs, we would reduce the 16.0 percent return presented over the past 15 years by the Wilshire 5000 Index to 15.8 percent for a Wilshire 5000 Index *fund*. The net return would exceed the 14.1 percent return achieved by the average managed fund by 1.7 percentage points.

Even that comparison gives managed mutual funds the benefit of a huge doubt, and, as a result, hardly gives index funds the credit they deserve. The comparison suffers from at least three distinct advantages: (1) it ignores fund sales charges; (2) it is biased in favor of funds that survive the entire period over which the comparison is made; and (3) it is not adjusted for taxes on income dividends and capital gains distributions.

Virtually all presentations of industrywide mutual fund returns suffer from their failure to take into account the initial ("front end") sales charges, which are incurred on about 75 percent of purchases of all mutual funds, and any redemption ("back end") charges paid by investors who redeem their shares after relatively short-term holding periods. (About 15 percent of funds subject investors to these penalty fees; the number of investors who redeem shares early and are subject to these fees is not possible to determine.) If investors pay a 5 percent initial sales charge and hold their fund shares for 5 years, their return would be penalized by about 1 percent per year; if they hold the shares for 10 years, the penalty is about one-half of 1 percent per year (these amounts rise if fund returns are positive; they decline if returns are negative). Many funds are sold without sales loads, so the effective industrywide penalty on performance probably reduced fund returns from 14.1 percent to 13.6 percent, or by at least 0.50 percent annually over the past 15 years.

Survivor Bias

Survivor bias is a second significant factor in enhancing fund returns. When we look at a 15-year comparison, for example, *we look at only those funds that have survived the entire period.* That turns out to be quite an accomplishment, for about one-fifth of all funds that existed at the start of a typical 15-year period are no longer around at its finish. They may have simply been liquidated, or, more likely, merged into other funds in the same fund complex. But, however they vanish, it is those that have failed to deliver competitive returns that tend to disappear. Their results have been carefully measured in several academic studies. In one of the most comprehensive studies of its kind, Princeton Professor Burton Malkiel (author of the best-selling *A Random Walk Down Wall Street*) found that, during the 10-year period from 1982 to 1991, 18 percent of funds—59 of 331, or nearly 1 of every 6—had come and gone.* During that period, the survivors enjoyed annual returns of 17.1 percent per year, but all funds together provided returns of only 15.7 percent per year. This survivor bias had therefore enhanced the annual returns *reported* by funds by fully 1.4 percentage points over the *actual* returns earned by the funds during that 10-year period. What is more, during the 15-year period ending in 1991, survivor bias accounted for an astonishing 4.2 percentage points annually. For the purpose of argument, then, let's conservatively reduce the average fund return reported for the past 15 years by 1 percent, moving the fund return after the sales-charge adjustment, mentioned above, to 12.6 percent. The gap below the Wilshire 5000 Index return of 16.0 percent then grows to 3.4 percentage points.

Tax-Efficiency

Another huge toll has been taken by taxes. Passively managed index funds, are tax-*efficient* given the low turnover implicit in the structure of the Standard & Poor's 500 Index (and, to an even greater extent, the all-market Wilshire 5000 Index). Actively managed funds are tax-*inefficient*, with portfolio turnover averaging upward of 80 percent per year. In fact, during the past 15 years, the original Vanguard index fund (based on the S&P 500 Index) outpaced 94 percent of all funds on a *pretax* basis, but actually outpaced 97 percent of all funds on an *after-tax* basis. I'll explore the matter of taxes in greater detail in Chapter 13, but based on those data, let's assume, very conservatively, that the relative managed fund performance is reduced by another percentage point for taxable investors.

---

* In a later study, Professor Mark Carhart found that fully one-third of all stock funds disappeared from 1962 to 1993, and the Malkiel study showed that, even in as short a period as 1988–1992, 100 of the original 686 funds disappeared, a mortality rate of 15 percent. More recently, in 1993–1998, the halcyon period of mutual fund prosperity, about 600 equity funds vanished.

The total reduction of (at least) 2.5 percentage points that is created in the real world by these three factors reduces the original managed fund annual return of 14.1 percent to 11.6 percent. The conversion of the pure Wilshire 5000 Index to include index fund operating costs, on the other hand, would reduce the return to 15.8 percent for the index fund. As far as we can tell, then, the annual spread in favor of the index fund is 4.2 percentage points per year. Whether you are a short-term, intermediate-term, or long-term investor, *that* shortfall truly makes a difference.

THE THORNY ISSUE OF RISK

There is a countervailing argument in favor of active managers: Equity funds fall short of the broad market index because they carry less risk. Equity funds hold cash reserves; index funds, by definition, remain fully invested and therefore are more exposed to the full force of market declines. Not only should the cash reserves held by actively managed funds in themselves lessen the shock of decline, but smart managers, recognizing that a market decline lies in prospect, can reduce stock holdings in order to raise substantial extra reserves and preserve capital.

Unfortunately for those who argue the merits of this superficially reasonable case, the record is bereft of evidence to support it. Equity fund managers, as a group, have shown no systematic ability to raise cash before major market drops or to reinvest that cash after market drops. Indeed, quite the reverse is true. Funds tend to hold large amounts of cash at market lows and small amounts at market highs. For example, funds held cash equal to only 4 percent of assets immediately before the 1973–1974 market crash, but increased it to about 12 percent at the ensuing low. Another example: At the beginning of the bull market in 1982, equity funds held cash equal to 11 percent of assets. In 1988, reserves still remained at 10 percent of assets. Yet, in mid-1998, just before the steepest stock market decline since 1987, reserves had dwindled to 4.6 percent of equity fund assets, one of the lowest midyear totals on record. Once again, the fund managers were wrong.

But the fact is that at any of those cash levels, cash is the tail and not the dog. Simple logic compels the conclusion that a 5 to 10 percent tail cannot possibly wag the dog represented by a 90 to 95 percent equity position. Indeed, the record of funds versus market indexes in periods of market decline confirms that the portfolios composed entirely of the higher quality, larger-cap stocks in the fully invested indexes have tended to display somewhat less volatility than the portfolios of the typical equity fund, which are composed of somewhat more aggressive stocks but seasoned with small cash positions.

On the record, index funds based on both the Standard & Poor's 500 Index and the Wilshire 5000 Index are somewhat *less* risky than the average mutual fund. *Morningstar Mutual Funds* calculates a risk factor for each fund based on its returns in the months in which it underperforms the risk-free Treasury Bill. *Morningstar's* data show that, over the past decade, a typical S&P 500 Index fund was fully 15 percent less risky than the average mutual fund; over the past five years, a typical S&P 500 Index fund was 19 percent less risky, and a Wilshire 5000 Index fund was 18 percent less risky.

Looked at in a different way, the standard deviation of return over the past decade has been: S&P 500, 14.3 percent; Wilshire 5000, 14.0 percent; average U.S. diversified mutual equity fund, 14.8 percent. Conforming to the *Morningstar* format, then, if the standard deviation of the average fund were rated at 1.00 for the decade, the S&P 500 Index fund would be rated at 0.97, and the Wilshire 5000 Index fund, at 0.95. (See Table 5.2.) Taken together, the *Morningstar* risk data and the relative standard deviations make it clear that, despite the fact that managed equity mutual funds do indeed maintain modest reserve positions—and have the ability to raise even more reserves in anticipation of market dips—their risk exposure has been systematically, and often significantly, greater than that of the fully invested broad market indexes.

TABLE 5.2

Risk: Average Equity Fund and Index Funds

	5-Year Morningstar Risk	10-Year Standard Deviation	10-Year Relative Standard Deviation	Cumulative Loss		
				8/31/87 to 11/30/87	5/23/96 to 7/25/96	7/16/98 to 9/3/98
Average Equity Fund	1.00	14.80	1.00	−28.3%	−9.5%	−20.3%
S&P 500 Index Fund	0.81	14.30	0.97	−29.8	−6.4	−16.9
Wilshire 5000 Index Fund	0.82	14.00*	0.95	−29.8*	−8.3	−18.8

*Wilshire 5000 Index; index fund not yet created.

The comparative record of managed mutual funds and market index funds in specific significant market declines confirms these data, even as it suggests that the risks carried by managed mutual funds relative to the market index funds have been rising as new, more aggressive funds have been added to the industry roster. More than a decade ago, in the largest market decline in the past generation, for example, both of the broad market indexes actually declined a bit *more* than the average fund. Each index fell about 29 percent during the brunt of the crash from August 31, 1987, to November 30, 1987, compared to a drop of 28 percent for the average fund. However, the Standard & Poor's 500 Index, with a larger relative gain before the fall and a larger recovery afterward, actually *rose* by 5.2 percent for the year. The average fund rose by just 0.5 percent.

In more recent declines, equity funds have become notably riskier. From late May through July 1996, for example, the 6.4 percent decline in an S&P 500 Index fund was 33 percent less than the 9.5 percent decline in the average fund, and the decline in an all-market index fund was 13 percent less. In the steep decline during the summer of 1998, the index funds again proved to be substantially more risk-averse, with the S&P 500 down almost 17 percent, the Wilshire 5000 down 19 percent, and the average fund down more than 20 percent. The more volatile funds formed during the late, great years of the bull market had simply made the industry more volatile. The leopard had changed its spots—but at the wrong time.

If we examine the record, using the various *Morningstar*-style categories of equity funds (large-cap value, small-cap growth, and so on), we find a highly consistent pattern of higher risk relative to *comparable* market indexes (not merely the S&P 500 Index) throughout the entire matrix. Risks assumed by funds have been particularly large among the various small-cap categories relative to comparable small-cap indexes. The net result is that index fund risk-adjusted returns have carried an even higher margin of advantage over actively managed funds than the raw (unadjusted) returns indicate. The style categories and these relationships are more fully described in the final pages of Chapter 6.

In all, it's hard to imagine why the specter of high risk continues to haunt the image of index funds. They decline precisely in step with the markets they measure. But so do managed funds—and even more markedly in recent years, as the industry has come to include more aggressive funds. The record simply doesn't support the premise that the modest positions in cash reserves held by actively managed funds provide an anchor to windward, nor the assertion that smart, agile portfolio managers systematically anticipate market declines and take defensive action. With fund cash reserves that were 50 percent lower at recent market highs than they were in the depressed markets of the early 1990s, quite the reverse appears to be true.

ALL INDEX FUNDS ARE NOT CREATED EQUAL

In this analysis of market indexes and index mutual funds, I have had to rely largely on the records of the original two index funds simply because, as the pioneers in the field, they are the funds with the longest records (23 years for the Vanguard 500 Index Fund, and seven years for the Total Stock Market Index Fund). But a caution is necessary: Both of these index funds are large; both are free of sales loads; both have operated at rock-bottom cost; both have maintained low portfolio turnover; and both have been administered with extraordinary efficiency, enabling them to track their target indexes with considerable precision.

The same cannot be said about all of the index funds that are now available in the marketplace. Of some 140 index funds, about 55 are modeled on the S&P 500 Index; four on the Wilshire 5000 Index; 46 on subsets of the overall U.S. stock market (large-cap growth and value, small-cap growth and value, and so on); 18 on international markets; and just 20 on the U.S. bond market. Instead of blindly choosing an index fund, investors must be careful to determine that the fund they select is indexed to the market segment they wish to emulate.

Surprisingly, one-third of all index funds carry either front-end or asset-based sales charges. Why an investor would opt to pay a commission on an index fund when a substantially identical fund is available without a commission remains a mystery. The investor who does so starts out on day one by falling as much as 5 percent or more behind the target index—behind the eight-ball, as it were—and falls further behind each year, as fund expenses take their toll. Suffice it to say that it would be silly for an intelligent investor to select an index fund that carries a commission.

It is equally nonsensical to select a fund that carries a high operating cost. Annual expense ratios of index mutual funds run from as low as a nominal 0.02 percent for funds available to very large institutional investors and 0.18 percent for publicly available funds, to as high as 0.95 percent, the rate charged by at least one established fund. That is simply too much to pay. (When a representative of that fund was asked how such a confiscatory fee could be justified, he responded, "It's a cash cow"—for the manager. Indeed it is. But a cash cow for the investor is a better option.)

Further, beware of the many funds that attest that their expense ratios are low, stating only in the fine print that fees are being waived for a temporary period or until a specific future date. What, really, is the point in your paying an artificially low expense ratio of, say, 0.19 percent for a few years, after which a much higher 0.50 percent fee may be assessed? It is at least possible that, by that time, your investment will have appreciated in value, and you will be subject to capital gains taxes that outweigh the obvious advantage of shifting to a truly low-cost fund. Be sure to read all the fine print about costs in the advertisements, and pay careful heed to the details in the fund's prospectus.

Next, there is the question of portfolio turnover. One of the great advantages of index funds is their tax efficiency. But some index funds, either because of constant heavy investor activity, or because of portfolio strategies based on the aggressive use of index futures, generate high portfolio turnover—sometimes as much as 100 percent or more—and consequently realize and distribute substantial capital gains. When tax-efficient index funds abound, there is simply no reason for taxable investors to select index funds that are tax-inefficient.

Further, all index funds are not created equal in operating efficiency. Some index fund managers, whether by virtue of skill, experience, or dedication, simply do a better job than others in the execution of portfolio transactions. Taking 1996 through 1998 as an example, the best managers of the Standard & Poor's 500 Index funds were actually able to outpace the returns of the index itself by as much as $\frac{1}{10}$ of 1 percent annually *before* the deduction of operating costs; the least successful managers fell $\frac{3}{10}$ of 1 percent (or more) behind. This difference in ability to match the index is pretty much ignored by the marketplace. But it should not be. Of what value is a manager, for example, who brags about an expense ratio (often temporary) of 0.18 percent and loses 0.30 percent in operating margin, resulting in a net shortfall of 0.48 percent to the index? Compare those results to the performance of a manager who charges 0.20 percent and exactly matches the index return, for a net shortfall of 0.20 percent. Investors should carefully examine the aspects of each manager's implementation of strategy for any index fund that is being considered.

Finally, index funds vary in the amount of unrealized capital gains in their portfolios. In the abstract, those with modest appreciation (or even losses) on their books might be favored over those with very large appreciation. But this factor should be weighed only in light of the countervailing advantages the funds may offer, as well as their susceptibility to heavy redemptions, their election of redemption-in-kind policies (thus obviating the need to liquidate portfolio securities), and their tax management strategies.

None of these little percentages may seem like much, but they can represent the difference between day and night for the long-term index fund investor. Even tiny differences in returns truly matter in a lifetime investment program. Consider the different approaches to index fund selection, given in Table 5.3. After a decade, $10,000 in the no-load, low-cost, efficient index fund would have grown to $30,500; in the worst outcome, the load, high-cost, inefficient fund would have grown to $26,500.

Such a hypothetical example is hardly absurd. It is real. Over the past decade, $10,000 invested in one efficient, low-cost, no-load S&P 500 Index fund would have grown to $54,000. Another putatively identical, but less efficient, higher-cost index fund carrying a 4.5 percent load, would have grown to only $47,000—truly a staggering gap between two S&P Index

TABLE 5.3

Net Returns of Index Funds with Varying Characteristics

	Assumed Gross Return	Sales Charge	Expense Ratio	Operating Efficiency*	Residual Net Return	Ten-Year Value of $10,000 Investment**
Market index No load Low cost	12%	0	0	0	12%	$31,100
Efficient No load Low cost	12	0	0.20%	0	11.8	30,500
Inefficient No load High cost	12	0	0.20	−0.20%	11.6	30,000
Inefficient Load High cost	12	0	0.80	−0.30	10.9	28,100
Inefficient	12	6%	0.80	−0.30	10.2	26,500

*Difference between target index and portfolio return before cost.
**Assumed 10-year holding period.

funds with the same portfolios. (This fund, as it happens, was the "cash cow" described earlier.) All index funds are *not* created equal.

INDEXING WORKS IN ALL MARKETS

That index funds are finally achieving grudging acceptance bears witness to the great success that index funds modeled on the Standard & Poor's 500 Stock Index have enjoyed by providing, in an era of extraordinary *absolute* stock market returns, superior *relative* returns as well. In addition, the all-market index fund, modeled on the Wilshire 5000 Equity Index, is beginning to make competitive inroads as it brings to full fruition the essential theory of indexing: That all investors, as a group, cannot possibly outpace the total (cost-free) return on the *entire stock market*. But the remaining detractors of index funds still hold to the position that indexing works only in efficient markets, such as those represented by the actively traded, very liquid large-capitalization stocks that overpoweringly dominate the S&P 500 Index and comprise 75 percent of the Wilshire 5000—and not in other presumably less efficient markets.

Plausible as that argument may sound, it is specious. The success of indexing is based not necessarily on some notion of market efficiency, but simply on the inability of all investors in any discrete market or market segment to outpace the universe of investments in which they operate. Efficiency relates to a market price structure that generally values all securities properly at any one time, which means that good and bad managers alike will have difficulty in differentiating themselves *either way*. In inefficient markets, good managers may have greater opportunities to outpace their universe. But the excess returns earned by good managers must inevitably be offset by inferior returns of the exact same dimension by bad managers.

However, costs of funds operating in so-called inefficient markets are higher than funds operating in efficient markets. For example, costs of U.S. small-cap funds are systematically higher than those of large-cap funds. In Chapter 6, we shall see that once the relatively higher risks that they assume are accounted for, managed midcap and small-cap funds have realized similar (if slightly *larger*) shortfalls to the indexes in their market sectors, compared to those their large-cap cousins have realized.

Costs of international funds are higher still, not only because of their higher expense ratios but because of much higher custodial costs, taxes, commissions, and market impact costs. As a result, not only do the exact same principles of indexing apply in international markets, but an even larger margin of index superiority is reflected in passively managed international index funds, as compared to actively managed international funds, as will be shown in Chapter 8. Indexing works—as it must—with high effectiveness in all the far-flung corners of the world of equity investing.

Table 5.4 illustrates how the total relationship between manager returns and index returns in efficient and inefficient markets might work. Note how the symmetrical pattern of precost returns quickly becomes asymmetrical after the deduction of costs. Put another way, the onus of costs erodes the superiority of the top equity managers, even as it magnifies the deficiency of the bottom-tier managers. But it does so by larger amounts in inefficient stock markets. Ironically, then, equity indexing should work *better* in inefficient markets than in efficient markets.

Indexing works in the bond market, too. Indeed, it is arguably even more valuable where high-grade fixed-income investments are concerned. Bond returns are typically lower than stock returns, so costs take a large toll on the gross annual returns earned by bond funds. The gross returns of competing bond funds tend to be similar, but the costs of most bond funds, as I shall note in Chapter 7, are excessive, giving low-cost bond index funds a remarkable head start. Finally, successful managers who achieve substantial superiority in precost returns are conspicuous by their paucity. There are, apparently, few Peter Lynches in the bond fund field. There are good managers and bad managers, as always, but no heroes who tower above all others.

The average bond fund has turned in an average annual return of 8.7 percent over the past 15 years, compared to 10.2 percent for the Lehman Aggregate (U.S.) Bond Index. That shortfall of 1.5 percentage points is

TABLE 5.4

Manager Returns vs. Market

	Before Costs		After Costs*	
	Top 10 Percent	Bottom 10 Percent	Top 10 Percent	Bottom 10 Percent
Efficient markets	+3%	−3%	+1½%	−4½%
Inefficient markets	+5	−5	+2½	−7½

*Assumed fund costs of 1½ percent in efficient markets and 2½ percent in inefficient markets.

largely accounted for by the estimated 1.3 percent annual expense incurred by the average bond fund (expense ratio of 1.08 percent plus portfolio transaction costs of perhaps 0.25 percent). Over a different time period, the first bond index fund, formed in 1986, has reflected a similar pattern of superior performance. Since its inception, its annual return has averaged 8.1 percent (net of operating expenses averaging about 0.20 percent and transaction costs of 0.10 percent). Its margin of superiority over the 7.4 percent return of the average bond mutual fund during the same period represents a 9 percent enhancement in returns over professionally managed bond funds. Chapter 7 will demonstrate how that same pattern of index superiority shines through in every major segment of the bond market—total, long-term, intermediate-term, taxable, and tax-exempt bonds alike. The success of indexing is not only theoretical, it is pragmatic. We *must* find it everywhere, and we do.

THE TRIUMPH OF INDEXING

An understanding of the fact that index funds have proven themselves by outpacing actively managed funds during the past near-quarter century is now pervasive. Experience has triumphed over hope not only in the academic community, where an apostle of active management is rarely found, but also in the financial media, where the conversion, if not complete, is pervasive. And not only in the world of successful professional investors—recall the comments by Warren Buffett, cited earlier in this chapter—but in the mutual fund industry itself.

Nearly all of the major no-load fund complexes have now begun to offer index funds—and not only index funds modeled on the Standard & Poor's 500 Stock Price Index. Even the major stock brokerage firms are offering index funds on a no-load basis, as is virtually essential. However, they make their index funds available only in investment management accounts, which entail, to whatever avail, an advisory fee that is charged directly to the client. I fear that this trend is less the result of enlightenment than of self-interest. Nonbelievers have been dragged—kicking and screaming—into the fray to meet a public demand that is now palpable. The need for traditional fund managers to fill out their product lines has outweighed their resistance to accepting the markedly lower fees that index funds must carry.

Nonetheless, an amazingly diverse group of index believers has emerged, and the comments from investment advisers who have seen the light reflect the truly remarkable acceptance that indexing now enjoys:

- Peter Lynch, the legendary former manager of the Magellan Fund, who established himself as one of the most brilliant stock pickers of his age: "Most investors would be better off in an index fund."

- Charles Schwab, founder of the largest mutual fund supermarket, which facilitates the selecting and trading of more than 1,000 individual actively managed mutual funds, with an emphasis, relentlessly advertised, on funds with exceptional past performance. But his heart belongs to indexing when it comes to his own dollars and the assets of institutions. Recently, his firm has even begun a vigorous promotion of its own (often relatively high-cost) index funds on television. Heed his words: "Only about one out of every four equity funds outperforms the stock market. That's why I'm a firm believer in the power of indexing."

- Internet adviser "The Motley Fool." While its partners' nostrums promise to "put you in a position to double the S&P 500, posting returns in excess of 20 percent per year," they praise indexing, albeit with faint damns. These self-styled gurus of the Internet acknowledge: "If you've had trouble with your investments, the index fund is there for you," and they state categorically, "*We* don't think there's any other fund out there worth buying."

- Perhaps most poignant of all, Jon Fossel, former Chairman of the OppenheimerFunds and of the Investment Company Institute, made the ultimate concession in response to the critical comments of an industry executive who had noted, "When it comes down to how we are performing, we are trailing in the market's wake." Fossel replied, "People ought to recognize that the average fund can *never* outperform the market in total" (italics added).

To state what must by now be obvious: The index fund is here to stay. What began as a controversial idea, bereft of public demand in 1975, has come to represent the standard of investment return—but the apparently unreachable star—for the mutual fund industry. At long last, we are witnessing the triumph of experience over hope. Actual experience has reflected the triumph of passively managed index funds over actively managed funds. Common sense has carried the day. In time, index funds will change the very fabric and nature of the mutual fund industry.

THE FUTURE OF INDEXING

Many changes for indexing can be expected during the years ahead. Some may reduce the substantial extra margins of return earned in the past by index funds over mutual funds with comparable portfolio characteristics. At least three possibilities exist:

1. Equity mutual funds might become fully invested. Cash has always been a drag on returns for the long-term equity investor. Yet most mutual funds hold significant cash reserves, presumably for liquidity purposes. As long as stocks earn higher returns than money market instruments, cash represents a substantial drag. As fund investors recognize the penalty that cash imposes on long-term returns—as well as the futility of paying an adviser 1.5 percent a year to manage cash reserves—fund managers may finally get the message.

2. Mutual fund costs might come down. Significant reductions in advisory fees are possible, if hardly likely, as the competitive implications of unmanaged, low-cost index funds become known, and as actively managed, high-cost funds realize that they must cut their fees to reduce the "fiscal drag" on performance that these fees represent. Lower fees might also come about as somnolent independent directors, if such there be, of mutual funds finally awaken and cut fund management fees that have reached excessive levels. Fees could easily be reduced without sacrificing the quality of management supervision, if managers simply eliminated their huge expenditures in areas that provide no benefit to mutual fund shareholders, such as marketing and advertising. I estimate that less than 10 percent of the expenses paid by mutual fund shareholders go to fund portfolio managers and research analysts who, as a group, are purported to have the ability to provide the returns that fund shareholders seek. There is ample room for fee reductions.

3. Fund portfolio turnover might decline from current excessive levels. In the old days (the 1950s, for example), mutual fund portfolio turnover rates were usually around 20 percent per year. Today, the average turnover rate approaches 100 percent a year. Because this turnover is costly, a wise manager attempting to outpace an approximate market index will one day more carefully assess the impact of portfolio turnover. As the huge tax cost of turnover to shareholders becomes known, investors may well demand lower turnover and more tax-efficient management strategies. Mutual funds, then, must learn from the lessons of indexing, and turn their focus from short-term speculation to long-term investment.

While lower costs, reduced reserves, and a focus on long-term investing could enhance industry returns and reduce the index advantage, there are at least three countervailing possibilities that may result in an *increase* in the index advantage.

1. Mutual fund expense ratios may increase. The trend toward replacing unpopular but obvious front-end loads with hidden loads in the form of 12b-1 fees has had the effect of raising reported fund expense ratios. In the absence of action by fund directors to drive other fees down, a continuing trend toward the use of 12b-1 fees will itself drive expense ratios even higher.

2. Fund portfolio turnover could, amazingly, increase, adding even further to fund costs. As market efficiency spreads from the large-cap segment (which is terribly efficient already) to midcap and small-cap stocks and international markets (as seems likely), managers might endeavor to capitalize on the increasingly rare mispricings that may be perceived to exist in individual securities by trading with even greater frequency.

(Continued)

3. Funds could lose even the opportunity to distinguish them-selves. Equity mutual fund assets now total some $2.5 tril-lion, 75 *times* their $34 billion total in 1976. Mutual fund managers now supervise some 33 percent of all individual stocks, compared with less than 2 percent two decades ago. With their higher turnover, fund managers are now simply trading stocks with one another, making it impossible to en-hance industrywide returns. In the future, it could be tougher than ever for mutual fund managers as a group, and even managers of individual funds, to differentiate their per-formance in an amount sufficient to overcome their fees and operating expenses.

Which of these countervailing sets of forces—one set reducing the index fund advantage, the other set increasing it—will prevail? While the raw power of indexing—now demonstrated by experience as well as by theory—could force major changes in the way fund complexes operate, I fear the industry will resist the changes that are necessary. But even if fund managers fail to experience the kind of epiphany that Saul experienced on the road to Damascus and come to accept the message of indexing—that would be too much to ask—changes may come in traditional fund policies because investors will demand them and the fund industry will at last develop an enlight-ened sense of self-interest.

CHAPTER

ON EQUITY STYLES
TICK-TACK-TOE

*I*n recent years, "style purity" has become the catchphrase of portfolio managers, investment advisers, and mutual fund investors. Mutual funds—sometimes enthusiastically, sometimes reluctantly—are defining their investment strategies and investment policies more clearly. The managers of individual stock funds today feel pressured to keep the portfolios they manage fully invested at all times, and to confine themselves to a given portfolio style that defines the fund's strategy—growth stocks versus value stocks, for example, or large-cap stocks versus small-cap stocks.

A powerful argument can be made that the choice of equity fund styles—like the choice of fund portfolio managers—is just one more example of industry witchcraft. Just as absolutely no brute evidence exists that past fund returns are the precursors of future returns, so there is little, if any, evidence that there are superior investment styles that prevail over time. In both cases, above-average returns and below-average returns revert to normal levels: Individual fund returns revert to appropriate market index norms, and equity styles revert to total stock market norms. (In both cases, I am speaking of fund returns *before* the deduction of costs.)

Why bother with styles at all? This is not a trivial question. There are powerful reasons for owning the entire stock market, or even large-capitalization blended (growth and value) funds, the particular fund style that most strongly tends to track (again, before costs are deducted) the total return of the market.

But if there is little, if any, evidence of persistence in the investment performance of an individual mutual fund relative to its peers, there is substantial evidence of persistence in the relative risks assumed by individual funds, largely because of the investment style they follow. Style, it turns out, *does* make a difference. And since style differences are persistent, sheer logic leads us to the conclusion that there is greater probability of persistence in *risk-adjusted* returns than in *total* returns earned by each fund. Selecting a particular fund style can enable investors to have an important degree of risk control. (Large-cap value funds, for example, have assumed about 50 percent less volatility than the average fund, and small-cap growth funds have assumed about 50 percent more.)

Most investors, properly in my view, will emphasize a strategy that focuses on funds in the large-cap category, especially blended growth and value funds, as a conservative, centrist approach to equity investing. Some investors may want to consider two other options: "stockpicking" funds without a clear mandate, but with a broad opportunity to rotate from one market sector to another; or funds that hew to the benchmarks of specific style categories. Investors who rely on style-specific funds can then reflect personal risk preferences or balance out the risks in an existing portfolio that is overweighted—or underweighted—relative to the market in one style or another. This latter case may be described as a risk-control strategy. Hovering over the entire strategy issue is another major investment decision: Whether, regardless of the investment style chosen, it should be implemented with a traditionally managed fund or with an index fund that emulates its style. My goal in this chapter is to help you deal sensibly with these challenges.

ENTER TICK-TACK-TOE

Consider the child's game of tick-tack-toe. There is simply no way to win, even if a genius is playing against an opponent of only moderate intelligence. Each player simply blocks the other player's next move. (A schematic version is shown in Figure 6.1.) Of course, if one player is slow to see the possibilities or lacks concentration, his opponent can win the game. Tick-tack-toe is a game that cannot be won. It is the consummate loser's game.

Curiously enough, the *Morningstar* "Category Rating" system, introduced in 1996, is played in a nine-box pattern identical to that of tick-tack-toe. Because of that similarity, the nine-box system for analyzing

FIGURE 6.1

Tick-Tack-Toe

X	O	X
X	O	O
O	X	X

fund investment styles raises this question: Does the search for fund performance resemble the search for three Xs (or Os) in a row? Or, put another way: If no one can win consistently when nearly all participants have at least average skill, is not fund selection also a loser's game?

More than two decades ago, Charles Ellis wrote, in *The Loser's Game*, that the premise that professional managers can beat the market appeared to be false. Then, the Standard & Poor's 500 Index was virtually the only standard used by financial institutions to measure market returns. (And even that index wasn't used very often!) The portfolios of most institutional managers and mutual funds were in fact dominated by a blended list of the large-cap stocks in the S&P 500. Today, other styles have emerged; some funds place extreme emphasis on value or growth, or on midcap or small-cap stocks. These various styles differ from one another both in the returns that they achieve (at least over interim periods) and in the volatility risk they assume (which proves to be fairly consistent over time). Good judgment dictates comparing funds with those in the same style categories.

COMPARING APPLES TO APPLES

To date, most evaluations of mutual fund performance have been fairly simplistic: How has a fund performed relative to "the market"? The Standard & Poor's 500 Stock Price Index is usually used as a proxy for "the market," despite the fact that it accounts for only about 75 percent of the capitalization of the U.S. stock market and is dominated by corporations with gigantic market capitalizations. (Its 50 largest stocks account for 35 percent of the entire market. The combined weight of the 6,900 "non-500" stocks in the market is 25 percent.)

Many funds resemble "the market" only tangentially. Practitioners of style analysis compare a mutual fund with other funds that are following a similar investment style, not with "the market." For many years, institutional investors represented this type of analysis by drawing a box with a vertical axis extending from large to small market capitalization, and a horizontal axis extending from value to growth (usually based on ratios of market-to-book value or price-to-earnings). Each account got an "X" somewhere along each axis. It wasn't a very complicated exercise, but neither was it a particularly simple way to evaluate comparative performance. A typical style box used by institutional investors is shown in Figure 6.2, which compares a large-cap growth portfolio (left) with a small-cap value portfolio (right).

Enter *Morningstar*. Its contribution—and it *is*, as advertised, "a more intelligent way to select and monitor mutual funds"—was to replace the institutional style box with a nine-box matrix (just like tick-tack-toe) in which each fund is, in effect, forced into a dual description: large-, medium-, or small-capitalization on the vertical axis, and value or growth at the extremes of the horizontal axis, with "blend" (a combination of the two) in the middle.

The beauty of this system is that it immediately makes it possible to quantify the vital statistics of each fund's performance relative to that of its peers, based on a combination of risk and return. Large-cap growth

FIGURE 6.2

Institutional Style Box

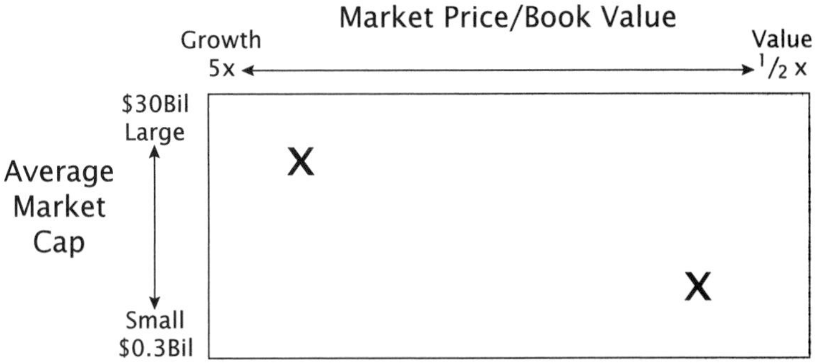

funds are compared with other large-cap growth funds; small-cap value funds are compared with other small-cap value funds; and so on. Under the *Morningstar* system, each fund then gets a Category Rating in a range from "one" (lowest 10 percent) to "five" (highest 10 percent). Both the top and bottom performance ratings are tough leagues to break into. Eighty percent of the funds are in the middle categories (45 percent in categories two and four; 35 percent in category three).

Figure 6.3 is the first of ten tick-tack-toe boxes in this chapter. It shows the mix of 741 equity funds with five-year records as of the beginning of 1997. These funds are tracked by *Morningstar*, which makes their detailed records readily accessible through its database. While this analysis is significant, achieving superior total returns in the long run, irrespective of style or category, is infinitely more significant. The task of the investor is to achieve the highest possible portion of the return of the total stock market, whether by style or skill.

The *Morningstar* Category Rating system accurately reflects general differences or similarities in the returns earned by the funds in various style categories. In the five-year period ended 12/31/96 that is analyzed in this chapter, similarities were most apparent. Only large-cap growth funds (annual returns averaging about +12 percent) strayed from the +13 percent to +15 percent returns of the other groups. The annual returns for each of the nine categories are shown in Figure 6.4.

FIGURE 6.3

Morningstar Style Boxes (741 Equity Funds)*

	Number of Funds		
	Value	Blend	Growth
Large	100	211	58
Medium	54	84	90
Small	52	32	60

*Funds with 5-year records as of December 31, 1996.
Data from Morningstar.

FIGURE 6.4

Annual Returns by Fund Category*

	Annual Returns (%)		
	Value	Blend	Growth
Large	13.8	13.2	11.9
Medium	14.2	14.0	13.3
Small	15.1	15.1	15.0

* 1992–1996.

FIGURE 6.5

Risk by Fund Category*

	Standard Deviation (%)		
	Value	Blend	Growth
Large	9.8	9.9	12.0
Medium	9.9	11.3	15.8
Small	11.6	13.9	18.7

* 1992–1996.

FIGURE 6.6

Risk–Return Ratio by Fund Category*

	Risk-Adjusted Return**		
	Value	Blend	Growth
Large	1.23	1.09	0.80
Medium	1.20	0.98	0.67
Small	1.15	0.93	0.69

* 1992–1996.
** Sharpe ratio.

Differences in risk, however, are much more sharply defined among the nine categories. Using standard deviation (described in Chapter 1) as a proxy for risk, the variability of returns over the five years has ranged from a low of 9.8 percent (large-cap value) to a high that is nearly double that figure: 18.7 percent (small-cap growth). Curiously, despite the nearly identical *returns* among the three small-cap categories, the differences in *risk* were extreme (11.6 percent for value and 18.7 percent for growth). Figure 6.5 shows these sharp differences in risk.

These differences in risk, in the face of the similarity of returns, give rise to large differences in risk-adjusted returns—in effect, the return earned per unit of risk assumed by the fund. Again, we use the Sharpe ratio, based on the number of percentage points of a fund's excess return (over the risk-free rate) for each percentage point of volatility. As Figure 6.6 shows, the differences in *risk-adjusted return ratios* are also extremely wide—in fact, almost double—from 1.23 for large value funds to 0.67–0.69 for mid-cap and small-cap growth funds.

Adjusting returns to take risk into account is an important consideration for investors. To understand why, consider this example: Assume that the market volatility is 10 percent and the market's annual rate of return is 14 percent. Reducing that return by an assumed risk-free rate of 4 percent would bring the market's risk-adjusted net to 1.00. Now consider two mutual funds with the same 14 percent return: Fund A has more volatility than the market (11 percent), and Fund B has less volatility (9 percent). Fund A would have a risk-adjusted return of .90; Fund B, a risk-adjusted return of 1.11. If investors in Fund B wish to assume risk that is slightly larger than the market and equal to Fund A, they could theoretically borrow 20 percent on their investment and place it in the fund, gaining 20 percent leverage. Their risk would increase to 11 percent, but their return would rise to 16.8 percent. Thus, their return would be 20 percent higher than their original 14 percent return. These 2.8 percentage points of extra return would be gained without assuming any more risk than Fund A. If the intelligent investor's goal is to earn the highest returns possible for a given level of risk, Fund A would clearly be the inferior investment.

I know this analysis is complicated. This example may clarify the concept: Assume that two funds had an equal volatility of 10 percent. A fund with a 1.20 risk–return ratio would return 16 percent, and a fund with a risk–return ratio of 0.60 would return 10 percent (assuming a risk-free rate of 4 percent). *The difference of 6 percentage points per year is hardly trivial.*

A Ratio Too Acute?

Although it is essential to consider fund returns in the context of fund risks, the Sharpe ratio is a bit of a blunt instrument to measure risk-adjusted returns. Past returns don't predict future returns. And although relative risks among funds have a good deal of consistency over time, standard deviation is only a rough proxy for a concept as elusive as risk. Further, weighting risk as equal to return in importance in the formula is completely arbitrary. Here is the reality of investing, as I see it: *An extra percentage point of standard deviation is meaningless, but an extra percentage point of return is priceless.* Large differences in risk are extremely important—there *is* a difference between a stock portfolio and a bond portfolio—but the expedient of weighting risk and return equally, in a simple formula, leaves much to be desired. In the final analysis, risk-adjusted returns, like beauty, may be in the eye of the beholder.

Despite these weaknesses, the Sharpe ratio is the principal instrument used by investment analysts to measure risk-adjusted returns. It presents a more complete picture of fund performance than raw return, and can help investors to evaluate the relative success of competing funds following the same broad investment strategies. Perhaps like all statistics, it can be remarkably useful, but only if its limitations are recognized.

Because the average returns for each of the nine boxes during the period were fairly consistent, the wide variations in risk-adjusted return ratios largely reflect the differences in the risks of the nine market segments. Before the advent of style analysis, it was difficult to associate these differences in risk-adjusted return with the performance of a particular market segment. Often, variations were attributed to differences in manager skill, rather than to the fact that one manager invested in small-cap growth stocks while another plied his trade among large-cap value stocks. Style analysis enables investors to appraise the ability of managers to use the tools they have chosen. The nine-box peer-group comparison, while by no means perfect, is the best available.

EQUITY FUNDS—RISKS, RETURNS, AND COSTS

What happens when we begin to evaluate equity funds on the basis of their investment styles, as measured by their *Morningstar* categories? I'm now going to attempt to answer this question, using returns and standard deviations of return during the five-year period from 1992 through 1996. The first example is the large-capitalization blend group—mutual funds that invest in giant companies that have both value and growth characteristics. Of the 741 funds analyzed by *Morningstar*, this category has 211—more than twice as many as any other group—and represents some 40 percent of the assets of all domestic equity funds ($450 billion of $1.2 trillion of equity assets in the *Morningstar* database at year-end 1996). It provides a solid platform on which to begin the analysis.

Table 6.1 shows the returns and risks for the large-cap blend group. The funds are ranked in four quartiles, based on total returns for the period. Even though returns rise, risk in this category remains virtually unchanged, and standard deviation remains remarkably constant over the quartiles. The risk-adjusted return ratio increases by the same magnitude as the total return, from a ratio of 0.74 to 1.37—fully 63 ratio points from the lowest to the highest, an astonishing 85 percent difference. And, this outcome for the large-cap blend (middle-of-the-road) fund category seems to be typical. Seven of the nine categories (the exceptions are small-cap value and medium-cap growth) have fairly steady risk scores, whether returns are high or low. Hence, the top *risk-adjusted* ratings were consistently earned by the funds with the highest total returns.

TABLE 6.1

Large-Capitalization Blend Funds (Ranked by Return)

Return Quartile	Five-Year Total Returns	Five-Year Risk	Risk-Adjusted Ratio
First (highest)	15.9%	10.1%	1.37
Second	14.1	9.8	1.22
Third	12.6	9.7	1.04
Fourth (lowest)	10.2	10.0	0.74
Average	13.2%	9.9%	1.09

But if risk does not account for these differences in return, what does? Is it manager skill, or luck, or something more tangible? One thing that *is* tangible is fund expenses. And it is one element of fund performance that has a powerful tendency to remain fairly persistent in a given fund.

So, I divided the funds into cost quartiles. The funds with the lowest expense ratios constituted the first quartile, and the funds with the highest ratios were placed in the fourth quartile. It will come as no surprise to anyone who has seriously studied investment returns—either on a theoretical academic basis or from pragmatic experience—that *cost matters*. In fact, the funds in the group with the lowest expense ratios had the highest net returns. At the same time, they assumed a nearly identical level of risk (volatility), and therefore provided distinctly higher risk-adjusted returns. The data presented in Table 6.1 are arrayed according to expense quartiles in Table 6.2.

We are now onto something important. *With risk astonishingly constant, high returns are directly associated with low costs.* In the large-cap blend group, the average risk-adjusted rating provided by the lowest-expense funds (1.23) is 24 percent higher than the 0.99 average rating for the highest expense funds. Expenses are clearly a compelling factor.

There is another way of viewing the relationship. If we relate returns to expense ratios for the 211 funds in the large-cap blend category by performing a statistical regression that measures the extent of their reciprocal dependence, the slope is −1.80 percent. Each 1 percent increase in expense ratio has, on average, reduced the net total return earned by fund shareholders by 1.80 percent. Our intuition might tell us that each point of cost should cost exactly one point of return, but something much more onerous is taking place. Although the causative factors are not exactly clear, one explanation seems to hold some merit: High-cost funds tend to have high turnover, and portfolio transactions carry a substantial cost of their own.

Given the finding in Table 6.2, it is relevant to add the expense ratios to the *net* returns to see how similar the *gross* returns would have been. Again, perhaps not surprisingly, the *gross* returns in each quartile are substantially the same, albeit with an advantage to the funds with below-average costs (see Table 6.3).

This example confirms my theory: *Cost is a key determinant of the relative returns earned by funds.* This reality prevails not only among large-cap blend funds, but also among the funds in all investment styles. Slightly less extreme than the slope for large-cap blend funds is the slope of the all-fund regression line: −1.30, meaning that each 1 percent of cost reduces

TABLE 6.2

Large-Capitalization Blend Funds (Ranked by Costs)

Cost Quartile	Five-Year Total Return	Five-Year Risk	Risk-Adjusted Ratio
First (highest)	14.2%	9.8%	1.23
Second	13.8	9.9	1.12
Third	12.5	9.9	1.03
Fourth (lowest)	12.3	9.9	0.99
Average	13.2%	9.9%	1.09

TABLE 6.3

Large-Capitalization Blend Funds—Net Returns versus Gross Returns

Cost Quartile	Five-Year Net Return	Expense Ratio	Five-Year Gross Return
First (lowest)	14.2%	0.5	14.7%
Second	13.8	0.9	14.7
Third	12.5	1.1	13.6
Fourth (highest)	12.3	1.7	14.0
Average	13.2%	1.1	14.3%

returns, on average, by 1.30 percent. Why high-cost managers display apparently lower stockpicking skills remains unclear.

The next question is: Do these relationships between return and risk prevail across the style boxes? The answer is: Yes, they do—remarkably well. Figure 6.7 shows the percentage difference between the risk-adjusted returns of the first-quartile (lowest-expense) funds and the fourth-quartile (highest-expense) funds, using the average risk-adjusted rating *for that style box* as the standard. For example, in the large-cap blend category, low-expense funds have risk-adjusted returns 14 percent greater than the average, and high-expense funds' returns are 10 percent lower than the average—a compelling 24 percent spread.

The consistency of the relative risk-adjusted ratings in each matrix is powerful. *In every box, low-cost funds provide above-average ratings. In every box but one, high-cost funds provide below-average ratings.* The only exception

FIGURE 6.7

Relative Risk-Adjusted Return Ratios*

	Low-Expense Funds				High-Expense Funds		
	Value	Blend	Growth		Value	Blend	Growth
Large	+0.19	+0.14	+0.09	Large	−0.34	−0.10	−0.13
Medium	+0.35	+0.13	+0.13	Medium	−0.25	−0.27	−0.12
Small	+0.03	+0.04	+0.01	Small	−0.07	+0.11	−0.04

* Using returns and risks for each *Morningstar* style box.

is in the small-cap blend category, where the funds in the highest-expense quartile provided a better rating (+0.11) than those in the low-expense quartile (+0.04). (This is the smallest group—32 funds—in any of the nine style categories, and therefore may be less reliable in a statistical sense.)

The strong implication of these figures is clear: Whatever style they seek, investors who don't seriously consider limiting selections to funds in the low-expense group and eschewing funds in the high-expense group should take off their blinders. Mutual fund expense ratios are published periodically in the financial pages of major newspapers, in financial magazines, and in fund evaluation services such as *Morningstar*. They are required to be stated in fund prospectuses. "Seek and ye shall find."

In the mutual fund world, forecasting the relative returns (to say nothing of the absolute returns) of an unindexed fund based on its past performance is indeed a fool's game—in general, a zero-sum game relative to other funds, and a negative-sum game relative to the market indexes, as I'll show shortly. Investing on an absolute basis is a positive-sum game; that is, over time, financial markets have provided positive returns. Yet past performance data are all we have . . . almost.

For those willing to look at them, we have cost data. And future fund expense ratios, unlike future fund relative returns, are highly predictable. We now know—as a certainty—that cost matters. It matters for equity funds in the aggregate; it matters far more for bond funds (as we will see in the next chapter), and infinitely more—indeed, cost is virtually every-thing—for money market funds. And we've seen how much it matters—in-deed, it is a prime differentiator—in the nine-box equity style analysis, where the pattern parallels that of a tick-tack-toe game.

Index Funds—Risks, Returns, and Costs

Why should you not act on the full implication of the thesis that cost mat-ters? The lowest-cost funds in the marketplace today are invariably index funds, so why not just buy index funds in each of the nine style boxes? This proves to be neither a specious argument, nor one bereft of common sense.

Figure 6.8 shows both the returns and risks of equity funds managed in that style, compared with the returns and risks of a low-cost index fund *following the same style.* The index funds are operating index funds in the three large-cap groups (Standard & Poor's/Barra Indexes), and hypotheti-cal index funds based on publicly produced indexes (with returns reduced by estimated fund costs of 0.3 percent) in the medium- and small-cap groups (Frank Russell Indexes). Figure 6.8 reflects the spread of risk and return in each category.

To summarize the outcome: The average *return* for all the funds in the index group was 1.4 percentage points above the average return for the eq-uity group—+15.1 percent vs. +13.7 percent. In six of the nine boxes, the

FIGURE 6.8

Index Funds vs. Managed Funds: Returns and Risks (Percentage Points)

	Added Index Fund Return				Reduced Index Fund Risk		
	Value	Blend	Growth		Value	Blend	Growth
Large	+2.8	+1.9	+1.4	Large	−0.9	−1.3	−2.5
Medium	+2.9	+1.5	−0.4	Medium	−1.3	−2.0	−4.5
Small	+3.1	+0.6	−2.8	Small	−2.8	−3.2	−4.8

The data from which these figures are derived appear in Appendix II.

passively managed market index fund outpaced the average return of the actively managed equity funds; in two cases, the results were about even; and in just one case (this time among the 60 small-cap growth funds), the actively managed funds did better.

But the average risk assumed by the equity mutual funds—and this is a truly remarkable finding—is far higher: 11.9 percent for the equity fund group, and 9.7 percent for the comparably weighted indexes. (Small- and medium-cap growth funds took particularly large extra risks.) The average risk for all 741 funds is fully 23 percent higher than the risk assumed by the index funds.

The net result is that the *risk-adjusted* ratios average 1.23 for the index group and 0.99 for the regular funds—an average premium of more than 24 percent in risk-adjusted return. It is a strikingly consistent premium, and, as shown in Figure 6.9, it is remarkably parallel across the matrix. The relative risk-adjusted ratings are so dramatically in favor of the low-cost index approach as to defy even the most optimistic (or, for active managers, pessimistic) expectations.

There is one exception to the pattern. I acknowledge that the results in the small-cap growth category could be considered an exception to the rule. In this particular five-year period, active managers for these 60 funds were able to overcome their costs and surpass the index. Yet, the relatively small size of the fund group in the sample, or perhaps the particular period presented, may have simply resulted in an anomaly in the data.

Overall, the magnitudes of difference are so large and so consistent as to devastate the concept of high-cost active management. In fact, I could

FIGURE 6.9

Risk-Adjusted Ratings of Index Funds versus Equity Funds

	Value	Blend	Growth
Large	+0.31	+0.22	+0.18
Medium	+0.35	+0.29	+0.16
Small	+0.46	+0.19	−0.06

barely believe the figures, but we checked them "eight ways to Sunday," and they are correct.

By way of example, the large-cap value figure of +0.31 reflects an index fund rating of 1.54 versus a mutual fund rating of 1.23. Lest this difference seem unimportant, consider this example of what a difference of 31 ratio points means. First, assume that Index Fund A and Managed Fund B have equal standard deviations of 10 percent. Second, assume a risk-free rate of 4 percent. Result: Index Fund A, with a risk-adjusted return of 15.4 percent (1.54 ratio) would enjoy a total return of 19.4 percent annually. Managed Fund B, with a risk-adjusted return of 12.3 percent (1.23 ratio), would enjoy a total return of 16.3 percent annually—a truly remarkable enhancement of 3.1 percentage points per year. Much of this spread is accounted for by the lower expense ratios and lower portfolio transaction costs for index funds. Further, the index funds would carry substantial tax advantages.

The matrix presented in Figure 6.9 demonstrates a striking pattern that appears to give the lie to the often-expressed—now even trite—notion that indexing works only in large-cap markets. *Given these data, that notion no longer has the ring of truth.* In each of the three broad size categories, the appropriate index funds hold a consistent advantage in risk-adjusted return—indeed, an advantage that *increases*, if only slightly, as capitalization size *declines*. Holding risk *constant* at the level assumed by the funds, the index fund would produce ascending excess annual returns as follows: large-cap, +3.6 percent; medium-cap, +4.2 percent; small-cap, +4.4 percent. Table 6.4 (on the next page), in which the index fund returns have been increased to statistically equalize risk, shows how these calculations were derived.

This pattern—and these truly remarkable differences—will surely surprise many casual observers of mutual fund data. To the extent to which our five-year period can be accepted as reasonable, the *Morningstar* Category Ratings may ultimately prove to be the biggest boon to spreading the gospel of indexing since the first S&P 500 Index mutual fund was founded in 1975.

GOD, PASCAL, AND WAR GAMES

As Peter Bernstein tells the story in his marvelous book, *Against the Gods*, Blaise Pascal, the father of probability theory, cast the question of the existence of God as a game of chance: "A coin is tossed. Which way would you bet: on heads (God is) or tails (God is not)?"

TABLE 6.4

Risk-Equalized Index Fund Returns

	Annualized* Return	Standard Deviation	Risk-Adjusted Return
Large-Cap:			
Managed funds	12.9%	10.5%	1.0
Index fund**	16.5	10.5	1.2
Index Fund Advantage	+3.6%	0	+0.2
Medium-Cap:			
Managed funds	13.8%	12.3%	0.9
Index fund**	18.0	12.3	1.2
Index Fund Advantage	+4.2%	0	+0.3
Small-Cap:			
Managed funds	15.1%	14.7%	0.9
Index fund**	19.5	14.7	1.1
Index Fund Advantage	+4.4%	0	+0.2

* December 31, 1991–December 31, 1996.
** Index return adjusted to equalize index risk and fund risk. Data before adjustment for large, medium, and small capitalization groups, respectively: percentage return, 15.0, 15.2, and 15.3; percentage risk, 9.0, 9.7, and 11.1.

Paraphrasing Pascal, consider the chances of being on the losing side of the bet. If you bet God *is*, you will live a holy life and give up a few enjoyable temptations, but that's all you lose. If you bet God is *not* and you are wrong, but you give in to all temptations, your evil life will cause you to be forever damned. *Consequences must outweigh probabilities.*

Turning to the stock market, Bernstein continues, if you believe it is efficient (and you are right), the best strategy is to buy an index fund. If you believe it is efficient (and you are wrong), you will earn the market's return, but a few actively managed funds will beat you. But if you bet that the market is not efficient and you are wrong, the consequences of underperforming with an actively managed fund could be very painful. The risk, in short, is much greater if you bet on inefficiency rather than on efficiency.

And that is ultimately the conclusion of equity style analysis in the mutual fund industry. No matter what fund style you seek, you should emphasize low-cost funds and eschew high-cost funds. And, for the best bet of all, you should consider indexing in whichever style category you want to include. Index funds boast the additional benefit of absolute fidelity to their investment style. Although there is no guarantee that, say, a small-cap growth manager will limit his investment selections to small-cap growth stocks, it's a certainty that a small-cap growth index fund will invest only in small-cap growth stocks. Rather than emphasizing particular styles, however, a simpler course would be for you to index your entire equity portfolio with the Standard & Poor's 500 Stock Index. A more conservative—and more certain—wager would be to index your portfolio to the *total* stock market.

If, because of high costs, investing with mutual fund managers is a (relative) loser's game (although almost surely a winner's game in absolute terms over the long run), is it not similar to another game—one between battling global armies? I answer the question by way of analogy, using an example from the 1983 movie *War Games*.

We are in the NORAD war room, where our generals are trying to ward off an incipient global nuclear war, precipitated by a young computer nerd who has cracked the U.S. security system. The boy says he can solve the problem he has created, and, with all other hope lost, the generals agree to let him try. He programs the U.S. air defense computer . . . with a game of tick-tack-toe.

Calculating at a furious pace, the computer realizes that neither opponent can win the game—or the nuclear war—and the screen goes blank. The action ceases. Peace reigns. Then these words appear on the computer screen: "A strange game. The only winning move is not to play . . . How about a nice game of chess?"

It is entirely appropriate to consider that mutual fund managers, with all their intelligence, training, and ability—and with all of the computer power at their command—are engaged in a vast competition with one another to draw the best stocks and discard the worst, all with a view toward winning the performance game and attracting the most dollars to manage. And all the while, consider that funds that do not play the game at all—the index funds—may be accumulating the most capital for their investors. So it is fair to ask: Have investment management games, like global warfare games, become losers' games, just like tick-tack-toe? The compelling evidence presented in this chapter suggests that the answer is "Yes."

A Dependence on Time

As all investors have come to learn, one way or another, the mutual fund returns presented in any analysis are time-dependent. Because markets and fund returns change from one period to another, the presenters of the data, through their ability to pick the period for analysis, have a powerful advantage in proving their case. Nevertheless, the analysis presented in this chapter is as fair and objective as I can make it. I deliberately selected the five-year period 1992–1996 (inclusive) rather than the more recent five-year periods ending in 1997 or 1998 because the return of the Standard & Poor's 500 Index relative to that of the average fund was considerably lower during the earlier period. My objective in this chapter was to minimize, to the extent possible, any arguable large-cap bias.

As to the choice of the length of the period, I chose five years simply because a shorter period (say, 3 years) would have been even less satisfactory, and a longer period (say, 10 years) would have cut the number of funds in the study by half, creating a less reliable sample. I freely acknowledge that we can conclude only so much with five-year numbers in a strong equity market, even though this period included two poor market years and three good ones—hardly unrepresentative of the market's long-term pattern. However, not only was the average annual return of the S&P 500 Index for the five years the lowest of any of the potential choices for the three periods (3, 5, and 10 years), but its return was also the lowest relative to the returns of the average managed equity fund. The table below compares relative returns during the 3-, 5-, and 10-year periods. The style analysis of the data presented in this chapter deserves testing in other periods and under a variety of market conditions.

S&P 500 Index Return vs. Average Equity Fund

Period	S&P 500	Equity Fund Average	Index Relative Return
Three Years	19.7%	15.4%	128%
Five Years	15.2	13.7	111
Ten Years	15.3	13.3	115

Periods ending December 31, 1996.

CHAPTER 7

ON BONDS

TREADMILL TO OBLIVION?

ond mutual funds can fill a useful role. They make it possible for investors to gain the extraordinary value of broad diversification over as many as 100 bonds or more, reducing risk without an attendant sacrifice in gross return. Bond funds are professionally managed, and most emphasize high-quality, investment-grade bonds in their portfolios. Many offer a particular range of maturities, from short (1 to 3 years) to long (10 to 20 years or more), with gradations in between, enabling investors to balance their income requirements with their tolerance for risk. Bond funds provide considerable flexibility to investors by facilitating purchases and liquidations of shares in small amounts. Some bond funds offer these important advantages at reasonable cost. Most, however, do not. Partly as a result, the once flourishing bond fund segment of the mutual fund industry has lost much of its attraction for investors.

The rise and decline of the bond fund empire is one of the most captivating, yet untold, chapters in the annals of the mutual fund industry. That story reminds us that the mutual fund principles of diversification and management—as valid today as they have ever been—cannot provide acceptable returns to investors when they are offset by excessive cost encumbrances. It also provides a picture of the complacency and over-reaching characteristic of many managers of fixed-income funds.

Surprising as it may seem, as recently as 1993, bond funds—then with assets of $760 billion compared to $749 billion in stock funds and $565.3

161

FIGURE 7.1A

Assets of Bond Funds and Stock Funds

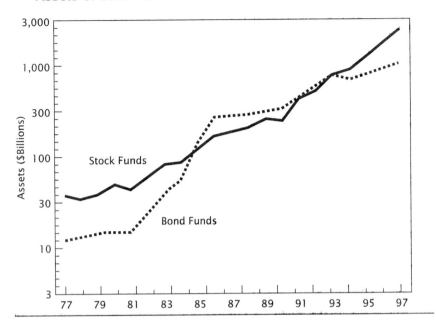

FIGURE 7.1B

Bond Fund Assets Relative to Stock Fund Assets

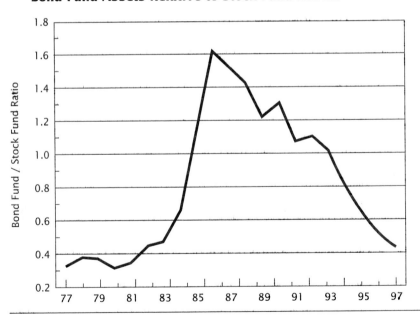

billion in money market funds—were the largest component of the mutual fund industry. In fact, they reached their peak relative importance seven years earlier, in 1986, when bond fund assets of $260 billion were 60 percent *larger* than the $160 billion invested in equity funds.

Since 1986, we have seen a powerful resumption of both of the long post-1982 bull markets. In the booming stock market, fund investors have enjoyed record returns (17.7 percent per year). A very good bond market also brought generous returns to bond fund investors (8.6 percent), but those returns paled in comparison with the returns achieved by stock funds. Partly—but only partly—as a result, bond fund assets of $1 trillion as 1998 began made an equally pale comparison with the $2.4 trillion assets of equity funds—some 60 percent *smaller*.

But the relative performance of the stock and bond markets was only one of two major causes of the huge decline in the relative importance of the once-dominant bond fund component of the industry. The other factor is this: As a group, bond funds have failed to provide investors with adequate returns relative to those achieved in the bond market itself.

Figure 7.1A shows the booming stock fund assets and the slowing of bond fund growth. The dramatic rise and decline in the importance of bond funds relative to equity funds are shown in Figure 7.1B. Once the equity market environment turns more sober, future bond fund returns may well prove to be more competitive with stock fund returns. But, unless the bond fund industry changes its ways and gives shareholders a fair shake, bond funds will be on a treadmill to oblivion.

MISERY LOVES COMPANY

I am not *quite* alone in my concern about today's bond funds as a group. My apprehension is shared by no less an investment professional than Peter Lynch, best known as the brilliant equity investor who served as portfolio manager of Magellan Fund during the 1970s and 1980s. He publicly shared, in a 1993 interview with *Barron's*, my positive conviction about the merits of stock index funds, and he has also echoed my misgivings about bond funds. "Their purpose in life eludes me," he says, adding:

> Bond funds [have been] consistently outperformed by individual bonds, sometimes by as much as 2 percent a year . . . [doing] worse the longer the funds were held. The benefits of expert management were exceeded by the expenses that were extracted from the funds to support the experts.[1]

What Is a "Commodity"?

I use the term "commodity-like" to define investment classes in which individual securities follow closely related patterns of return. The classic example would be long-term U.S. Treasury bonds. Each issue is backed by the full faith and credit of the U.S. government; each has a long-term maturity; and each has a similar duration. A change in the level of interest rates affects each one in a similar pattern. Investment-grade short-term corporate bonds also share common characteristics and return patterns. Widely diversified packages of GNMA securities (issued by the Government National Mortgage Association, and backed by loans, mortgages, and a U.S. Treasury guarantee) also have parallel characteristics. Each of these examples fits the definition of "commodity-like" that typifies the various types of bonds.

In his opinion: "Since one U.S. Treasury bond or Ginnie Mae certificate is the same as the next, there is little a manager of one of these funds can do to distinguish himself from competitors."

But the Magellan Fund manager, I think, overstates the case. Bond funds do serve a purpose. Unlike bonds themselves, they usually maintain relatively fixed maturities, enabling an investor to choose a suitable maturity (long-, intermediate-, or short-term) and have it remain relatively constant over time. And there are some competent professional bond fund managers that stand out, although, sadly, only a very small fraction among them make their services available at costs that justify the portfolio management skills they offer.

Nonetheless, Peter Lynch revealed a simple investment truism: In highly efficient market segments comprising commodity-like securities, it is extremely difficult for even the most brilliant money managers to garner a significant margin of advantage—*before* the deduction of costs. It follows, then, that it is virtually impossible for them to avoid providing returns to the shareholders of the funds they manage—*after* the deduction of fund costs—that match market returns. When costs are excessive, the shortfall in return is excessive, too.

Fund expenses exert a powerful influence on bond fund returns. Over a recent five-year period, for example, the return of an average corporate bond *fund* lagged the return of the corporate bond *market* by an average of 1.5 percent per year. Strikingly, this disparity from market returns contains within itself a second important disparity. That average gap of 1.5 percent consisted of a 1.3 percentage point shortfall for the no-load bond funds, and a 1.8 percentage point shortfall for the much larger group that charges sales loads (front-end loads or hidden annual 12b-1 fees). The same pattern is apparent in the government bond and municipal bond arenas (see Table 7.1).

Facing the situation that this differential cost structure exemplifies, Peter Lynch presents the sales charge issue in this way: "Another mystifying aspect of bond fund mania [and, I would agree, when he wrote his 1993 book, *Beating the Street*, it was almost a mania] is why people are willing to pay a . . . sales charge, a.k.a. load, to get into bond funds." He is not *really* mystified, however, for that question quickly led him to "Peter's Principle #5: There's no point in paying Yo-Yo Ma to play the radio."[2] Once again, we agree. Yet, apparently without challenge from fund directors, or managers, or even investors, fully three of every five bond funds get away with charging a sales load. Indeed, three-quarters of the assets of all bond funds are owned by shareholders who have paid a sales load as the price of admission to a game that, as a rule, is not worth playing.

TABLE 7.1

Returns of Bond Funds vs. Bond Indexes, 1992–1997

	Index	Average Return of Managed Funds		Shortfall to Index	
		No Load	Load	No Load	Load
Corporate	8.2%	6.9%	6.4%	−1.3%	−1.8%
Government	7.9	7.2	5.4	−0.7	−2.5
Municipal	6.4	6.0	5.3	−0.4	−1.1

Note: For each market index group—corporate, government, and municipal—the return is an average of the appropriate Lehman Bros. short-, intermediate-, and long-term indexes. The returns of corporate, government, and municipal funds reflect a similarly weighted average of short-, intermediate-, and long-term funds.

A FLAGRANT EXAMPLE

Let me cite just one example of the impact of costs on returns in that most efficient of all bond markets: short-term government bonds. The funds in this category carry an annual expense ratio handicap of 1.03 percent. Expense ratios range from as low as 0.69 percent for the *average* no-load fund to 1.49 percent for the *average* load fund (and their expense ratios do not even include the initial sales charges). Just to make the point clear, imagine this: for the average no-load bond fund, cost would consume 13 percent of the recent 5.0 percent yield on the U.S. Treasury 2½-year note; for the average load fund, it would consume 29 percent. That penalty could fairly be described as confiscatory.

Assuming a 5.0 percent yield for the Treasury note, the net return of a fund with a 1.5 percent cost would be 3.7 percent. Raising that 3.5 percent to 5.0 percent would require the manager to earn an extra 1.5 percentage points—i.e., an enhancement of more than 40 percent! What do you think are the chances that a mutual fund manager could select a portfolio of short-term Treasury notes that would somehow add nearly 40 percent to the return of a short-term Treasury portfolio—that is, enough to overcome the cost handicap and merely match the market's return? If you were to argue that the chances are 1-in-10,000 (I doubt they are that good!), my next question would be: What chance would you have of identifying that manager *in advance?* It doesn't seem like a bet worth making. Yet high-cost short-term government bond funds, some of which carry sales loads, are rife in the industry.

And it gets worse. Some funds, desperate to provide market yields, make a practice of purchasing Treasury notes at a premium and then publishing a yield—and actually paying a dividend—that fails to amortize that premium. (In fairness, the funds are also required to report an "SEC yield" that is net of amortized premiums.) Result: Higher income now, a guaranteed capital loss later, when the bonds, purchased at a premium, mature at par value. For a horrible example, consider that shareholders of one fund—which had more than $1 billion in assets—experienced a decline in net asset value from $10.19 per share in 1991 to $8.62 as 1998 began—a capital loss of 15 percent for a "safe" investment in U.S. Government-guaranteed short-term paper.

These negative examples of what is happening in the bond fund arena set the stage for a comprehensive examination of the role of costs—expense ratios and sales charges—in shaping returns. *All bond funds are not created equal.* Bond index funds differ from actively managed funds. Low-cost funds differ from high-cost funds. Different managers have different skill levels. In all, some bond funds give investors the right to overpay; others (a much smaller number) give investors the right to a fair shake. The principal conclusion may be obvious: *Cost matters.*

How Much Does Cost Matter?

To determine just *how much* cost matters, let's examine the extent to which cost undermines returns in four large, diverse groups of bond funds, in each of which policies are based on clearly defined maturities and port-folios are invested largely in high-quality issues. The four largest bond fund segments are: (1) long-term municipal bonds; (2) short-term U.S. Government bonds; (3) intermediate-term U.S. Government bonds (in-cluding GNMAs); and (4) intermediate-term general (largely, investment-grade corporate) bonds. In all, 448 funds—representing bond fund groups that account for about 60 percent of all bond fund assets in the *Morn-ingstar* list—are included in our study, clearly a representative sample.

The results are consistent and uniform. In three of these four seg-ments, the low-cost quartile outpaced the high-cost quartile by an amount very closely equivalent to the difference in expense ratios; that is, each quartile had about the same gross return, and costs accounted for substan-tially all of the return differences. In the fourth case, returns in the low-cost quartile ran only slightly above returns in the high-cost quartile, but the high-cost funds held portfolios that were significantly riskier in every respect. In each case, the measurement of risk was based on three factors:

1. Duration,* a better measure than average maturity when evaluat-ing a fund's sensitivity to interest rate risk.

2. Volatility, a measure of the variations in a bond fund's monthly re-turns relative to the average taxable or tax-exempt bond fund.

3. Portfolio quality, using ratings by Standard & Poor's Rating Ser-vices. [Investment-grade bonds are rated from AAA (highest) to BBB (lowest).]

---

*Although duration is a complex mathematical concept, it measures an important factor: the sensitivity of a bond price to changes in the general level of interest rates. A short-term bond fund with a portfolio duration of, say, 2.0 would move up or down in price by 2 percent for each change of one percentage point in interest rates; a long-term bond fund with a portfolio duration of 12.0 would move up or down by fully 12 percent for each change of one percentage point in rates.

In general, the lowest-cost group had the lowest duration, the lowest volatility, and the highest quality. *The lowest-cost group had not only the highest returns, but also the lowest risks.* Bond fund investors simply cannot afford to ignore that message.

Long-Term Municipal Bonds

First, consider high-quality long-term municipal bonds. I began with a look at the entire set of funds in this group, using five-year returns as reported by *Morningstar Mutual Funds*. There are 92 funds in this group. The scatter diagram (Figure 7.2) presents, for each fund, the annual rate of return (vertical axis) and the annual expense ratio (horizontal axis). For purposes of illustration, I also show the results of a hypothetical municipal bond index fund, although it would be difficult to replicate, reducing the return by assumed annual costs of 0.20 percent.

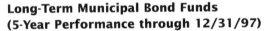

FIGURE 7.2

**Long-Term Municipal Bond Funds
(5-Year Performance through 12/31/97)**

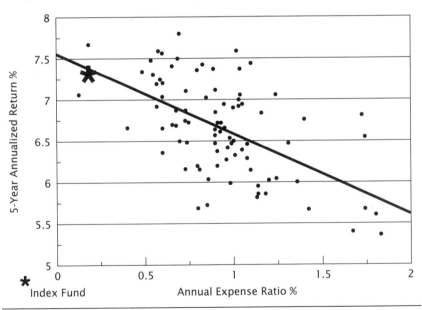

The obvious conclusion: Returns go down as costs go up. It's as simple as that. In fact, as the trend line on Figure 7.2 shows, each percentage point reduction in costs, on average, increased returns by 1.04 percentage points. Perhaps the managers of the high-cost funds weren't quite as smart as the managers of the low-cost funds. But we can be sure that cost is a prime determinant of the relative returns of long-term municipal bond funds.

Dividing the funds into four quartiles, ranging from the highest-cost to the lowest-cost funds, we see a direct relationship between low cost and high return (Table 7.2). Expenses in the low-cost quartile were 0.9 percentage points *lower* than in the high-cost quartile, and returns were 0.9 percentage points *higher*. Equally obvious is the fact that, in both high-cost and low-cost funds, the *gross* returns earned by the funds were actually the same (7.7 percent). The advantage provided by the lowest-cost managers lay in the fact that they consumed the smallest percentage of the returns available in the long-term tax-exempt bond market—6 percent, versus 18 percent for the high-cost managers. The expenses of the low-cost hypothetical index fund consumed only a tiny fraction (3 percent) of return, an efficiency that can hardly be found wanting.

How about the possibility that differences in volatility, in quality, or in duration played a role? The differences in duration and volatility that exist among the regular long-term municipal bond funds *favor* the lowest-cost

TABLE 7.2

High-Quality Long-Term Municipal Bond Funds: Returns and Costs

Cost Quartile	Five-Year Net Return	Expense Ratio	Five-Year Gross Return	Return Consumed by Cost
First quartile (highest cost)	6.3%	1.4%	7.7%	18%
Second quartile	6.7	1.0	7.7	13
Third quartile	6.9	0.8	7.7	10
Fourth quartile (lowest cost)	7.2	0.5	7.7	6
Index fund*	7.4%	0.2%	7.6%	3%

*Lehman Ten-Year Municipal Bond Index, less assumed expense ratio of 0.20 percent.

TABLE 7.3

High-Quality Long-Term Municipal Bond Funds: Risk Characteristics

Cost Quartile	Duration	Volatility*	Quality AAA	AA	A	<A
First quartile (highest cost)	8.5 years	1.20	66%	15%	7%	12%
Second quartile	8.0	1.10	58	16	12	14
Third quartile	8.1	1.13	56	20	9	15
Fourth quartile (lowest cost)	8.0	1.11	60	20	10	10
Index fund	6.9 years	NA	54%	27%	15%	4%

Data from Morningstar.
* Relative to municipal bond funds of all maturities.

funds, but the difference is slight. And, as Table 7.3 shows, their portfolios also have the smallest position in the lowest-grade bonds. The clear conclusion: With risk almost a constant, the winning return in long-term municipal bond funds is achieved by the group with the lowest costs.

Despite earning a higher net return than any of the quartiles, the index fund carried, by a wide margin, the lowest risk. Its volatility rating was not available, but its duration was the shortest; its portfolio quality, with only 4 percent below A-rated, was among the highest, and its return, as shown in Figure 7.2, was outstanding.

Short-Term U.S. Government Bond Funds

For our second example, we'll move all the way down the maturity spectrum to short-term funds, with U.S. Government bond funds as our example. Returns and costs for the entire group (100 funds) are displayed in Figure 7.3.

We reach the same conclusion: Returns go up as costs go down. The trend line shows that each 1.00 percentage point reduction in costs increased returns by 0.90 percent. There are some good reasons why it turns out to be a little less than a full point; we'll get to those after we sort out the funds by cost quartile (Table 7.4). Note that an index fund—which

FIGURE 7.3

**Short-Term Government Bond Funds
(5-Year Performance through 12/31/97)**

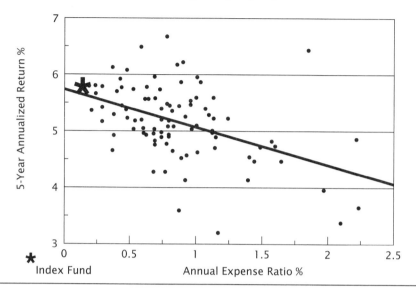

★
Index Fund

TABLE 7.4

**Short-Term U.S. Government Bond Funds:
Returns and Costs**

Cost Quartile	Five-Year Net Return	Expense Ratio	Five-Year Gross Return	Return Consumed by Cost
First quartile (highest cost)	4.5%	1.6%	6.1%	26%
Second quartile	5.1	0.9	6.0	15
Third quartile	5.2	0.7	5.9	12
Fourth quartile (lowest cost)	5.5	0.4	5.9	7
Index fund*	5.8%	0.2%	6.0%	3%

*Lehman Short (1–5) U.S. Government Index, less assumed expense ratio of 0.20 percent.

would be easy to create in this market segment—would again be a powerful competitor.

Note that the lowest-cost funds provided a gross return of 5.9 percent, or, after a 0.4 percent expense ratio, a net return of 5.5 percent. The high-cost funds earned a bit more (6.1 percent), but, after a heavy 1.6 percent expense, delivered only 4.5 percent to investors—more than a full percentage point less.

Here again, we see a direct relationship between low cost and high return. The question comes down to this: Which would you rather have, managers who pick short-term government bonds for you and take 26 percent of what they earn, or managers who pick the same bonds and take 7 percent of the return for their efforts? In short, would you rather earn 93 percent or 74 percent of the market return?

As it turns out, return is not the only issue here. We might expect that other things would be equal in such a generic asset class as short-term government bonds. But let's at least examine the possibility of inequalities in risk characteristics, including duration, volatility, and quality, as shown in Table 7.5.

Here, we learn something worth knowing: The low-cost fund group not only delivers the highest returns but it also assumes the lowest risks, measured both by duration and price volatility. (The index fund duration is the same as that for all funds as a group.) Because the funds are in the short-term U.S. Government category, nearly all holdings are in U.S. Government bonds, and credit quality is excellent throughout, although only

TABLE 7.5

Short-Term U.S. Government Bond Funds: Risk Characteristics

Cost Quartile	Risk Characteristics		Quality	
	Duration	Volatility*	Government	Corporate
First quartile (highest cost)	2.3 years	0.69	92%	8%
Second quartile	2.4	0.70	95	5
Third quartile	2.4	0.58	99	1
Fourth quartile (lowest cost)	1.9	0.53	97	3
Index fund	2.3 years	NA	100%	0%

*Relative to taxable bond funds of all maturities.

the index fund holds 100 percent governments. The slight lowering of risk as cost declines helps to explain why each point of reduction in cost accounts for slightly less than a full point of higher return. It also suggests that high-cost managers assume higher risks in a futile attempt to provide competitive yields.

Low-cost short-term government bond funds—and the very low-cost index fund—let you have your cake and eat it, too. They provide the highest returns, hand in hand with the lowest risks, truly a winning combination.

Intermediate-Term U.S. Government and GNMA Funds

Now let's move from long and short maturities to intermediates. Perhaps the best test of our thesis is the relationship between costs and returns among intermediate-term U.S. Government and GNMA funds. (Both have demonstrated very similar returns over time, and *Morningstar*—properly, I think—includes both in a single 169-fund category.) By now, this pattern of cost and return is familiar, but let's look at it again in Figure 7.4.

FIGURE 7.4

**Intermediate-Term Government Bond Funds
(5-Year Performance through 12/31/97)**

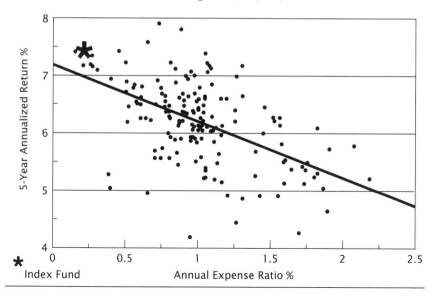

In this case, with each percentage point reduction in cost, return rises by 1.10 percent, a similar pattern to what we've seen in long-term and short-term bond funds. It hammers home the validity of the central thesis: in bond funds of *all* maturities, cost and return are inextricably inter-linked. Table 7.6 reflects our thesis once again. The low-cost quartile earns about the same gross return (7.2 percent) as the three others, but delivers a net return (6.6 percent) that is 10 percent higher. And the index fund once again distinguishes itself, earning among the highest returns of any of the funds.

Quartile by quartile, then, we see substantially similar gross returns, but a large gap remains in net returns, substantially all of which is engen-dered by cost. If there are differences in risk, they too are quickly resolved in favor of the lowest-cost funds (see Table 7.7).

Average *durations* of the higher-cost funds are about the same as the low-cost intermediate-term government fund group in total, but it turns out that the low-cost funds carry about 20 percent lower *volatility* than their higher-cost peers. The index fund duration is more than 20 percent lower. Portfolio composition is fairly uniform. So, with duration, volatil-ity, and portfolio quality all in the same ballpark, cost carries the day, dollar for dollar. The index fund once again distinguishes itself not only with a strong relative return, but with a low relative risk.

TABLE 7.6

Intermediate-Term U.S. Government and GNMA Funds: Returns and Costs

Cost Quartile	Five-Year Net Return	Expense Ratio	Five-Year Gross Return	Return Consumed by Cost
First quartile (highest cost)	5.4%	1.6%	7.0%	23%
Second quartile	6.2	1.1	7.3	15
Third quartile	6.3	0.9	7.2	13
Fourth quartile (lowest cost)	6.6	0.6	7.2	8
Index fund*	7.2%	0.2%	7.4%	3%

*Weighted average of Lehman GNMA (5–10 years) U.S. Treasury Indexes, less assumed expense ratio of 0.20 percent.

TABLE 7.7

Intermediate-Term U.S. Government and GNMA Funds: Risk Characteristics

Cost Quartile	Duration	Volatility*	Quality Government	Corporate
First quartile (highest cost)	4.5 years	1.18	95%	5%
Second quartile	4.7	1.06	90	10
Third quartile	4.2	1.04	97	3
Fourth quartile (lowest cost)	4.5	0.98	90**	10
Index fund	3.4 years	NA	100%	0%

*Relative to taxable bond funds of all maturities.
** Of the 42 funds in the quartile, 25 are 100 percent in governments; the 17 outliers bring the average to 90 percent.

Intermediate-Term Corporate Bond Funds

One more example sends the same message, but sends it in a different language and hammers home the point. In the intermediate-term corporate bond fund category, net returns are fairly constant irrespective of costs, though the lower-cost funds still tend to deliver slightly higher returns to investors. The index fund again proves to be a singularly excellent performer, making its mark high atop the group. Its low costs enable it to provide higher returns, and it holds *only* investment-grade corporate bonds, none of which carries a rating below BBB.

As you can see in Figure 7.5, the slope of the return/cost line runs downward, but not as steeply as in our previous examples. The slope shows that each percentage-point reduction in cost provides a 0.3 percent increase in return.

This same pattern becomes clear when we examine the four cost quartiles (Table 7.8). The low-cost group provided a market return advantage of 0.2 percent—7.3 percent versus 7.1 percent—over the high-cost group, although its cost advantage was a much more substantial 0.7 percent—0.6 percent versus 1.3 percent.

FIGURE 7.5

**Intermediate-Term Corporate Bond Funds
(5-Year Performance through 12/31/97)**

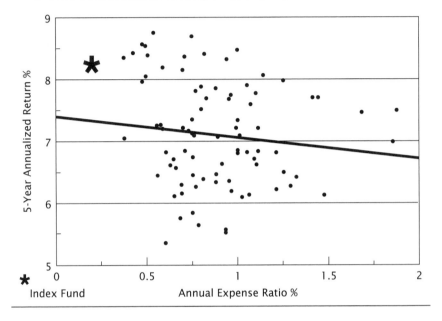

*
Index Fund

TABLE 7.8

Intermediate-Term Corporate Bond Funds: Returns and Costs

Cost Quartile	Five-Year Net Return	Expense Ratio	Five-Year Gross Return	Return Consumed by Cost
First quartile (highest cost)	7.1%	1.3%	8.4%	15%
Second quartile	7.2	1.0	8.2	12
Third quartile	7.3	0.8	8.1	10
Fourth quartile (lowest cost)	7.3	0.6	7.9	8
Index fund*	8.2%	0.2%	8.4%	2%

*Lehman (5–10) Investment Grade Index, less assumed expense ratio of 0.20 percent.

How have these high-cost managers been able to offset most of their large-cost handicap? Was it because their high fees somehow endowed them with greater management skills? Or did they reach out for higher yields by assuming higher risks? Table 7.9 provides a clear answer to that question: They took more risks.

As Table 7.9 makes clear, with each higher level of cost—without a single exception—the managers assumed higher risk. They seem to have been determined to provide competitive returns, and, given their higher costs, they had no recourse but to assume higher risks. This apparent relationship, as far as I know, has remained undisclosed. But it is there, in the form of higher duration, higher price volatility, lower portfolio quality: a striking difference between the lowest-cost portfolios (83 percent in governments and A-rated corporates, and 9 percent in below-BBB bonds) and the highest-cost portfolios (only 57 percent in governments and investment grades and 19 percent in below-BBBs). The same direct dollar-for-dollar trade-off between return and cost that we've seen before has been supplanted in part by a reverse trade-off between risk and cost. It is in corporate bond funds that the trade-off is at its most obvious. Nonetheless, lower-cost funds, despite assuming far lower risks, garner slightly larger returns.

What the data reveal about the corporate bond index fund is rather striking. As you would expect, part of its value-added is low cost, but it

TABLE 7.9

Intermediate-Term Corporate Bond Funds: Risk Characteristics

Cost Quartile	Duration	Volatility*	Quality			
			Government	AAA-A	BBB	<BBB
First quartile (highest cost)	5.2 years	1.14	21%	36%	24%	19%
Second quartile	5.1	1.08	34	36	18	12
Third quartile	4.8	1.04	42	33	15	10
Fourth quartile (lowest cost)	4.6	0.99	49	34	8	9
Index fund	5.4 years	NA	0%	70%	30%	0%

*Relative to taxable bonds of all maturities.

also gains from a moderately long duration (5.4 years vs. 4.9 years for the managed funds), and a credit risk that *may* be a bit higher (no government bonds, but no bonds below BBB either). In fact, the corporate bond group, as defined, includes hybrid corporate–government funds, and the index fund wins, not only because of low cost, but also through the higher returns it amasses by living up to its definitional purity as a truly *corporate* bond fund.

WHAT ABOUT MANAGEMENT SKILL?

Our analysis of the relationship between bond fund cost and returns seems rather conclusive: Cost matters. But cost is not the *only* ingredient that shapes returns. If it were, the first three scatter diagrams presented in this chapter would not have such a varied pattern. In fact, the dispersion around the trend line can be measured at an average R-squared* of less than 0.36. (1.00 would place every fund right on the line, meaning that cost explained not 36 percent but 100 percent of return.) The return of a bond index fund compared to a bond index would be explained almost entirely by the costs it incurs, plus an element of market-matching skill by its managers. The low cost of the bond index fund (assumed to be 0.2 percent) largely explains its superiority over managed funds.

Although both duration risk and volatility risk contribute to the dispersion of returns, management ability is also a material force in shaping returns. And there are indeed some skilled professional managers at work in bond funds. The best of them are competent, experienced, and wise in the ways in which the fixed-income markets work. Their funds may or may not be operated under disciplined portfolio guidelines relating to quality and maturity, and only investors can decide which type of strategy they prefer. But each fund should clearly describe its strategy for all to see. Beyond strategy, some portion of the record—as in all aspects of investing— will be based on skill and some portion on luck. The two are not easy to separate, nor is enduring skill easy to identify in advance. Past returns earned as a result of management ability provide little, if any, assurance about the future.

---

* R-squared is a measure of the mutual association between any two factors. In this example, the level of investment expenses explains, on average, 0.36, or 36 percent, of the level of bond fund returns. All other factors combined, such as risk, portfolio turnover, and management skill and luck, account for the remaining 0.67, or 67 percent.

What course, then, should the investor follow? Common sense would dictate making bond fund selections primarily from among funds in the lowest-cost quartile, the better to maximize the chances of enjoying returns above segment norms and of avoiding at least the highest-cost quartile. Bond index funds would be exceptional options, but few such funds exist. (Given that their benefits go almost entirely to fund shareholders rather than fund managers, there is little monetary incentive for managers to offer them.) Nonetheless, it will always be possible—and always challenging—to garner an advantage by owning a fund that provides both skilled management *and* low cost. The investor who is able to "accentuate the positive and eliminate the negative" in this way will be rewarded.

SALES CHARGES EXACERBATE THE COST ISSUE

Before I examine the issue of awareness of bond fund shareholders about the trade-off between return and cost (and, to some degree, risk), I should note that the comparisons just presented ignore the outright sales charges that are payable when investors purchase shares, or when they redeem shares within five years of purchase. (However, hidden 12b-1 sales charges, where applicable, are included in the expense ratios I've shown.) Thus, my analysis gives a benefit of enormous doubt to funds that charge the traditional front-end and the newer back-end sales charges.

Ironic as it may seem, funds that charge sales commissions dominate the high-cost groups, and no-load funds dominate the low-cost groups. For example, among the 21 intermediate-term corporate bond funds in the higher-cost quartile, 17 entail front-end sales charges for investors, and none is pure no-load. Among the 22 funds in the lower-cost quartile, on the other hand, only four entail front-end sales charges, and 18 are pure no-load. Industry data ignore the impact of these charges, but investors ignore them at their peril.

But they *do* ignore them. In the industry's two principal distribution channels, no-load bond fund assets of $165 billion are dwarfed by the $482 billion in assets of broker-distributed high-cost bond funds carrying sales charges (including $122 billion of assets managed by the brokerage firms themselves). Two things are apparent about the brokerage firms that manage bond funds: (1) they charge high management fees, and (2) despite what would seem an insurmountable expense hardship for their clients, they are able to levy sales charges on them, too. From the point of view of the clients, that has proven to be a very expensive combination.

A dispassionate observer of the passing parade of contradictions within these giant national brokerage firms would be mystified. On the *third* floor of their buildings (let's call it the institutional trading floor), their bond traders are bickering over a "tick" (in the parlance of the trade, a tick is ½₂ of a percentage point on a $1,000 bond, or about 31 cents). The traders are prepared to commit mayhem for ⅟₁₆, and to take out swords and pistols, ready to kill, for ⅛ (four ticks). Yet, on the *first* floor of the same building (call it the retail sales floor), their account executives seem able to utterly ignore the baneful impact of 32 ticks (one full percentage point)— or even 50 ticks (1.6 percentage points)—that are laid on their customers year after year. It may make a lot of sense for the sellers, but it makes no sense for the buyers.

Fee Dollars Are "Real Money"

Broker-managed funds are not alone in charging high prices. Despite their profound impact on returns, fees have run amok throughout the bond fund arena. Even large funds with fee *rates* below industry norms are paying fee *dollars* to their advisers in amounts that are truly astonishing—they amount to, using current parlance, "real money." For example, one of the largest GNMA funds (with assets of $8 billion) paid its investment manager $44 million in 1997, although the fund has achieved returns that fail to even match the returns of an unmanaged index of GNMA securities. (The fund also pays 12b-1 fees of $9 million and administrative expenses of $10 million.) How much of that $44 million fee could the manager be spending on management? If we assume there are two portfolio managers, one or two credit researchers (after all, the credit quality of GNMAs is guaranteed by the U.S. Treasury), several bond traders, and a certain amount of occupancy and overhead costs, perhaps the aggregate cost could reach $5 million. (However, an even larger GNMA fund, with higher returns, as it happens, pays its investment adviser just $1 million.) Where does the other $39 million of the fee go? The only obvious place is the pocket of the fund manager. Why should some of it not go into the pockets of fund shareholders in the form of lower fees, thereby providing them with a portion of the staggering economies of scale that fund management involves?

One can only wonder what defenses are available against overreaching when advisers in the high-cost quartile of bond funds are consuming some 20 percent of fund returns, leaving only 80 percent for shareholders, who

TABLE 7.10

How Costs Consume Bond Fund Returns over Time

| End of Period (Years) | Initial Investment of $10,000 | | | |
| | Capital Value | | Capital Lost | |
	6% Return	5% Return*	Amount	Percent*
1	$ 10,600	$10,500	$ 100	17%
10	17,900	16,300	1,600	20
20	32,100	26,500	5,600	25
30	57,400	43,200	14,200	30
40	102,900	70,400	32,500	35

*Lost capital as percentage of market appreciation.

have, after all, ponied up 100 percent of the fund's capital. These shareholders are not receiving a fair return on their investment. Even worse, the percentage of benefits received by shareholders *declines* with the passage of time. Yet those who buy and sell funds ignore the cumulative impact of high costs in commodity-like segments of the bond market that provide relatively modest returns. Currently, bonds yield about 6 percent on average; even a 1 percent cost reduces that return to a 5 percent yield for fund shareholders, a reduction of 17 percent. Table 7.10 shows the impact of that difference on a $10,000 initial investment over time. The reduction in final value engendered by a cost of 1 percent rises to 20 percent over a decade, and to a truly confiscatory 35 percent after four decades. Ignorance of this cumulative cost may be intellectual bliss. But it is financial devastation.

How to Avoid Excessive Costs

Certain defenses, although too few in number, exist for avoiding the fee overreaching that is suggested by the return–risk–cost trade-off in the bond fund arena. Those same trade-offs exist for equity funds, but they tend to have a larger impact on the lower returns that have characterized bonds over time. Unfortunately, few of the defenses seem to be working. The National Association of Securities Dealers (NASD), the self-regulatory organization that oversees brokerage firms and fund distributors, imposes a requirement of suitability for brokers in their choice of investments for their clients. But when low-cost options exist in the bond fund arena, how can a fund that consumes 20 percent or more of the market returns be "suitable"? The Securities and Exchange Commission (SEC) requires full disclosure. However, the financial fact that higher returns (or lower risk) are associated hand in hand with lower costs is not mentioned, let alone fully disclosed, to investors in bond fund prospectuses.*

If stricter discosure does not come to pass, enabling investors to make these judgments, and if fund directors do not place the interests of shareholders ahead of the interests of fund advisers and reduce fund fees, then how are shareholders to protect themselves? Rely on common sense. Read the prospectuses carefully. If they are not clear or forthcoming, demand answers. Carefully consider risk, defined by volatility, duration, and portfolio quality. And, above all, seek well-managed bond funds that are available at low cost.

Low-cost bond fund options do exist today. *But there are not very many.* Only one of every 20 bond funds in the *Morningstar* five-year database has an expense ratio below 0.50 percent, which I regard as the *upper limit* of a fair cost. These funds consistently rank in the high range of returns among the top-quartile performers. Why aren't there more low-cost options? When will investors demand them and advisers supply them? Why aren't there more bond index funds? The grand total, as far as I can tell, is 20—an astonishing total in light of the data presented here. That paucity is appalling in commodity-type market segments where fund cost is a critical determinant of returns to shareholders, and where an index fund can be run for 20 basis points or less. Why can't the industry resolve these critical anomalies—clean up the mess, if you will—that have been created by these exorbitant fees?

Bond fund investors should no longer suffer excessive costs. They deserve substantial reductions in fees and loads from the vast majority of funds that are charging fees that become more confiscatory with the passage of time. The preceding table illustrates the treadmill that leads to ever more inadequate bond fund returns, and finally approaches oblivion for the incremental return on the investor's capital. Continued failure to provide adequate returns will surely lead to the fall of the near-$1 trillion bond fund empire, itself a treadmill to oblivion that would represent some form of poetic justice. But I would rather see a treadmill that leads to the

---

*These problems are even more predictable and more evident in the money market fund category. However, they are completely ignored there as well.

oblivion of exorbitant sales charges and excessive management fees. If that happens, the valuable investment characteristics of bond funds could emerge, and the bond funds segment of the mutual fund industry could be restored to the favor it deserves in the marketplace.

I hope that regulatory and self-governance mechanisms will finally work. But, failing that outcome, it is up to investors to eschew high-cost bond funds when they make their selections, to desert high-cost bonds if they own any, and to seek out well-managed bond funds operating at low cost, and bond index funds that track high-quality bond market indexes. Finally, the future of the bond fund industry is up to bond fund investors.

CHAPTER 8

ON GLOBAL INVESTING

ACRES OF DIAMONDS

"Acres of Diamonds" is the title of a classic lecture by Dr. Russell Conwell, founder of Temple University. He delivered his talk the world over during the 1870s and 1880s, long before this era of mass communication, and his words inspired millions of people. Dr. Conwell told the story of an ancient Persian named Al Hafed, a wealthy man who sought even greater riches. One night, he dreamed of finding a great diamond mine. Soon after, he set off on a search for it that would take him to every corner of the ancient world.

The quest forced Al Hafed to spend all his wealth. Despondent, he cast himself into the sea at the Pillars of Hercules, sinking beneath the foaming crest of the tide. Later, on Al Hafed's very property in Persia, so Dr. Conwell's story goes, "his successor led his camel to the garden brook and noticed a curious flash in the shallow stream, and pulled out a black stone with an eye of light, reflecting all of the colors of the rainbow." He had discovered in Al Hafed's garden the Golconda diamond mine, which was to yield some of the world's greatest diamonds, including the Kohinoor diamond that is treasured among England's crown jewels.

The moral of the story is clear and simple: Stay home and dig in your own garden, instead of tempting fate in an alien world. You will find "acres of diamonds" right where you are.

The more I read about investing outside the United States, the more I think about this story. I am not suggesting that the U.S. economy is a new Golconda, nor that investing in overseas ventures is parallel to death in a foreign land. But here in America we have, at least at the moment, the most productive economy, the greatest innovation, the most hospitable legal environment, and the finest capital markets on the globe. With 5 percent of the world's population, we produce 25 percent of its goods and services. It is safe to say that America is the envy of almost every other nation. As U.S. citizens, we should count our blessings every day.

If our diamond lode is within our own borders, shouldn't the investments we choose for our portfolios stay here, too? I believe that would be a sensible strategy. Overseas investments—holdings in the corporations of other nations—are not essential, nor even necessary, to a well-diversified portfolio. For investors who disagree—and there are some valid reasons for global investing—I would recommend limiting international investments to a maximum of 20 percent of a global equity portfolio.*

THE GLOBAL PORTFOLIO EXTREME

Today's conventional wisdom suggests otherwise. In recent years, pension and endowment funds have gradually built their holdings of foreign equities to significant levels, often at the expense of their U.S. equity positions. More than 1,000 U.S.-operated equity mutual funds—one out of every four—invest primarily in international equities, and even our largely domestic funds have nearly 7 percent of their assets invested in foreign issues. The global investing strategy is a favorite of academic theorists, some of whom recommend that the ideal equity portfolio should consist of holdings of each nation's stocks at their world-market weight. As of mid-1998, such a strategy would have yielded the following weightings:

Nation	Percent
United States	48%
Japan	9
United Kingdom	10
Germany	5
France	4
Emerging markets	4
Other	20
Total	100%

---

* An *international portfolio* includes only foreign issues. A *global portfolio* includes both U.S. and foreign issues. These definitions are consistent with industry parlance.

Note that more than half of the assets of this "ideal" portfolio for a U.S. investor would be placed outside the United States.

This strategy rests primarily on a simple premise: Because foreign markets have experienced patterns of volatility that are different from those of the U.S. market (and, to an important degree, different from one another), their inclusion in a portfolio of U.S. equities would reduce the portfolio's total volatility and hence provide higher *risk-adjusted* returns. Other arguments advanced in favor of the strategy include: the enhanced stability inherent in a more diversified economic base; higher potential growth rates; and cheaper valuations in world markets. But these are speculative arguments that may or may not prove valid.

The other side of the story was well presented, in late 1997, by *Wall Street Journal* columnist Roger Lowenstein.[1] Describing the strategy as "Global-Investing Bunk," he wrote that "this faddish bit of investment wisdom was exposed as nonwisdom in 1997." Citing the collapse in Asian stocks, he challenged the notion that "the 'sound' investor is one who has moved a goodly chunk of his money out of the society he knows to countries with which he is unfamiliar, each according to its market weights." Lowenstein concluded that "while gambling in every country is wiser than gambling in one, not gambling at all is wiser still."

CURRENCY RISK—AND RETURNS

I, too, have serious reservations about a full market-weighted global strategy. It involves a very heavy layer of one particular risk that an equity investor never need assume: currency risk. Returns earned from investing in stock valued in one's home currency are measured in the coin of the realm in which the investor earns, spends, and saves. (Sometimes to your advantage as a citizen, to be sure, sometimes not.) Even if foreign investments were to provide the same rate of return—measured in their local currencies—as U.S. investments, the returns earned might be very different, depending on the strength or weakness of the dollar in world markets. A *strong* dollar *reduces* the returns earned by U.S. investors in foreign markets; a *weak* dollar *increases* the returns earned in foreign markets.

In the very long run, because the mechanics of government financing and international trade should equalize currency values, foreign currency risk relative to the U.S. dollar should be a neutral factor in global markets. But over interim periods, the road to parity may be rocky. For example, during the 30-year history of the Morgan Stanley Capital International

Europe, Australasia, Far East (EAFE) Index, the U.S. dollar was weak from 1970 through 1980, strong through 1984, and very weak until 1995. Since then, it has rallied nicely. On balance, however, the dollar in 1998 is worth roughly what it was worth in 1980. These fluctuations led to considerable misunderstanding about the returns earned in international markets. A fine example came during the decade that ended in 1994. The upper section of Table 8.1 shows that foreign returns for U.S. investors (i.e., in dollar terms) were far higher than returns on U.S. stocks during that decade.

Given this scenario, investors could easily have been (and probably were) led to believe that foreign markets had outpaced the U.S. market and therefore promised better future growth. The 3.6 percent enhancement in annual return—over a very strong U.S. market—had led to 137 percentage points of extra capital accumulation over a decade. Why not jump on the bandwagon?

Why not, indeed? Because the excess returns in international markets were, to an important degree, an illusion. Although investors had earned a handsome return in the currency markets, their returns from foreign stock markets were, in fact, rather ordinary. Measured in *local* currencies, international market annual returns *lagged* the U.S. market by 4.1 percentage points annually, just a bit more than the margin by which they appeared to

TABLE 8.1

Global Returns for the Ten Years Ended December 31, 1994

Global Market*	Annual Return	Cumulative Return
	Measured in Dollars	
U.S. stocks	+14.3%	+282%
International stocks (U.S. currency)	+17.9	+419
Shortfall of U.S. stocks	−3.6%	−137%
	Measured in Local Currencies	
U.S. stocks	+14.3%	+282%
International stocks	+10.2	+163
U.S. advantage	+4.1%	+119%

*S&P 500 and MSCI-EAFE Indexes.

lead it. The inordinate weakness in the dollar had more than doubled the cumulative international return, as shown in the lower section of Table 8.1.

I believe that the performance of foreign stocks for U.S. investors, in the long run, will be determined by each nation's fundamental returns (based on dividend yields and earnings growth), rather than by currency returns. Taking into account the national economic growth rates around the globe during the 1990s—and comparing them to the powerful global reach, entrepreneurial energy, and technology leadership we see in our nation today—it would be logical to expect U.S. growth to exceed the growth in other nations.

On the other hand, the United States may well be at the pinnacle of its economic cycle, while many of the European powers, Japan, and the emerging markets—beset, respectively, with high unemployment, over-extended financial institutions, and deep recessions—may have reached some sort of nadir. Further complicating the matter, it is never clear whether these economic factors are accurately reflected in present market valuations. The race for superior market returns around the globe is never an easy one to call.

But there *was* what seemed to me an easy call in 1994. As it turned out, that call has proven correct so far: such weakness in the dollar could not continue indefinitely. Given that likelihood, past performance data so heavily influenced by the weakness in the dollar were deeply flawed. Looking to the future without being aware that the weak dollar had added 7.7 percentage points annually to foreign stock returns would result in highly exaggerated expectations. In fact, from the close of 1994 through mid-1998, the dollar's strength was restored and actually *reduced* foreign returns by an annualized rate of 4.6 percentage points.

THE GLOBAL EFFICIENT FRONTIER

Many investors reject the full market-weight global strategy but endorse a more sophisticated form of analysis that sets the structure of the global portfolio. The analysis involves the calculation of an *efficient frontier*, which is designed to determine the precise allocation of assets between U.S. and foreign holdings. The goal is a combination that promises the highest return at the lowest level of risk (i.e., the lowest volatility of return acceptable to the investor). I am skeptical of this approach as well, for the efficient frontier is based almost entirely on *past* returns and *past* risk patterns. That bias may be unavoidable—after all, history is our only source of hard statistics—but past relative returns of stock portfolios and (albeit to a much lesser degree) past relative volatility are not always harbingers of the future, and may even be counterproductive.

Consider, for example, the efficient frontier that would have been drawn at the end of 1988, the high-water mark for relative returns in international markets. As shown in the upper section of Table 8.2, the optimal combination of the highest return for the lowest risk—and, for aficionados of the theory, the requisite asset allocation—would have called for 50 percent invested in foreign stocks and 50 percent in U.S. stocks. How would it have worked out? Not particularly well. Indeed, after 1988, that portfolio proved to be rather insufficient, if not decidedly inefficient. With an annual return of 11.4 percent (compared to 19.2 percent in the United States), not only did it sharply lag the return of the all-U.S. portfolio, it also actually proved subject to slightly *higher* risk than the U.S. portfolio (standard deviation of 12.6 percent versus 12.2 percent). That combination of return and risk is hardly a winning combination.

Today, an investor putting money to work using this theory would settle on a rather different global portfolio. Based on history, the efficient frontier is backward-looking. So the investor currently seeking maximum return and minimum risk would select an efficient portfolio based on the

TABLE 8.2

"The Efficient Frontier"

	Annual Return	Volatility Risk*
	Decade Ended December 31, 1988	
100% U.S. stocks	16.2%	16.4%
100% International stocks	22.3	17.0
Most efficient global portfolio:		
50% U.S.—50% international	19.6	14.4
	9.5 Years Ended June 30, 1998	
100% U.S. stocks	19.2%	12.2%
100% International stocks	5.8	16.9
Most efficient global portfolio:		
80% U.S.—20% international	16.6	11.8

*Monthly standard deviation.

returns of the respective markets over the *past* decade, when the results were as shown in the lower section of Table 8.2.

Given a decade of high returns and low volatility in the United States—and the reverse in the rest of the world—U.S. stocks now represent 80 percent of the portfolio, nearly double their weight a decade earlier. Will this new global allocation lead the followers of the efficient frontier theory in the right direction? We have no way of knowing. But experience leads us to conclude that it is rather unlikely to provide the optimal answer.

Another problem with the efficient frontier theory, it seems to me, is that extremely small variations in risk may separate the optimal portfolio from those deemed less efficient. For example, in the decade ending in 1988, the standard deviation of an 80/20 U.S./international mix was 15.1 percent, compared to 14.4 percent for a 50/50 mix (purportedly most efficient). That difference—less than a single percentage point—is so small as to be almost invisible to any real-world investor, particularly one who is not willing or able to engage in the arcane methodology required for calculating standard deviations of monthly return, leaving aside whether such deviations are a valid proxy for risk.

Based on the nine and a half years ended in June 1998, the central tolerances are equally minuscule. For example, the 11.8 percent deviation for the hindsight-based 80/20 U.S./international efficient portfolio with the lowest risk would have offered a reduction of less than one percentage point below the 12.2 percent figure for a portfolio holding 100 percent in U.S. equities. For intelligent investors to allow their entire portfolio strategy to be based on these truly trivial past differences in risk—really an elusive proxy for risk—seems a wholly unwarranted triumph of process over judgment.

Contrasting the periods ending in 1988 and June 1998, Figure 8.1 crystallizes two important realities of the global efficient frontier: (1) vast shifts in the frontier may take place over a decade, and (2) variations in risk near the efficient point of each curve are inconsequential, despite large variations in asset allocation. Slavish reliance on history seems particularly flawed in markets where currency fluctuations create substantial extra risk.

There is, in the final analysis, only one risk that equity investors need to assume: *market risk*—the inevitable truth that *all* stock portfolios fluctuate in value. For better or worse, most investors choose to assume two additional risks: *style risk*, or choosing mutual funds and stock portfolios

FIGURE 8.1

Which Efficient Frontier? U.S. versus International Holdings

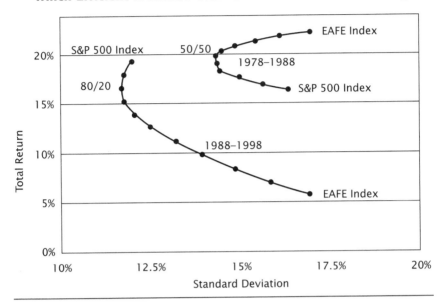

with a particular bias, such as those focused on large-value stocks, or small-growth stocks, or any other stocks whose returns are expected to vary from the total stock market over time; and *manager risk*, or selecting a mutual fund whose portfolio manager may or may not provide the optimal portfolio within the fund's style category.

Leaving aside for the moment the wisdom of assuming those two extra risks—which nearly all investors take for granted—I see no reason for investors to assume yet a third extra risk: *currency risk*. But, to those who, in their own wisdom and judgment, accept the thesis that global investing is necessary, I reaffirm my rule-of-thumb recommendation: Limit international holdings to no more than one-fifth of the equity portfolio.

INTERNATIONAL ECONOMIES AND FINANCIAL MARKETS

So far, I have not dealt with one of the most obvious risks of putting money to work abroad: the contrasts between the governments, economies, and financial systems of most foreign countries and those of the United States.

As a theoretical matter, those risks tend to be subsumed by the marvelous arbitrage pricing mechanism that is implicit in the financial markets. Through this mechanism, market prices are assumed to take into account all existing information about a stock—including all stocks of all nations—and, through the decisions of informed buyers and sellers, to reach a price that accurately balances potential risk against prospective reward.

In retrospect, the record clearly shows that huge shifts take place in the relative positioning of national economies—sometimes over an extended period of time, and sometimes with remarkable speed. The financial market is a stern taskmaster that brooks few compromises. Consider Japan. A decade ago, U.S. investors were worried that the Japanese economy, "The Rising Sun," would eventually dominate the world. In Tokyo, soaring stock prices escalated the total capitalization of Japanese stocks to nearly half of the world's entire market capitalization. Japan's dominant 43 percent share was half again the size of the U.S. market's then-28 percent portion.

Since then, Japan's economy has withered while most other economies (especially that of the United States) have flourished. The Japanese government's fiscal and monetary policies have seemed to hurt rather than help that nation's economy, and its banking system remains overextended and permeated with problem loans. The Nikkei stock market index has fallen from 27,700 yen to 15,800 yen in mid-1998, about half its value a decade ago.

Meanwhile, other world markets have prospered. In the United States, during the same period, the Dow Jones Industrial Average increased from 2,140 to 8,950—a 320 percent rise. The European markets (according to the MSCI-EAFE-Europe Index) rose 275 percent in local currency terms. Japan's astonishing fall from grace was reflected in its global weighting in mid-1998: 9 percent of world markets, or one-fifth of its 43 percent weighting a decade before. During the same period, the U.S. market has grown to 48 percent of the value of the world's total capitalization, or more than half again our 28 percent portion in 1988. Note the striking similarity of our world market share in 1998 to Japan's a decade earlier. Whether that parallel will continue with a comparable erosion in the years to come remains to be seen, but it is worth thinking about. Clearly, if you believe it will happen, you should overweight foreign holdings. Table 8.3 reflects the relative changes in the capitalization of world markets in 1988 and mid-1998. Bear in mind that those dramatic shifts took place during less than a decade—a rather brief span of financial history.

Reversal of Fortune?

In the early autumn of 1998, the total U.S. stock market was up about 3 percent for the year, and international markets were down about 7 percent. Stock markets in Western European nations were higher, but virtually all other global markets had tumbled. Japan was down about 20 percent, the emerging markets were off about 40 percent, and the Russian markets had plummeted almost 80 percent. To add insult to injury, weaknesses in local currencies of most foreign nations constituted a significant portion of the losses suffered by U.S. investors.

This additional enhancement of the relative returns on U.S. stocks can be interpreted in one of two ways: (1) it further validates the "Acres of Diamonds" thesis of this chapter; or (2) it makes the opportunities for U.S. investors abroad even more attractive than they were earlier. After all, there is considerable substance to the argument that returns in international and U.S. markets will revert to the mean of a uniform global return on stocks over the long term, as happened, on balance, from 1960 through 1997.

Even in these days of U.S. ascendancy, who can be absolutely confident that the U.S. dollar, having soared, will not tumble? Or that a rival nation (or block of nations, such as the European Community) will not supplant the United States as the world economic leader? Or that present world market values are now priced in anticipation of the worst outcomes around the world and the best outcome in the United States? The answer is: No one, least of all I. Reversals of fortune in the financial markets have proved to be more the rule than the exception.

But a trap awaits investors who decide the best is yet to be for foreign markets. It is the trap of market timing. Reversals of fortune often come when least expected. It is easy to be too late, or too early, to take advantage of them, as was the case after their big 1997 tumble. Maybe the worst is finally over abroad. But maybe it is not. We just don't know.

TABLE 8.3

Capitalization of World Markets, 1988 and 1998

	December 31, 1988	June 30, 1998
United States	28%	48%
Japan	43	9
United Kingdom	8	10
France and Germany	5	10
Other countries	16	23
Total	100%	100%

A current example of the risk involved in global investing is Southeast Asia. Through mid-1997, many global investors had looked to these emerging markets as offering an unusually favorable opportunity for earning superior long-term returns. And, during the 1980s and 1990s, both the economies and the markets of Indonesia, South Korea, Malaysia, Singapore, Thailand, and the Philippines had indeed distinguished themselves. In the newly global economy, their populations and economies were growing apace, and soaring stock returns doubled their weight in world markets, from 1.9 percent in 1991 to 3.8 percent as 1997 began. But, by autumn of 1997, their government-dominated financial systems weakened, their currencies plummeted, and their economies slumped.

Rare was the Southeast Asian market that did not tumble by 40 percent or more in local currency terms and another 40 percent in dollar terms. Declines of 80 percent or more in value were the norm for U.S. investors—all in the span of just a few months. With other world markets marching upward, the relative weight of the Southeast Asian markets tumbled by an astonishing 70 percent. As 1998 began, their weight was 1.2 percent of world markets, or less than one-third of their weight only a year earlier, when they reached the pinnacle of their popularity with fund investors. The problems persisted in 1998, and these emerging markets continued to deteriorate. These reversals have given investors a humbling lesson in the risks of global investing. Those risks are especially high in nations where U.S. standards for accounting, financial transparency, and liquidity have not yet been attained.

THE RECORD OF GLOBAL INVESTORS

Perhaps the fairest way to evaluate the investment merit of global investing is to rest the case on neither abstract academic theories nor anecdotal market evidence, but on the results achieved by real global managers who, unbounded by national borders, put the money of investors to work each day, selecting individual stocks from whichever of the world's markets they favor. While few funds that follow global strategies have operated for a full decade, the evidence so far is not very inspiring.

In the 10 years through 1997, global funds realized total returns averaging only 11.2 percent annually, a far cry from the 18.1 percent rate of return for the Standard & Poor's 500 Index. At the same time, these funds' risk (standard deviation) averaged 14.3 percent, or slightly *larger* than the 14.1 percent risk of the S&P 500. Further, the average return achieved by the global funds conceals a substantial risk: wide variations in the performance of individual managers. Returns ranged from a high of 15.5 percent annually for the top performer to less than half that (6.9 percent) for the bottom performer. So, investors' returns varied widely, depending on which fund they chose.

During the past five years, a broader list (57 global funds) has operated, but the managers again failed to distinguish themselves. Their average return of 14.1 percent was lower than the 15.9 percent return of the Morgan Stanley Capital International All Country World Index (all countries weighted by their market capitalizations), and their average risk (standard deviation) of 13.1 percent was higher than the index's 12.3 percent. The global managers made two mistakes. The first was their *strategic bet* against the U.S. market. Their fundamental policy decision to invest heavily (as did the global index itself) outside the United States came during an era when our nation's market returns proved to be the highest of any major market in the world. Their second error was a *tactical bet* against the U.S. market. With a 30 percent commitment to U.S. stocks at the end of 1997, compared to 47 percent of the target index, they were heavily underweighted. All in all, their record provides less than a ringing tribute to global strategies and global strategists alike.

CONSTRUCTING YOUR OWN GLOBAL PORTFOLIO

There is, of course, another way to go about the process of global investing. If you decide that investing outside the United States offers opportunities for greater returns, along with the possibility of reducing the short-term volatility of your holdings, you may simply decide for yourself the amount of your portfolio that will be allocated to non-U.S. stocks, thus balancing your U.S. investments with others from foreign nations.

But what has been the record of overseas stocks? During the great worldwide bull market of the past 15 years, returns on international stocks have fallen short of the returns available in the U.S. stock market. While the EAFE Index was growing at a 15.3 percent rate through 1997, the Standard & Poor's 500 Index achieved a 17.5 percent growth rate. Mutual funds in each area failed to match the returns of their target indexes. Surprisingly, though, international mutual funds in fact did slightly better than their U.S. counterparts.

In the past 10 years, however, international funds and indexes alike fell far short of their U.S. counterparts. The average international fund provided an annual return of 9.0 percent, one-third less than the 15.5 percent return for the average U.S. fund. As a result, there was an astonishing difference in the final capital accumulated on an investment of $10,000 in each category. For foreign funds, the capital grew to $24,000; for U.S. funds, the capital reached $42,000. During this period, curiously, while the average U.S. fund again lagged behind the unmanaged index, international funds actually outpaced their target indexes. (I'll discuss this anomaly shortly.)

Because very few international funds existed in the 1950s and 1960s, valid 40- and 30-year comparisons of fund and index returns are not available. However, looking at the 25-year record, the 9.9 percent return for the average foreign fund fell well short of the 11.9 percent return for the EAFE Index—hardly an unsurprising outcome. Such a difference in annual return has a profound impact on long-run accumulations. An initial $10,000 investment in the average foreign fund would have increased to $107,000, representing a shortfall of fully $60,000 from the $167,000 accumulated in the EAFE Index.

Using the longest possible period—the entire history of the EAFE Index—as a basis of study reflects a remarkable outcome. From 1960 through 1997, the annual rate of return of the S&P 500 Index of U.S. stocks—11.5 percent—was *precisely identical* to the return of the EAFE Index of international stocks. As we shall see in Chapter 10, there were lots of swings to and fro between these two categories, but in the long run international investing failed to add any incremental return to U.S. portfolios. "Chasing the will o' the wisp" may be too strong a formulation to describe the quest for superior returns in overseas markets. But then again, history suggests that it may not be.

INDEXING IN INTERNATIONAL MARKETS—A BETTER WAY?

By any measure, the long-term record of actively managed international funds leaves much to be desired. But, to the extent investors are persuaded to diversify globally, there is another method for approaching international markets, and it should prove to be a better way in the long run. That method is simply investing in an international index fund.

Indexing provides financial advantages that should prove greater in international equity markets than in the United States market. First, average operating expenses are considerably higher for international mutual funds; they run about 1.7 percent, a cost increase of 0.3 percent over U.S. funds. Second, although portfolio turnover is lower among international funds (about 70 percent per year—still a very high figure), transactions cost considerably more in international markets. Liquidity costs, trading costs, stamp taxes, and custodial fees are all higher, and they may result in transaction costs that total as much as 2 percent (or more) of assets each year. Thus, the annual handicap to be overcome may approach 4 percent, nearly double the plus-2 percent handicap faced by U.S. equity managers. At this cost level, it is virtually impossible for most managers to provide superior net returns.

An international index fund incurs the same type of costs as managed funds, but in much lower amounts. Specifically, a low-cost international equity index fund need pay no investment advisory fee and, largely because of that fact, would incur an expense ratio of one-third or less of the international fund norm of 1.7 percent. For index funds investing in the developed markets of Europe and the Pacific, the expense ratio should not exceed 0.50 percent; for emerging markets portfolios, it should not exceed 0.75 percent.

Even more important is the fact that index portfolios sailing in international waters should experience minimal portfolio turnover—ideally, less than 5 percent annually. That rate would be one-fourteenth of the 70 percent average turnover rate of actively managed international funds, a particularly important advantage in costly foreign markets. The low turnover should limit the transaction costs of international index funds to about 0.5 percent of assets per year.

Combined, the operating expenses and the transaction costs of international index funds should generally average less than 1 percent annually, compared to nearly 4 percent for actively managed international funds. Over an extended period of time, international index funds could well be in a position to deliver a natural advantage of some three percentage points in annual return over managed funds. This truly substantial margin is one and one-half times the 2 percent natural advantage that U.S. index funds have enjoyed in recent years.

Yes, No, and Maybe

Have these indexing advantages proved out in practice? The answer is unequivocal: "Yes, no, and maybe." To understand the "yes" part, you need only consider the ultimate realities of markets and managers, from which there is no recourse. Investors owning all stocks in a given market will achieve the market's gross return before the deduction of the costs of investing. These same investors, in the aggregate, will inevitably fall short of the market's return after costs are deducted.

"Maybe" enters the picture simply because we have access only to very incomplete data about the records of all investors in these markets. International funds offered in the United States own only a small portion of all foreign stocks—about $330 billion, or roughly 2 percent of all international equities. Such a small sample for comparison may not yield valid conclusions about the relative performance of their managers.

Here is where the "no" comes in. We simply cannot be certain that the 3 percent annual advantage in returns for index funds, which I have assumed will prove out over the long run, will occur without fail in all interim periods. Over sufficient time, however, I expect that U.S. managers will be neither smarter—nor dumber—than their counterparts throughout the rest of the world, and that the 3 percent margin will hold true on a long-term basis.

Let's examine the validity of the 3 percent assumption by dividing the international market into its two largest components: Europe and the Pacific. In Europe, the market is highly diversified among a variety of nations: the United Kingdom accounts for 30 percent of the total value of the European index; Germany, 15 percent; France, 13 percent; Switzerland, 11 percent; the Netherlands, 8 percent; Italy, 6 percent; other nations collectively, 17 percent. Not only do the managers of European funds tend to have fairly similar weightings, but the markets of the various European nations are often affected by similar economic and financial factors, and more often than not have followed parallel paths.

The records of funds that invest in Europe clearly validate the index approach to international investing. In the decade through 1997, the average European fund provided an annual return of 10.2 percent, compared to 14.6 percent for the European stock index. Taking into account index fund total costs of up to 1 percent, the advantage would be 3.4 percent per year, the rough equivalent of the 3 percent gap that I postulated on the basis of the drag of high managed fund expenses and high transaction costs. In this period, "Yes," the index advantage proved out nicely.

In the Pacific, the answer is equivocal. The limited data available—the records of U.S. managers owning but a tiny portion of Pacific stocks—would suggest "Maybe." But the principal reason for any discrepancy is that the stock market of a single country—Japan—totally dominates the weight, and hence the return, of the Pacific index. A decade ago, Japanese stocks made up fully 93 percent of the market value of the region's stocks. Even after its fall from grace, this single market carried 80 percent weight in the region. (The MSCI-Pacific Index includes neither China nor the emerging markets of Southeast Asia, which are represented in the MSCI Emerging Markets Index.) But, given the diversification requirements applicable to diversified U.S. mutual funds—imposed by policy or mandated by legal requirements—Japan represented a far smaller weight, an average of just 38 percent of the Pacific portfolios under the direction of U.S. managers.

As a result of this reduced exposure to a fallen, if giant, market over the past decade, Pacific funds provided a positive annual return of only 4.4 percent—modest to a fault, but well in excess of the negative return (–1.2 percent) for the Pacific index. The handful of mutual funds investing primarily in Japan did slightly worse, lagging the Japan-dominated regional index with a negative return of –1.8 percent. Given the small number of Pacific funds (only 3 in 1988, 57 in 1998), these results do not shake my faith that indexing works in all markets.

Beyond the established markets of Europe and the Pacific are the emerging markets. It is to these emerging markets that investors seeking explosive economic growth often turn. Ignoring the extra risk—which recently became so obvious in these markets—would be naïve, but aggressive investors seeking extra return would be well advised to limit their emerging market exposure to a reasonable portion of their international exposure. While the record of index funds investing in emerging markets is short (only four years), the results so far are encouraging. But, given the brevity of the period, a verdict of "Maybe" is fair enough. Nonetheless, in the fullness of time, such index funds should garner a meaningful edge over active managers.

Turning now to the *total* international market as measured by the EAFE Index (which does not include the emerging markets of smaller nations), we can surely reaffirm the earlier analysis with a ringing verdict of "Yes." During the past quarter century, the shortfall of the average U.S. managed international fund was 2.0 percentage points annually to the 11.9 percent annual return of the EAFE Index. The full 25-year period (through 1997) included a 15-year segment in which the EAFE Index won by an annual margin of 5 percentage points, followed by a 10-year segment in which it lagged by 2.5 percentage points annually. The change was caused entirely by the shift of Japan from market leader to market laggard during the past decade. If the answer for the short-term investor is "Maybe," the answer for the long-term investor is "Yes." Indexing works.

Some international funds can and do defy the odds that so heavily favor index funds. In general, they are funds that tend to have these characteristics: highly experienced managers in place for an extended period; relatively low portfolio turnover; and modest operating costs and advisory fees. (This pattern is unusual in the international fund field, but it is pervasive among the winning funds.) Nonetheless, times change, managers are replaced, policies are revised, and expense ratios often move upward. For the long-term investor interested in spreading investments around the globe via mutual funds, international index funds offer a sensible approach.

THE ACCIDENTAL TOURIST

In this day and age, it would hardly pay to ignore the impact, on every nation on earth, of the globalization of economies and financial markets. Our nation is no exception to this trend. Indeed, it is arguable that the United States has been the leading force in creating and sustaining globalization. But it seems to me that, for American investors interested in capitalizing on the global trend, the solution lies within our own borders. Seeking to earn higher returns by holding global portfolios has been our version of Al Hafed's fruitless search in "Acres of Diamonds."

American companies have become major global powers. A recent study by Morgan Stanley Dean Witter was right on point: "If you invest in the Standard & Poor's 500 Index as a whole, you own a diversified global portfolio." While some 77 percent of revenues of the companies in the S&P 500 Index comes from North America, 23 percent comes from other nations: 13 percent from Europe, 2 percent from Japan, and 8 percent from the emerging markets of Asia (5 percent) and Latin America (3 percent).

Some of the largest companies in the S&P 500 Index have a truly vast global reach, with half of their revenues or more generated outside of the United States: Coca-Cola, 67 percent; Intel, 58 percent; Microsoft, 55 percent; American International Group, 54 percent; and Procter & Gamble, 50 percent.

Along with peers that have lower international exposure, many of these companies have come to be known as "fortress" companies. They are ostensibly able to control their own growth by the sheer power of their global recognition and marketing muscle. Naturally, although they are subject to business conditions in international economies that are themselves influenced by local currency valuations, in their own businesses they usually hedge most—if not all—of their exposure to currency risk by the use of futures. But with 23 percent of their aggregate revenues and 28 percent of their net income coming from outside of the United States, the companies in the S&P 500 Index clearly provide a significant global exposure. U.S. investors need not venture directly into foreign lands.

The past record shows that U.S. stocks with heavy international interests have tended to be highly correlated with other less globally oriented U.S. issues, while foreign markets seem to march to a different drummer. Thus, diversifying by owning foreign stocks directly is apt to be more effective in reducing the volatility of a portfolio's monthly returns. But, as I argue throughout this book, short-term volatility is not to be prized at the expense of long-term return.

"ACRES OF DIAMONDS" REVISITED

Large *additional* exposure to foreign stocks to investment in foreign nations is not essential. In terms of risk and return, the record of the past— whether prologue to the future or not—does not provide compelling reasons to abandon the acres of diamonds that can be unearthed at home in order to seek unknown diamond lodes abroad. Dr. Conwell's theme was: "Do what you can, with what you have, where you are today." He focused on opportunities in Philadelphia, but he also recounted examples of finding great wealth all over America—from Pennsylvania to New England, to North Carolina and California. He used John D. Rockefeller and oil as one example, and Colonel John Sutter and gold as another.

Dr. Conwell was always careful to dignify the search for wealth with a higher purpose. "I say you ought to be rich," he would intone. "You have no right to be poor. There are so many opportunities right here."

But he would quickly add: "We all know that there are things more valuable than money, some things grander and more sublime." The thrill of earning money to build one's own home and the nobility of helping those in need, he noted, were among "those things greatly enhanced by the use of money."

If he lived in today's world, Dr. Conwell would doubtless talk about the accumulation of financial wealth for a comfortable life and a peaceful retirement. I have no way of knowing whether he would also advocate investing in corporations whose home is in America. But, with the legend of Al Hafed in mind, it is easy to imagine that he would stake his claim on a portfolio that was fully invested in U.S. equities.

However precarious the perch, America is sitting on top of the world as the 1990s end. If our pride in that achievement is false, a mighty fall may be coming. It happened in Japan a decade ago, and it can happen here. Such a fall from grace by the United States, however unlikely, is not impossible. Investors must consider for themselves the relative returns and risks around the globe and then allocate their portfolios accordingly. But for me, if some latter-day Conwell were to quote Roger Lowenstein's wise advice in *The Wall Street Journal*, I'd agree: "You can lead a happy investment life without leaving home."

ON SELECTING
SUPERIOR FUNDS

THE SEARCH FOR THE HOLY GRAIL

K nowledgeable observers realize that the central task of investing is to gain the highest possible portion of the long-run return achieved by the class of financial assets in which they invest. *But they recognize and accept that the portion will be less than 100 percent.* As I have indicated in Chapter 4, a market index fund can provide 99 percent of the annual returns earned by its stock market benchmark, while the average actively managed stock fund can be expected to provide about 85 percent. While the future relative returns of managed funds are uncertain, it is difficult to imagine that they will rise to anywhere near 99 percent. Low-cost index funds, on the other hand, are almost certain to reach the 98 to 99 percent level, consistently over time.

As I noted earlier, even industry leaders are coming to recognize these realities, explicitly acknowledging (at least in one case) that "the average fund can *never* outperform the market." In fact, even those whose business is the promotion of actively managed funds cannot ignore these two poignant realities of the marketplace: (1) investors, as a group, do not, cannot, and will not beat the market; and (2) the overwhelming odds are against any particular mutual fund's doing so consistently over an investment lifetime. The real world of investing is not at all like Garrison Keillor's mythical Lake Wobegon, where "all of the children are above average."

Recognizing these powerful odds against any individual fund's outpacing an unmanaged index, the mutual fund industry has implicitly

205

conceded this point. Reflecting the concession, much of the industry is engaged in a hell-bent mission to take hold of the finest instrument ever created for long-term investing and transform it into a vehicle for inter-mediate-term—and even short-term—speculation.

Intelligent investors must accept the fact that, over time, the fund (or funds) they select, irrespective of past performance, will inevitably revert toward the mean. But the mean here is defined as the market mean *reduced by the costs the fund incurs*—advisory fees, operating expenses, and market-ing costs (in all, the expense ratio)—plus the cost of buying and selling portfolio securities (transaction costs). In the world of mutual funds, as we've seen, these costs are extremely high. The annual expense ratio of a median equity fund is now 1.5 percent, and rising. Transaction costs are difficult to quantify with precision, but with the high portfolio turnover rates generated in mutual funds an estimate of 0.5 percent to 1 percent an-nually hardly seems excessive. Current "all-in" costs, then, can be conser-vatively estimated at upward of 2 percent per year.

Given these realities, the search for the holy grail of market-beating long-term returns has been every bit as frustrating to fund managers and fund investors in the twentieth century—and will surely be so in the twenty-first century—as the search for the Holy Grail of the Last Supper was to the legendary knights of King Arthur's Round Table in the sixth century.

THE EQUITY FUND RECORD

Let's first examine the records of equity mutual funds in what I'll call the modern era. I'll use the period since the beginning of the great U.S. bull market in stocks, from August 1982 to mid-1998. This period is particu-larly relevant because it embraces the time during which equity fund assets became the largest pool of assets, holding more than 21 percent of the value of the U.S. stock market, and during which mutual fund expense ra-tios and portfolio turnover activity rose to the highest levels in history. Over this 16-year span, the annual returns of those equity mutual funds that survived the period averaged 16.5 percent before taxes, providing 87 percent of the return of the total stock market, as measured by the 18.9 percent returns on the all-market Wilshire 5000 Equity Index.* Given the

---

*The gap of 2.4 percent (18.9 −16.5) is somewhat larger than my earlier 2 percent estimate of fund costs, in part because of the drag created by the lower returns on the cash reserves typically held by actively managed funds.

rise in fund costs, it seems certain that this gap between fund returns and market returns will widen in the future.

These undeniable facts about fund returns, fund costs, and the relevance of past fund records have led to the boom in index funds today. If you can't beat the market—no one speaks of *meeting* the market—why not join it? An all-market index fund, operated at a total cost of 0.2 percent (one-tenth of the industry norm), would have provided an annual return of 18.7 percent, or nearly 99 percent of the total market return during the same period.

The comparison of 99 percent of *annual* market return for an index fund and 87 percent for a managed fund, as we now know, conceals a much larger gap than merely 12 points. The *terminal* value of the initial investment of $10,000 in the index fund on August 2, 1982, would have been $153,100; the terminal value of the same investment, for the same time period, in a traditionally managed active fund would have been $113,700. Thus, the index fund provided 97 percent of the accumulated growth in value of the investment in the index itself while the average managed fund provided only 70 percent of its accumulated growth. In Chapter 14, I will explore in greater detail the mathematics that explain why the managed fund shortfall rises so steeply over time. For now, let's just call it "the tyranny of compounding."

If these numbers frighten you, consider that, in all probability, you "ain't seen nothin' yet." Assuming only that the bull-market tree doesn't grow to the sky and the stock market gives a more modest account of itself, the performance gap will get larger. For example, let's hold costs constant and take stock market returns down to, say, 8 percent annually over 15 years. The results would be a net return of 7.8 percent for the index fund (98 percent of the market return) and 6 percent for the managed equity fund (75 percent). At the end of 15 years, the $10,000 investment would be valued at $30,900 in the index fund versus $24,000 in the managed equity fund. Now, the accumulated growth of the index fund represents 96 percent of the growth in the index investment, while the managed fund share tumbles to 64 percent. Tyranny, as it were, has increased the cumulative performance gap from 27 percentage points in the past bull-market era to 32 percentage points in what may well be a more realistic depiction of the foreseeable future. But whatever the future holds, the wide gap between fund returns and market index returns is not a very happy prospect for the fund industry. It means that managed mutual funds accepted at least implicitly by investors as the holy grail of high performance during most of the great bull market, will again fail to meet the test of time.

ENTER THE INDEX FUND

My study of historical performance relationships similar to these (although considerably less unfavorable to the funds), almost 25 years ago, encouraged me to start the fund industry's first market index mutual fund, modeled on the Standard & Poor's Composite Stock Price Index as I chronicled in Chapter 5, "On Indexing." After a shaky start, and minuscule assets, Vanguard 500 Index Fund turned on its jets and became both an artistic and a commercial success.

Despite its initially chilly reception, the index fund now commands the attention of executives throughout the mutual fund industry. Although uncopied—even shunned—for a full decade, the first index fund has now been joined by some 140 competitive index funds. A few have been formed by missionaries (or converts, and "there's no one more religious than a convert"), but most by opportunistic no-load firms, "eating crow" and dragged—kicking and screaming—into the fray by the institutional 401(k) savings plan market. Some have reasonable expense ratios, but most of them are the result of temporary fee waivers. Many have unacceptably high expense ratios. And an appalling one-third of index funds even charge sales loads or 12b-1 fees. Their sponsors ignore the fact that minimal cost accounts for virtually all of the index advantage. About two-thirds of the U.S. equity funds are targeted against the S&P 500 Index.

The indexing concept, however, is much broader than the S&P 500 Index fund. Even though the theory of indexing works most effectively against the total stock market, the all-market index fund (based on the Wilshire 5000 Equity Index) is only at the beginning of its acceptance. What is more, indexing also works well for investors who, for one reason or another, seek to earn higher returns in specific broad market sectors. Funds modeled on growth indexes and value indexes, as well as small-cap and mid-cap indexes, will also grow in acceptance. It is only a matter of time until someone has the good sense to offer index funds that match each of the nine Morningstar style/market-cap boxes. As shown in Chapter 6, index funds would have produced highly effective risk-adjusted returns in each box. Index funds are in the incipient stage in the international stock markets and in the bond market, too, but they will become far more important there in the years ahead.

Index funds are threatening to become the holy grail of mutual fund investing—the optimal way to approach the return of the markets—and deservedly so. During 1998, index funds claimed an estimated 25 percent of the net new cash flowing into equity funds, up from just 10 percent in 1990.

Assuming that investors continue to see the merit of indexing strategies as the best means to outpace the long-term returns of actively managed funds—a point that the past data abundantly demonstrate—how can sponsors of traditional funds compete? Material cuts in the fees they charge seem unlikely because their profits would be slashed. A reduction in portfolio transaction costs is also unlikely, for it would result in unacceptably radical changes in today's silly, but chic, high-turnover investment policies. So what are they to do?

THE INDEX FUND ELICITS A NEW INDUSTRY MANTRA

Fund sponsors must respond in some other way to the challenge of indexing. They must create a new holy grail, and that is the very path that much of the fund industry is following. The idea is to have investors actively manage their own fund portfolios, the better (or so the theory goes) to achieve returns that provide, not merely 99 percent of the market's return, but well over 100 percent. The new strategy seems to entail ingredients like these:

- Don't own a fund for the long term.
- Treat funds as stocks. Own lots of them and change them frequently.
- Exercise your freedom of choice—often.
- Dash to the nearest fund supermarket, and swap funds free of trading costs (or so it is incorrectly alleged).
- Heed the ads for those handsome past performers whose returns are advertised on your television screen.
- In all, the message seems to be "switch and get rich."

This grotesque transfiguration of the long-term nature of fund investing is now well under way. Equity fund investors currently hold their shares of a given fund for an average of but three years.

But does it work for people to trade their mutual funds like stocks? Are there methods for selecting and swapping mutual funds that might result in superior returns? Are there strategies that have worked in the past? In this chapter, I'm going to examine that question from four vantage points: first, the theoretical world of academe, from which massive studies of fund performance have emanated; second, the real world of fund selection, reflected in the records of funds that have actually outpaced the market in the past; third, the records of advisers who recommend fund portfolios; and fourth, the records of funds that invest in other funds (funds-of-funds).

SELECTING WINNING FUNDS—AN ACADEMIC ACTIVITY

Given the ability of computers to spit out endless performance comparisons, multiple regressions, and complex formulas, our academics have tested, well, *everything*. While a lot of data mining may well be involved in what is duly recorded on this subject in *The Journal of Finance*, *The Journal of Portfolio Management*, the *Financial Analysts Journal*, and similar publications, these respected and thoughtful scholars have no axe to grind. And they have carefully examined the record to determine whether there are past factors that may persist over time and thus may be valuable in selecting funds that will provide superior future returns.

The Sharpe Study

What have the academics found? We'll start with the guru of the academic profession in the mutual fund arena, Professor William F. Sharpe of Stanford University. He carefully examined the 10-year records of the 100 largest equity funds (measured each year), accounting for more than 40 percent of the assets of all such funds. He then compared their returns with the returns of comparably weighted market-sector indexes, including a U.S. Treasury bill component (thereby accounting for the persistent performance lag created by fund cash positions).[1]

Dr. Sharpe properly acknowledged that the cost advantage ascribable to large funds probably provided superior relative returns for his sample of funds, but found nonetheless that the average return of the funds he studied fell short of the multi-index return by 0.64 percent per year over the past decade. (It should go without saying that using the 100 largest funds in itself creates a substantial bias in favor of successful funds.) The shortfall could not be deemed significantly different from zero, but the data surely undermined any belief that a typical actively managed equity fund can outperform a passive alternative. (The data would have been even less favorable to the funds if Sharpe had included sales charges.)

Dr. Sharpe then singled out those fund managers who seemed to have demonstrated skill in selecting stocks over various interim periods, and examined whether the success continued in future periods. He investigated common measures for judging funds—size, past performance, and the Sharpe Ratio of risk-adjusted return. The best evidence of some level of performance consistency appeared in the results for the previous 12 months (i.e., selecting a fund on the basis of its year-earlier performance slightly improved the chance of seeing that performance continue). An investor who had held the top 25 funds—the top quartile in Sharpe's study—shifting funds as needed on that basis year after year, would have added an annual return of 0.8 percent relative to the index return over the subsequent 5- and 10-year periods. (An investor who had holdings in the bottom quartile would have underperformed by 0.5 percent per year over the 5-year period and 1.3 percent annually over the 10-year period). Even disregarding the extra taxes incurred by switching funds regularly, this rate of return would seem a rather shaky basis for an investment strategy.

Do winners repeat? Sharpe summarized his results this way: "If the past 10 years are indicative of the next 10, one might answer in the affirmative" (although, I would note, the positive margin is modest to a fault). However, perhaps Sharpe's "neutral position" (not proven) is more appropriate, for he conceded that "the evidence is far from conclusive, statistically or economically."

The Carhart Study

Mark Carhart, of the University of Southern California, is another respected scholar who tackled the issue of persistence in fund performance. He evaluated 1,892 diversified equity funds over 16,109 fund years (amazing!) from 1962 to 1993.[2] First, he found that "common factors in stock returns [value vs. growth, large cap vs. small cap, high beta* vs. low beta] and investment expenses almost completely explain persistence in equity fund returns." Properly adjusting for the customary failure to consider the effect of the subaverage returns of funds that have gone out of existence, Carhart confirmed Professor Burton Malkiel's conclusion, described in

---

* Beta is a measure of a fund's volatility relative to a stock market index (usually the Standard & Poor's 500 Index).

Chapter 5, that survivor bias has enhanced past annual returns reported for funds over the 1982–1991 decade by about 1.4 percent per year. Dr. Malkiel also found some limited evidence of persistence during the 1970s, but none during the 1980s.[3]

Looking at past one-year returns relative to those of the subsequent year, Carhart concluded, among other things, that relatively few funds stay in their initial decile ranking, although funds in the top and bottom deciles maintain their rankings more frequently than the 10 percent that mere chance would suggest. The 17 percent of funds repeating in decile one seems less than compelling. The 46 percent of funds repeating in decile ten, on the other hand, is quite imposing, a performance that seems largely explained by the fact that many low-decile funds tend to be trapped there by their high costs. In his conclusion, Carhart warns: *"While the popular press will no doubt continue to glamorize the best-performing mutual fund managers, the mundane explanations of strategy and investment cost account for almost all of the important predictability of mutual fund returns."* [Italics added] Translation: Relying on past records to select funds that will provide superior performance in the future is a challenging task.

The Goetzmann-Ibbotson Study

In another study, William Goetzmann and Roger Ibbotson tested the repeat-winner hypothesis over two-year, one-year, and monthly intervals from 1975 to 1987.[4] For all periods, they ranked equity mutual funds in terms of both raw returns and risk-adjusted returns, and then split them into two categories: winners (top 50 percent) and losers (bottom 50 percent). Their analysis indicated that investing in winners slightly increased the chance of outperforming the return of the all-fund average in the subsequent period, an important measure because funds that underperformed by reason of high expenses tended to repeat their shortfalls.

By way of example, their study of growth mutual funds over two-year periods revealed that past top performers had a 60 percent chance of being winners over the subsequent two years. Therefore, one might conclude that the chance of a fund's being better than average in four subsequent two-year periods would have been about one in eight. Exceeding the average fund return in each succeeding two-year period, in short, was hardly an odds-on wager—and the odds would have been far worse if sales charges and taxes had been taken into account.

To make matters worse for those who advocate the merits of enhancing returns by moving from one fund to another, *even relatively consistent winners might be losers relative to the market index.* Goetzmann and Ibbotson explicitly conceded that picking winners—even when defined as funds in the top quartile, based on their performance relative to their peers—may not be enough to beat the market. They concluded: "While the 'repeat-winner' pattern may not be a guide to beating the market, it does appear to be a guide to beating the pack over the long term." In the face of index fund competition, then, to what avail is a strategy that relies on evidence suggesting a tenuous persistence of a fund's performance relative to its *peers*, when unaccompanied by any evidence—in fact, with considerable evidence to the contrary—of performance persistence that outpaces the *market?*

All of these academic labors in the statistical vineyards suggest that there is little, if any, persistence in performance. That is, the researchers have found no way to evaluate fund past returns and predict future winners with confidence. What is more, even if other studies, on other days, suggest that there *is* a secret—a new holy grail, as it were—such a record of past persistence itself would not necessarily be evidence that the same persistence would prevail in the future. The fact is that market conditions change; fund portfolio managers change (and rapidly at that); fund organizations change; and fund strategies change, often influenced by the asset growth that success begets as we shall see in Chapter 12. This panoply of changes undermines the very relevance of the past, and effectively eliminates any link between past and future performance.

With that seemingly conclusive background from the theoretical world of academia, let's now look at fund selection in the real world of investing. We'll consider first, the actual records of the funds that *did* beat the market during the long bull market; next, the investment advisers who recommend mutual fund portfolios; and finally, the actual records of funds-of-funds, which invest solely in other mutual funds.

FUNDS THAT HAVE BEATEN THE MARKET— THE DISAPPOINTING REALITY

Despite the serious lag of mutual fund returns during the great bull market, one out of every six managed equity funds succeeded in outpacing the market's return. Of the 258 general equity funds that survived that period (the industry was far smaller in 1982), 42 succeeded in outpacing the 18.9 percent return of the Wilshire 5000 Equity Index (a lower hurdle, to be sure, than the 19.8 percent return of the S&P 500 Index). But only 12 of those 42 (one of every 21 survivors) did so by a margin of 1.5 percentage points. If we assume that the funds' annual tracking error, relative to the

A Fund Manager Concedes

Literally *no* brute evidence exists to support the proposition that, out there somewhere, just waiting to be found, is a holy grail that will contain a message describing how to select, in advance, funds that will outpace the Standard & Poor's 500 Index on the basis of past performance.

The mutual fund industry's tacit acceptance of this reality has now become explicit for at least one fund adviser. In mid-1998, Morgan Stanley Dean Witter, manager of some $160 billion of assets in load and no-load mutual funds, published a report entitled "Risk and Repeat Performance in Mutual Funds." After examining the total returns of 660 equity funds during the two successive five-year periods comprising the 1987–1997 decade, the report concluded: "Of the funds in the best quartile of total return in the first period, only 28 percent remained in the top quartile in the second period, and 51 percent remained in the top half. *Alarmingly, this figure is indistinguishable from 'random' results (which would put 50 percent in the top half) . . . supporting a 'null' hypothesis in which there is no repetition of top performers.*" [Italics added.]

Despite the randomness of fund returns, however, fund risk profiles are quite persistent. Fully 63 percent of the funds with the highest volatility in the first period remained in the top quartile during the second period, 2½ *times* the random expectation of 25 percent. Similarly, 55 percent of the funds with the lowest volatility remained in the bottom quartile in the subsequent period, more than double what chance would suggest.

Combining random returns with persistent volatility, the report concluded the obvious: Past risk-adjusted performance is more likely to be predictive than absolute performance alone. It then noted that "the S&P 500 ranked in the top quartile of risk-adjusted performance throughout the first and second periods." Since "the bottom line is that risk-adjusted past performance is a superior predictor of future performance," it follows that Morgan Stanley has concluded that the S&P 500 Index should continue to provide superior performance in the future. That this conclusion also strongly echoes my conclusion is not surprising. That the echo chamber from which it resounds lies in the corridors of a major mutual fund manager is astounding.

index, was a fairly modest 3 percent, then only a return of 1.5 percent in excess of the index return would represent statistically significant outperformance. Based on their actual tracking errors, only 3 of the 12 funds—only about one in each 100—cleared the hurdle of statistical significance. Nonetheless, it's instructive to examine all 12 funds.

A bit of microanalysis shows that these 12 funds were a rather motley group. Six carved out their entire long-term margins in the early years, when their assets were small, and have been mediocre performers for years. That leaves six legitimate top performers. Interestingly, and importantly, all six had the same portfolio managers throughout all or most of the period (the managers' average age is now 57); two closed to new cash flow before their assets reached $1 billion.

The 12 winners could not have been easy to identify in advance; at the outset, their shares were owned by relatively few fund investors. (Their aggregate 1982 assets totaled $1.8 billion, only 3 percent of total equity fund assets.) In any event, despite their acknowledged past success, no one can be sure of the extent to which it may recur in the future, whether or not their managers stay on the job or retire and rest on their laurels. Today, could investors be highly confident of superior returns if they selected one of the four legitimate fund champions that remain open to investors? It would seem, at best, a counterintuitive decision for an intelligent investor.

THE INVESTMENT ADVISERS WHO SELECT FUNDS— ANOTHER DISAPPOINTMENT

Next, let's examine the public records of advisers who recommend mutual funds. For the past five years, *The New York Times* has published, each quarter, the records of equity fund portfolios selected and supervised by five respected advisers who began their task on July 7, 1993. During this period, not one of the portfolios has come close to matching the record of the Vanguard 500 Index Fund, which was chosen by the *Times* as the appropriate comparative standard. The advisers' average annual return of 11.8 percent provided 59 percent of the annual return of the market, and the Index fund provided 99 percent (see Figure 9.1). While some of these advisers chose equity portfolios that were designed to be somewhat less risky (i.e., less volatile) than the 500 Index itself, the decline in the Index during the third quarter of 1998 proved to be but 85 percent of the decline in the average fund portfolio of the advisers.

In any event, providing only 59 percent of the market's annual return during a five-year period in which even the *average* fund provided 70 percent

FIGURE 9.1

The Experts Speak: Five Advisers, $50,000 Investment

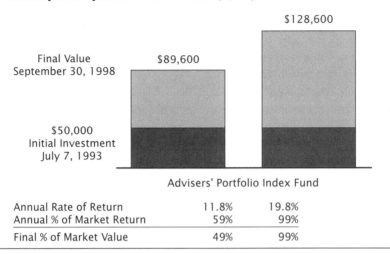

	Advisers' Portfolio	Index Fund
Annual Rate of Return	11.8%	19.8%
Annual % of Market Return	59%	99%
Final % of Market Value	49%	99%

represents a failure that verges on the astounding. To make matters even worse, when it comes to the capital accumulated during the full period, the average portfolio of the advisers provided just 49 percent of the final growth of the S&P 500 Index, while the Index fund provided 99 percent. Selecting winning funds, even by experts, is hardly bereft of challenges.

Another, longer-run evaluation of the success of advisers in selecting fund portfolios is the *Hulbert Financial Digest*. It reports that, of 59 advisory newsletters that it has tracked for a full decade, the average adviser's portfolio has provided a return of +7.9 percent. This return represented 58 percent of the market's return of 13.7 percent, as it happens, almost identical to the 59 percent figure achieved by the advisers whose returns have been reported by *The New York Times* study in a much shorter period. Only eight newsletters outpaced the market with their recommendations. Interestingly, and perhaps not surprisingly, that is very close to the one-in-six chance of superiority that the mutual funds themselves have displayed since mid-1982. For better or worse, during this bull-market era, many of these advisers recommended portfolios that were far more conservative than the stock market itself. On average, however, they carried a risk that closely approximated the risk of the market. With average risk but well-below-average return, their risk-adjusted return (measured by the Sharpe

Ratio) amounted to just 42 percent of the market's risk-adjusted return, and only three advisers higher risk-adjusted returns than the index. In all, the accumulated evidence regarding the ability of the experts to select winning funds remains not only negative, but far worse than what informed intuition might suggest.

RETURNS OF FUNDS-OF-FUNDS—
YET ANOTHER DISAPPOINTMENT

The third real-world test consists of the actual records of funds-of-funds—mutual funds that select other mutual funds for their portfolios. And these records are the most deplorable of the lot. The funds-of-funds not only lag the market—we now know that five of every six funds have done *that*—but they seriously lag even the style categories of the funds in which they invest, in part because of the extra layer of costs they almost universally add. For example, in the year ended June 30, 1998, of the 14 funds-of-funds investing in large-blend (value and growth) funds, 4 ranked in the 96th to 100th percentiles (one was dead last) and 5 ranked in the 90th to 95th percentiles. The champions, if that's the right term, of this undistinguished group ranked in the 65th percentile, lagging two-thirds of the peer funds from which they made their selection. In all, the 93 funds-of-funds with full-year records achieved about what might have been expected from a random selection of funds that was reduced by an added layer of costs of more than 1 percent: an average of the 68th percentile compared to their regular fund-style peers.

I present the one-year results only because so few funds-of-funds have been around very long. Over the past decade, when only nine of them existed at the outset, the record was a bit worse: they lagged 69 percent of the funds in their peer group. But excluding the single fund that did *not* add a layer of extra expenses (it *outpaced* 72 percent of its peers), the ranking quickly dropped down, with the remaining eight funds-of-funds achieving only a 75th percentile ranking among comparable regular funds. This neighborhood is hardly posh but is surely familiar, clearly reaffirming the one-year numbers presented above. To make matters even worse, managed funds-of-funds typically turn over their own fund portfolios at an average rate of about 80 percent per year, a short-term focus that inevitably impinges on the long-term returns they earn. The combination of high fund turnover and high fund costs, with two extra layers of cost—from high turnover and excessive operating expenses—has clearly proved to be a formula for failure.

Given the transitory nature of the one-year data, and the existence of a limited number of funds over the past ten years, perhaps the most relevant evidence is found in the three-year data. The past three years give us the opportunity to examine 35 funds-of-funds that have existed during the period, comparing each with its peer group: 11 large-cap, medium-cap, and small-cap stock funds; 4 international stock funds; 16 balanced (hybrid) funds, and 4 bond funds. The average fund-of-funds achieved a 66th percentile ranking, closely confirming the one- and 10-year findings. The average fund-of-funds returned an average of 15.5 percent for the period, a 2.4 percentage point shortfall to the average return of its peer group. Since more than half of this lag is created by the average expense ratio of 1.3 percent (1.7 percent excluding those funds that levy no additional fees) they added on, clearly the "experts" managing them had no particular selection ability sufficient to offset the costs of their services. Figure 9.2 shows the ranking of the 28 funds-of-funds among the 35 fund total that added on such fees in terms of their percentile rankings. It clearly reflects the powerful odds against successful fund selection for expensive funds-of-funds. It is a loser's game.

To make matters worse, I believe it would be optimistic to expect that a 66th percentile rank can be sustained. Those funds-of-funds that bear an extra layer of fees have carried their own expense ratios averaging 1.7 percent (one-fourth incur expense ratios of 2 percent or more) piled on to the all-in costs of the underlying funds (averaging about 2 percent). Total annual costs borne by shareholders then reach to almost 4 percent. Such an extra deduction—assuming that their managers, on average, pick average funds—should produce about a 75th percentile rank. In any event, it would take naïveté to undreamed-of heights to believe that such a heavily loaded package of funds could ever outpace appropriate market indexes. Yet the funds-of-funds industry, as it were, is booming. Some 70 new such funds have been formed since June 1995, bringing the total to more than 120. But the record is bereft of evidence that the game is worth the candle.*

---

*A personal anecdote: When Robert Markman, an independent investment adviser who is a long-time foe of indexing, formed his own fund-of-funds early in 1995, I made so bold as to wager him $25 that an index fund modeled on the S&P 500 would prove a better investment than his MultiFund Moderate Growth Portfolio, the portfolio he identified as having a strategy that would outperform the S&P 500 over the following five years. With 3½ years having elapsed, the results so far: Vanguard 500 Index Fund +124 percent, Multi Fund Moderate Growth Portfolio +58 percent. The bet isn't due to be settled until April 1, 2000, so I'm not yet banking the money. But if the S&P 500 Index generates, say, a 6 percent annualized return in the next 1½ years, the Markman Portfolio will have to rise at a 34 percent annual rate! That will be no mean challenge for this fund-of-funds portfolio.

FIGURE 9.2

Funds-of-Funds—Total Returns Relative to Peer Group*
(June, 1995–June, 1998)

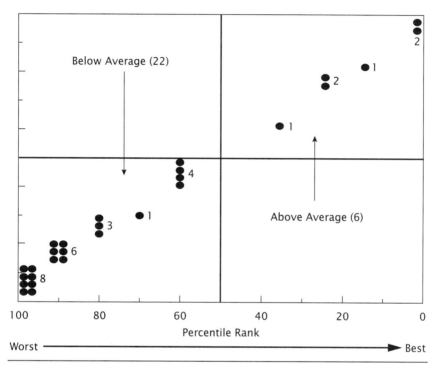

* Excludes seven funds-of-funds that levy no additional expense ratio.

A Caveat

Before leaving this subject, I want to emphasize a critical distinction among funds-of-funds: whether or not they add an extra layer of costs. As these costs are added, the odds against superior returns relative to regular mutual funds escalate. However, funds-of-funds that levy no extra costs (there are only a handful) do not carry this handicap. The record clearly supports this distinction. While funds-of-funds that bear extra costs have provided returns that have outpaced only 32 percent of comparable mutual funds over the past five years, funds-of-funds that do not bear extra costs have outpaced 79 percent of comparable funds.

It goes almost without saying that investors who consider owning funds-of-funds should look first at those that (a) do not add this extra layer

"I CAN SUMMON SPIRITS FROM THE VASTY DEEP . . ."

In *Henry IV*, part 1, Shakespeare tells us of Glendower's bragging, "I can summon spirits from the vasty deep." To which Hotspur responds, "Yes. But when you summon them, will they come?" That is a good question to ask when appraising the past performance of mutual funds. Any professional analyst of fund performance—or any armchair investor, buttressed by *Morningstar Mutual Funds*—can summon from the quagmire the names of the best-performing mutual funds of the past—those that have outpaced their peers and representative market indexes. That is the easy part.

The tough part is having the future winners come when they are summoned now. Even if yesterday's solid performers do appear, abundant statistical evidence suggests that they won't repeat their superiority tomorrow. Yet, investors persist in believing that they can select, in advance, funds that will outperform the broad market indexes. That expectation is easy to understand. Some funds manage to outpace the indexes over substantial periods of time, offering seemingly incontrovertible proof of management superiority that will endure. But it rarely does. By the time a long-term record of superiority has emerged, the outstanding mutual funds with outstanding records may already be colliding with an immutable principle of the financial markets: Reversion to the mean.

Discussed at length in the next chapter, mean reversion is a first principle of financial physics. Even the funds with the very best past records have a strong—and, in the long run, overpowering—tendency to gravitate to average gross returns, and, hence, below-average net returns. This tendency is reinforced by the fact that mutual funds with outstanding returns tend to attract large cash inflows from investors, and, as a result, are gradually stifled in their search for return superiority. The business of investment management—like the business of selecting portfolio managers—is fallible, tough, and demanding, particularly for mutual funds carrying the dead weight of excessive costs. Surely, summoning the spirits from the vasty deep—calling for the top performers to repeat their past success—is far easier than having them come and answer our call for continued excellence.

of costs, (b) themselves focus on low-cost funds, and (c) carry no sales loads. There is no reason that such funds cannot provide competitive returns, or, as they have during the past five years, returns exceeding the norms of their peer funds.

No Holy Grail Here—Academic or Pragmatic

Whether we consider academic studies (many of which, I presume, included tests of predicting future returns that were found wanting and were never published), or the pragmatic and unforgiving actual results of the funds with the best long-term records, or the picks of fund advisory services, or records of funds-of-funds, the odds of selecting mutual funds that are top performers in the future have proved extremely poor. The chances that individual fund investors will find the holy grail that will identify *in advance* the future's superior performers seem equally dismal.

Before this era of performance evaluation on a relative basis and sophisticated return attribution on a factor basis, equity mutual funds with active managers who achieved the best sustained long-term records represented the pinnacle of performance excellence. In recent years, the acceptance of such funds as representing the holy grail has been endangered by the clear performance superiority of the index fund, and by its rapidly increasing acceptance. As a result, much of the industry has, at least implicitly, mounted a counterattack. If only a rare fund can hope to go toe-to-toe with the market on a long-term basis, aggressive fund distributors seem to argue, let's gain an edge by encouraging investors to abandon the conventional buy-and-hold fund strategy and switch opportunistically among funds. To be sure, the thesis leaves aside the self-evident fact that, although *some* investors may, against all odds, succeed in outpacing the market by astute selection of funds, investors *as a group* must underperform the market by the amount of their costs. This brute fact remains firmly in place.

In short, the traditional investor strategy of holding managed mutual funds for the long term has not provided the holy grail of market-superior returns—not by a long shot. Nor will the current fad of switching rapidly into and out of funds. The index strategy, by definition, must provide less-than-market returns—but only by a slight margin. And that is the true holy grail: achieving through a diversified investment portfolio a return that is as close to 100 percent of the market return as is possible. The odds remain high that few equity mutual fund portfolio managers will beat the stock market, and that, over the long pull, even those who win will not do so by a very wide margin.

After all, fund managers are mere mortals who operate in highly efficient markets. The bogus fund-switching strategy in vogue today, implicitly designed to counter the index strategy by misleading investors into thinking that, individually, they can somehow out-fox the market, is certain (I choose that word carefully) to be a loser's game. And the argument that a fund-of-funds can somehow emulate the result of a long-term buy-and-hold index fund strategy by adding a fee averaging 1.7 percent per year on top of the 2 percent cost incurred by the average fund flies in the face of reason. Abundant and compelling past evidence reinforces the validity of this elemental conclusion.

For fund managers, the most effective response to the challenge of the index fund is not a chimera—ever to chase the market return but never capture it—but common sense. Fund managers must reduce fees to equitable levels, return to the traditional fund philosophy of long-term investing, and limit the asset levels of the portfolios they manage to a size appropriate to their strategies and objectives. These changes should make the returns of actively managed funds more competitive with those of passive index funds. Taken together, each of these small steps toward manager competitiveness would constitute one giant forward step for the mutual fund shareholders. The golden rule—Put the investor first!—is the best route to the holy grail we should all be seeking. If this industry fails to implement this golden rule, low-cost index funds will continue to provide the last best chance for investors to find the holy grail of optimal investment returns.

PART III

ON INVESTMENT PERFORMANCE

Ultimately, we are concerned primarily with the performance of our investments. One of the investment principles least recognized by individual investors—reversion to the mean, that eternal force of gravity that seems to hold the financial markets in its grip—remains a fact of life in the world of investing. The fund industry ignores the subject, but my analysis shows that, whether considering the returns of individual funds, or of different investment styles or of the stock market itself, superior returns finally revert to some sort of long-term norm. Very large mutual funds, once they have reverted to the norm, rarely rise again. The problems raised by the growth of this industry to giant size further compound the performance problem. Given the clear handicap of size, many large funds appear to have embraced "investment relativism," in which portfolios are structured to resemble the popular market averages, adding some stability to their returns, but at the expense of superiority—a costly prescription for failure.

Mutual funds routinely ignore taxes when they present their performance, but investors cannot ignore taxes. Yet most funds, apparently blind to the needs of their taxable investors, continue to engage in rapid-fire portfolio transaction activity, which generates excessive taxes without providing any apparent countervailing advantage, even to those investors who hold shares in tax-deferred accounts. I suggest several solutions to this tax problem, including reshaping present fund policies and designing new funds that serve the needs of taxable investors. The final chapter of this section discusses the important role of *time* in shaping long-term investment performance. This temporal dimension interacts with each of the three spatial dimensions of investing, enhancing *return*, reducing *risk*, and magnifying the impact of *cost*—conclusions completely consistent with what common sense would suggest. As we return to the theme of long-term investing with which Part I began, we now come full circle in considering the three major investment challenges—investment strategy, choices, and performance—that face mutual fund investors.

CHAPTER 10

ON REVERSION TO THE MEAN

SIR ISAAC NEWTON'S REVENGE ON WALL STREET

At first blush, the principle of reversion to the mean might seem a slightly dry and uninspiring subject. I assure you, it is anything but that. This principle from the theoretical world of academe has proven to be wholly pragmatic in the very real world of the financial markets. It is evident in the relative returns of equity mutual funds, in the relative returns of a whole range of stock market sectors, and, over the long term, in the absolute returns earned by common stocks as a group. Reversion to the mean (RTM) represents the operation of a kind of "law of gravity" in the stock market, through which returns mysteriously seem to be drawn to norms of one kind or another over time. This application of the universal law of gravity might even be characterized as Sir Isaac Newton's revenge on Wall Street.

As investors, many of us have chosen mutual funds as all or part of our investment programs. Whether funds are a part of your portfolio or not, you have probably carefully considered your own financial circumstances and risk tolerances, and decided on your optimal allocation of assets between fixed-income investments and stocks. And if you share in the powerful and rarely challenged ethic of our era—that common stocks are virtually certain to provide the highest returns of any major asset class over the long term—a substantial portion of your program may well be invested in equity funds.

Assuming that is the case, how should intelligent investors who select mutual funds undertake the task of choosing them? Let me start with my own assessment of how *not* to go about it: basing selections principally, or even importantly, on the records of exceptional past performance that are published and promoted by the hyperbolic marketing machine that drives the mutual fund industry today. You will be well served if you ignore those claims. The overpowering lesson of history—as I have been trying to persuade you in earlier chapters—is: *In the long run, a well-diversified equity portfolio is a commodity, providing rates of return that are highly likely to resemble closely and finally fall short of, those of the stock market as a whole.*

By the end of the period over which you may accumulate your nest egg, be it 10 years or 50 years, the odds are that a fund's *gross* rate of annual return will approximate that of the stock market. I choose the word *gross* with care. Given the excessive costs borne by most mutual funds—including the fully disclosed (if often ignored) direct expenses (used for operating, marketing, and investment advisory costs, and for generous profits for managers) plus the hidden costs of fund portfolio transactions—the *net* rate of return of the funds as a group and, over the long run, of individual funds, has tended to lag the market by from 1½ to 2½ percentage points annually. These differences in annual returns, if extended over long periods of time, will make a dramatic difference in your final capital.

Mutual Fund Champions Come Down to Earth

In periods as short as one year, many mutual funds—especially small, aggressive ones—can and do defy the odds. In some decade-long periods, perhaps one out of five funds succeeds in doing so by a material amount. But in the very long run, there is a profound tendency for the returns of high-performing funds to come down to earth, and, almost as inevitably, for the returns of low-performing funds to come *up* to earth, as it were. (In fact, bottom performing funds tend to remain there because of high expenses. Since these expenses persist, upward moves of these funds are impeded.) Indeed, as I shall show, the distance traveled in the course of these descents and ascents tends to be directly proportional to the earlier distance above or below the market's return. *Reversion toward the market mean is the dominant factor in long-term mutual fund returns.*

Let me clarify with an example using the past two full decades to perform this test: the 1970s (which provided uncharacteristically modest

equity returns) and the 1980s (which returned the favor by providing unusually generous returns—a sort of RTM example in a different context;
I'll come to that later). In performing this analysis, I've used middle-of-
the-road growth-and-income funds and growth mutual funds. These
funds include the large, well-known funds that carry risks at about the
same level as the Standard & Poor's 500 Composite Stock Price Index.

Figure 10.1 shows how the four quartiles of funds, ranked by fund performance relative to the S&P 500 Index in the 1970s, regressed toward the
market mean during the 1980s. Note, for example, that the top quartile of
funds provided annual returns averaging an imposing 4.8 percentage
points above the Index during the 1970s, but ended up 1.0 point behind
the norm during the 1980s, a downward reversion of 5.8 points compared

FIGURE 10.1

Fund Annual Returns Relative to Market Index

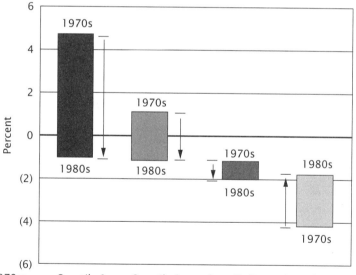

Ranking in 1970s:	Quartile 1	Quartile 2	Quartile 3	Quartile 4
Annual Returns Relative to S&P 500 Index				
1970s	4.8%	1.1%	−1.1%	−4.1%
1980s	−1.0%	−1.1%	−2.0%	−1.8%
1980s Reversion	−5.8%	−2.2%	−0.9%	2.3%

to the Index. By the same token, the bottom quartile fell 4.1 points behind the Index during the 1970s but reduced that gap to 1.8 points behind the Index during the 1980s, an upward reversion of 2.3 percentage points. (Note that in the second and third quartiles, there is much less change in returns, because these returns were close to the mean in the first decade.)

The consistency of this pattern was equally striking; 33 of the 34 funds in the top quartile reverted toward the market mean during the 1980s, with two-thirds of the formerly superior funds actually falling behind the Index. For what it's worth, that one exception is a fund that provided a remarkable excess return of fully 11 percentage points per year during the 1980s. However, it has performed a classic RTM maneuver so far during the 1990s, providing an annual return precisely equal to the Index, an equally remarkable 11-point annual mean reversion. Over the past four years alone, it has lagged the Index by 5.6 percentage points annually. Sometimes, the manifestation of RTM requires patience!

Because it operates in a theoretical world, devoid of operating and transaction costs, the unmanaged S&P 500 Index is not only a tough target but an elusive one. (It has a strong bias toward stocks with very large market capitalizations.) Even though I have chosen the mutual fund categories dominated by large-cap funds with volatility characteristics similar to those of the Index, the capitalizations of the stocks in their portfolios are somewhat smaller. Nonetheless, during the two decades—a time frame that obviously includes a considerable bias in favor of the funds by including only those that survived the period—the comparative differences were not large. During the first decade, these fund survivors actually outpaced the annual returns of the Index by a slight 0.1 percent, a somewhat uncharacteristically favorable outcome, only to fall 1.5 percent behind during the second decade, a more normal result.

In any event, to put that issue to rest, I present in Figure 10.2 a similar tabulation in which the same funds are *compared with one another*. Figure 10.2 shows how, in each quartile, the mutual funds have regressed toward the mean of the fund group itself, rather than toward that of the Index. Again, RTM is the order of the day: the top quartile funds lost 3.9 points of their former 4.7-point advantage. Fully 30 of the 34 top-quartile funds reverted. In the bottom quartile, 33 funds improved their relative records, and only one failed to do so. The bottom-quartile funds reverted upward by 4.1 points, recouping precisely what they had lost in the prior decade. RTM is sending a powerful message about the futility of evaluating funds based on their past returns. The patterns of Figures 10.1 and 10.2 are virtually

FIGURE 10.2

Fund Annual Returns Relative to Average Equity Fund

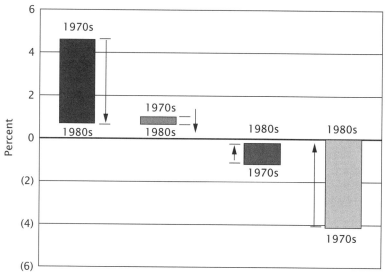

Ranking in 1970s:	Quartile 1	Quartile 2	Quartile 3	Quartile 4
Annual Return Relative to Average Fund				
1970s	4.6%	0.9%	–1.2%	–4.1%
1980s	0.7%	0.6%	–0.3%	0.0%
1980s Reversion	–3.9%	–0.3%	+0.9%	+4.1%

identical despite a change in the standard of reversion from the market average to the fund average. The RTM principle remains firmly intact.

To reinforce the point, we repeated the same test over the past 20 years. Comparing the decade 1987–1997 with 1977–1987, the top quartile reversion to the market mean was a slightly larger 6.9 percentage points—from 5.1 percentage points ahead of the index to 1.8 percentage points behind the index—with all 44 funds reverting toward the mean, including fully 35 that fell below it. In the bottom quartile, with many of the returns retarded by excessive costs in both periods, 22 of the 44 funds improved their relative annual returns. The average return for these funds actually failed by a minuscule margin to revert (moving from 3.7 to 3.8 percentage points behind the index), a result brought about solely by the fact that two funds—notorious for their consistent and abject failure—turned in average *annual* returns

29 percentage points short of the market. (Absent those funds, the reversion took the bottom quartile funds upward from 3.2 to 2.6 percentage points behind the index.)

We also repeated the test for 1977–1987 and 1987–1997 using the average return of the funds themselves rather than the average return of the market index as in the previous test. Here, with fund costs taken into account, the pattern is again remarkable symmetry. In the top quartile, 41 of the 44 funds reverted downward; in the bottom quartile, 40 of the 44 funds reverted upward. On average, the downward reversion for the top group was 4.3 percentage points; the upward reversion for the bottom group, again held back by high costs, was 3.2 percentage points. Clearly, the general rule of reversion to the mean in mutual fund returns, no matter which time period or which standard we use, is consistent, highly predictable, and, finally, universal.

Mutual fund marketers assume—usually correctly—that most investors are completely unaware that today's top performers are overwhelmingly likely both to be tomorrow's ordinary participants in the stock market, and to parallel the average of their peers. In other words, today's Beau Brummels are tomorrow's Joe Six-Packs. Indeed, despite compelling evidence of that outcome, fund advertisers consistently hawk top performers. Fund organizations know full well that today's idols have feet of clay. But as long as there are believers in witchcraft, the purveyors of witches' brew will create and peddle elixirs and panaceas, engendering costly and counterproductive investment choices that inevitably come to grips with yesterday's realities, not tomorrow's.

No study exists that suggests the opposite conclusion: that the very few long-term winners that have emerged (usually, through highly superior returns in their *early* years, when they have very small assets and few shareholders) can be selected *in advance*. But perhaps there is a better way of reaping superior future performance than by sowing superior past performance. Let us turn to a second category of RTM, and a second reflection of Sir Isaac Newton's revenge on Wall Street.

GRAVITY AND STOCK MARKET SECTORS

Large-cap growth and value funds must provide short-term returns that roughly track those of the stock market before costs are deducted. But over the long run, because of costs, they must fall significantly short. Should investors seeking superior long-term returns concentrate on stocks in selected *sectors* of the stock market that may have characteristics that lead to outperformance? Alas, there seems to be no enduring systematic bias in favor of a particular market sector. RTM seems consistently to turn even what often appear to be long-term secular trends into mere cyclical phenomena, albeit often of considerable duration.

Let's look at four examples: (1) growth stocks versus value stocks, (2) high-grade stocks versus low-priced stocks, (3) large-cap stocks versus small-cap stocks, and (4) U.S. stocks versus international stocks. The net result of all four examples (I tip my hand here) is that, in each of these key market sectors, RTM is alive and well.

Growth Stocks vs. Value Stocks

We begin with growth stocks (generally, those with above-average earnings growth, price–earnings ratios, and market–book ratios) and value stocks (lower in each case, and offering above-average yields). For this study, I've examined 60 years of growth funds (mutual funds with stated growth objectives and a record of above-average volatility) and value funds (seeking both growth *and* income, and demonstrating average to below-average volatility).*

In recent years, the conventional wisdom has been to give the value philosophy accolades for superiority over the growth philosophy. Perhaps this belief predominates because so few observers have examined the full historical record. Nonetheless, over the long run, as shown in Figure 10.3, RTM proves powerful and profound. In the early years, growth funds controlled the game and were clearly the winners from 1937 through 1968. At the end of that long era, an investment in value stocks was worth just 62 percent of an equivalent initial investment in growth stocks. Value stocks then enjoyed a huge resurgence through 1976, redressing almost precisely the entire earlier deficit. (This recent history—covering only 8 of the entire 60 years—has created the value stock mystique.) Then, growth stocks outperformed through 1980, and value stocks have pretty much dominated through 1997. (As it was to happen— RTM at work again?—growth stocks returned with a fury to preeminence in 1998.)

---

* Before published industry norms for the two groups became available in 1968, I relied on a sample of funds whose objectives, portfolios, and annual returns made this distinction clear.

FIGURE 10.3

Growth Funds vs. Value Funds (1937–1997)

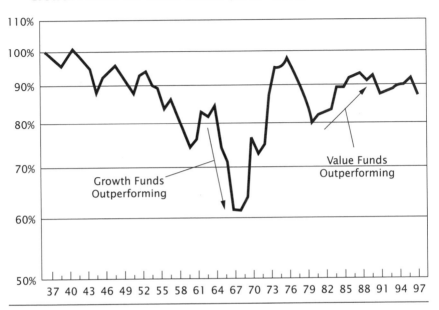

When all of these cyclical fluctuations for the full six decades were linked, the terminal investment in value stocks was equal to about nine-tenths of the investment in growth stocks. For the full 60-year period, the compound total returns were: growth, 11.7 percent; value, 11.5 percent—a tiny difference. I'd call that match a standoff—and another tribute to RTM.

High-Grade Stocks vs. Low-Priced Stocks

My second example of market sector RTM is high-grade versus low-priced stocks. This series—not much considered by investors during the past decade—has been published by Standard & Poor's Corporation on a consistent basis since 1926. As shown in Figure 10.4, the swings in market preeminence have been much briefer than with growth and value stocks. The most sustained trends have been evident during the past four decades. Low-priced stocks enjoyed a six-year feast from 1962 through 1968. It was followed by a complete reversal in favor of high-grade stocks—a six-year famine that lasted through 1974.

FIGURE 10.4

High-Grade Stocks vs. Low-Priced Stocks (1925–1997)

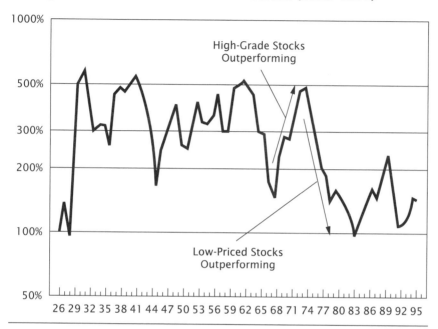

Continuing a cycle that seems vaguely to parallel the seven-year cycle of biblical prophesy, the next feast for low-priced stocks lasted for nine years, through 1983, and was followed by a seven-year famine through 1990, followed by a brief feast that appears to have ended in 1992. When all was said and done, for the full seven decades, each dollar initially invested in high-grade stocks was valued at about 1.4 times the investment in low-priced stocks—almost exactly where it was at the end of 1927, which was a truly great year for high-grade issues. Even including the distorting effect of that single opening year, high-grade stocks provided a historical return of 6.7 percent versus 6.2 percent for low-priced stocks (in both cases, excluding dividends). Nonetheless, the power of RTM is apparent in the chart.

Large-Cap Stocks vs. Small-Cap Stocks

Now to my third sector. One of the seemingly indestructible myths of investing is that stocks with small market capitalizations outpace stocks with large market capitalizations over time. Having accepted this proposition, its proponents then explain why, in terms easily understood: "Small caps carry higher risks, therefore it follows, as the night the day, that they must earn higher returns." This reasoning would seem to make consummate good sense. But, in fact, as shown in Figure 10.5, the cycles of small-cap superiority have been relatively spasmodic. From 1925 through 1964—a period of fully 39 years—small caps and large caps provided identical returns. Then, in just four years, through 1968, the small-cap return more than doubled the large-cap return. Virtually that entire margin was lost during the next five years. By 1973, small caps were about at par with large caps for nearly the full half-century. The small caps' reputation was made largely during the 1973–1983 decade. Then, perhaps inevitably, RTM struck again in a fifth cycle. Paralleling the observation of the poet Thomas Fuller in 1650, it was darkest for the large caps just before the dawn, for the sun has shone brightly upon them since 1983.

On balance, for the full period, the compound annual return on small-cap stocks was 12.7 percent, compared with 11.0 percent for large-cap

FIGURE 10.5

Large-Cap Stocks vs. Small-Cap Stocks (1925–1997)

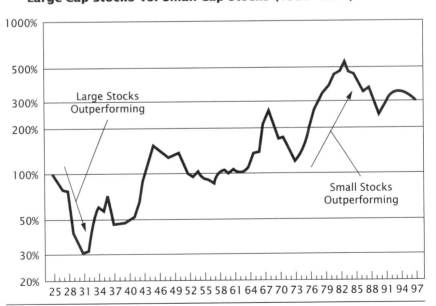

stocks. This difference resulted in a terminal value for small-cap stocks that was three times that of large-cap stocks, as shown in Figure 10.5. But, given the dominance of small caps in a single decade, I'm not sure I'd rely on it. (Certainly the truly awesome strength of large caps, in a so-so 1998 for small caps, meant it was not wise to accept uncritically the small-cap thesis.) Without the relatively brief cycle of small-cap domination in 1973–1983—only one of seven decades in the period—large caps were actually *superior*. When that period is excluded, annual returns were: large caps, 11.1 percent; small caps, 10.4 percent. In any event, the relationship between large caps and small caps, if not entirely dominated by RTM, is permeated with the force of market gravity.

U.S. Stocks vs. International Stocks

For U.S. stocks versus international stocks, no historical chronicle compares in length to those I've used for my first examples of RTM. I rely here on all the available data, covering only the past 38 years. As shown in Figure 10.6, there is profound evidence for my thesis. Here, I'll compare the

FIGURE 10.6

U.S. Stocks vs. International Stocks (1959–1997)

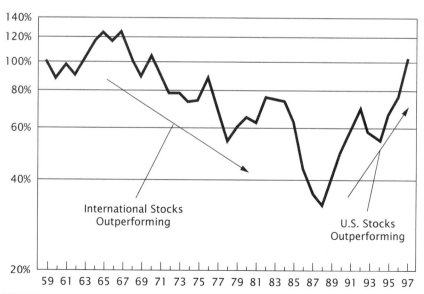

returns of the S&P 500 Index and the Morgan Stanley Capital International Europe, Australasia, Far East (EAFE) Index, expressed in dollars rather than local currency terms to reflect the experience of U.S. investors. There were frequent swings to and fro, but the ratio of cumulative value slightly favored the EAFE Index for the first 24 years (through 1984). The compound returns were: EAFE, 9.7 percent; S&P, 8.4 percent.

Then EAFE exploded, outpacing U.S. stocks by fully two times during the brief 1984–1988 cycle. During the subsequent nine years, U.S. stocks completely repaid the compliment, more than redressing that short flash of EAFE brilliance. For the full period, the compound returns on U.S. stocks and international stocks were identical: 11.5 percent. The relative value of each initial dollar invested by the investor who stayed in the United States was worth precisely the same as the dollar invested by the investor who traveled abroad. Over the long run, RTM has clearly manifested itself in global equity markets.

Back to Sir Isaac Newton

I've now illustrated the powerful force of the law of relative market gravity, although perhaps not with Sir Isaac Newton's precision. His discovery of the law of universal gravitation has been described as the high point of the scientific revolution of the seventeenth century. To be sure, the utility value of mean reversion to investors in diversified equity funds and in stock market sectors will hardly be the high point of this fading century. Indeed, Newton's third law: "Every action has an equal and opposite reaction,"* is perhaps an even better translation of what happens in financial markets. But RTM, even though it may take decades to appear, is a principle borne out by history. Intelligent investors will ignore it at their peril. I'm staking my own investment strategy on the fact that it will continue to exist.

COMMON STOCKS RETURN TO EARTH, TOO

There is a third important area of mean reversion: the long-term returns of common stocks. Unlike stock mutual funds and stock market sectors, RTM relates here to absolute, not relative, returns. For more than two

---

*For the record, Sir Isaac's equation is: Gravitational force equals the gravitational constant times the relative masses of two objects divided by the distance between them squared.

centuries, over rolling 25-year periods, the U.S. stock market has demonstrated a profound tendency to provide real (after-inflation) returns that surround a norm of about 6.7 percent. As shown in Figure 10.7, the swings around this norm are reasonably narrow, and returns are much below 4 percent in only 5 periods.

In short, real returns have ranged between roughly 4 percent and 10 percent in 93 percent of the 25-year periods—a remarkable record of consistency. RTM is alive and well in the stock market. The standard deviation of annual returns in 25-year periods—about half of an investing lifetime for most investors today—is plus or minus 2.0 percent from the norm. In fairness, in a time frame of 10 years, the standard deviation is 4.4 percent; in an investment lifetime of 50 years, it is a minuscule 1 percent. Time horizon makes a meaningful difference.

The root cause of these consistent long-term returns is fundamental: corporate dividends and corporate earnings growth. And, using data we have available from 1871 forward, we can measure the extent to which these two financial fundamentals have dictated the returns earned on

FIGURE 10.7

Rolling 25-Year Real Stock Returns

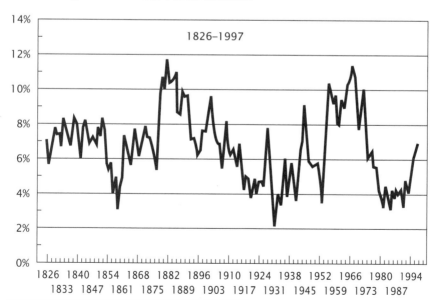

equities. The sum of real corporate earnings growth plus dividend yields since 1871, again averaged over rolling 25-year periods, produces a total *fundamental* return on stocks of 6.7 percent. This figure precisely matches the *actual* real stock market return of 6.7 percent, meaning that the role of speculation was neutral over time. This precise equality of the two returns during this 127-year period is a remarkable tribute to the long-run rationality of the financial markets.

Lord Keynes Redux

In the shorter run, the irrationality in stock returns is created by the speculative element. Stock market irrationality can be measured by the ephemeral—but critical—factor represented by the stock market's price–earnings ratio. If, following Lord Keynes, we use the term *investment* to describe the fundamental return based on earnings and dividends, we use the term *speculation* to describe this second determinant of stock prices: the price that investors will pay for each dollar of corporate earnings. If the power of fundamentals dominates market returns in the very long run, the power of speculation dominates market returns in the shorter run. Speculation is, ultimately, temporary and fickle. Over time, investors have been willing to pay an average of about $14 for each $1 of earnings. But if, in their optimism, they are willing to pay $21, stock prices will leap by 50 percent *for that reason alone.* If, in their pessimism, they are willing to pay only $7, stock prices will fall by 50 percent. The changing price of $1 of earnings creates powerful leverage indeed, *but it doesn't last forever, nor even for an investing lifetime.*

Even over periods as long as a quarter century, however, there have been variations in returns based on the esoteric force of speculation rather than on the rock foundation of investment. But they have been reasonably subdued. The combination of dividend yields and earnings growth has remained the predominant driver of return. Figure 10.8 presents the differences between the two since 1871. (It was not until then that reliable figures on earnings and dividends began to be developed.) Actual returns fell within a range of plus or minus some two percentage points of fundamental returns in 88 of the 102 periods of 25 years since 1871. I am struck by the fact that there seem to be six waves—each with roughly 15 years' duration—from the peak-to-valley (and vice versa) role of speculation. Just for fun, I've delineated these six waves—arguably, three grand RTM cycles—in Figure 10.8.

FIGURE 10.8

Actual Stock Market Real Returns vs. Fundamental Returns Rolling 25-Year Periods

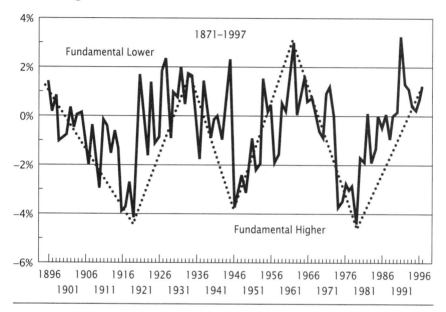

To illustrate how these differences between fundamental and actual returns have worked in the past, let's compare the role of investment and speculation in two very different climates (Table 10.1). In both examples, I rely on nominal, rather than real, stock market returns. When investors moved from pessimism to optimism, as in 1942 to 1967, a fine fundamental return of 12.8 percent was supplemented by a speculative return of 2.6 percent. This additional return represented the annual impact of the upward revaluation represented by a 95 percent increase in the price of $1 of earnings, from $9.50 to $18.10, bringing total return to 15.4 percent. On the other hand, when optimism turned into pessimism, as in 1958 to 1983, the reevaluation of $1 of earnings reduced the price of $1 of earnings by 40 percent, from $19.10 to $11.80. The annual impact of this reduction was −1.9 percent over the full 25-year period, taking the fundamental return from 9.7 percent to 7.8 percent. With $1 of earnings today selling for $27, I suppose it's fair to say that our future expectations ought to be held in check.

TABLE 10.1

Rolling 25-Year Nominal Stock Returns

	Pessimism to Optimism 1942–1967	Optimism to Pessimism 1958–1983
1. Fundamental component		
A. Dividend yield	6.0%	3.2%
B. Earnings growth	+6.8	+6.5
Total fundamental return	12.8%	9.7%
2. Speculative component	+2.6	−1.9
3. Total market return	15.4%	7.8%

My purpose in again discussing the overpowering force of fundamental factors in driving stock returns is to reinforce the fact that the economics of capitalism and competition seem somehow to have established a historic limit of 4 percent real (6 percent nominal) returns on long-term earnings growth. What has captivated the U.S. stock market today—and what has helped to drive the stock market during these glorious recent years—is the notion that earnings growth has moved to a new, distinctly higher, plateau. Indeed, during the past 15 years, real returns have averaged fully 12.6 percent—nearly double the long-term norm, and a return significantly exceeded in only nine of the 182 15-year periods since 1816—and even then not by very much. Even if the coming decade produces only a 3 percent real return, the quarter-century return would be 8.6 percent, still well above the long-term norm of 6.7 percent. But the remarkable returns earned on stocks since 1982 have raised important questions about whether the old shackles of fundamental returns have been ripped away, freeing America to enter a new era of corporate profitability. The central question of the day is: Are stocks reverting to a new, higher mean?

A New, Higher Mean?

In mid-1997, as the bull market roared to new heights, the respected firm of Morgan Stanley Dean Witter headlined its investment strategy bulletin, "A New, Higher Mean to Revert To?"[1] The bulletin began by saying, "as the fat returns from U.S. equities keep piling up, you have to wonder if in this brave new world, the historical returns of 6 percent to 7 percent real are obsolete, and have to be revised upward." It then took the middle ground. "This golden age for equities won't last forever . . . but the mean for equities is probably somewhat higher than in the past, and famine will follow feast as it always has." The bulletin concluded that the new mean market return would be "7 percent to 8 percent real, but below the 10 percent today's bulls talk about. The real returns of around 12 percent generated for a decade now are simply not sustainable. Over time, returns will have to gravitate back toward the new mean."

If—*if*—a real return of 7 percent to 8 percent is in fact the new mean, as the strategy bulletin seemed to imply, stocks would then have been overvalued (i.e., overpriced relative to the fundamentals) by about 20 percent. In such an environment of revaluation, a protracted period with real stock returns in the 3 percent to 5 percent range would be expected. At that level, stocks would face serious competition from bonds. Bonds, now with nominal yields of about 5¼ percent, should provide real returns of about 3½ percent to 4 percent on average over the coming decade, at considerably lower risk.

Given the hazardous nature of market forecasting, however, and the powerful odds against being right *twice* (selling at or near the highs, and buying back at or near the lows, a winning strategy of extraordinary unlikelihood), the possibility—even the probability—of inferior risk-adjusted returns on stocks should prompt, not aggressive investment actions, but thoughtful consideration about investment goals.

INVESTING TO COPE WITH THE FORCE OF GRAVITY

The academic aspects of RTM—what the historical statistics tell us—suggest that mean reversion is alive and well. It has been manifested in almost every aspect of investing: in shaping relative returns for individual mutual funds; in shaping the relative performance of diverse stock market sectors; and in determining the absolute levels of long-term stock returns, albeit perhaps at a prospective level that may be somewhat higher than in the past. If, as an academic matter, you accept this thesis, what actions does it imply for the wholly pragmatic business of investing? How can this history help to ensure that you and your family will have an optimal opportunity to accumulate capital?

As we saw in Chapter 3, much comfort can be found in an appropriate asset allocation mix. Today's financial markets seem to carry a higher-than-normal risk component, but I do not believe that investors should abandon equities. In a retirement plan, for example, I would suggest balancing the potential risks and returns by centering on a 70 percent equity/30 percent bond program. I'd shade equities higher (up to 90/10) for those at the beginning of their accumulation programs, provided that they have a healthy appetite for returns, a strong stomach for risks, and an extended time (15 to 40 years) before retirement. For anyone who is making regular investments that are modest relative to the capital already salted away, and who has more conservative instincts and a shorter time horizon (1 to 15 years), I'd shade equities lower—perhaps all the way down to 35/65. *No one knows what future returns the financial markets will provide.* A balanced approach has been validated over centuries, not because it provided the highest returns (it clearly didn't), but because it achieved solid long-term returns without excessive short-term risks—hardly an unacceptable outcome.

With the stage thus set, however roughly, for future market returns, what does RTM suggest about equity investment strategy? Since RTM prevails among all market sectors such as growth stocks and value stocks, large-cap stocks and small-cap stocks, and U.S. stocks and international stocks, most investors should own equity funds that represent a broad cross-section of the U.S. stock market, in which large-cap stocks are the predominant component. Investors who believe they can garner a performance edge by selecting (or even overweighting) funds with different investment styles and strategies should be aware of the risks involved in doing so. For those who believe that the clear lessons of history are pointing us in the wrong direction (always a risky bet), an equally risky bet remains: Determining which of these countervailing segments will in fact prove to be superior in the years to come. If, for example, large-cap and small-cap stocks do not revert to the market mean over the next 10 to 20 years, an investor has to guess which of the two is more likely to provide superior returns. It is for this reason that I prefer, on both theoretical and practical grounds, index funds that track the total U.S. stock market. With their extraordinarily broad diversification, over a wide-ranging spectrum of large-, mid-, and small-cap stocks alike, these funds are the ultimate response to the power of RTM in the stock market.

A decision to own an all-stock market index fund also solves the problem of fund selection. Why fly in the face of historical evidence by trying to select individual mutual funds in the hope of picking a big winner? Given the power of mean reversion in the returns of individual mutual funds, an index fund provides the most reliable participation in the future returns of equities as a group. Surely it has proved its worth in the past.

Notwithstanding my preference for the total market fund, a Standard & Poor's 500 Index fund is by no means an unacceptable choice. This large-cap index fund carries a 75 percent weight in the U.S. stock market, and cannot diverge widely from the total market, even in short-term periods. RTM suggests that its long-run returns will closely parallel those of the total market. Given low costs, either index fund should provide investors with the best possible opportunity to earn returns approaching 100 percent of the market return.

THE CROWN JEWELS

In this modern era of investing, the descriptive phrase "the crown jewels"—the family's most valuable asset—has taken on new meaning. Investors aspire to something far more important than diamonds, rubies, and sapphires. They aspire to accumulate sufficient capital to reach their personal financial goals. A comfortable and independent retirement is a major goal for most investors. When the time for retirement comes to the breadwinner, the family's most valuable asset—its crown jewel—will almost certainly be the capital value of the retirement plan. Tax-deferred plans are especially valuable jewels because tax deferral, combined with low-cost investing, is the most valuable weapon in the long-term investor's arsenal. Limited only by the provisions of the Internal Revenue Code, you should put every penny you can spare into your IRA or your 401(k) or 403(b) thrift plan.

An investment program that carries the theoretical armor of RTM, the mathematical armor of regular investing, and the protective armor of a balanced strategy, combined with the powerful weaponry of compound interest, deferred taxes, and low cost, would be applauded by Sir Isaac Newton. Even as the proverbial apple drops to the ground, so too do high-performing mutual funds and surging sectors of the stock market. The returns achieved in the most productive eras of the stock market itself, given enough time, have dropped to normal levels. Newton's law of gravity, applied to the manifold mean reversion of returns in the financial markets, should also help you to think through and develop an intelligent financial plan and to implement it with simplicity and common sense, the better to accumulate a retirement fund of generous proportions. Powerful evidence of reversion to the mean in the financial markets is found not only in academic studies, but in pragmatic experience. As you accumulate capital, be sure to use the concept to your benefit.

CHAPTER

ON INVESTMENT RELATIVISM

HAPPINESS OR MISERY?

*M*ore than at any time in the history of the financial markets (or so it would seem), the quest for investment success has come to center on relative performance over the short term. We have entered what we might call "The Age of Investment Relativism." All eyes seem focused on a comparison that has become as much a part of investors' lives as the daily fluctuations in the stock market: "How did my equity portfolio perform relative to the Standard & Poor's 500 Composite Stock Price Index?" Our happiness or misery seems to depend on how we answer that question.

Some 150 years ago, the impecunious and mercurial Mr. Micawber (in Charles Dickens's *David Copperfield*) bestowed happiness or misery according to the following formula: "Annual income, twenty pounds, annual expenditures nineteen six, result happiness. Annual income, twenty pounds, annual expenditures twenty pounds six, result misery."

Too many mutual fund portfolio managers and shareholders now seem to operate in a system representing a new form of Micawber's formula: Market return, 17.8 percent, my return, 18.3; result happiness. Market return, 17.8 percent, my return, 13.2; result misery.

That last set of returns, in fact, describes the shortfall of the average domestic equity mutual fund compared to the stock market (as measured by the S&P 500 Index) over the past 15 years: 17.8 percent versus 13.2

percent. The 4.6 percentage point gap suggests why most equity fund managers are likely to be feeling considerable professional misery—albeit, perversely, along with stunning personal financial gain—as the 1990s end. While, given the great bull market, most fund investors have hardly felt much financial misery, it seems only a matter of time until they recognize not what was, but what might have been.

If the question were simply "Did the professional investment advisers outpace the market over the past 15 years?" the answer is clear. Most advisers did *not.* Indeed, as a matter of basic mathematics and elementary logic, most advisers *cannot* outpace the market over the long run. They ought to disclose, candidly and forthrightly (indeed passionately) to shareholders and prospective investors alike, not only the absolute rates of return they have achieved—in individual years and over the long term—but how those returns compared to the returns that would have been achieved by an *appropriate* benchmark standard accepted by manager and investor alike as a prime measure of success over the long pull. (While the Securities and Exchange Commission has required this type of comparative disclosure in fund investment reports since 1994, it is more often than not deeply buried in the text.)

A Powerful Bogey

But, while the change is almost never disclosed to investors, mutual fund managers seem to have decided to shift from a long-term to a short-term focus. Indeed, a powerful focus on *quarterly* relative performance has developed, fostered by reporting in the media, by performance-sensitive institutional investors, and by individual investors seeking the latest leaders in short-term fund performance. Advisers have responded as you would expect. Performance is almost invariably based on a single standard—an omnipresent "bogey" (a Scottish word meaning "goblin," and few advisers regard it in kinder terms): the redoubtable S&P 500 Composite Stock Price Index.* Curiously, we often see weekly and even daily comparisons after a significant market *drop*, but rarely after a sharp rally. The reason: Market indexes are, by definition, 100 percent invested at all times, and

---

* I must confess to being amused by the irony that the "bogle" was the earliest known goblin, already part of Scottish literature in 1500. Some years ago, I was called "Beta Bogle, the data devil." Given my role in forming the first index mutual fund, it is entirely possible that active managers place me in the goblin category.

managers await (so far, to no avail) confirmation that their cash reserves will offer significant protection in declining markets. While the 30-stock Dow Jones Industrial Average remains our basic measure of *daily* market swings, the market-value-weighted S&P 500 is used almost invariably in making relative return comparisons over longer periods.

Today, institutional pension officers scowl over their bifocals as they review the quarterly performance comparisons in regularly scheduled meetings with their investment advisers. Individual investors receive the data each quarter, either in real time on their computers, or later (shocking!) in the next morning's newspaper. Such short-term focus can be only counterproductive.

These rat-a-tat volleys of comparative information are of relatively recent vintage. Indeed, mutual fund sponsors were prohibited by the Statement of Policy of the National Association of Securities Dealers (NASD) from publishing "total returns"—even *without* making comparisons—from 1950 through 1965. But, the total-returns teetotalers of the old days became the social drinkers of the early 1970s. It may not be stretching things to say that, by the early 1990s, they were on the verge of becoming alcoholics.

Does it really matter whether today's omnipresent S&P comparisons have been fomented by the information overload in this miraculous age of communications technology? Or by the self-styled sophistication of institutional clients, who seem to have vested interests in frequently changing advisers? Or by the appetite of mutual fund investors for fund winners over the short term? Or by the overly aggressive marketing of funds? Whatever the reason, relative investment performance—investment relativism, if you will—is the order of the day.

Managers should still be held to a performance standard, but two problems must be recognized: managers are too often held to a single standard, irrespective of investors' objectives, and the measurements, far from being appropriately based on long-term investment returns, are overwhelmingly dominated by extremely short periods. We might well ask: To what avail?

Despite the overpowering performance success of the S&P 500 during the past five years—and therefore the improved returns achieved by many closet index funds—large-cap trees do not grow to the sky, and some retribution may lie ahead. (Investors who believe that large-cap stocks are somehow destined for permanent ascendancy, of course, would fare better in a low-cost *true* S&P 500 Index fund.) But in the long run, investors will not be well served when fund managers, caught up in the perception that beating the market each quarter is happiness and losing is misery, use the S&P 500 Index as the mandatory measuring stick for their own portfolios. All too often, the script reads: "S&P technology stocks, 14 percent of the value of the index, 21 percent of my portfolio; GE, 3 percent of the S&P, 1.2 percent of my portfolio," and so on. The manager then attempts to rectify such mismatches. In this practice, clearly, the benchmark supplants judgment. Portfolio managers invest not on the basis of analysis and conviction, but in relation to a market standard, gingerly shading the weights of their portfolio holdings somewhat higher or lower than those of the benchmark. In the absence of genuine managerial judgment, the implicit questions quickly follow: "Is my 'bet' [as it is usually described] the right one? Or should I align my portfolio more closely to the Index?" A lot of casino capitalism, by managers and investors alike, is being labeled as *investing*, and *betting*—even betting not to lose—may be the best word to characterize a strategy of overreliance on the composition of an unmanaged and relatively unchanging market index.

THE RISE OF CLOSET INDEXING

Taken to extremes, the process seems to work something like this: "I think Coca-Cola stock is grotesquely overvalued. But, in case it keeps going up, I'm going to buy a 1.5 percent portfolio position for protection. Since that's less than Coca-Cola's 2.0 percent weight in the S&P 500 Index, I'll have a good defensive position versus the Index when Coca-Cola takes the tumble it so richly deserves."

Isn't that philosophy the antithesis of professional investment management? Yet hasn't it become the formula followed by nervous portfolio managers anxious to hold their jobs? Isn't it the result of the marketing department's holding sway over the investment department? In each case, my finding would be: Guilty as charged.

Such a closet indexing strategy is, in my view, more pervasive than most investors realize. But, whether it permeates a portfolio or takes place at the margin, I've never seen it disclosed in a fund's prospectus. (The handful of quantitative funds with a specific goal of adding incremental returns to a specific market index, however, ordinarily disclose their strategy.) In fairness, when it applies, it applies primarily to the managers of funds investing in large capitalization stocks. Closet indexing is a relatively simple process when the 10 largest stocks in the S&P 500 Index represent nearly 20 percent of the Index. Even if it creeps into the small-cap side of the business, closet indexing seems unlikely to permeate it. In the Russell 2500 Small Cap Index, the largest 10 stocks constitute 2.4 percent. But the fact is that large-cap stocks dominate the financial markets, with the 500 large-cap stocks constituting the S&P 500 Index accounting for some 75 percent of the total value of all U.S. stocks. Large-cap-dominated strategies account for roughly three-fourths of the assets of all equity mutual funds, and an even higher proportion of institutional assets.

Closet indexing may well be having an impact on stock returns. I never ascribe causality to any of the myriad factors that affect the price of a stock, but it seems more than coincidence that, from 1996 through June 1998, the largest gains among the blue-chip stocks whose capitalizations dominated the market came to those stocks in which mutual funds held the *smallest* relative positions. The five largest stocks in the S&P 500 Index that were most *underowned* by mutual funds returned almost 50 percent annually, compared to an average gain of roughly 24 percent for the remaining 495 stocks. In other words, the Lucents and Microsofts—so large that even the enormous mutual fund industry owns just a modest percentage of their equity—have led the market forward.

Could it be that active managers, in their passion to compete with the passive S&P 500 Index, are primarily responsible for driving up the price of the underowned large stocks, giving it, over the past three years, when it surpassed 95 percent of equity funds, the most formidable record of outpacing active fund managers in history? Are managers forcing their portfolios to become more Indexlike, so as to avoid serious shortfalls in the quarterly comparison sweepstakes? And, if so, are managers sowing the seeds of their own performance inferiority today? Stranger things have happened.

The overarching goal of this era of investment relativism seems to be the avoidance of inferior short-term returns relative to the S&P 500, rather than the achievement of superior absolute long-term returns. If this industry ever had a chance to produce another Peter Lynch, or perhaps the next Warren Buffett, that chance is disappearing fast. Since quantitative science entered the business of mutual fund performance in the mid-1980s, relativism has become the basis of a comprehensive performance measurement system. *Beta* (risk, measured by the fund's price volatility relative to the S&P 500 Index) and *alpha* (the fund's rate of return, adjusted for risk, relative to the Index) have entered our lexicon. We also have the Sharpe Ratio, which measures a fund's excess return over a Treasury bill relative to its

"IF IT LOOKS LIKE A DUCK . . ."

Given the focus on measuring large-cap funds, in particular, against the Standard & Poor's 500 Index, many large funds have clearly become closet index funds, emulating the Index, albeit not so closely as to abandon all hope of surpassing it. Just when a *casual focus* on the weightings of portfolio holdings in industry groups and individual stocks relative to the S&P 500 Index becomes an *obsession*, and then crosses the line to become a firm (if undisclosed) *policy*, will rarely be clear. But there are several pieces of evidence for investors to consider in evaluating whether a fund has become a closet index fund. (Each of them can easily be found in *Morningstar Mutual Funds*.)

1. *Asset size.* When large funds grow very large, they inevitably become less flexible in their policies, concentrating their portfolios on stocks with large capitalizations.

2. *Portfolio composition.* Funds with 80 percent or more invested in large-cap stocks, similarly weighted to the industry groups in the Index.

3. *Individual portfolio holdings.* Funds with, say, more than 15 of their 25 largest holdings among the 25 largest stocks in the Index.

4. *Correlation.* An R^2 statistic of 0.95 or more, meaning essentially that 95 percent of the fund's return has been determined by the return of the Index.

The managements of the funds that become—to all intents and purposes—closet index funds, of course, vigorously deny that such is the case. An executive for one huge fund company put it this way: "It's okay for a manager not to own Microsoft [now the largest stock in the 500 Index] but I don't want someone doing that inadvertently or unconsciously." Read: "If the stock is going up, that manager had better have a darn good reason for not owning it." Another form of denial is "Less than half of our stocks are in the Index," without acknowledging that 80 percent of the *value* of its portfolio is. Self-serving denials by management may be less useful than the wisdom of the old saw: "If it looks like a duck, and it walks like a duck, and it quacks like a duck, it *is* a duck." Or at least an odds-on candidate to be a duck.

risk (standard deviation)—not to be confused with the Selection Sharpe Ratio, an information ratio that measures excess return over a benchmark standard—conventionally, of course, our devilish friend, the S&P 500 Index. And these formulas, once the exclusive domain of professionals, are even discussed by individual investors at coffee breaks and cocktail parties. I do not believe that this focus on simplistic mathematical precision is a healthy state of being for managers, nor for their clients, nor for the market itself. Yet there is no end in sight—no *omega* on the horizon to the spread of closet indexing strategies. In fact, as industry assets grow, their growth is almost sure to accelerate.

THE INDEX FUND: VILLAIN OF THE PIECE?

The most important reason for the defensive reaction of fund managers to index comparisons and the rise of closet indexing is the index fund itself. The S&P 500 *Index* is a mean adversary, but the *index fund* is the real villain of the piece. Once upon a time, managers defended themselves by using a simple retort: "Yeah, but who can buy the market?" Later, the more sophisticated response was: "Yeah, but the index is theoretical, and it would cost a lot to buy, so you wouldn't be able to nearly match the index." By making it possible for even the smallest of investors to buy the market, low-cost index funds have given the lie to these foolish make-weight arguments. But even though I founded the first index mutual fund way back in 1975 (perhaps the bogle goblin really *was* the data devil), index funds did not begin to catch the fancy of investors and become a formidable competitor for their assets until the late 1990s.

To the extent that it *is* becoming the investment of choice, the index fund is taking its rightful place within the mutual fund industry. It is the odds-on favorite to outpace three of every four managers. For the market as a whole, low-cost investing in a highly diversified portfolio of stocks—a loose but accurate description of an index fund—ineluctably beats investing in a diversified portfolio of high-cost funds over the long run. Admittedly, the S&P 500 Index has had a particularly good run over the past 15 years. But the S&P 500 stocks also make up 75 percent of the total market. In the long run, their aggregate return *should* parallel the total market. An index fund targeted on the Wilshire 5000 Index, of course, will match the market over the long term and the short term alike. In any event, the index fund marketplace, now dominated by S&P 500 strategies, is increasingly moving in the direction of all-market indexing. Over time, this broader strategy may well become the principal choice for institutional indexers and fund indexers alike.

The time must also come when investors, analysts, and the media use indexes from market segments as the standards for funds with particular investment styles (i.e., large-cap value, small-cap growth, and so on). As I pointed out in Chapter 6, the advantages of an index strategy are equally apparent in all market-cap categories and in all investment styles. As a result, market-segment index funds are likely to take their proper place in the marketplace, and indexing in all its forms should continue to gain even greater acceptance by investors.

WE'RE ALL QUANTS NOW

There is more bad news for fund managers. Another form of indexlike competition—quantitative investing—is emerging, and I'm confident that it too will take its place in the field. The widespread use of quantitative techniques and computers to screen and value individual stocks and stock groups in the traditional security-analyst-based management process has spread to what is called quantitative investing, computer-driven investment policies that rely rigidly and exclusively on mathematical formulas to set strategy or to select stocks for investment portfolios. ("We're all quants now.") Current industry estimates place the assets managed by quants at $100 billion, and the growth rate has been strong.

Some of these quantitative strategies might fairly be described as the ultimate forms of investment relativism. But they must not be confused with closet indexing. With fully disclosed policies and strategies, they are hardly hidden in a closet. Their strategies are rigorous and controlled, not random and intuitive, and their costs are often well below conventional norms. It's far less costly to run a computer program than to employ a large portfolio research and management staff.

Through a strategy typically known as enhanced indexing, such funds seek explicitly to outpace a particular market index, all the while attempting to severely limit variations from the index return (so-called "tracking error"). Most use sophisticated computer models to select a diversified portfolio of stocks whose characteristics are closely aligned with the target index in such areas as industry sectors, and market characteristics in such areas as price–earnings and market-to-book ratios. The first mutual fund in this category, begun in 1986 and operated at a cost far below industry norms, has bettered the index itself, but only slightly. The margin it achieved, however, was sufficient to give it a meaningful edge over an index fund (by reason of its costs, low as they were) in long-term accumulation. The overall evidence of success in such disciplined and/or sector-neutral strategies, as they are known, is quite mixed, but my guess is that these strategies will ultimately prove attractive to investors who realize the value of indexing but can't quite enter an index fund and abandon all hope that they can identify in advance active managers who will outperform the index results. Provided that quantitative funds become available at costs competitive with those of index funds—and succeed in providing extra returns—enhanced indexing may also represent an important challenge to the status quo.

MEASURING MANAGERS—WHERE DOES YOUR MANAGER STAND?

Faced with the new competition from index and quantitative funds, how should traditional managers respond, and what issues should shareholders consider? If closet indexing is a wrong or even a counterproductive response—as I believe it is—what is the right response? First, a given: Advisers should freely acknowledge to investors that they should be expected to outpace an agreed-on market performance standard *over the long run*, and that they will strive to do just that. What else is an adviser *supposed* to do? How else can we measure whether the economic value being created is sufficient to justify the cost of retaining the adviser in the first place? The all-embracing standard need not be—*it should not be*—the S&P 500 Index, although it obviously would seem to be for large-cap funds that are a blend of growth stocks *and* value stocks. For managers who purport to have open charters to invest wherever they wish, broader all-market indexes seem most appropriate. They should no longer be virtually ignored.

Other index styles are appropriate standards for other types of funds. Indexes measuring returns for each style/market-cap "box" will also become part of our world. It is simply unrealistic for small-cap or mid-cap managers to replicate (that is, to parallel) the long-term record of an all-market index. Their performance should be measured against the market segment(s) in which they choose to participate. Weighted indexes combining appropriate levels of large-cap and small-cap stocks, value and growth stocks, and international stocks surely make sense for funds that define their investment policies in these terms. Blame the fund *investor* if he or she selects a fund with a small-cap strategy that fails to outpace the return

of the total market over the long term, even though it outperforms the
small-cap universe. But blame the fund *manager* if its small-cap fund fails
to outpace the small-cap universe, even if its long-term return surpasses
the return of the total market.

Both investors and managers should consider the role of bonds and
cash reserves in the asset mix of the target index. Stock indexes (and index
funds), to state the obvious, hold neither. A balanced fund should be measured against a balanced mix of stocks, bonds, and reserves. And it would
not necessarily be foolish for an adviser to an equity fund that, in order to
moderate risk, holds a fairly consistent 5 percent to 15 percent position in
cash reserves to use a similarly adjusted stock/reserve benchmark.

It is important for investors to understand that it is next to impossible
to market-time a changing cash reserve position. The mutual fund industry, in fact, tends to hold reserves in a thoroughly counterproductive fashion, with large reserves at market lows and small reserves at market highs.
(Paradoxically, some market timers use fund cash reserve positions as a
timing indicator; they believe it is a reliably *contrary* indicator.) Most important of all, given a positive stock market over time, investors must
understand that whether a fund has a steady reserve position or a varied
one, they will pay a commensurate price in the rate of return they earn. To
be sure, the volatility of the fund may be marginally reduced. But investors must understand, as I have noted, that over the long run *a percentage point increase in volatility is meaningless; a percentage point increase in return
is priceless.* The sharp contrast between those two powerful, and I think
virtually unarguable, axioms should give advisers and investors ample food
for thought.

"If You Can't Beat 'Em, Join 'Em"

Faced with the competition of index investing and quantitative investing
in this age of investment relativism, too many managers are responding in
the most ineffective manner possible: closet indexing. *But shaping an inchoate and undisclosed policy around the structure of an index is, ultimately, managerial suicide.* It is the ultimate concession to the unarguable economic
value of a low-cost, passively managed index fund over a high-cost, actively
managed traditional fund. That this policy is undisclosed, or even denied,
is not its primary failing, however. The problem is simply that the more a
fund's fees and expenses exceed index fund levels (say, 0.20 percent per
year for the low-cost index funds) and its portfolio turnover surpasses
nominal levels, the more likely its attempt to emulate the index will result

in failure. (Low expenses, low turnover, and a fully invested participation in equities are the hallmarks of index fund excellence.) In short, today's *chance of victory*, as small as it demonstrably is for active managers, will become tomorrow's *certainty of defeat* if managers offer tacit index funds with high fees, high portfolio turnover, and even a modest position in cash reserves. And it is mutual fund shareholders who will pay the price.

Relativism suggests that managers are becoming more *similar* to the enemy: "If you can't beat 'em, join 'em." But, in the long term, being *different* gives an individual manager at least a fighting chance to win the battle for extra market return. Holding to a clearly differentiated strategy—and keeping a tight lid on fees and other costs—to cope with the realities of index competition is better than just standing there and hoping, as Mr. Micawber did, that "something will turn up."

Fortunately, not all fund managers subscribe to the new relativism. Indeed, some of the better mutual fund managers find it repugnant. A recent article in *Money* magazine suggests that investment relativism is caused by "aggressive marketing executives who see short-term numbers as the best way to attract new shareholders."[1] One top portfolio strategist says: "That's the marketing side of the business talking, not someone with a fiduciary duty." Another portfolio manager asserts: "Relative investing is ridiculous." Still another routinely consults what he describes as his Eleventh Commandment: "Thou shalt not do relative investing." Warns yet another: "Relativity worked well for Einstein, but it has no place in investing."

Mutual fund managers who elect to be different (I wish there were more of them) need to make it absolutely clear to shareholders that their returns will not closely track the quarterly returns, nor even the annual returns, of a market index. They should make it equally clear that their expectation is to outpace the market *over the long run* (or alternatively, that they don't expect to outpace it, and why they don't, which would be an interesting statement indeed). Today's pervasive short-term comparisons are merely noise—a discordant element that ill serves managers and investors alike. In this context, I borrow a phrase from William Shakespeare to describe the short-term noise in the market: "A tale told by an idiot, full of sound and fury, signifying nothing."

Relativism is the triumph of process over judgment. I believe that it is possible for some managers to apply judgment born of wisdom and experience in the selection of a stock portfolio that will outpace the market over time, without assuming undue risk. Those managers will be extraordinarily difficult to identify in advance, but investors have a fighting chance to win if they seek experienced professionals with individuality, training, experience, savvy, determination, contrarianism (or sheer iconoclasm), and a capacity for hard work. The Puritan Ethic is not all bad! Importantly, these winning managers will limit the assets of the funds they manage, relative to the market capitalizations of the asset classes in which they utilize their expertise, and suppress their proclivity to actively trade the portfolio rather than to analyze, buy, and hold stocks for the long term.

Some successful managers, rather than being concerned with short-term relative risks, will run fully invested equity positions with relatively low portfolio turnover, in order to capitalize on the fundamental long-term opportunities offered by investing in carefully selected equities. Rather than slavishly relying on short-term standards, others will succeed simply by investing according to the courage of their convictions and holding cash reserves when they judge market risk as excessive. Both groups will manage their funds at reasonable costs, allocating their fee revenues toward human talent and investment productivity, not marketing profligacy designed, not to improve investment returns for fund shareholders but to advance the management company's own profitability. To be successful in an environment where indexing, and perhaps quantitative, strategies will become increasingly pervasive—and fully competitive—the successful mutual fund investment manager must serve the shareholder's interest—first, last, and solely.

Dickens Returns

In another Charles Dickens novel, *A Tale of Two Cities*, these famous words come first: "It was the best of times. It was the worst of times." For the past 16 years, we have witnessed the best of times for the stock market: a bull market of unprecedented magnitude, creating happiness and wealth beyond measure for both fund managers and fund investors. But it also could be seen as the worst of times (though it is hardly perceived that way yet) for fund owners, who will surely be filled with misery when they realize what might have been—the wealth that might have been created for them if their funds had generated returns approaching, or even exceeding, the returns generated by the stock market itself. The record of the age that has brought investment relativism to the fore and left common sense in the dust has been less than a ringing tribute to the implied promise of professional managers to their shareholder-clients: to provide superior long-run returns.

CHAPTER

ON ASSET SIZE
Nothing Fails Like Success

*I*n the short span of two decades, mutual funds have grown from a mom-and-pop cottage industry to a financial behemoth. The great American mutual fund boom has multiplied equity fund assets fully 82 times, from $34 billion 20 years ago to $2.8 trillion presently. The old saying, "Nothing succeeds like success," surely describes the industry today. As the great 16-year bull market has soared, investors have flocked to mutual funds in numbers not even dreamed of two decades ago.

But there is a contrary expression: "Nothing *fails* like success." The massive asset size and transaction volume of mutual funds (by portfolio managers and shareholders alike) have created serious problems, along with an important set of limitations for the industry. If small is beautiful, mutual funds are not as pretty as they once were.

The industry today differs not just in degree but in kind from what it was as recently as a decade ago. As a result, the past is unlikely to be prologue. The way we look at equity mutual funds must change, to reflect today's realities and those that we will continue to face in the years ahead. The history of mutual fund performance relative to the market is not likely to be very relevant to how mutual funds perform in the future. Nonetheless, despite having had the opportunity to outpace the market in an earlier era, mutual funds failed to do so by a wide margin.

Isn't Bigger Better?

Mutual funds—now holding $2.5 trillion of U.S. equity securities—control more than 21 percent of corporate America. At the start of 1982, just before the great bull market began, when the total value of U.S. equities was $1.3 trillion, fund holdings totaled $40 billion, or just 2.8 percent of the total. (See Figure 12.1.) This extraordinary eightfold increase in percentage ownership, so rarely noted, has important implications. And the control continues to grow. By the century's end, one of every four shares of stock—or four of every ten shares, if we include shares held in other investment accounts run by mutual fund managers—may well be effectively controlled by mutual funds.

In 1982, mutual funds constituted largely a stand-alone industry that was focused almost entirely on its own business. Few were units of financial conglomerates that also provided asset management services directly to individuals and institutions. Today, only three of the 25 largest fund complexes provide their services solely to mutual funds. The conglomeration of fund complexes with one another, and with banks, trust companies, insurance companies, and brokerage firms (to say nothing of railroads, glass makers, and airlines), national and international alike, has reached epic proportions.

FIGURE 12.1

Fund Manager Ownership of U.S. Stocks

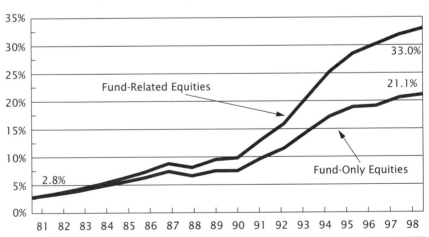

As a result, the ownership of equity securities by mutual funds alone severely understates, by fully *one-third*, the importance of the investment power and impact of the firms that manage funds. These firms also manage separate investment accounts for institutional clients and wealthy individuals. Their value, currently estimated at $1.5 trillion, brings the total ownership of stocks by accounts managed by mutual fund advisers to some $4 trillion, or some 33 percent of the $12 trillion market capitalization of U.S. equities. Such a concentration of ownership—without parallel in American financial history—continues to grow apace.

But that ownership, in a sense, is not the most important issue. Given the vigorous, highly active investment strategies adopted by most mutual funds—annual portfolio turnover in equity funds has soared to nearly 90 percent—as much as half or more of all U.S. stock transaction activity is accounted for by this relatively small group of managing institutions. It is not ridiculous to assert that they *are* the market.

What are the implications of that situation? Let's begin by focusing on mutual fund ownership of individual securities. Figure 12.2 shows fund holdings of the 10 stocks with the largest U.S. market capitalization. Note the curiously wide range of holdings: less than 5 percent of Coca-Cola; some 6 percent to 10 percent in Exxon, General Electric, Microsoft, and Intel; nearly 19 percent of Merck. Compare these to the overall average share ownership of 21 percent of all stocks owned by the industry. These

FIGURE 12.2

Fund Ownership of the Ten Largest Stocks*

	Held by Mutual Funds
General Electric	9.8%
Microsoft	9.3
Coca-Cola	4.5
Exxon	6.5
Merck	18.8
Pfizer	12.6
Wal-Mart	12.7
Intel	9.4
Procter & Gamble	8.3
Bristol-Myers Squibb	16.0

*As of June 30, 1998.

high-performing—and obviously underowned—stocks led the way in the 1996–1998 bull market, and helped drive the index fund boom.

Since index funds and index pools held 8.0 percent of the total value of the Standard & Poor's 500 Stock Index, it follows that they owned 8.0 percent of the shares of *each one* of the large stocks in the Index. (Their portfolios contain an equal percentage of the shares of each stock.) So the prices of these giant issues may have been given some of their upward momentum, not by the demand of index funds, but by the demand created by *active* managers who were fearful of their underweightings and anxious to lose no further ground to the spectacular index fund returns.

In its ownership strategy, then, the fund industry has a substantial relative bias against the equities with the largest market capitalizations, and in favor of midcap and small-cap shares. Figure 12.3 shows that, in this pattern of ownership, participation rises as capitalization levels decline. Compared to a "par" of about 21 percent—their share of all U.S. stocks—fund ownership equals 15 percent of the 100 stocks with market capitalizations over $23 billion. This percentage grows uniformly as capitalization size shrinks, to 21 percent of the 300–600th largest stocks, to 36 percent of the 100 stocks ranked 901 to 1,000 in size, falling then to 21 percent of the remaining 6,300 stocks with capitalization of less than $500 million. This reversal of trend for very small stocks presumably relates to their limited liquidity.

FIGURE 12.3

Fund Ownership by Market Capitalization

Equities Grouped by Size	Equity Fund Holdings*
1–100	14.8%
101–200	18.7
201–300	20.2
301–400	20.9
401–500	21.0
501–600	21.7
601–700	23.6
701–800	25.4
801–900	29.2
901–1000	35.7
1001–7300	21.6

*As of June 30, 1998.

One implication of the industry's giant size is that these dominant ownership percentages represent the "big stick" now carried by mutual funds (and their associated asset pools) in corporate governance. The funds so far have followed President Theodore Roosevelt's advice to speak softly when carrying a "big stick," but their institutional brethren in the state and local government pension fund arena have shown no similar restraint. Nonetheless, it is fair to say that the latent power of fund ownership, added to the dynamic power represented by the ownership of the huge state and local asset pools, has helped bring about the truly revolutionary focus on creating shareholder economic value that has helped awaken corporate America to the responsibilities it owes its owners. In this somewhat perverse sense, funds can be said to have helped create the great boom in earnings that U.S. corporations, by focusing intently on shareholder value, have enjoyed in recent years.

Another implication of the funds' giant size is that mutual fund shareholders have played an increasingly powerful role in shaping stock market returns. The increase of fund ownership from less than 3 percent to 21 percent of U.S. stocks in 16 years has meant that fund shareholders themselves have fueled the demand for stocks, which has helped drive stocks upward. But these same fund shareholders have also created new risks to market liquidity. To the extent that they demonstrate a herd instinct, shareholders could endanger the very liquidity that mutual funds pledge to offer. The fact that this obvious and implicit risk has so far manifested itself only by adding to the demand for stocks should not blind us to the reality that any significant run of fund redemptions would create downward pressure, perhaps of major dimension.

SIZE AND FUND INVESTMENT RETURNS

But the final implication of the dominant fund ownership of stocks—fund performance relative to the market—is my main focus here. I believe that the industry's giant size is apt to impede—indeed eliminate—any potential that mutual funds as a group might otherwise have had to offer superior returns. Paradoxically, if the growth of mutual funds, by helping to add value in the corporate world, has had a positive impact on stock returns, it has also had a negative impact on the value that the fund industry can add for its own shareholders. Simply put, it is at least possible to imagine that a mutual fund subset owning less than 3 percent of the stock market could outpace the market itself, but it is virtually inconceivable that a fund subset owning 21 percent could do so. And to suggest that a subset of 33 percent (including funds and their associated asset pools), and doing one-half of all stock transactions at that, could turn the trick would tax one's credulity. In an efficient market, an aggregation of one-third of all investment assets does not outpace the other two-thirds. It is simply too much to expect.

In 1975, I gave the Vanguard directors data on fund returns for the period from 1945 to 1975. Compared to the Standard & Poor's 500 Index, the average equity fund had experienced an annual shortfall of −1.6 percent. That figure dropped to a cumulative −0.8 percent through 1981. Since then, funds have fallen behind the S&P 500 Index by a far larger amount, −3.7 percent annually in the period from 1981 to June 1998 (although part of that increased margin is accounted for by the large-cap bias of the Index). Most of it is doubtless caused by the rise in both mutual expense ratios and costly portfolio turnover.

The industry as a whole, given its massive size, is truly in a straitjacket. The fleet-footed cheetah has become the lumbering pachyderm. Any chance, however remote, that mutual funds as a group can outpace a suitably weighted market index (one that includes large and small stocks in similar proportions to those of the industry) is "gone with the wind."

Put another way, if equity funds as a group are to outpace the market, the last best hope is through minimization of the fiscal drag that makes winning the game so tough. Funds could: reduce advisory fees, marketing costs, and expense ratios; reduce excessive and costly portfolio turnover; and reduce the long-term drag of cash holdings, so easy to do in an age when futures contracts on market indexes are available. None of these trends has developed to date. In the highly unlikely event that they do develop, they could help improve fund returns and give more fund managers the opportunity to live up to their own professional reputations and the expectations of fund shareholders. Funds as a group would continue to trail the market by the amount of their costs, but by a slimmer margin. *Such changes could help reduce the industry's return shortfall against the indexes. But, given the industry's massive size, there is no longer any chance to eliminate it.*

REAL SIZE, REAL PROBLEMS

What's true for the industry is also true for large individual fund components. These dominant mutual funds have reached mammoth size—indeed, two large funds, the $75 billion actively managed Magellan Fund and $64

FIGURE 12.4

Five Largest Equity Funds

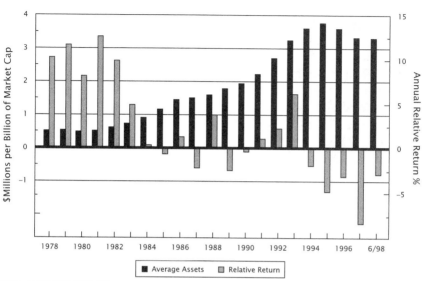

billion Vanguard 500 Index Fund,* each have more assets than all equity mutual funds combined held at the start of 1983. Seventeen other funds now have assets above $20 billion each. All told, the 48 stock funds with assets of $10 billion and above control more than $1 trillion of equities.

What happens when funds grow to large size? Consider the experience of five of the largest actively managed equity funds whose aggregate assets grew from $500 million to $37 billion during the 1978–1998 period uniformly their performance deteriorated. Figure 12.4 shows their average annual returns, relative to the Standard & Poor's 500 Index, along with their asset size relative to the total stock market. The pattern is familiar: profound reversion to the mean (RTM), the same situation that we witnessed in Chapter 10. While RTM is one of the most pervasive rules of the

---

*An index fund has no particular size limitations simply because its portfolio holds the same percentage of each corporation's shares. It does no active trading of these stocks, nearly buying or selling shares of each in proportion to the net cash flow from investors purchasing (or redeeming) the shares of the index fund.

financial markets, there are exceptions that can persist for periods as long as 15 years or more. As documented in Figure 12.4, however, the attainment of huge size turns that rule from near-pervasive to all-pervasive. From the start of 1978 to the end of 1982, these five large funds amassed a large performance edge over the Standard & Poor's 500 Index, outpacing the benchmark by 10 percentage points per year. They achieved that performance edge when they were relatively small (indeed, their performance fostered their growth), with average assets of $500,000 for every $1 billion of stock market capitalization. They lost the edge when they attained elephantine size. Since the start of 1994, with relative assets reaching $3.5 million for every $1 billion of stock market capitalization, these five actively managed funds have lagged the Standard & Poor's 500 Index by more than 4 percentage points per year. In other words, as the managed funds' relative assets rose sevenfold, their relative performance suffered a net decline of more than 14 percentage points annually. This size increase almost certainly played a major role—probably a starring role—in this remarkable example of reversion to, and then below, the mean.

Measuring a Fund's Real Size

Consider for a moment a question that is almost never part of the public debate about fund size: What is the relevant *unit* of size? Rather than the size of the fund itself, the unit of measurement ought to be the total asset base of the organization that manages an individual fund. By this standard, a large fund may in fact be two to three (or more) times the size that it appears to be. To the often-pervasive extent that other funds in the same complex (or institutional accounts managed by the same organization) own the same stock—given *firm-wide* policy constraints on percentage ownership of a given stock, transaction allocation procedures, and limitations on market liquidity—the problems of size are magnified proportionally.

Here are two real-world examples. One fund is by far the largest actively managed equity fund in the world, a $75 billion fund that finally closed its doors to new individual shareholders in 1997, when assets stood at $60 billion, all the while leaving the doors wide open to its millions of existing retirement plan investors. In five of its largest equity positions, it held a total of 40 million shares. But just ten of the sister funds supervised by its management company owned nearly 130 million shares. To the extent that the remainder of this giant fund's portfolio duplicates this ratio, it's fair to say that the fund (sort of) closed its doors at an asset level, not of $60 billion, but effectively an asset level of $200 billion. That decision, if you believe the press releases, passes for discipline in this industry.

Another example is the second largest actively managed equity fund, with assets of $47 billion. Along with just two sister funds managed by the same firm (the fourth largest equity fund, with $45 billion, and the thirty-second largest, with a mere $10 billion), five of its largest portfolio holdings represent one-third of the shares owned by three funds in aggregate. If we assume that this ratio approximates the relationship between its entire portfolio and *all* of the other fund and institutional accounts managed by the firm, this fund's effective size is $105 billion, with all of the constraints that implies. And yet none of the funds (or managed accounts) in this complex has yet been closed to the flow of new money.

It seems clear that funds that have created a record of remarkable returns at relatively small asset levels have a pronounced tendency to lose that edge when they get large. There is also considerable anecdotal evidence that highly volatile funds that have been successful tend to become far less volatile when they get large. In either case, whatever utility a fund's past record of performance *may* have had becomes completely irrelevant as giant size takes hold. Surely shareholders should be made aware of the extent to which these circumstances exist, for they relate directly to the validity, viability, and relevance of the long-term records that are presented in fund promotional material as gospel. "Past performance does not guarantee future returns," the customary industry boilerplate, is but a pale recognition of this phenomenon.

WHAT'S SIZE GOT TO DO WITH IT?

There are three major reasons why large size inhibits the achievement of superior returns: the universe of stocks available for a fund's portfolio declines; transaction costs increase; and portfolio management becomes increasingly structured, group-oriented, and less reliant on savvy individuals.

A Shrinking Universe

The shrinking universe of investment opportunities that comes with size is quite obvious. There are legal and practical constraints on security ownership. To ensure broad diversification, managers rarely wish to have their funds hold many investment positions in excess of 3 percent of fund assets.

Further, because dominant ownership positions may well constrain market liquidity as shares are purchased and sold, only a rare firm will wish to have very many positions representing as much as 10 percent of a corporation's shares outstanding.

Taken together, these two limitations—on diversifying assets and on maintaining liquidity—have a clearly calculable relationship to the number of major portfolio positions that can be held at a given level of fund assets. For example, assuming a 2 percent maximum holding and a 10 percent maximum ownership, a manager of a $1 billion portfolio in mid-1988 would be able to choose from among 3,080 stocks (Figure 12.5). But if the portfolio were $5 billion, the number would be 1,272 stocks, a drop of more than half. At $20 billion, it would drop by nearly two-thirds, to 470 stocks. And if the constraint on ownership engendered by the risk of illiquidity were 5 percent of a company's shares outstanding (probably, given industry practice, a more realistic figure than 10 percent), only 257 issues would be available. This net reduction of 92 percent from the original

FIGURE 12.5

Universe of Stocks Available to Purchase

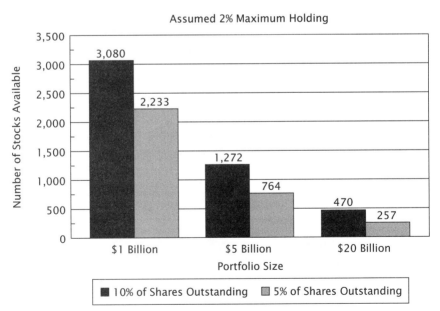

number entails limitations on portfolio selection that are as important as they are obvious.

The manager of a large portfolio could try to escape some of the problems of size by having larger numbers of holdings in smaller concentrations. (The largest fund, for example, owns 483 stocks.) But the performance of each holding, by definition, would have a smaller impact on the performance of the portfolio. Also, the manager could structure a strategy around industry subsets such as Internet participants, modem manufacturers, circuit board makers, and so on, rather than pick individual stocks. But the fundamental point remains intact: large asset size reduces drastically the number of important portfolio positions that can be included in the investable universe available to a portfolio manager of a large fund.

Higher Transaction Costs

A second factor is that the cost of portfolio transactions increases with size. As a general rule, managers could do far worse than reciting, "the larger the number of shares traded, the greater the impact on price," and quickly adding, "the higher the percentage of a day's (or week's) volume, the greater still the price impact," followed by, "the greater the urgency to complete a transaction, the greater again the price impact." These general conclusions would then follow: (1) short-term strategies are more costly to implement than long-term strategies; (2) momentum trades are more costly than trades based on fundamentals; (3) information-sensitive trades (based on purported market knowledge) are more costly than information-less trades (i.e., index fund transactions); and (4) aggressive trades made with speedy execution as the goal are more costly than opportunistic (contrarian) trades.

Mutual fund size, *as such*, is not the problem. No transaction costs are associated with the huge long-term holdings of American Express, Walt Disney, and Gillette owned by Mr. Buffett's Berkshire Hathaway—even though those positions represent, on average, fully one-half of those of the entire mutual fund industry—or of Coca-Cola, in which his 200 million shares are almost double the 112 million shares held by all funds combined. (Now we see how funds can be so underrepresented in Coke!) Why? Because he doesn't buy or sell them very often. The shares of Berkshire Hathaway aren't redeemable on demand, so he won't need to sell them until he wishes to do so—at his price (i.e., opportunistically). If he

"A FAT WALLET IS THE ENEMY OF SUPERIOR INVESTMENT RESULTS"

Asset size is an issue for all investment institutions that manage huge accumulations of capital. The statistical evidence is quite convincing. Truly outstanding managers have become an endangered species. In a 1998 article entitled "Where, Oh Where, Are the .400 Hitters of Yesteryear?"[1] portfolio strategist Peter L. Bernstein found strong evidence that the margin of outperformance of the most successful investment managers (including mutual fund managers) has been steadily shrinking over the past 40 years.

His statistical study struck a responsive chord with Warren E. Buffett, quoted above, who expressed the view that the culprit of the trend toward mediocrity was asset size rather than heightened competition for winning performance, as Mr. Bernstein had suggested. Mr. Buffett said that "about 75 percent of the difference in our performance between now and in the distant past is accounted for by size. We have always known that huge increases in managed funds would dramatically diminish our universe of investment choices. [The Berkshire Hathaway assets he supervises now total $64 billion.] Obviously performance would be much diminished if we had only 100 securities available for possible purchase compared to, say, the 10,000 available when our capital was microscopic."[2]

Here is how he described what happens to performance when the portfolio wallet fattens: "For the entire 1950s, my personal returns using equities with a market cap of less than $10 million were better than 60 percent annually. At our present size, I dream at night about 300 basis points" (i.e., 3 percentage points per year better than the market).

The mutual fund industry has been facing the same issues of size as has Mr. Buffett for at least a decade. But the giant fund firms are hardly as candid as Mr. Buffett in articulating the challenges of "a fat wallet," let alone acknowledging the constraints that large accumulations of assets impose on earning superior returns.

should want to get out in a rush, he would doubtless have to accept a considerable price sacrifice. But that is hardly his style.

I have heard of only one manager in the mutual fund industry who has examined the impact of trading costs—commissions, bid–ask spreads, market impact, opportunity cost—in his own firm, *and* has had the courage to make the results public. He is John C. Bogle, Jr., portfolio manager for the three mutual funds of Numeric Investors—all quantitatively run, high-turnover accounts. (Full disclosure requires me to note that he is my oldest son. Apparently, the apple doesn't fall very far from the tree.) After examining more than 20,000 trades, he reports these costs: trades in value stocks, 0.6 percent of the dollar amount of the trade; trades in small-growth stocks, 1.8 percent; trades in which shares represent one-eighth of daily volume, 0.5 percent; shares representing two days' volume, 2.3 percent. He concludes that the hidden drag of transaction costs rises as the size of purchases and sales becomes a larger fraction of market volume—an effect that, he states, "exists for every style, for every size, and for every manager." He recently closed two of his three funds at asset levels of $100 million each. *That* is discipline.

More universally, based on data provided by the Plexus Group, typical total trading costs for an investment manager are estimated to be about 0.8 percent of the amount of transaction value. If a fund has a turnover of 50 percent per year (in effect selling one half of the stocks in the portfolio and then reinvesting the proceeds in other stocks), purchases and sales together would be equal to the fund's average assets. Thus, the fund's annual return would have been reduced by 0.8 percent, or 8 percent of an assumed 10 percent return. At 100 percent turnover, the annual performance penalty—other factors held constant—would be 1.6 percent. These hidden transaction costs, added to the expense ratio of 1.5 percent for the average equity fund, would create an aggregate fiscal drag of more than 3 percent per year—consuming almost one-third of a 10 percent annual return.

My own estimates of industry-wide transaction costs are well below these figures, which vary with investment objective, style, transaction activity, and fund size. But there seems little question that transaction costs have some direct correlation with asset size. Smart managers—and most fund managers *are* smart—have to be particularly alert when the assets they manage increase relative to the market. The managers must add some sort of value that exceeds their growing transaction costs. If they can't get smart—and as individuals in a group they can never all outsmart each other—they must fall further behind the cost-free returns earned on unmanaged market indexes composed of securities similar to those represented by the fund's style. The evidence strongly suggests that no extra value has been forthcoming.

The Triumph of Process over Judgment

The third reason that large size impairs outstanding returns is less obvious. But the handicap it imposes on the managers of a fund organization is no less real. As an organization expands, the impact of an individual portfolio manager wanes, and the impact of an institutional investment process waxes. No longer are there a few portfolio managers with messy desks, bright ideas, and decisive minds, supported by a handful of analysts and traders, and modest administrative backing. Now, there is a horde of funds (as many as 100 or more), plus an organization chart, an investment process, committees to approve transactions and then to appraise them, meetings, exhaustive legal and regulatory filings, red tape, and a focus on process ("Who's in charge here?") rather than on judgment ("What should we own?"). The manager who used to invest heavily in his best ideas can no longer afford to do so.

Wall Street Journal columnist Roger Lowenstein is one of the few journalists who has recognized this phenomenon. He recently wrote: "Picking stocks, like writing stories, is a one-at-a-time endeavor. It is done best by individuals or small groups of people sharing their ideas *and buying only the very best.* A small fund family managing selective portfolios . . . can succeed as a group, but no large institution . . . can order dozens of managers to outperform. The image can be branded, but not the talent. The people matter more than the name."[3]

Nothing *Does* Succeed Like Success—For Fund Managers

My hypothesis that "nothing fails like success" has been laid out before you. To show why it must be so, I've presented compelling evidence based not only on common sense but on statistics. My reasoning is hardly counterintuitive. Given the industry's present size (which seems rather unlikely to shrink back to where it was a decade, or even five years, ago) and its growth rate, the problems connected with giant size are far more likely to intensify than abate. Is it not significant that no one—as far as I know—has ever seriously presented the converse case? No financial journal has published a paper entitled, in essence, "Asset Size: Remarkable Benefits to Mutual Fund Investors." No member of the personal finance press has advised, "For Truly Superior Performance, Go with the Giants," nor offered a defense that meets a lower standard: "Large Funds: The Easiest Way to Beat the Indexes." Probably the most favorable comment a manager of any large portfolio would dare make on the subject is: "Size doesn't significantly impair my ability to do my job." But I'm not at all sure that it would be said with much enthusiasm or conviction, or even with a straight face. To me, the case that asset size (a fat wallet, in Warren Buffett's words) is the enemy of performance excellence is so obvious that it defies serious debate.

Why do funds allow size to get out of hand? Because, for advisers, "nothing *does* succeed like success." The *management company* loves large size because the dollar amount of the advisory fees it receives rises almost linearly with fund assets. The larger the assets, the larger the fees. And the management company's profits grow at a still higher rate, even as returns to fund shareholders are impaired. Why? Because the huge leverage of economies of scale has been arrogated by advisers to their own benefit rather than to the benefit of the fund shareholders they serve.

The industry is growing apace, largely because American investors, excited by the continuing bull market, have developed an appetite for mutual funds that seems virtually insatiable. Individual fund complexes are growing at a parallel rate. Their growth is not only accepted, but is being accelerated by aggressive marketing campaigns, often at the expense of the investors who own the fund. The chief catalysts are fund advisers who have everything to gain, financially speaking, and nothing to lose by building funds to such a size that their past performance is irrelevant and their future performance is destined for mediocrity: the return of the market, reduced by the fund's management fees and transaction costs.

To Dream the Impossible Dream

Mutual fund investors owe it to themselves not only to be aware of the problems of burgeoning size in an industry that seems to applaud giant fund complexes, but also to become a force in their resolution. Albert Einstein said, "Any intelligent fool can make things bigger, more complex . . . it takes a touch of genius—and a lot of courage—to move in the opposite direction." It may be an impossible dream, but there are some decidedly real-world solutions, some rules that managers can follow, if only they are given the incentive to do so. If enough investors demand change and "vote with their feet" by selecting funds that follow these rules, and by moving their investments out of funds that ignore them, progress will come. Here, then, are the imperatives that would be followed by wise and responsible fund managers:

1. *Change the fund's strategy, but not its objectives.* Whatever happened to long-term strategy? From less than 20 percent in the good old days, fund portfolio turnover has increased to nearly 90 percent per year. Whatever else it may have accomplished, it has not improved fund returns relative to the market. In fact, fund returns have arguably deteriorated. Why don't the leopards of the mutual fund industry change their spots and go back to those good old days? (Returning to the industry's traditional 15 percent turnover rate might be even better.) I imagine the answer is: Most managers prefer to be short-term traders (today's *average* holding period is roughly one year) rather than long-term investors (if an average holding period of seven years, which would reflect a 15 percent turnover, is sufficient to qualify for that description).

The present situation, however, is likely to persist. First, because the new breed of portfolio manager *likes* turnover. Perhaps these managers are aggressive by temperament. They're highly intelligent and well educated, and they want to apply their talents, such as they may be, actively and often. Second, and perhaps even more important, managers in this industry make the big money if they can deliver flashy short-term fund performance. A steady-as-you-go, buy-and-hold portfolio has become an anachronism. The way to garner assets for a new fund is to build a record the financial press will write about. The money then flows in, leading to soaring advisory fees and strong profits for the managers. No one worries much that the fund's character (and its performance) must change when it grows large. The attitude seems to be, "We'll worry about that tomorrow."

2. *Close the fund to new investors.* When a fund reaches a size at which it can no longer implement its strategy because of a constricting number of stocks in its universe, or because of the increasing likelihood of significantly influencing prices through active buying and selling, why not close the fund? So far, even as the problems of dealing with size have become imminent, only about two out of every 100 funds have closed, including a few that have done so at far higher asset levels than would seem appropriate. But most funds seem to ignore the problem and so face deteriorating relative returns and reduced opportunities to distinguish themselves, to the detriment of shareholders who purchased their shares because the fund had distinguished itself in the past. As John C. Bogle, Jr., has said, "Managers and trustees have turned a blind eye toward the interest of the shareholder, in favor of their own interest in the ever growing stream of revenues."

Sad to say, the status quo seems likely to persist simply because the profitability of a fund "franchise" to the manager is linear: the larger the fund, the larger the return to the *adviser*. This incentive seems to supersede any interest in providing the optimal return to the *shareholder*. If investors and financial advisers were to place their investment heft behind the fair resolution of this issue, and if the financial press were to give it the attention it deserves, fund managers might finally be forced to act and close funds at appropriate levels.

3. *Let the fund grow, but add new managers.* One obvious solution to the problem created when a fund begins to get too large to implement its earlier strategies is to bring in a new portfolio manager and allocate part of the existing portfolio and future cash inflow to the new firm. (I recommend a new firm because bringing in a new manager from the existing firm would not solve the liquidity problem.) However, only a few large fund groups have used multimanager structures, assigning two to four external managers to supervise an existing fund. Given the true arm's-length negotiations that are implicit under this arrangement, advisory fees paid to the new external advisers are apt to be far below industry norms. This situation presents the paradox of why the "in-house" adviser for a given fund receives a high fee, but an external adviser for a sister fund receives a fee a fraction as large. (Investors should raise that question with their fund's management or its directors. I'd love to hear the answer.)

The retention of an external manager comes to grips with the size issue by allowing a fund to grow without the loss of—and perhaps with an increase in—investment efficiency. However, the solution also creates a new problem. How likely is it that the portfolio run by the new adviser will add value? Won't two managers simply offset each other with inevitably alternating periods of good and bad returns? What about four managers? Or six? There is clearly a law of diminishing returns, and it may begin to come into play as early as the addition of the first manager. We just can't be sure. In any event, use of this strategy is rare.

4. *Lower the basic advisory fee, but add an incentive fee.* If the goal is to maintain a generous incentive for the manager without jeopardizing the relative returns to the investor, why not cut the regular fee and add an incentive that is paid only to the extent that the fund's returns exceed the returns of an appropriate market index? A simple example: Cut the fee from 1.00 percent to 0.75 percent, and add an incentive of 0.25 percent. The problem (for the manager) is that the incentive must be symmetrical. A fee penalty of 0.25 percent would be imposed if the fund falls short, in which case the total fee would tumble to 0.50 percent. But fair is fair. Do the job and get paid; fail and take the consequences. Or fairer yet, make the standard, not the index return, but the index return *plus* the margin of excess return over the index that the fund had achieved in, say, the prior five years. This is likely to be the performance the shareholders are expecting, and the mutual equity of such a structure seems quite obvious.

Alas, these two types of incentive fee solutions (especially the second one) seem unlikely to be adopted unless fund shareholders demand their implementation. Basic incentive fees, never common in this business, are becoming even more rare. Barely 100 of 7,000 mutual funds now make use of them. Managers would rather receive something (a high fee) for nothing (the fee is paid whether performance is good or bad). Nonetheless, any challenge to the existing fee culture of the industry is conspicuous only by its absence.

5. *Offer a mutual fund that is size-proof, with minimal turnover and a nominal fee.* Given the evidence of the importance of transaction costs and management fees in shaping past returns and the fact that the huge present size of the industry, combined with the higher level of fees, may make the attainment of even the present standard of mediocrity more difficult to attain in the future, wouldn't a low-turnover, low-cost fund provide a solid alternative for mutual fund investors? Of course it would. But "long-term investing" seems to have vanished from the lexicon of most portfolio managers, in part because it is apparently difficult to identify first-class enterprises that will have staying power and in part because most of today's managers are an active, impatient lot. Taking this rule to its logical conclusion suggests an index fund, but an index strategy, while it clearly provides superior profits to investors, provides minuscule profits to the advisers.

You Can Make the Dream a Reality

Rare indeed is the fund organization that has taken any of the above suggestions very seriously—so far. Portfolio turnover is high and shows no sign of diminishing, despite some fragile evidence that unit transaction costs are rising. Few funds have closed, and many of those that have closed have done so far later than their growth demanded. The use of external managers is as rare as ten-carat diamonds. Expense ratios are rising, most notably for the horde of new funds being formed. Incentive fees not only remain conspicuous by their rarity, but are indeed being abandoned. Fund innovation—in other areas, clever to a fault—has ignored the opportunity to create funds that are more cost-efficient and more tax-efficient. (I present one structure for such a fund in the next chapter.) The best existing proxy for dealing with the challenges of large size—the index fund—is a pariah that is accepted largely because trustees of institutional thrift and retirement plans (which, paradoxically, gain no performance advantage from tax efficiency) are demanding it for corporate employees. As fund investors, you are among the 50 million Davids who, together, can hurl a rock that will get the attention of the Goliath fund management companies and stun them into recognizing the problems of asset size.

Compared to its beginnings, the mutual fund industry is different today: different in the aggregate, different in its power in the financial markets, different in its investment limitations, different in its costs and its impact on the stock market, different in the way its investment decisions are made and implemented. Any reliance on history as a guide to the future accomplishments of individual mutual funds, and of the fund industry itself, is tenuous at best.

If present growth rates continue, in only a few years, mutual fund managers could control perhaps four-tenths of all U.S. equities and account for as much as three-fourths of all equity transactions. Why isn't the industry more forthright about the issue of size? Why can't we face up to the fact that our burgeoning asset growth has already changed the character of most giant funds, and indeed, of the industry in the aggregate? Liquidity matters. Cost matters. Taxes matter. And size can kill. The challenge of performance excellence is becoming more formidable and more impregnable to attainment, even by skilled professional portfolio managers. If funds won't deal with these questions, investors must persist in raising them. If left unresolved, their impact on funds' performance and future returns may be profound.

No firm—I repeat, *no* firm—is exempt from these issues, and hence no fund investor is exempt. Investment firms and investors alike must have the wisdom to face this dissonant music. The mutual fund industry's fabulous success is living proof that "nothing *succeeds* like success." But that rule may well be sowing the seeds of its own antithesis: "Nothing *fails* like success." Investors must consider all of the implications of investment size, not only for the funds whose shares they own, but for the industry colossus they have helped to create.

CHAPTER

ON TAXES
THE MESSAGE OF THE PARALLAX

Often, a small change in vantage point can engender a large change in perception. So it is with the parallax, exemplified by the angle created by the 2¼-inch distance between our eyes, which enables us to visualize objects in three dimensions. As I discussed in Chapter 3, mutual fund investment has four dimensions, return, risk, cost, and time. It is conventional to consider investments on the basis of return and risk, but I believe that adding cost as a third dimension provides a far better understanding of investment returns generally, and mutual fund returns in particular. Thus, I apply the principle of the parallax to mutual funds.

The impact of cost is greatly magnified when we consider not only the substantial operating and transaction costs of mutual funds, but the cost of taxes as well. The profound impact of taxes on fund returns is a subject too long ignored. Fund managers may feel that they can afford to ignore it, but fund owners ignore it at their peril. With an estimated $700 billion of capital gains currently on the books in mutual fund portfolios, it is high time for the subject of taxes to receive the exposure it deserves. To be sure, an investor's goal is not simply to minimize the tax burden, but rather to achieve the highest possible net returns. Paradoxically, however, a focus on minimizing taxes seems not only not to diminish, but to enhance pretax returns.

277

Given the remarkable increase in potential tax liability that has come hand-in-hand with the 16-year bull market, it's especially timely to acknowledge taxes as a major aspect of the cost of investing in mutual fund shares. Alas, it is too late to discuss the taxes that fund investors paid, by April 15, 1998, on the $180 billion of capital gains that the industry realized during 1997. But although taxes paid on those gains are water over the dam, the issue has hardly vanished. Tens of billions of gains realized and distributed in 1998 must be reported on tax returns for 1998, and tax on them paid by April 15, 1999.

At this point, a caution: the huge $700 billion estimated unrealized tax liability is a very volatile number; it is highly sensitive to changes in the level of the stock market. In a market decline, unrealized gains come right off the top. A 25 percent market decline, for example, would eliminate the industry's entire potential net tax liability, even as a 25 percent market increase would double it. Please bear this high leverage in mind as you consider the impact of taxes on the returns you earn on your fund investments. Also, remember that the substantial gains already realized but not yet distributed will be distributed and will become taxable to shareholders, even if the industry's unrealized gains were entirely erased by a market decline. Almost no matter what the market does, substantial capital gains will be distributed to fund investors for many years, for the large amount of unrealized gains on fund books is unlikely to be washed entirely away.

It is ironic that the mutual fund industry's high turnover policies have exacerbated the tax issue. As managers turn over their portfolios in an ongoing attempt to beat the market—all the while failing to do so—this activity places a further burden on the backs of taxable shareholders: a cost increase that substantially magnifies the existing shortfall to the market reflected in the reported (pretax) returns of the overwhelming majority of mutual funds.

Earlier, I noted that during the 16-year bull market through June 1998, the average equity mutual fund provided a return of 16.5 percent versus 18.9 percent for the total stock market. This shortfall of 2.4 percentage points per year—engendered importantly by annual costs of about 2 percent—*may* not look excessive when subtracted from a market providing an annualized return of nearly 20 percent. But, over time, it would consume fully one-fourth of a 10 percent return, to say nothing of confiscating one-half of a 5 percent return.

Consider for a moment what is called "Alpha." It is a vital measure of a fund's return relative to the stock market, adjusted to reflect the relative risk assumed by the fund. The statistics are quite clear. (*Morningstar Mutual Funds* is the best-recognized source.) They show that the average mutual fund has provided an Alpha—a risk-adjusted return relative to the market of *minus* 1.9 percent per year—"negative Alpha," as it is known—during the past decade. In other words, the annual return earned by fund investors was almost 2 percentage points less than they might have expected. This number roughly equals the industry's annual costs. It is no accident that Alpha is normally quite similar to fund total operating and transaction costs. But it doesn't take into account the hidden cost of taxes.

TAXES—THE INDUSTRY'S BLACK SHEEP

The tax issue is the black sheep of the mutual fund industry. Like a cousin who can't get her life together or an uncle who drinks too much, taxes are kept out of sight and out of mind. But investors cannot afford to turn a blind eye to this issue. For it is the fund shareholder who pays the taxes on a mutual fund's income dividends and on any capital gains distributions generated by the fund's constant staccato of portfolio sales, and—at least in the recent bounteous bull market—by the realization of enormous taxable capital gains. The dichotomy is that a portfolio manager's performance is measured and applauded on the basis of *pretax* return—never mind that the Internal Revenue Service confiscates a healthy share of it. Few portfolio managers spend their time agonizing over the tax consequences of their decisions.

Ever since the creation of the first mutual fund in 1924, the industry has essentially ignored the tax issue. Indeed, for decades, funds were sold as much on the basis of "looking for more income" as on the basis of total return. (In the 1940s and early 1950s, stock yields averaged 8 percent and bond yields averaged 2½ percent. Imagine!) The industry often sloughed off the difference between income dividends and capital gains distributions. They were added together to arrive at a "total distribution yield," a practice not legally permitted since 1950. In recent years, as tax-deferred IRA accounts and 401(k) corporate retirement plans have come to the fore, tax considerations have gotten even less attention. In fact, investors in tax-deferred retirement plans, which as a group hold 40 percent of the assets of equity funds, are now the driving force in industry growth. Investors in these accounts need burden neither their minds nor their checkbooks with tax issues.

But the owners of the other 60 percent of fund assets do not have the luxury of ignoring tax considerations. Each year, they must pay taxes on the fund distributions they receive. Yet mutual funds do not provide adequate disclosure about the tax implications of their investment strategies, portfolio turnover expectations, and gain realization policies. Look under the "Dividends, Capital Gains, and Taxes" heading in a typical fund prospectus, and you'll find something like: "The fund distributes annually substantially all of its net income after expenses and any capital gains realized from the sale of securities. Dividends and short-term gains are taxable to you as ordinary income; distributions of long-term capital gains are taxable to you as long-term capital gains." That is proper disclosure as far as it goes. *But it doesn't go nearly far enough.*

Portfolio managers, fund sponsors, and distributors *know* that funds don't pay much, if any, attention to tax concerns. Rather than ignore this important fact, they ought to call it to the attention of investors. Here's my try at a much needed prospectus disclosure:

> The fund is managed without regard to tax considerations, and given its expected rate of portfolio turnover, is likely to realize and distribute a high portion of its capital return in the form of capital gains which are taxable annually, a substantial portion of which are likely to be realized in the form of short-term gains subject to full income tax rates. (Some funds might be entitled to modify the last phrase.)

There would seem to be only two reasons that the disclosure of that known fact does *not* find its way into today's prospectuses: inadvertence, or some sense that it would hurt the fund's marketing effort by encouraging investors to focus on the negative impact of excessive taxes on their total returns. Whatever the reason, I believe that the sentence quoted above should be included as a prominent part—if not the opening sentence—of the disclosure of fund tax considerations in the prospectus. Full disclosure must be the order of the day.

The Remarkable Value of Tax Deferral

The serious problem created by the relatively prompt realization of capital gains by funds is that investors must pay taxes on them almost immediately. Yet the truly enormous value of deferring capital gains taxes seems almost universally ignored. To put it simply: A tax that is deferred is the functional equivalent of an interest-free loan from the U.S. Treasury Department, with a maturity equal to the number of years of deferral. You

will probably owe the tax someday, but you don't have to pay it until then.*
Just imagine the value of a 10-year interest-free loan, or even a 25-year
loan. Better still, calculate it. A $1.00 loan repayment deferred for 10 years
has a present value of 47 cents; with a 25-year loan, that figure is just 15
cents! But mutual fund history suggests that as few as 5 percent of all fund
holdings can be expected to be held for 10 years, and thus gain that 53 cent
bonus on each dollar deferred for a decade, to say nothing of the bonus of
85 cents per dollar over a quarter century.

As of late 1998, mutual funds were carrying an estimated appreciation
of a cool $700 billion (25 percent of equity fund assets), representing a po-
tential liability to their taxable shareholders of some $100 billion. As much
as $200 billion of net gains have been realized during 1998, and distrib-
uted at year-end. The remaining $500 billion of those gains have not yet
been realized, but, assuming that market prices hold constant, will ultimately be realized and subject to taxes. The mammoth distribution of
gains realized in 1998 will likely constitute about $150 billion in long-
term gains and $50 billion in short-term gains. Perhaps $80 billion of the
$200 billion will be received by investors in tax-deferred retirement pro-
grams. The $120 billion received by taxable investors for 1998 gains, then,
will carry an estimated tax liability of more than $30 billion. One can only
hope that they are ready to pay it.

External circumstances could exacerbate the situation in 1999. If a
market decline were to cause net liquidations of fund shares, it would *increase* per-share distributions. Conversely, a rising market might bring in
new money at ascending prices, which would *dilute* per-share distributions.
That is why mutual fund unrealized gains, relative to the rise in stock
prices, have been small so far. Curiously, investors don't seem to object to
paying $10.00 per share for a fund with a potential tax liability for, say,
$2.50 in unrealized capital gains in its portfolio. In a down market, when
share prices tumble, it is possible, if not likely, that relatively new fund investors, with unrealized losses, would nonetheless receive substantial taxable capital gains distributions. (Fund accounting practices give rise to
strange outcomes.) Forewarned is forearmed.

With all this background, let's look at the impact of taxes in a longer-
term context. On the income distribution side, perversely enough, the tax

---

* In fact, the tax *never* need be paid if the investment, at the investor's death, is bequeathed
to a beneficiary. Then, the original cost basis is "stepped up" to the market value at the
time of death.

impact is, in a sense, beneficial. In late 1998, equity mutual funds were earning gross income—before expenses—at a rate of about 1.9 percent. (Their equity holdings yielded about 1.2 percent; their 10 percent position in bonds and cash reserves yielded about 7 percent.) But annual fund expenses averaged 1.5 percent, so equity fund investors were receiving a puny yield of less than 0.5 percent on which to pay taxes. *Expenses were consuming some 75 percent of fund income.* In the paradoxical world of mutual funds, the higher the expense ratio, the more "tax-efficient" the income component of total return. But there is such a thing as paying too much for tax efficiency, as reflected in that perverse example. In a sense, mutual fund expenses represent a tax rate of 75 percent on gross income, deducted before the regular taxes are even paid. It is "Alice in Wonderland" writ large.

Alpha Takes Another Hit . . . From Taxes

The impact of taxes on the capital component is another story altogether. Here, "tax-inefficient" is the operative term for mutual funds. The tax blessing, as it were, in the income component of return is overwhelmed by the tax bane on the far larger capital component. A simple example: During the past 15 years, the average equity fund enjoyed an average annual return of 14 percent. Let's assume 3 percent of the return came from income and 11 percent from capital, of which 8 percent was realized. Let's further assume that 30 percent of the capital gain was realized on a short-term basis. (These assumptions closely parallel actual industry experience.) On the income side, the tax bite, assuming a 33 percent average rate, would reduce return by 1 percent. On the capital side, with a 33 percent rate on short-term gains taxable as income, and a 25 percent tax rate on long-term gains, taxes would claim 2.2 percent of return. In all, taxes would have reduced the reported returns of the average equity fund from 14 percent to 10.8 percent, while leaving risk unchanged.[1]

The fact is that taxes have a hugely negative impact on relative returns. An outstanding article by Robert H. Jeffrey and Robert D. Arnott in *The Journal of Portfolio Management*, "Is Your Alpha Big Enough to Cover Its Taxes?"[2] concludes that it is not. I'll add: No, your Alpha is being eaten alive by taxes. That situation is made somewhat more dire by the fact that equity funds, as we've seen, largely because of their investment costs, already have had a *negative* Alpha of *–1.9* percent annually over the past 10 years. On an after-tax basis, that negative Alpha nearly triples to *–5.1* percent. Professional investors all know that successful investing is a tough game. But fund costs and taxes, some paid unnecessarily, make it even tougher. Even if *some* individual investors are aware how much tougher the game is when fund expenses and taxes are deducted from the manager's returns, *all* fund investors should be told the facts—and the figures—with candor. That 5.1 percent slice confiscated more than one-fourth of the stock market's return in the past decade.

FUND PORTFOLIO TURNOVER SOARS

It's important to recognize that what's happening here is largely the product of the inordinately high portfolio turnover rates of mutual funds. Twenty-five years ago, fund portfolio turnover averaged 30 percent; today, it averages nearly 90 percent. Individual investors may hold stocks for decades, and families may hold them for generations, but mutual funds are rushing to buy and sell their stocks with seemingly carefree abandon based on transitory changes in prices and without concern for tax consequences. This behavior sharply reduces the returns generated for their taxable owners.

Further, some fund managers are so trigger-happy that many of the gains are short-term in nature (less than one year) and are taxed at ordinary income rates. In recent years, some 30 percent of fund gains fell into this category, but with the end of the long-standing limitations on "short-short" gains under the so-called Taxpayer Relief Act of 1997, this figure could well increase. Now, portfolio managers can feel free to realize an unlimited percentage of the fund's income in the form of gains realized in less than 30 days. For mutual fund shareholders, the economic value created by this change in the law is dubious in the extreme.

It is highly unlikely that fund turnover will slow so greatly that it will mitigate the gain realization issue. Reducing a fund's turnover from 150 percent to 100 percent simply doesn't matter. Substantially *all* gains are realized fairly quickly. Authoritative studies suggest that turnover rates would have to be reduced to 20 percent or less to engender a material lessening of the tax burden. But *any* turnover, by forcing shareholders to give up the value of that implied interest-free loan, has a negative impact on the net returns enjoyed by investors.

What happens when the basic strategy of a fund calls for limited turnover? Something very good for fund investors. The amount of tax due falls, and the after-tax return rises accordingly. It is that simple. As taxes are deferred, returns rise significantly with each additional year that an investor elects to hold fund shares. And through tax elimination—for example, if an investor's heirs receive the shares with a stepped-up cost basis at the time of the investor's death—after-tax returns leap ever higher.

FUND MANAGER TURNOVER DOESN'T HELP

Even if, as a policy matter, good intentions exist to reduce turnover, it soars—and substantial gains are realized—when a new portfolio manager is brought in to manage a fund. This event happens with increasing frequency in this era of manager turnover. "Superstar" managers may be lured away by huge stipends, or entrepreneurial instincts, or the fact that the large asset size of the funds they manage has impeded their ability to deliver outstanding returns. But whatever the case, fund portfolio managers currently have an average tenure of only five years.

To say that these are critical issues for taxable mutual fund investors would be a powerful understatement. As James P. Garland, president of the Jeffrey Company, has observed, "Taxable investing is a loser's game. Those who lose the least—to taxes and fees—stand to win the most when the game's all over."[3] Garland compared the hypothetical after-tax returns of an investor in a typical fund and a tax-managed index fund over the 25-year period from 1971 to 1995. During this period, the Standard & Poor's 500 Index earned a compound rate of return of 12.0 percent (*before* taxes). After expenses and taxes, the average mutual fund compounded at 8.0 percent, and the tax-managed fund compounded at 10.2 percent. (See Figure 13.1.)

After relinquishing 16 percent of final fund total returns to the fund manager and 44 percent to the government, a fund investor retained but 40 percent of the theoretical tax-free market return. For a tax-managed index fund, 6 percent of the final value accrued to the manager and 27 percent to the government; the investor retained 67 percent. For an investor who began the period with an investment of $1 million, the net result was a final capital pool of $11.3 millon in a low-cost tax-managed fund, compared to $6.8 million for an investor in a typical mutual fund.

With decidedly mixed emotions, I tell you that the Garland methodology seriously *overstated* the net return of the typical fund. It assumed a fund expense ratio of 1 percent and ignored fund portfolio transaction costs. As I have noted, however, all-in costs incurred by funds today average 2 percent or more. The methodology also assumed that all capital gains were realized on a long-term basis (28 percent tax) when, in fact,

FIGURE 13.1

Cost—The Third Dimension: Fund Expenses Plus Taxes, $1,000,000 Investment, 25-Year Returns (1971–1995)— Market Return 12.0%

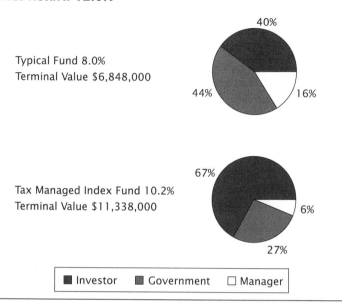

Typical Fund 8.0%
Terminal Value $6,848,000

Tax Managed Index Fund 10.2%
Terminal Value $11,338,000

■ Investor   ■ Government   □ Manager

perhaps one-third of fund gains were actually taxable at a (then) short-term rate of 36 percent.* The study also moderately *understated* the results of the tax-managed index fund. It assumed an 0.3 percent expense ratio when 0.2 percent would have been more realistic. But, even giving the benefit of a very large doubt to the typical fund, the impact of taxes and expenses on mutual fund returns is astonishing.

A Good Solution: The Index Fund

At this point, you are probably thinking that you should forget about mutual funds, at least for taxable accounts; or that there must be a better way to achieve the valuable diversification that mutual funds clearly provide. Well, there *is* a better way. You *can* avoid suffering the negative consequences of

---

*Currently, the maximum tax rate on long-term gains is 20 percent and the maximum tax rate on short-term gains (and ordinary income) is 40 percent.

both high costs *and* excessive taxes, and come as close to achieving a positive Alpha as the law of the financial markets allows. A relative handful of funds operates at a minimal cost and with a minimal tax burden. Most are broadly based market index funds (for example, those based on the Standard & Poor's 500 Index) or index funds replicating the entire stock market (the Wilshire 5000 Equity Index). And they are working well (especially the Wilshire index) because significant changes to their composition rarely take place.

Let's begin with a baseline: the after-tax return of the S&P 500 Index. We'll deduct income tax from the dividends, assume no capital gain realization, and defer all capital gains taxes. With a pretax return of 17.2 percent over the 15 years from June 1983 to June 1998, and assuming an estimated tax impact of −1.5 percent (largely because of *income* taxes), the after-tax return turns out to be 15.7 percent, 91 percent of its pretax return.

Now let's turn to the real world and calculate the comparable figures. For an average mutual fund, the 15-year pretax return was 13.6 percent and taxes were 2.8 percent, producing an after-tax return of 10.8 percent—a flow-through of 79 percent. For comparison, Table 13.1 shows the record of the Vanguard 500 Index Fund. Its pretax return was 16.9 percent, of which taxes consumed 1.9 percent, leaving a net return of 15.0 percent. As a result, the Index Fund's rank rises from the 94th to the 97th percentile. The former advantage is shaped largely by the high costs incurred by the typical actively managed mutual fund; the latter, by the heavy tax burden engendered in this typically high-turnover industry.

During this 15-year period—admittedly, a good time frame for the giant-cap stocks that dominate the Index—the focus on low costs helped

TABLE 13.1

S&P 500 Index Fund and Average Mutual Fund

	Rate of Return Fifteen Years Ended 6/30/98	
	Before Taxes	After Taxes
Index fund	+16.9%	+15.0%
Average mutual fund	+13.6	+10.8
Index fund advantage	+3.3%	+4.2%
Funds outpaced by index fund	94%	97%

place the index fund near the top of the mutual fund industry. Its focus on tax minimization took it even higher, bringing it nearly halfway toward being number one. Outpacing 97 percent of all equity funds on an after-tax basis over a decade and a half hardly seems a shabby accomplishment for a passively managed fund lacking even the putative advantage of a skilled portfolio manager.

Once again, these numbers overstate to some degree the returns of regular mutual funds, because the underperforming mutual funds drop out of the race and thus out of the return calculations. And the powerful impact that this survivorship bias has on reported industry returns is no trivial matter, as I've shown in Chapter 5. If the return of the average mutual fund, displayed in Table 13.1, were to be corrected for this bias, then the fund underperformance would have been even more dramatic.

In fairness, however, the index *fund* returns are also lower than the returns of the Index, because they are reduced by portfolio transaction and operating costs. No matter how modest, these costs exist in the real world. From 1983 to 1998, for example, the Vanguard 500 Index Fund's returns of 16.9 percent before taxes and 15.0 percent after taxes compared to 17.2 percent and 15.7 percent respectively for the Index itself.

Results Confirmed

The results of this analysis have been confirmed by other independent studies. The most rigorous study was prepared by Joel M. Dickson and John B. Shoven of Stanford University. They found that during the 10-year period ending in 1992, an actual mutual fund modeled on the S&P 500 Index provided an annual after-tax return of 13.4 percent compared to 10.7 percent for the median equity mutual fund. That advantage of 2.7 percentage points annually moved the index fund up from the 79th percentile to the 86th percentile, leaping over 10 of the 31 funds in their 147-fund sample that had provided higher pretax returns.[4]

There is a high degree of certainty that the low-cost advantage of indexing will persist. But there may be a lower level of certainty that the deferral of gain realization will persist. First, index funds, by virtue of their low turnover, should build up their *unrealized* gains, over time. At some point down the road, a portion of those gains may be realized. Second, despite the intention of an index fund to avoid realization, it could be susceptible to a run of shareholder redemptions that could force it to liquidate highly appreciated portfolio holdings. Nonetheless, given the huge value of tax deferral for a long period, and its considerable value even for a limited period, it is difficult to visualize a circumstance under which the potential tax advantage offered by index funds, *relative to traditional actively managed funds*, will not persist.

A BETTER SOLUTION: THE TAX-MANAGED FUND

New funds are finally being developed that should provide an even better solution than the regular index fund to the tax problem faced by mutual fund shareholders. In 1994, one fund group, interested in improving the tax efficiency of conventional index funds, developed the industry's first series of low-cost, tax-managed funds. The most popular form is based on:

- Using a market index strategy, but emphasizing growth stocks and holding lower-yielding equities, in order to minimize the tax burden on income.

- Realizing, to the maximum possible extent, losses on the sale of portfolio holdings that have declined (a practice known as "harvesting losses"), and thereby offsetting realized gains when they occur.

- Replacing the holdings sold at a loss after 30 days. (During the interim, their absence from the portfolio could engender a small lack of precision in matching the index.)

- Limiting its shareholder base to investors with a long-term focus by charging a penalty—a transaction fee, *payable to the fund and its remaining shareholders*—if shares are redeemed within five years of purchase. Such a penalty is designed to minimize the possibility of abrupt share redemptions.

- Maintaining the same rock-bottom costs that characterize the lowest-cost index funds.

Based on the relatively short experience of these tax-managed funds, this approach seems to be working well. Thanks to the penalty provisions, redemptions are a tiny fraction of industry norms; speculative market-timing short-term investors have been conspicuous by their absence; and no capital gains have yet been realized. What is more, they have provided excellent returns relative to comparable actively managed funds.

More recently, others in the industry have begun to respond; more than a score of other purportedly tax-managed funds have been formed.

But few follow an index strategy, and few have taken tangible measures, such as penalty fees, to limit redemptions. The funds' expense ratios are no lower than the norms for other managed funds, relinquishing another key advantage. Overall, except for their intention to "lean against the wind" to avoid excessive turnover, their investment objectives are conventional. Further, it is not clear what will happen when they experience the inevitable portfolio *manager* turnover. Together, these potential negatives are apt to make it difficult to reduce materially either the tax bite or the bite that operating expense ratios take out of Alpha.

When properly structured, however, tax-managed funds seem destined to become a strong force in the mutual fund field—made even stronger, I believe, by the reduction of taxes in the Taxpayer Relief Act of 1997. Under previous law, the 28 percent capital gains rate was 12 percentage points below the 40 percent maximum marginal income tax rate. The new rate is 20 percent—that is, 20 percentage points below the 40 percent income tax rate. This change raises the tax discount on long-term gains from 12 percentage points to 20 percentage points—an increase of fully 1.7 times and a further enhancement to the value of long-term deferral. But high-turnover funds—holding stocks for less than a year on average—continue to subject shareholders to full income tax rates on their short-term gains, and sacrifice the considerable value of tax deferral on their long-term gains.

A NEW IDEA, SIXTY YEARS OLD

With all of the high-priced creative and imaginative talent in the mutual fund industry, why hasn't someone, somewhere, dreamed up a still better way to enhance after-tax mutual fund returns? Surely the opportunities abound. Let me describe one idea. Start with a fund that simply buys a large sampling of high-quality blue-chip growth stocks, and holds them unless fundamental circumstances change radically. Where do we find a budding Warren Buffett to manage it? Honestly, I don't know. As an alternative, how about a fund that buys, say, the 50 largest stocks in the Standard & Poor's Growth Index universe? (That's 80 percent of the capitalization of the growth universe and 30 percent of *the entire stock market*.) The fund holds these 50 stocks, without rebalancing as prices change. If there is a merger, keep the merged company. If a company is bought for cash, reinvest the proceeds in the next largest growth company or in the fund's other holdings (the choice probably won't matter).

No manager would be needed, so the fund would incur only bare-bones operating costs, perhaps totaling an expense ratio of 20 basis points. Minimize exposure to shareholder redemptions by imposing stiff redemption fees and/or strong limitations on daily liquidity (perhaps open the fund for redemption only on the last day of each quarter). Finally, when shares are redeemed, don't sell stocks to meet the redemption. Pay the investor in shares of the highly marketable securities in the portfolio ("redemption in kind"). Explain in advance that this is what you will do. Those investors will realize the same tax that they otherwise would on any gains, and the fund's tax integrity will be preserved. These procedures will make the fund unattractive to quick-triggered opportunists—a good outcome for shareholders. And, over time, these sound policies will make it commensurately easier to attract serious long-term investors, who will otherwise become an endangered species.

The potential rewards are huge. In a stock market that averages a 10 percent pretax return, the average fund (assuming a 2 percent expense ratio) might provide a pretax return of 8 percent and an after-tax return of 6.5 percent. A low-cost, buy-and-hold fund with a 10 percent gross return and expenses of 0.2 percent should achieve a net return of 9.8 percent before taxes and 9 percent after taxes. This is a conservative hypothesis, for the hypothetical after-tax spread of 2.5 percent is well below the actual after-tax shortfall of 4.3 percent that actually existed between active funds and the S&P 500 Index during the past 15 years.

For long-term investors, these numbers would be little short of dynamite. After 25 years and net of all taxes, $100,000 invested at the outset would have grown to $483,000 in the actively managed fund. But the buy-and-hold fund would have reached $862,000, or almost double that amount. It is surely fair to conclude that both fund expenses and taxes matter—in large magnitude.

The potential risks are small. Here are the mathematics: The 30 percent of the entire investment universe currently represented by the 50 largest growth stocks would have to *underperform* the remaining 70 percent of the market by more than 3.0 percentage points per year for 25 years—at which point, the choice between the two funds would be indifferent. The powerful forces of efficient financial markets would likely repel any such challenge. History reflects the fact that growth stocks and value stocks have provided virtually identical returns over the past six decades (see Chapter 10). Such a defeat for our hypothetical fund could be accomplished, over the long-term, only against all odds. The surprising, if simple, fact is that broad diversification makes it just as difficult to achieve significant *underperformance* relative to the market as to achieve significant *overperformance*. In short, the risk–return equation appears highly favorable, thanks simply to the minimization of the fiscal drag of costs—operating expenses and tax penalties alike. That's the three-dimensional view from this pair of eyes.

A look at history might help to evaluate the risk that growth stocks, even when purchased at notably high valuations, will underperform the market over the long run. Jeremy J. Siegel helped to answer the question with his study of the performance of the famous Nifty Fifty growth stocks of the "go-go" era of 1965 to 1972. In an article in *The Journal of Portfolio Management*, Professor Siegel showed that a frozen portfolio, equally weighted in those 50 highly valued stocks and purchased at the start of 1971 (near the peak of the market) marginally outperformed the stock market as a whole over the subsequent 25 years.[5] Some of the 50 did well: Philip Morris was the champion, up 21 percent per year, with McDonald's (+18 percent), Coca-Cola, and Disney (each +16 percent) in close pursuit. Some did poorly: MGIC Investment finished last on the list, losing more than 4.6 percent per year; Emery Air Freight (–1 percent) did nearly that badly; and Polaroid (+2 percent) and Xerox (+5 percent) also ranked near the bottom.

On a pretax basis, the Nifty Fifty portfolio earned an average annual return of 12.4 percent, an advantage of just 0.7 percentage points over the stock market return of 11.7 percent. But on an after-tax basis, this relative advantage grew significantly: The Nifty Fifty portfolio advantage increased to fully 2 percentage points per years (9.8 percent versus 7.8 percent). These long-term past returns, earned on a static portfolio oriented to growth, in retrospect bought at a high price, surely validate this concept. At the end of the period, an initial investment of $10,000 in the Nifty Fifty portfolio, after the deduction of taxes, was worth $98,000 versus $63,000 for the stock market as a whole. The average mutual fund, of course, trailed far behind the market during that period.

Nothing New under the Sun

There is, Ecclesiastes tells us, nothing new under the sun. That ancient maxim, in a sense, applies to this "new" idea. A tiny coterie of mutual fund historians might still remember a similar fund formed in 1938, which gave early credentials to the buy-and-hold idea. Structured as a fixed trust, Founders Mutual Fund picked an equal-weighted portfolio of 36 of the blue-chip stocks of the day, and held them until 1983, when the fund abandoned the strategy. At the end of that 45-year period, *Founders*

Individual Stocks versus Mutual Funds

In recent years, the flight of investor capital out of individual stocks and into mutual fund shares has reached landslide proportions. For investors in tax-deferred IRAs and corporate retirement plans, that's a good thing in many ways; while their costs are often far too high, funds provide individual investors with far greater diversification and more professional investment oversight than they otherwise might have enjoyed. For taxable investors, however, the benefits of mutual funds are eroded considerably by their realization of capital gains prematurely. When these gains are distributed—as they must be, under Federal law—fund shareholders lose the remarkable advantage of tax-free compounding, and often receive gains realized in holding periods so short that the gains are subject to taxes, not at the top 20 percent rate on long-term gains, but at the rate of up to 40 percent applied to gains realized by the fund on portfolio securities held for twelve months or less.

In the real world of capitalism and competition, one would have expected the industry to have provided, long ago, a wide array of mutual funds with objectives and strategies that would meet the needs of taxable investors. That seemingly inevitable development, however, has yet to gather momentum. I believe the reasons lie in the industry's complacency about investors' lack of awareness of the impact of taxes (perhaps itself inevitable, given the magnificent stock market environment), as well as its hesitancy to offer new funds with objectives and strategies that, at least to some degree, resemble the passive, minimum turnover, high quality, and low costs of index funds. As much as it would serve the interests of investors, that concession would hardly serve the financial interest of most management companies. There has been little innovation (even the new "old" fund I've described in this chapter has yet to be offered to investors), and they are left with few satisfactory choices.

Still, investors—or at least substantial investors who have the means to diversify on their own—are not without recourse. *They can simply abandon mutual funds and buy stocks directly.* To some degree, such a strategy may increase their risk, although much of the risk involved in stock selection can be diversified away by owning, say, 15 to 20 stocks of blue-chip growth companies in unrelated lines of business. But the strategy surely ought to increase returns, for the tax burden of fund investing (added to the ever increasing cost of fund ownership) can be remarkably reduced. By offsetting the added risk with more-than-commensurate after-tax reward, canny investors can markedly enhance their long-term returns.

When they own individual stocks, investors are in a position to control their own gain realization. They can best determine, for their own personal and family situation, answers to questions like these:

- Should I realize gains on a short-term basis and pay a 40 percent penalty tax?
- Even if my gains are long-term, will I be able to reinvest more productively the 80 cents or more of each $1.00 of sales proceeds that I will net after taxes?
- Should I buy and hold forever, with the hope and expectation that at least one, or two or three, of my selections will become home runs, obviating the impact of my (all too likely) bad choices?

Tax control is a crucial issue for investors. If the mutual fund industry is unwilling to offer productive investment strategies to provide tax control, substantial investors will be forced to travel another route. *This industry has no monopoly on managing the assets of the intelligent investor.*

held the same 36 stocks it had owned at the outset. Among them were IBM, Procter & Gamble, duPont, Union Pacific, and Eastman Kodak—not only durable (by definition), but successful enterprises.

Prior to the change in its strategy (I couldn't locate any record of its first five years), the Founders portfolio earned an average annual pretax return of 10.3 percent, compared to the return of 11.4 percent on the Standard & Poor's 500 Index—a gap predictably engendered in part by the fund's operating costs of 0.5 percent. Interestingly, its return was identical to the 10.3 percent return of Massachusetts Investors Trust (MIT, the largest equity fund throughout the entire era). I could not precisely calculate after-tax returns, but the record shows that Founders distributed only minimal gains during the period, while MIT distributed substantial gains. In short, Founders won the after-tax race.

A similar fund, Lexington Corporate Leaders Fund, formed in 1935 and invested in 30 stocks, has, impressively by fund industry standards, virtually matched the Standard & Poor's 500 Index (15.6 percent versus 15.7 percent) over the past 22 years (the earliest comparison available using Morningstar's database). This comparison, along with the Founders data, proves one thing and one thing only: a fund selecting a fixed initial list of large blue-chip stocks—and holding it, come what may—can give a fully competitive account of itself on an after-expense, pretax basis. By so doing, it can generate a substantial margin of after-tax advantage relative to other funds. The industry owes it to intelligent, tax-conscious investors to make such a fund available.

Tax Strategies

The objective of this chapter has been to help taxable fund investors develop intelligent investment strategies that will maximize the after-tax returns they receive from their mutual fund investments. Given the mutual fund industry's heavy reliance on extraordinarily high portfolio turnover—which is highly tax-inefficient—the best choices are: well-structured managed funds with extremely low portfolio turnover (a universe in which there are surprisingly few fund choices); passively managed index funds focused on the entire stock market or on huge market segments such as the Standard & Poor's 500 Index; index-oriented tax-managed funds investing in large growth stocks; and funds offering fixed portfolios, once they are again made available to investors.

But there is another key issue in investors' tax strategy. Qualified retirement plans [401(k), 403(b), IRA] have become critically important in the accumulation of family capital. Allocation of investments between a regular taxable account and a tax-deferred account has become a decision of great moment. Common sense would seem to suggest that income-oriented assets such as bonds should be placed in the tax-deferred account, and growth-oriented assets such as stocks, which have historically provided a large share of their returns as capital gains, should be kept in the taxable account. The logic is simple: current income is taxable at rates as high as 40 percent, whereas capital gains are subject to rates as low as 20 percent. Even more important, the realization of capital gains can be deferred indefinitely, effectively gaining an interest-free loan from the U. S. Treasury.

Through their disregard for taxable shareholders, however, mutual funds have turned that common sense on its head. John Shoven has examined the allocation of stock funds and bond funds between taxable and tax-deferred accounts.[6] He found that, over a 30-year period, most investors would accumulate the greatest level of terminal wealth by keeping *stock funds* in a tax-deferred account, and holding *tax-exempt* municipal bond funds in a taxable account. In his analysis, he assumed that gross returns on stocks were 12 percent and gross returns on municipal bonds were 5.4 percent.

Why wouldn't it be more rewarding to keep corporate bond funds (which, in his study, returned 7.2 percent) in the tax-deferred wrapper, and place stock funds in a taxable account? After all, as long as the stocks' capital gains are unrealized, a stock fund won't sacrifice very much of its 12 percent gain to the IRS, and the investor will earn higher returns from corporate bonds than from municipal bonds.

That seemingly obvious policy simply doesn't work, mostly because the mutual fund industry pays little heed to the needs of taxable shareholders. Largely because of excessive turnover, a typical equity fund manager might transform a 12 percent pretax return into an 8.5 percent after-tax return. Through the serial distribution of long-term and even short-term gains, the manager needlessly sacrifices 30 percent of the stock market's gain to the tax collector. Given the distribution patterns of most equity funds, Professor Shoven concludes, the long-term investor can accumulate the greatest amount of terminal wealth by keeping stock funds *inside* the tax-deferred account and tax-exempt municipal bond funds *outside*.

But it need not be that way with all mutual funds. The Shoven study also presents an illustration showing the after-tax returns of an account in an index-type fund with much lower portfolio turnover. Table 13.2, comparing Fund A, a conventionally managed stock fund, with Fund B, an

TABLE 13.2

After Tax Returns of Tax-Inefficient and Tax-Efficient Stock Funds

	Dividends and Short-Term Gains	Long-Term Capital Gains	Accrued Capital Gains	Pretax Returns	After-Tax Returns
Inefficient Fund A	4%	6%	2%	12%	8.5%
Efficient Fund B	1	1	10	12	10.8

index stock fund, summarizes Professor Shoven's findings. Both stock funds earn the same 12 percent pretax return, but Fund A distributes a full 10 percentage points of this return—4 percent as short-term gains and income and 6 percent as long-term capital gains. Fund B distributes just 2 percentage points of its 12 percent return—1 percent as income and 1 percent as long-term gains. Once Shoven accounts for the taxes due on these distributions, Fund B boasts a 2.3 percentage point advantage over Fund A—a 25 percent premium in after-tax return.

Armed with a tax-efficient stock fund, investors can accumulate more capital by inverting Professor Shoven's unconventional prescription, and holding taxable bond funds inside their pension account and *tax-efficient* stock funds outside their pension account. After a 30-year holding period,

TABLE 13.3

Wealth Accumulated with Use of Tax-Inefficient and Tax-Efficient Stock Funds*

	Stocks in Pension Fund, Municipal Bonds Outside	Taxable Bonds in Pension Fund, Stocks Outside	Difference
Inefficient Fund A	$104,000	$ 72,000	−$32,000
Efficient Fund B	104,000	112,000	+8,000

*Assumed returns: municipal bonds, 5.2 percent tax-exempt; corporate bonds, 7.4 percent pretax, 4.4 percent after tax; common stocks, 12 percent pretax, 8.5 percent after tax in Fund A, 10.8 percent after tax in Fund B.

based on a $10,000 investment—$5,000 in stocks and $5,000 in bonds— the final value would be as shown in Table 13.3.

The use of a highly tax-efficient stock fund, then, would turn the equation upside down. An investor utilizing bonds in the pension account and stocks in a typical tax-inefficient fund outside accumulates $72,000, a $32,000 shortfall relative to the capital accumulated with the Shoven allocations. But when the same 50-50 strategy utilizes a tax-efficient stock fund, the accumulation totals $112,000, an excess of $8,000 relative to the capital accumulated with the Shoven allocation. The tables have been turned upside down. Using bonds in the pension account changes a *shortfall* of $32,000 into an *excess* of $8,000 (along with an estate tax advantage, since the cost basis of the taxable stock account is stepped up to market value at death).

Most investors may well decide to keep some stocks and some bonds in both taxable and tax-deferred accounts. But especially for those investing sizable sums—more than the $10,000 to $12,000 annually that, under current tax law, can be invested in tax-deferred accounts such as a 401(k) plan or a traditional IRA—the Shoven study offers sensible guidance to the optimal allocation of assets between a retirement fund and a conventional savings account. The decision must be a major focus of the investor's tax strategy.

THE PARALLAX VIEW

Investors must realize the importance of not merely minimizing taxes, but also maximizing after-tax returns. They must consider all three of the spatial dimensions of mutual fund investing: return, risk, and cost. Taxable investors must unfailingly recognize that taxes are costs—and substantial costs at that—and it is high time for mutual fund managers to do so as well. While there seems little need for additional conventional mutual funds offering the same old strategies, there is ample need for new funds designed solely to serve taxable investors. A fixed trust owning a diversified list of 50 U.S. blue-chip growth stocks is one alternative. In this global day and age, a sister fixed trust with a list of 75 of the largest growth stocks in the world is another. Both lists would be handsome. But, whatever stocks are chosen, the fixed trust must be operated at minimal cost, and structured to limit cash flows.

The ideas and concepts in this chapter, however obvious and painfully simple, are fully consistent with my parallax view of the mutual fund industry today. The new fund I've discussed is not, like so many funds in recent years, another transitory fad to capitalize on the strategy of the moment. It is based on a durable concept that capitalizes on age-old basics. Instead of focusing on what's most marketable to speculative investors in the short term, the industry should offer what's most serviceable to intelligent investors in the long term. The timing of introducing such a fund is risky, but so is the timing of all new funds. The markets of the world, particularly those in the United States, may look overextended today, but my earlier advice applies here: Never think you know more than the market. No one does.

It is high time for mutual fund managers to awaken to the critical issue of taxes, review their investment policies, and consider whether the industry's 30 million taxable shareholders are getting a fair shake. Mutual funds do not have a monopoly on the affections of investors. If fund managers persist in ignoring the tax consequences of their decisions, investors have the option of owning a diversified list of individual stocks held directly, and maintaining personal control over the realization of gains. Other tax-efficient means of investing are also emerging, notably the unit trusts known as "Spiders" and "Diamonds," essentially index funds replicating, respectively, the S&P 500 Index and the Dow Jones Industrial Average, and listed on the American Stock Exchange. That competition will, finally, have to be confronted if mutual funds are to remain the investment of choice for America's families.

CHAPTER

ON TIME

The Fourth Dimension—
Magic or Tyranny?

The language of geometry has proved a particularly fertile source of imagery and metaphor in my efforts to describe the elements of intelligent long-term investing. In the past, I have used the triangle to describe the eternal interplay of reward, risk, and cost in shaping investment returns, but a triangle exists only as a flat, two-dimensional surface. An elongated cube, which has the three spatial dimensions of length, breadth, and depth, is a more useful geometrical figure for those three key elements of investing. It better represents the complicated and simultaneous interplay among the dynamic vectors of return. But, as Albert Einstein pointed out, we live in a universe that is not only spatial, but temporal. He identified time as the Fourth Dimension, and so it is in the world of investing, too.

In other words, investment return has four dimensions. Three are the spatial dimensions: length (which I'll describe as reward), breadth (risk), and depth (cost). But there is also a temporal dimension: time. Figure 14.1 shows how the four dimensions interact. Never make an investment without having a clear idea of the impact each dimension will have, and never develop a financial program that doesn't meet the same standard.

I'll first review my earlier comments on the dimensions of reward, risk, and cost, and then, turn to the time dimension. These four dimensions are interlinked in tantalizing ways—sometimes obvious, sometimes

---

FIGURE 14.1

The Four Dimensions of Investing

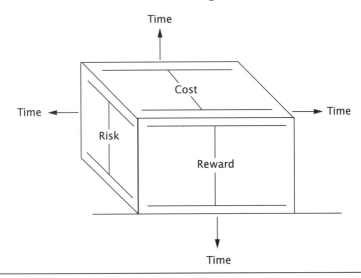

Time

Cost

Time ← → Time

Risk

Reward

Time

---

subtle. The intelligent investor cannot afford to ignore any of them. The challenge is to weigh each of them properly in the light of the investment goals to be achieved. Doing so with common sense and discipline is the key to the development of a sound investment program.

REWARD—THE FIRST DIMENSION

In Figure 14.1, I used "length" to describe reward, simply because it is the longer of the two straight-line dimensions of a surface. Reward must be given primacy as a factor in the process of wealth accumulation. Looking back at the past 15-plus years, during which mutual funds have become, overwhelmingly, the investment of choice for America's families, reward almost seems taken for granted. During that period, the total stock market has garnered an astonishing annualized return of 17.2 percent. As a result, an investor who placed $10,000 into the stock market at the end of 1982 would now have an investment worth $117,000 if costs and taxes were ignored. (Would that they could be!) During this era of abundance for so many investors, building a portfolio of assets has seemed easy.

Financial markets have, however, demonstrated a truly remarkable tendency to revert to the mean over time. It would be unwise to lose sight of the fact that the 12.6 percent real (inflation-adjusted) return of the past 15 years—almost double the long-term norm of some 7 percent—has been exceeded in but nine of the 181 periods of similar duration since 1802. It hardly seems probable that such a return shall soon be repeated: the investment fundamentals are clearly less compelling today than in mid-1982, when the bull rampage began, and when stocks were priced at a multiple of 7.9 times earnings. In late-1998, at 27 times earnings, they are more than three times as richly valued. In 1982, $1.00 of dividends could be purchased for an initial investment of $16 (a yield of 6 percent). Today, $1 of dividends costs $71 (a yield of 1.4 percent), almost four times as richly valued. (While it is said that dividends don't matter any more, I remain unconvinced.) Surely, if $71 for $1 of dividends is not too high a price, there must be *some* price that *is* too high to pay.

RISK—THE SECOND DIMENSION

As you survey the inevitably uncertain prospects for reward in the near term, which are perhaps greater at this level of the stock market than during the entire investment lifetime of most investors today, you must necessarily consider risk, the second dimension of investment return. In investment terms, risk is to reward what breadth is to length in spatial terms: the *lesser* of the two sides of the plane. That is not to say that risk is unimportant. It is crucial. But I simply do not accept its being counted *equally* with reward. Indeed, as I noted in Chapter 1, faith in the future, an essential element in investing, entails the implicit assumption that return will exceed risk. If the potential return does not exceed the potential risk, why invest at all? But risk is one of the hallmarks of equity investing, and fear of loss is often the investor's greatest concern. Conventionally, risk is measured with precision, albeit imperfectly, in terms of standard deviation, although that is a backward-looking measure that is more accurately a measure of price volatility rather than risk. (The two are not exactly the same!)

In weighing the first and second dimensions of return, an investor relies on measures of risk-adjusted return, of which the consummate measure is the Sharpe Ratio, essentially the relationship between the return of a portfolio and its volatility. As I noted in Chapter 6, however, counting one unit of risk as the equivalent of one unit of return seems simplistic, for at the margin it hardly seems rational to weight a meaningless difference of one percentage point of volatility equally with a priceless difference of one percentage point in long-term reward. Nonetheless, some investors have trained an almost singular focus on risk-adjusted return. In an effort to reduce portfolio volatility, institutional investors, and many individual investors as well, have increasingly diversified beyond the liquid financial markets of the United States. They have moved into international stock and bond markets, and have sampled a variety of nontraditional alternative assets: hedge funds and relatively illiquid assets such as venture capital, private capital of more seasoned enterprises without public markets, and hard assets such as real estate and energy. (Gold, once considered the consummate contracyclical holding, has lost its luster, presumably because of nearly two decades of languishing returns.)

Since they moved into the mainstream of institutional investing, these types of investments have rarely distinguished themselves, but the strategy may yet succeed. If the relative returns of international equities, after lagging for a decade, were merely to revert to their long-term means, they might well enhance the results of an equity portfolio. And it is probably reasonable to assume that, in the long run, illiquid investments such as venture capital and private equity should carry premiums over freely marketable issues, suggesting that a significant commitment in these areas could also enhance returns for investors to whom liquidity is not a major concern.* A pallid past, then, may well be the precursor of a favorable future, in which both reduced volatility and enhanced returns are achieved by the use of nontraditional asset classes.

This sequence of events, however, is merely conjecture. But make no mistake: each of these alternative asset classes carries its own outsized special risks, risks that investors are not required to assume. Besides, the *individual securities* in each class often carry extraordinarily high risk—inherently, a far greater risk than owning large, highly marketable, liquid U.S. stocks. Investors should carefully consider the implications of a decision to invest in alternative assets—holding investments that *individually* carry higher risks, with the goal of reducing the risk of the equity portfolio *as a whole*—and be fully aware of the paradox that decision entails.

---

*Independent studies indicate that such alternative investments have provided returns in the range of 15–20 percent annually during 1992–1997. Compared with the 18 percent return on the S&P 500 Index during the same period, and taking into account the leverage in many alternative investments, such returns would not be considered very impressive.

COST—THE THIRD DIMENSION

The first two elements, reward and risk, are well-accepted dimensions of investment return—indeed, usually to the complete exclusion of the third dimension. For example, how often do we read "risk/reward ratio" rather than "risk/reward/cost" ratio? Yet the impact of cost both on reward and on risk cannot possibly be overstated.

Cost matters. It matters in every far-flung corner of the world of investing, but it matters most where it is the highest. Throughout this book, I have catalogued the exceptionally high costs that characterize much of the mutual fund industry, and their impact on net fund returns that are astonishingly sensitive to cost. Add up the operating expense ratio of the average equity mutual fund (1.5 percent), plus the minimum estimated average portfolio transaction costs (0.5 percent), and the total cost of a no-load fund is at least 2 percent per year. If the fund charges a traditional front-end sales load (as most funds do), the minimum initial commission, amortized over a 10-year holding period, would come to 0.5 percent per year, bringing the total annual cost to 2.5 percent. For the one-fourth of all funds with the highest fees, the total cost would come to 2.5 percent per year (or 3.0 percent if high-cost load funds were used).

As I noted at the close of Chapter 3, even a 2.2 percent annual cost could consume 22 percent of a normal market return of perhaps 10 percent annually in nominal terms, and fully 30 percent of return if 2.5 percent inflation reduced it to a real return of 7.5 percent. Compounded over 10 years, this cost would consume 30 percent of the aggregate *nominal* return, and fully 36 percent of the aggregate *real* return. Looked at another way, a 2.2 percent cost would confiscate an astonishing 63 percent of the normal equity risk premium of 3.5 percent. Fund expenses are hungry ogres, not easily sated.

Not even included in these calculations is the appetite for consuming returns manifested by taxes, the equally famished cousins of the expense ogres. And as I noted in Chapter 13, mutual fund portfolios are typically managed with utter disregard for tax considerations. Fund managers not only fail to defer gain realization to the latest possible moment, but they also realize huge portions of gains long before they become eligible (after one year) for the 20 percent maximum rate on long-term gains. Perhaps one-third of all fund gains are realized in holding periods of less than one year and taxed at up to the maximum 40 percent rate applicable to ordinary income.

LONG-TERM INVESTING—THE CANNY SCOTS

While bona fide long-term investing seems almost entirely absent from the U.S. mutual fund scene, there are exceptions around the globe. A recent article in *The Wall Street Journal* reported that money managers in Scotland are following a path untrodden by most U.S. fund managers. At Walter Scott and Partners in Edinburgh, the firm focuses on a concentrated portfolio, which "holds a maximum of 50 stocks, and changes no more than six names annually—turnover of less than 15 percent. The firm's managers ignore stock-market benchmarks, and shrug off market turmoil." A spokesman notes that "Stock markets may go up and down a wee bit, but our goal is to have shares in companies that can grow their cash. At the end of the day, you're investing in a business you expect to grow. And compound growth is the most valuable tool of any investment manager."[1]

During the recent years of soaring markets, taxes on capital gains realized and distributed by mutual funds may well have penalized investment fund returns for taxable shareholders by another 2.2 percentage points each year, doubling the impact of the 2.2 percent annual cost penalty. During the 1995–1998 period alone, furthermore, the average equity fund actually lagged the total stock market by an annual rate of five percentage points, even *before* taxes were deducted, so taxes would have taken that shortfall to more than seven percentage points. Wise fund investors will ignore the third dimension of return, cost—specifically, fund investment expenses *and* taxes—at their peril.

TIME—THE FOURTH DIMENSION

With this review of the three *spatial* dimensions of return—length, breadth, and depth, as illustrated by return, risk, and cost—we move to the fourth dimension: time. Albert Einstein's General Theory of Relativity is generally credited with developing the concept of time as the fourth dimension of the universe, and time is an equally useful concept in the world of investment return.

In the investment world, the importance of time in shaping returns has been honored more in the breach than in the observance—more in theory than in practice. We speak of the value of long-term investing, and we say kind words about long-term investors. But when asked to list them, it is hard to name two. Who comes to mind after Warren Buffett?

In the mutual fund industry, as noted at the outset of this book, we clearly invest for the short term; fully one-third of equity fund portfolios have turnover of more than 100 percent each year. If our marketing policies and fund supermarkets are any indication, we seek short-term investors, too. And we get them: shareholders are turning over their own equity funds at an average annual rate of more than 30 percent. These numbers reflect incredible mobility; in both cases, they reflect foolish short-run strategies. In the search for investment return, I have no doubt that they are counterproductive. Looking across large classes of shareholders, I sometimes suspect that wealthy private investors may be the only significant group that prizes a long-term strategy and practices low portfolio turnover. And I am hardly above suggesting that the reliance on such a strategy may be precisely why these families are wealthy in the first place. Experience need not be painful to teach a powerful lesson. And fund investors and managers alike should learn from that experience.

Among all strategies, market index strategies have the longest time horizons. An all-market index changes only at the glacial pace of the entire market. Initial offerings of stocks are small in relative weight, and when firms vanish by merger or bankruptcy, no portfolio transactions ensue. The annual portfolio turnover of an all-market index fund rarely exceeds 2 to 3 percent, essentially an average holding period of 33 to 50 *years*. That long horizon is surely a significant factor in the formidable relative pretax returns that index funds have provided, as well as in their almost unparalleled superiority in providing after-tax returns.

Time and Reward—"The Magic of Compounding"

Given Einstein's role in bringing time to the fore as the fourth dimension of our universe, it is hardly surprising that he is often quoted (perhaps apocryphally) as having described compound interest as "the greatest mathematical discovery of all time." Indeed, the powerful link between time and reward is often described as the "magic of compounding." The longer the time horizon, the greater the power of compounding investment returns in transforming an initial outright investment, or a series of modest annual investments, into a truly breathtaking terminal value.

Let's begin with two basic cases of the magic of compounding. Figure 14.2 shows the results of a single initial investment over time. This is a

FIGURE 14.2

The First Dimension: Reward and the Magic of Compounding

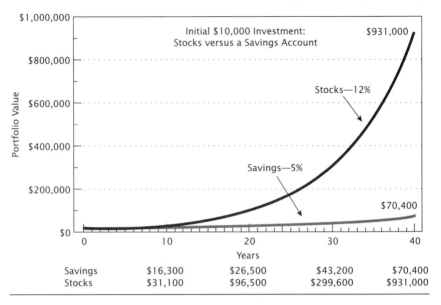

	0	10	20	30	40
Savings		$16,300	$26,500	$43,200	$70,400
Stocks		$31,100	$96,500	$299,600	$931,000

typical mutual fund industry format for comparing the result of an initial investment of $10,000 in stocks, held for a working lifetime of 40 years, earning a high return of 12 percent annually, with a fixed-income alternative that is earning the much lower annual return of 5 percent. The 12 percent return approximates the rate of total return on the stock market over the past 40 years; the 5 percent return approximates the recent yield of U.S. Treasury bills.

The investment in stocks builds its reward over savings year after year. Figure 14.2 shows how this edge in reward grows over the decades. The returns on stocks produce a final reward of $931,000; the returns on savings produce a final reward of $70,400. "Magic" is hardly too strong a word for this awesome differential.

Table 14.1 shows a second example of compounding for an investor whose goal is to invest regularly and accumulate $500,000 of assets. The hypothetical investor is 25 years old and expects to retire at age 65. After making the necessary calculations (using the same return assumptions), the choice comes down to (a) investing $43 per month in stocks for 40 years; or (b) investing $328 per month in savings for the same 40 years.

TABLE 14.1

Monthly Investing to Build $500,000 in Assets—$43/Month in Stocks versus $328/Month in Savings*

Number of Years	Cumulative Monthly Investments		Final Value	
	Stocks	Savings	Stocks	Savings
10	$ 5,100	$ 39,300	$ 9,900	$ 51,100
20	10,200	78,600	42,500	135,200
30	15,300	118,000	150,000	273,800
40	20,400	157,300	500,000	500,000

*Assumed rates of return: stocks, 12%; savings, 5%.

Here we see precisely the same compounding, but it is working in a different fashion. The same capital accumulation (consistent with the investor's objective) occurs in each case, but infinitely smaller investments are required to reach the goal if stocks are chosen over savings (assuming both that the past returns are achieved, and that the investments are in a tax-deferred account). The cumulative $43 monthly investment in stocks ($516 per year) totals $20,400 over 40 years; the cumulative $328 monthly investments in savings came to $3,936 per year, a total of $157,300 by the end of the period. The stock investment required only one-eighth the investment to reach the requisite $500,000 total. Magic is at work again.

The magic of compounding becomes even more apparent if we examine the results for three investors who delay beginning their programs. Instead of beginning to invest at age 25, one waits for 10 years, the second waits for 20 years, and the third waits for 30 years. It's not easy to acquire the habit of thrift, especially when spending is so much more fun than saving. Fun, yes. But expensive fun. Whether they invest or save, the cost of delay for investors ascends steeply with the passage of time.

Using the stock account only, and again assuming a return of 12 percent over the past 40 years, the cost of delay is shown in Figure 14.3. The difference between putting away $43 a month ($516 a year) if you begin early, but a staggering $2,174 a month ($26,088 a year) if you let 30 years elapse is astonishing. As shown in Figure 14.3, the fairly gradual slope that early investors must climb becomes, for investors who wait too long, an Everest-like peak that defies even the most resourceful mountaineers. (A

THE RULE OF 72

"The Rule of 72" provides a wonderful illustration of the magic of compounding. To quickly approximate how many years are required to double the value of an investment, simply divide the rate of return into 72: a 4 percent return takes about 18 years; 6 percent, 12 years; 10 percent, 7 plus years; and so on.

The table below shows how quickly money grows over various time periods at various rates. Note how the reward of higher return increases over time. At 4 percent, it takes 72 years—a very long time horizon—for the original investment to multiply sixteen-fold. But at 12 percent, it takes 24 years, only one-third the time, to grow sixteen-fold. After some 30 years, the investment compounding at 12 percent annually multiplies 32 times over, a multiple that the 4 percent rate would not reach until 90 years had elapsed. More magic.

The Rule of 72 also works in another useful way for investors putting money away today so that they can receive income tomorrow. For any given rate of return, the Rule of 72 shows how many years you must regularly invest a given sum before you can stop investing and then start withdrawing the same amount *without depleting your capital.*

For example, if you invest $500 per month at a 6 percent rate of return (72 divided by 6), after 12 years you could regularly withdraw $500 per month and still leave your principal untouched. After 24 years, you could begin to make withdrawals of $1,500 per month. After 36 years, you could withdraw $3,500 per month, and still preserve principal. But if your rate of return was 12 percent, your waiting time would be shorter: 6 years to begin $500 monthly withdrawals, 12 years for $1,500, and 18 years for $3,500. After 24 years, you could withdraw $7,500 per month without impairing your principal—fully five times the amount possible at the 6 percent rate of return.

Caution: The table may suggest that the stock market works off some sort of actuarial table. It does not, under *any* circumstances. If future stock returns are lower than 12 percent—hardly an inconceivable outcome—future retirement income would be reduced. For example, a monthly investment of $500 made at 12 percent would permit $7,500 withdrawals after 24 years without depleting capital. But if the return were 8 percent, the permissible monthly withdrawal after 24 years would be only $2,670. So be cautious about projecting past returns into the future, and be conservative in the returns you assume.

Using the Rule of 72

Compound Rate	2 Times	4 Times	8 Times	16 Times	32 Times
4%	18 years	36 years	54 years	72 years	90 years
6	12	24	36	48	60
8	9	18	27	36	45
10	7	14	21	28	35
12	6	12	18	24	30

FIGURE 14.3

How the Slope Steepens with Time

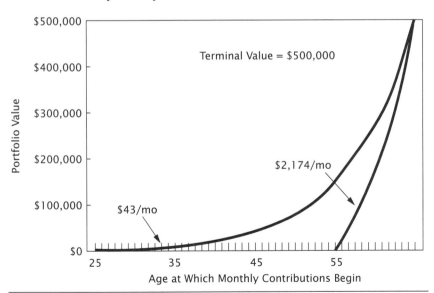

Note: Monthly investment required at age 35, $143; age 45, $505.

delay of 10 years more than triples the monthly outlay, to $143; a delay of 20 years multiplies the monthly outlay 12-fold, to $505.)

Time and Risk—"The Moderation of Compounding"

Almost as striking as the interplay between time and reward is the relationship between time and risk, particularly in the stock market. As your time horizon increases, the variability of stock market returns declines. As the years roll on, compounding moderates market risk. Furthermore, the risk of earning the stock market's long-term return declines quite steeply during surprisingly short spans. For example, merely extending your time horizon from one year to five years telescopes the absolute range of stock returns from +67 percent to −40 percent all the way down to a range of 27 percent to −11 percent. By the same token, the normal level of risk extremes (measured conventionally by one standard deviation), falls precipitously, from a high of 25.1 percent and a low of −11.1 percent in one year to a high of 14.4 percent and a low of −0.6 percent over five years. Extending the period to 10 years reduces the range of annual returns from a high of 11.2 percent to a low of 2.4 percent.

In the risky business of investing in stocks, most of the risk reduction is accomplished in a decade. Add five years, and the range of returns is reduced to a high of 10.3 percent and a low of 3.4 percent over 15 years. Add another full decade, and the range is only slightly different—high 8.7 percent, low 4.7 percent—a minuscule reduction after 25 years. Doubling the period to a full half-century scarcely reduces risk any further. The annual range of annualized returns on stocks dwindles to a high of 7.7 percent to a low of 5.7 percent.

Figure 14.4, showing how risk diminishes with the passage of time, is based on the data in Figure 1.3 in Chapter 1, now cast as a sort of half-mountain and its mirror image. *Descending the slope of risk is far easier than ascending the slope of reward.* Of the maximum decline in risk over an investing lifetime, fully six-tenths has been accomplished by holding stocks for 5 years, eight-tenths by holding them for 10 years, and nine-tenths by holding them for 15 years. But, lest we forget, risk, while reduced over 15 years, is hardly eliminated. While the normal ranges, as shown in Figure 14.4, are fairly narrow, the extremes are wide. During the best 15-year period, the annualized return was 14.2 percent; during the worst, a loss of −1.4 percent annually. No actuarial table here! The investor's time horizon itself makes investment risk an elusive concept, one inevitably interlinked

FIGURE 14.4

The Second Dimension: Risk and the Moderation of Compounding

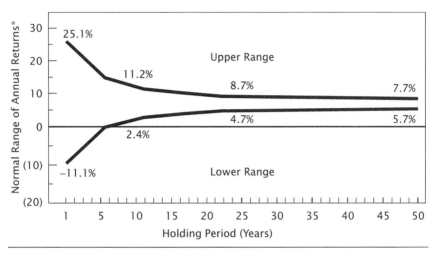

* Normal range based on one standard deviation of return (middle ⅔ of observations).

with investment reward. The fourth dimension significantly shapes our perception, not only of the first dimension of investment return, but of the second dimension.

Time and Cost—"The Tyranny of Compounding"

My earlier discussion of the interaction of time and reward included Figure 14.2, showing the typical fund industry representation of the virtues of investing in equities versus putting savings in a fixed-interest account. But fund investors do not earn the full market return. As a group, they cannot possibly do so, because fund investors incur costs, and costs are subtracted directly from the *gross* returns funds earn. Only the net returns are passed along to fund shareholders.

The mutual fund industry almost *never* shows the relationship between time and cost. If shown, the chart would be a rather disturbing one. It would present the same time period, the same stock market return of 12 percent, and the same $931,000 end result. But a second line would show the results assumed for a 10 percent mutual fund return: the market return reduced by estimated all-in annual equity fund expenses of 2 percent.

FIGURE 14.5

The Interaction of Time and Cost: Growth of $10,000 over 40 Years

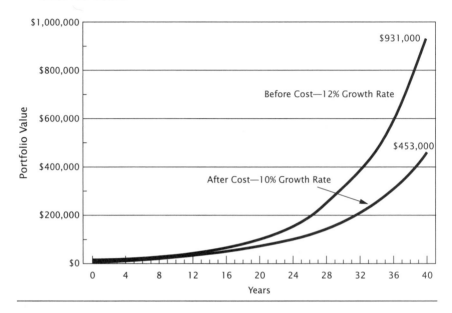

At 10 percent, the line still grows, nicely sweeping upward as the years pass, but to a 40-year total of only $453,000—*less than half of the value generated by the stock market's return.* Over the full 40-year period, costs have confiscated fully $478,000. Put another way, more than half the market's return has been consumed by the industry's costs. Figure 14.5 depicts pre-cost and post-cost returns.

This evidence, brutal but factual, reflects "the tyranny of compounding."* Figure 14.6 compares the extra capital (over and above the initial investment) earned with a gross return of 12 percent with the capital earned with a net return (after-cost) of 10 percent. In the first year, a gross return of 12 percent increases a $10,000 investment by $1,200, but the investment with a net return of 10 percent grows by $1,000, or 83 percent of the $1,200 provided by the market. After 10 years, the value of the costly investment has fallen to 76 percent of the market, and after 25 years to 61

---

*Journalist Jason Zweig calls this effect "the black magic of de-compounding."

FIGURE 14.6

The Third Dimension: Cost and the Tyranny of Compounding

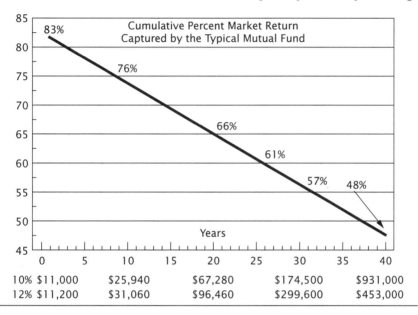

10%	$11,000	$25,940	$67,280	$174,500	$931,000
12%	$11,200	$31,060	$96,460	$299,600	$453,000

percent. After 40 years, the capital earned in the fund is worth just 48 percent of the capital that would have been accumulated in the market.

Cost matters. I use the phrase once again. Small differences in compound interest lead to increasing, and finally staggering, differences in capital accumulation. This phrase, however, illustrates not only the *magic* of compounding, but the *tyranny* of compounding. A higher cost investment loses ever more ground to a lower cost investment as the years roll on, leading to sharply lower capital accumulation. Like time and reward and time and risk, the dimensions of time and cost are also interlinked.

The other major cost of investing—taxes—also leads to sharply descending relative returns over time, so the tyranny of compounding gains further momentum. Based on the analysis presented in Chapter 13, which assumed a market return of 12 percent and an after-cost, after-tax mutual fund return of 8 percent, we can conclude that the combined appetites of the expense and tax ogres resulted in a truly staggering shortfall over just 25 years. The final capital value would have been only 37 percent of what the precost, pretax market return would have suggested. If, using the same net rates of return, the time line were extended to 40 years, the final values would have been $931,000 and $217,200. *Only 23 percent of the projected capital would have been accumulated.* The tyrannical impact of fund expenses combined with taxes paid on fund dividends and capital gains distributions, if almost completely ignored by the mutual fund industry, can no longer be ignored by fund investors. The sheer weight of evidence that cost matters is simply too compelling.

THE DIMENSIONAL IMPERATIVE

When navigating the financial markets, the long-term investor must keep in mind the four basic dimensions of long-term return—reward, risk, cost, and time—and must apply them to every asset class. Never forget that these four dimensions are remarkably interdependent.

> *Reward and risk go hand-in-hand. The conventional wisdom of finance teaches that if one is to increase, so must the other, and vice versa. Cost has a significant impact on both reward and risk. Lower costs make it possible to earn a higher return without assuming extra risk, or to hold reward constant and reduce risk. And because the passage of years multiplies the aggregate reward, moderates the volatility risk, and magnifies the burden of cost, time interacts with each of the three spatial dimensions of investing.*

If your basic objectives are long-term in nature, awareness of this interdependence will give you a strong advantage in planning the voyage of the flagship represented by your own investment accounts. During the long voyage that you take to reach your goal of accumulating capital, the financial markets will inevitably experience crosscurrents, tidal shifts, high winds, rough seas, and rugged storms. Today's bright skies, sprightly breezes, and calm waters won't last forever. But those of you who are looking to far horizons, who are able to accept a bit more short-term risk in the pursuit of enhanced long-term returns, who are conscious of the destructive power of cost, and who are able to use time to its highest advantage, will win the battle for investment survival, if only you have the wit and the wisdom to stay the exciting course that lies ahead.

PART IV

ON FUND MANAGEMENT

This part turns from the investment focus of the first three parts of the book to an examination of *why* so many mutual funds have failed to measure up to the implicit expectations of investors. The problems are grounded in the nature and structure of today's mutual fund industry. We have moved this industry away from our guiding principles to new principles that ill-serve fund investors. No longer is the prudent, disciplined stewardship of fund portfolios the core function, around which all others are satellite. Rather, the distribution of shares through aggressive advertising and selling techniques has become the industry's core function, dictating both the way we manage funds and the kind of funds we offer, as well as the prices at which we offer them. Management has been replaced by marketing as the talisman. Technology, despite the incredible blessings it has brought to the information available to fund investors and to the enhancement of the services we provide, has become our bane. Technology, in fact, has facilitated the metamorphosis of mutual funds from their role as the providers of sensible long-term investment programs to proxies for individual common stocks, to be actively traded by short-term investors in marketplaces resembling casinos.

With the affairs of mutual funds controlled by external management companies, considerable tension exists between the interests of fund shareholders and fund managers, a separation of ownership from control that has been counterproductive for shareholders. Yet, most fund directors seem oblivious to these issues, and fund boards, seemingly uncritically, routinely rubber-stamp contracts with underperforming managers and acquiesce in a steady round of management fee increases. A new structure under which funds would manage themselves may be called for. In the final chapter of Part IV, I explore the implications of new governance structures that would better serve the interests of shareholders. Such commonsense structural changes, I argue, could once again make prudent investment management ascendant over aggressive marketing as the focus of the industry, with great benefit to fund investors.

CHAPTER

ON PRINCIPLES

IMPORTANT PRINCIPLES
MUST BE INFLEXIBLE

One hundred and thirty-four years ago, in what proved to be his final public address, Abraham Lincoln said: "Important principles must be inflexible." He was right. In my judgment, the single most important principle on which the mutual fund industry was founded—and under which it has prospered—not only has become far too flexible, but is apparently being abandoned. This chapter will describe how this process has disengaged us from our roots, propose some solutions, and, along the way, suggest the role that mutual fund shareholders might play in a renaissance that will make this a better industry.

What are the mutual fund industry's founding principles? Management, diversification, service (including daily valuation of fund shares, liquidity, full disclosure, and convenience). Of these principles, management is the most important. Fund management, in my view, should be defined by a spirit of trusteeship, professional competence and discipline, and focus on the long term. That vital principle and these three critical components are in the process of losing their role as the driving force—in the long run, the *life* force—of the mutual fund business.

That is a strong statement, but I consider it a fair description of what is going on in the industry at present:

- *Trusteeship* implies making the interests of fund shareholders our highest priority and charging a reasonable price for our services. It is being supplanted by a focus on asset gathering—on distribution of fund shares. We seem to worship at the shrine of the Great God Market Share, the exorbitant cost of which is borne by fund shareholders.

- *Professional competence and discipline*, originally applied to investment fundamentals, are being focused on speculation. The earmarks include rapid turnover in fund investment portfolios (*averaging* 85 percent per year!), funds' concentration on ever narrowing segments of the stock market, and far too many gunslinger portfolio managers.

- *Focus on the long term*, which once defined the eminent suitability of mutual funds for long-term investors, has become a focus on the ownership of fund shares for the short term, a second level of speculation. Even more baneful, fund shareholders are being enticed to use their mutual funds as vehicles for rapid switching—sometimes to take advantage of market timing, but too often, to simply jump on the bandwagon of the latest hot fund. That, too, is speculation.

These trends are ominous, for investors as well as for the industry. More important, these trends are hardly good for our nation's system of capital formation. Sixty years ago, Lord Keynes wrote: "When the capital development of a country becomes the by-product of the activities of a casino, the job is likely to be ill-done." His warning is equally valid today. The mutual fund industry is developing a form of *casino capitalism*, featuring rapid trading in the financial markets and in the mutual fund marketplace, with an excessive portion of the amounts that are wagered going to the croupiers. Unfortunately, the terminology of gambling has begun to permeate the world of investing.

DISTRIBUTION DRIVES THE INDUSTRY

In the mutual fund industry, distribution has become more important than management, and asset gathering is superseding trusteeship.* My

---

*I believe that my characterizations of the mutual fund industry in the aggregate here are fair, but it would be unfair not to acknowledge that some industry participants take a more enlightened view. They exist, though I am confident that they constitute a fairly small minority.

concern regarding these trends is hardly new. When I wrote my 1951 senior thesis at Princeton, I chose as my topic a tiny young industry that had $2 billion of assets under management—roughly 4/100ths of 1 percent of today's $5 trillion total. Even then, I explicitly concluded that funds should give their shareholders a fairer shake by cutting fees and sales charges, and by making "no claim to superiority to the market averages." More fundamentally, I urged that the focus of the industry should be, above all, on serving shareholders, "the function around which all others are satellite." At the close of the final chapter of my thesis, I underlined this citation: *"The principal function of investment companies is the management of their investment portfolios. Everything else is incidental to the performance of this function."*

If that principle ever existed, it is on the way out today. Distribution of mutual fund shares seems to have become the principal function of investment companies. Listen to the manager of the largest mutual fund: "It's like the difference between making movies and distributing them. It's better to be in the distribution business, given that you have access to everybody else's business." This is, of course, a plug for the mutual fund casino, the so-called "fund marketplace." The idea is: "Buy any funds that catch your fancy, but buy them from us." Trade often, and, by shifting the cost of trading from your own account to the amorphous, voiceless mass of the longer-term shareholders of the funds, do it "for free." Today, the average holding period for an equity fund investor appears to be about 3 years; in 1970, before the days of "free switching," it was something like 12½ years.

MANAGEMENT VERSUS DISTRIBUTION

Note how far such a strategy departs from what I regard as the two most basic principles of investing in mutual funds: Invest for the long term, and its corollary, don't expect miracles from management (another quote from my Princeton thesis). What I've called casino capitalism is diametrically opposed to those two principles. Paradoxically, the head of by far the largest mutual fund casino (known accurately, but rather sadly, as a "supermarket") agrees with both of them. His own personal investment principles are evidenced in his actions: He owns funds as long-term investments. In his own words, "in market timing . . . there are so many things working against you . . . the decision making, the emotional part, the analytics of making the right decision . . . the cost, the taxes." And he owns passively managed index funds. "I'm more of an indexer . . . if you get an

S&P index return, you'll be in the 85th percentile of performance. Why would you screw it up?" Yet the firm he created seems to be built on two countervailing principles: "Pick hot managers," and its corollary, "Switch and get rich." Maybe it is my Calvinist streak, but I am troubled by the idea that one's personal investment principles can so blatantly contradict the investment principles of one's business. President Lincoln would not have been amused.

These examples from two of our industry's current leaders buttress my concern that the industry is on the way to abandoning its fundamental principle—management—and replacing it with another principle—distribution at all costs. Why is this a problem? First, distribution is extremely expensive, and the costs are borne by mutual fund shareholders in the form of ever-rising expense ratios. The annual equity fund expense ratio has risen by some 50 percent in 15 years (from 0.97 percent of assets in 1981 to 1.55 percent in 1997), even as assets have exploded (see Figure 15.1). With equity fund assets up from $40 billion to *$2.8 trillion*, I estimate that annual costs paid by equity fund shareholders alone (taking into account that large funds typically have somewhat lower ratios than small funds) have risen from $320 million to *$34 billion* in this period—a hundredfold increase, far larger than the seventyfold increase in equity fund assets. If fund expense ratios in this industry had simply remained fixed, the costs borne

FIGURE 15.1

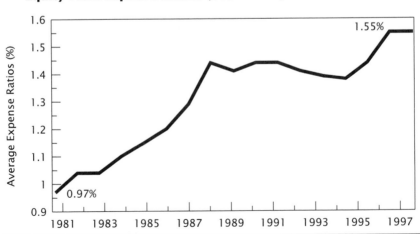

Equity Fund Expense Ratios (1981–1997)

by mutual fund investors would presently be $27 billion—a $7 billion saving. And, because there are staggering economies of scale in portfolio management and research, expense ratios should have substantially *declined*, and savings should have been enhanced by even more billions.

The second problem with this focus on distribution is that, ordinarily, no significant benefits flow to shareholders as a result of large size; in fact, large size is generally detrimental. Shareholders are paying the piper but are not able to call a better tune. In the real world, higher costs harm shareholders by widening the gap between financial market returns (in effect, market index returns) and the returns earned by market participants. This is patently true of money market funds, where maturity and quality are constrained by federal regulation. It is also profoundly important in high-grade bond funds (consider a short-term U.S. Treasury bond fund, for example), and increasingly obvious in the equity fund arena, where passively managed, low-cost market index funds outpace most actively managed equity funds.

The disjunction of these two trends produces an overwhelming irony: enormous amounts of the expenses paid by fund shareholders are not benefiting those very same shareholders. In effect, high fees are paying for huge profits to fund managers (or their public stockholders, who are just along for the ride), who, as a group, are consistently underperforming the financial markets in which they participate.

This situation has developed largely because of the gradual deterioration of the guiding principle that management is the central function of mutual fund companies—the function around which all others should be satellite. This is not just a question of principle, but of compliance with federal law as set forth in the Investment Company Act of 1940, which clearly states that investment companies must be managed in the interest of their shareholders.

What can be done to reverse these ominous trends? How can fund investors get a fair shake? After preaching this gospel for a long, long time, I'm starting to lose heart about the possibility that mutual fund independent directors—despite being required by law to place the interest of fund shareholders first—will ever try to stem a tide that, truthfully, needs to be reversed. Can we rely on competition to do the job it usually does so well in our economy, but has failed to do in the mutual fund industry? Price competition has proven to be an unlikely product of a roaring bull market where a 16.5 percent annual rate of return for equity funds is the bonus of a lifetime. Never mind that the total stock market's annual return was

18.9 percent, and that we are not apt, in our lifetime, to see its like again. The lion's share of the fund shortfall versus the market return was caused by mutual fund costs. In a less generous stock market, with better-informed investors, competition should, finally, carry the day.

For competition to work, however, investors need information before they can develop knowledge, and knowledge before they can develop wisdom, and wisdom before they can develop a commonsense financial plan. There is more than enough information available about the past returns, prospective risks, and actual costs of mutual funds. The problem is that not all of this information is made public. Too often it falls victim to inadequate disclosure, or selective disclosure, or even nondisclosure. And even when information is fully disclosed, it is usually ignored by investors who don't recognize its importance, or—in today's exuberant market environment—don't think it is particularly relevant. Demanding investors—especially if better informed by probing, thoughtful commentators—can play a huge role in forcing the industry to return to its founding principles.

Information That Can Make a Difference in Your Fund Investments

Let me point out six areas of information in which you, as an investor, can better educate yourself: (1) cost; (2) fee waivers; (3) performance; (4) proxy voting; (5) alternative investment strategies; and (6) investment guidance.

You can profitably use this information in the fund selection process, in the proxy voting process, and in deciding which of your fund holdings might no longer warrant inclusion in your portfolio. "Voting with your feet" is the most effective way to bring about positive change. But if you contemplate redeeming your fund shares, don't forget to consider their tax cost basis. In these bountiful days of market appreciation, the funds you own are apt to have a bit of a lock on your money.

Cost Information

Cost is just as important to fund investors as risk and return because excessive cost—other things being equal—either directly reduces return or increases the potential risk assumed to achieve a target return. As discussed in Chapter 3, cost has profound implications for asset allocation strategy, the most critical decision an investor faces. A high-cost portfolio must have a significantly higher stock position and a lower bond position to generate a return equal to that of a low-cost portfolio. This is a message that you must always bear in mind.

Thanks to a vigilant Securities and Exchange Commission (SEC), fund prospectuses now do an adequate job of showing the impact of expense ratios and sales charges. They show the actual costs of both, as well as hypothetical illustrations of their combined impact on the returns earned by mutual fund investors who hold their shares for periods of 1, 3, 5, and 10 years. Indeed, the SEC has just upped the ante. The old standard of cost disclosure was based on an exceedingly modest $1,000 investment, so the 10-year cost of, say, $185 for owning an average fund looked trivial. Now the disclosure standard is based on a $10,000 investment, and the cost is $1,850. An investor—at least one who looks at the prospectus—just might decide that is a pretty large bite. In any event, over 10 years, costs would consume fully 18.5 percent of that initial fund investment—a clear and compelling piece of information. For a very low-cost fund, it might be only $200, or 2 percent—and that represents a striking difference from $1,850. I recommended this change to the SEC a few years ago, and I'm delighted that it is now in place. It will help investors to focus on the critical factor of cost. But the other heavy cost of fund ownership is not disclosed: The transaction costs that the fund incurs in the turnover of its portfolio. The costs can be only vaguely inferred from the turnover figure itself, which is reported in the prospectus. But the indirect cost of turnover often rivals the direct fund costs that are disclosed. Funds ought to be required to estimate them and disclose them in their prospectuses.

I have also urged—so far, without success—that a comparison of a fund's expense ratio with that of its peer group be required in the annual report. Over extended periods, costs often make the difference between top-quartile (or, for that matter, bottom-quartile) returns and average returns. But today, in a typical annual report, it is difficult to find even the one mandatory reference to a fund's expense ratio. (Hint: Look for it at the end of the report, on a single line buried deep within a 14-line table of "Financial Highlights," right before the ever-scintillating "Notes to Financial Statements" and the "Report of Independent Accountants.") The SEC even asks for more than that in the prospectus; witness the 10-year cost table I mentioned above. Investors should urge funds to give increased prominence to costs, and to discuss their impact on returns. Investors also deserve information about the tremendous portion of fund *income* that is consumed by costs. Currently, costs reduce the income yield of the average equity fund by fully 75 percent—from *gross* income of 1.9 percent to *net* income (after the deduction of expenses) of less than 0.5 percent—a yield that is clearly a pittance. Yet the percentage reduction in income is not even disclosed.

Fee Waiver Information

Don't take only my word for the fact that costs are important. The fund industry knows it, and a few lower-cost funds designed for high-net-worth investors even feel compelled to advertise that "other factors held equal, lower costs lead to higher returns." When costs *are* used as a marketing weapon within the industry, we see, not true cost reductions that benefit fund shareholders, but "teaser rates" in the yields on money market funds, for example, accomplished by fee waivers and expense absorptions for "a temporary [and unspecified] period of time." Such cost reductions are designed to mislead shareholders about a money market fund's sustainable yield. How can it be proper to annualize a money market yield that may endure for only one day after an advertisement appears? Make no mistake: costs are essentially the sole determinant of relative yields on money market funds, and investors care about those yields.

Consider this example: one money market fund grew, within less than two years of its inception in 1989, from $100,000 to $9 billion in 1990 by temporarily waiving fees. Then, the adviser reinstated the full, typically onerous, fee without having the courtesy to notify the shareholders. The fund's assets gradually dwindled to $1.6 billion. Smart investors obviously fled the fund as they gradually experienced the yield reduction firsthand, but many less observant investors remain in the fund. It is a sad commentary on the relationship of marketing (it worked) to management (it failed).

Investors should seek realistic information that shows a fund's true yield after the deduction of all expected costs, and should generally ignore the teaser rate created by the fee waiver. Funds should no longer be permitted to publish yields that are subsidized, unless the subsidy has been guaranteed for, say, at least three years. The same approach should be taken with index funds that temporarily provide low expenses in order to appear competitive in the marketplace. (One of the largest S&P 500 Index funds, waiving fees so as to appear as the lowest-expense such fund, openly acknowledges to the trade press that it does not expect to remain in that enviable position after its subsidy expires. Interestingly, however, the prospectus makes no such disclosure to investors.) Arguably, investors should consider taking advantage of these low rates while they last. Doing so, of course, requires considerable vigilance thereafter, in order to observe when the fee waiver terminates. Discouragingly, the clear duty to notify shareholders of this event is ignored by fund sponsors.

Performance Information

Within the fund industry, it is no secret that the conventional rates of return to measure a fund's performance (time-weighted, on a per-share basis), with few exceptions, reflect performance that is significantly higher, and in many cases radically higher, than the returns actually earned by its shareholders (dollar-weighted, on the basis of total net assets). The present conventional measure is simple, convenient, and useful, but it doesn't tell the whole story. How relevant is this measure for a fund that begins a period with, say, $50 million in assets and ends with $3 billion? Is it easier to manage, or even, heaven forbid, to manipulate a small fund's portfolio? Can even a manager who is not playing games in the IPO market sustain his or her success when the fund being managed is 60 times as large?

The answers to these questions are not without significance to investors. For whatever reason, the fund with the highest (conventionally measured) return in the entire industry—annually, about 20 percent per share—in the decade ended July 31, 1996, had a dollar-weighted return of −4 percent during that same period. There is a difference, and investors should be aware of it. Urge your fund to report dollar-weighted returns, along with time-weighted returns, in its prospectuses and annual report.*

In this context, you are entitled to a clear explanation of the fund's early performance before you invest. Its manager is apt to be tight-lipped on the subject, but there is usually an important story that ought to be told. For example, during 1995, the 10 top-ranking general equity funds—all quite new, and with, on average, less than $100 million of assets—rose 67 percent, more than double the 31 percent gain for the average general equity fund. How? Twenty 5 percent positions, each of which rose 67 percent?

---

* Unlike the conventional time-weighted total return, which simply measures the change in a fund share's net asset value, with this figure adjusted for any dividends paid, a dollar-weighted total return relates the varying returns earned by a fund to the varying level of assets managed by the fund. The returns earned when a fund is managing a greater level of assets are accorded greater weight than those earned when the fund has a smaller level of assets. In effect, the dollar-weighted return reflects the experience of the average investor who owns the fund's shares.

Inconceivable. Twenty positions—4 up 180 percent, and the other 16 up 39 percent on average? Possible, but unlikely. Eighty positions, because the 20-stock portfolio had an average holding period of three months? Most likely of all. No wise observer would expect these funds to outpace the market by three times over again. And they didn't. Their average gain was 5.9 percent in 1996 and 5.6 percent in 1997, which put them 25 percent *below* the total stock market for the full three-year period. Less seasoned observers, who base their investment decisions on past performance, could have been warned of the peril if they had had information about the nature of those surprisingly large returns.

You are also entitled to better risk disclosure, although it is easier to state the obvious need than to fulfill it. Risk is a highly complex issue, and I believe that the central issue is a fund's specific risk relative to the total stock market. Most investors are generally aware of the nature (if not the dimension) of *stock market risk,* so we should focus on the second and third elements of risk: *objective risk* (large-cap value versus small-cap growth, for example) and *manager risk* (how good is the fund adviser within its objective group?). While manager risk is unpredictable, objective risk remains remarkably consistent over time. Both elements are nicely subsumed by a simple comparison of a fund's total quarterly return with that of a broad market index. Figure 15.2 displays the two returns and shows the general nature of a fund's risk tolerance (or intolerance). In a large-cap index fund, the bars in the chart would be almost identical; in a small-cap aggressive growth fund, they would be quite different. Emphasizing that relative risk is more predictable than future return, I recommended that such a chart be included in fund prospectuses. While it did not adopt that suggestion, the SEC did add a requirement that a fund disclose the highest return and the lowest return it earned in any quarter during the prior decade. This disclosure is a big step forward, but it would have been far more useful to have also shown the stock market returns during each of these quarters, in order to indicate whether the fund is taking more or less risk than the investor wishes to assume.

Proxy Voting Information

Too few mutual fund investors take the trouble to read the proxy statements disseminated by their funds. These statements rarely highlight proposals that shareholders approve an increase in advisory fees, and *never* publicize them. The media generally receive releases that brag about

FIGURE 15.2

Risk Measure: Contrasting Quarterly Returns 1988–1998 (as of June 1998)

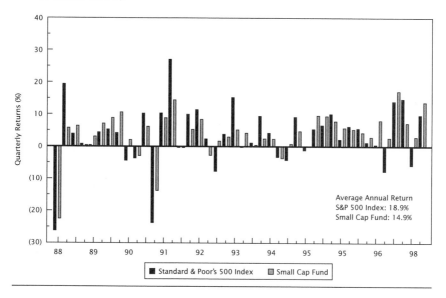

Average Annual Return
S&P 500 Index: 18.9%
Small Cap Fund: 14.9%

■ Standard & Poor's 500 Index   ☐ Small Cap Fund

performance, or a star manager, or record cash flows, rather than releases that discuss matters that the fund's managers hope will remain hidden from shareholders. Managers know that if investors are better informed, they are more likely to "just say no," or to "vote with their feet" and redeem their shares. The only way to avail yourself of this opportunity is to pay careful attention to your fund's proxy, even though it is rife with tortuous prose. If you merely vote in your own interests as a shareholder, the mutual fund industry's wanton tendency to increase advisory fees and add distribution fees will be curbed.

Given the inattention of shareholders—or perhaps their confidence that the directors of the fund will protect their interests—abuse occurs. Operating behind a veil of public ignorance, for example, a major fund complex was able, within the space of a year, to raise its fees by 100 percent. First, in December 1991, fund shareholders were sent proxies requesting approval of a new investment advisory fee contract that would raise fees by 50 percent. The base fee would increase by 25 basis points, from 0.50 percent of assets to 0.75 percent. The reasons cited were the increased cost and complexity of investment management and research activities, and the fact that the fund's fees were (heaven forbid!) "below average." Not disclosed—a serious lack of disclosure, in my view—was the effect of the fee increase on the pretax profits of the adviser, which likely rose by as much as 100 percent. Shareholders duly approved the proposed increase.

Armed with this surge in profitability, only seven months later (this may not surprise you), the adviser sold itself—for a cool $1 billion—to one of its competitors. It then asked the fund's shareholders to approve not only the change in control, but another 0.25 percent fee increase—this time, a 12b-1 distribution fee in that amount. Another surge in profitability for the adviser (and its new owner) surely followed, presumably adding considerable value to the price that had been agreed on for the sale. The new fee raised the expense ratio to 1.19 percent, or about 60 percent above the 0.75 percent level at which it had reposed less than a year earlier. (With asset growth, the annualized fees paid to the adviser then rose from some $45 million to $100 million, or 125 percent.) Nonetheless, the fund directors had reviewed the proposal, as they are obliged to do under the law, and found that this new fee, as part of the merger package, imposed "no unfair burden" on the fund. Presumably impressed by this endorsement by the fund's ostensibly independent directors, and uninformed about the additional, larger increase in the adviser's profits, shareholders again dutifully approved.

This brief anecdote provides in microcosm a two-step process that is far from rare in the fund industry: Increase the fees paid for management, without any specific disclosure about how much, if any, of the revenues might be dedicated to additional portfolio supervision and research expenditures and how much to marketing expenses and to the adviser's profits; and add further distribution fees (because the sales of the fund's shares "potentially could increase," as compensation to dealers becomes more attractive), without disclosing the fact that higher sales volumes hold absolutely no benefit to shareholders. If there is a better example of the clash of the cultures—management versus distribution—I'd be hard pressed to find it. Fund advisers ought to be required to disclose their revenues, expenditures (showing management, marketing, and administrative costs separately), and the profits they earn from each fund they manage, and from the funds as a group.

Imagine the reaction of consumers if a "Big Three" automaker increased the average price of its new cars by 60 percent—from, say, $16,000 to $26,000. This would never happen in the competitive automobile marketplace, where there is real price competition, but it does happen, time and again, in the mutual fund marketplace, where such competition is conspicuous only by its absence. The advisory fees paid by a fund are not set by the market, but normally recommended to the fund board by the agreement of the fund president and the president of the investment adviser, *who are usually the same person*. (Now *that* is a tough scenario for arm's-length negotiation!) Shareholders owe it to themselves to pay at least as much attention to the prices they pay for their funds as to the prices they pay for their cars.

Information about Alternative Investment Strategies

The mutual fund industry has been built, in a sense, on witchcraft. Enchanted by a long bull market and the conventional (but illusory) notion that "the pros"—and especially "hot managers"—can do better than mere mortals, investors are ignoring the drumbeat theme of experience: Fund net returns, sooner or later, revert to the market mean and finally below it. Investors owe it to themselves to be aware that traditionally managed mutual funds are not the only way to invest. Holding individual stocks for the long term may not only be wise, but far more tax-efficient. And market index funds are also a promising, if counterintuitive, choice. The record is clear that a low-cost index fund *has* provided enhanced returns for long-term investors. Our prominent casino man, quoted earlier, said that it *will* provide returns better than 85 percent of all stock funds ("Why would you screw it up?").

I know that index funds are boring. They aren't sexy; they don't make news; their managers, if never morons, are rarely geniuses; they don't "beat the market." It is ironic that it is only in recent years that the index funds (after more than two decades of operating experience) have received the attention they deserve. That recognition, sadly, is based more on the truly sensational results of the S&P 500 Index during the past three years (top 6 percent of funds, almost certainly unrepeatable in any future three-year period) than on its outstanding long-term record. Index funds are now "hot," but that's a silly reason to invest in them. It is high time to focus not on their short-term performance, but on their principles. It is also time to focus on, not merely index funds, but *low-cost* index funds. Low cost, broad diversification, and tax efficiency are virtually the only essential merits of this passive management strategy. Some 40 index funds have sales charges, and 25 others have expense ratios of 1 percent or more. As William Safire would say, "Fugeddaboudit."

Investment Guidance Information

No matter how much—or how little—you agree with me on the long-run impact of reversion of fund performance to the mean, and the role of cost in performance, you ultimately want advice about which funds you should own. For too many investors, the choice comes down to which funds they believe will provide the highest future return. Investors don't consider the role of cost or the rule of reversion to the mean, but usually look solely to the past "track record." They are led in this direction by publications that lionize the latest superstar manager or publish lists of "the best mutual funds for the next decade" (or even the next year, or even an unspecified period). But investors would be well served if publications accepted the obligation to critique, in retrospect, their *own* performance with the same doggedness that they critique fund performance. "Sauce for the goose is sauce for the gander." Disclosure of how funds on "recommended lists" performed *after* their appearance would surely make investors skeptical about the foresight of such lists. Whether from the media or the funds themselves, intelligent investors should demand accountability.

One biweekly national magazine has produced an "Honor Roll" of funds each year, and has been doing so for roughly a quarter century. Its honor roll funds, on average, have produced a rate of return of +12.5 percent per year since 1973, compared to +14.7 percent for the Wilshire 5000 Index, which outpaced the honor roll fund average in 14 of the past 15 years. What is more, the honor roll funds seemed to carry a bit more risk than the Wilshire 5000 Index, declining more than the Index in all four down-market years during the 24-year period. Why shouldn't the magazine report these facts to its readers each year, as it updates its statistics and adds and deletes funds from the roll?

A monthly national magazine, in a recent article, published the results of its "picks from the past," but did not compare them with a market index, nor present a cumulative average return for its 10 picks. It did inform readers: "We're reasonably content with our picks." One can only imagine why they should be. Their list produced a two-year return of 14.7 percent, only about two-thirds of the 20.1 percent annual gain in the Index for the same period. Would any investor be "reasonably content" with such performance? Why? Investors deserve full disclosure from those who purport to purvey investment guidance to them.

ESPERANTO-TYPE CRANKS

I return here to my central theme: If you agree with my thesis, you can help yourself by seeking full disclosure about fund costs, fee increases, performance and risk, alternative investment strategies, and fund guidance, important information that will help you to soundly evaluate mutual funds. By doing so, you can help redress the imbalance that is increasingly tilted in favor of fund distribution at the expense of fund management. I believe, profoundly, that returning to our first principles will provide bountiful benefits to mutual fund shareholders.

Let me expand on this theme with a parallel of politics and mutual funds. I turn to Esperanto: "a language of supreme universality." According to *New Yorker* political correspondent Michael Kelly, an Esperantist is "sort of a unified-field theorist, a believer in the *one great idea* that will fix anything, an overarching concept that puts it all into context."[1]

Mr. Kelly cites 1996 vice presidential candidates Jack Kemp and Al Gore as "Esperanto-type cranks—men who, if they may not have ambitious intellects, have the ambition to be men of ambitious intellects." Jack Kemp, Kelly writes, is "a glory of capitalism man, believing that if the money machine can ever be built just right and oiled just so, it will drive the world forever in humming happiness." Al Gore is described as "a believer in systemology—that everything is connected to everything else, holistically, and that fixing it all is just a matter of getting all the systems running right, beginning with one's own and working outward from there." Kelly concludes: *"The driving dream of every Esperanto-type crank is that if he could only explain things to enough people carefully enough, thoroughly enough, thoughtfully enough—why, eventually everyone would see, and then everything would be fixed."* [Italics added]

Had he been considering mutual funds rather than politics, Mr. Kelly could easily have described my strong and simple beliefs in a similar fashion. Please do not mark me as just another Esperanto-type crank, but carefully consider my driving dream that most of this industry's shortcomings would be fixed if we returned to our first principles: focus on management, not distribution; on professional competence and discipline, not gunslinging and speculation in casinos; on trusteeship and adding value through low costs, not asset-gathering and dissipating value with exorbitant costs.

This change will happen—and this is the "one great idea"—only if we move to a system in which the focus of mutual fund governance and control is shifted. Today, it almost invariably reposes with the executives and owners of mutual fund management companies, who seek good fund performance, to be sure, but also seek enormous personal gain, and seem incapable of successfully balancing the obvious direct conflict in apportioning the two. It is imperative that this conflict be resolved. Mutual funds must be operated under the enlightened governance of directors who are responsible solely to the shareholders of the mutual funds themselves, for whom *fund* performance is the sole measure of profit.

In recent years, the principles of management—including trusteeship, professional competence and discipline, and focus on the long term—have been compromised by the demand for distribution and asset gathering above all else, and their return to preeminence seems a long way beyond the horizon. But tomorrow is another matter, and now that I've explained it to you, I hope, "carefully enough, thoroughly enough, thoughtfully enough, why, you will see, and then everything will be fixed," as Michael Kelly wrote. As Thomas Paine stated so eloquently, "A thing moderately good is not so good as it ought to be. Moderation in temper is always a virtue; but moderation in principle is always a vice." The kindest thing that can be said about mutual fund principles is that they have been "moderated." Now is the time to demand that the important and traditional principles of this industry must be inflexible. If investors demand change, their interests will be served.

CHAPTER 16

ON MARKETING
THE MESSAGE IS THE MEDIUM

In 1967, a "New Age" writer named Marshall McLuhan wrote a book entitled *The Medium Is the Massage*. His point was that, in the hectic pace of modern life, the lightninglike speed of communications over the airwaves had come to control the very messages that were sent. What we were witnessing on television, on entertainment and news programming alike, was a far cry from what we had read in books and newspapers. In the news media, for example, the balanced reportage, rich in detail, that had been a hallmark of the best newspapers gave way to superficial 30-second sound bites on the events of the day. Now, three decades after the publication of the McLuhan book, the Internet has become a whole new medium of receiving and processing information, and the speed and reach of communications have been increasing at an exponential rate. McLuhan was ahead of his time, and his observations seem even more profound today.

In discussing the role of marketing in the mutual fund industry, I'm going to take two liberties with Mr. McLuhan's title, reversing the order and changing "Massage" to "Message." Doing so gives me a fitting title for this chapter: "The Message Is the Medium." For in this industry, marketing is now in the driver's seat. What the industry *offers* to investors now shapes what funds actually *provide* and the cost at which they provide it. Using an old, uncomplimentary business expression: "We used to be a business that sells what it makes, but we've become a business that makes whatever sells." The marketing message has overtaken the investment medium; the cart now pulls the horse.

During most of the first half-century after the industry's inception in 1924, mutual funds were focused largely on the stewardship of shareholders' assets. They were managed by investment advisers charged with the responsibility of managing other people's money. And they were distributed by separate principal underwriters. In fact, many of the largest fund companies assumed neither the responsibility for, nor the cost of, distribution and marketing services. But at an accelerating rate over the past decade, the focus has clearly turned toward marketing and away from management. The implications of that trend are ominous.

Four principal problems are created by this overemphasis on marketing. First, it costs mutual fund shareholders a great deal of money—billions of dollars of extra fund expenses—which reduces the returns received by shareholders. Second, these large expenditures not only offer no countervailing benefit in terms of shareholder returns, but, to the extent they succeed in bringing additional assets into the funds, have a powerful tendency to *further reduce* fund returns. Third, mutual funds are too often hyped and hawked, and trusting investors may be imperiled by the risks assumed by, and deluded about the potential returns of, the funds. Lastly, and perhaps most significant of all, the distribution drive alters the relationship between investors and funds. Rather than being perceived as an *owner* of the fund, the shareholder is perceived as a mere *customer* of the adviser. At that point, the mutual fund is no longer primarily an *investment account* under the stewardship of a profession *manager*, but an investment *product* under the control of a professional *marketer*.

YOUR MONEY IS NO OBJECT

Marketing and distribution are highly expensive functions, and money is no object. But it is the money of the *fund shareholders*. Yet, the fund manager reaps the benefits of that money, earning rising fees as the assets roll in. At the outset of the growth curve, some beneficial economies of scale may accrue to a fund's shareholders, but the principal benefits of growth accrue to the manager. And as assets increase to boxcar levels, funds often become musclebound, bereft of the ability to follow the investment strategies that engendered their early success.

Newspaper and magazine advertisements and television commercials that foster the "branding" image now cost fund investors as much as $1 billion per year. Other marketing efforts—direct mail, literature, and promotions—are also hugely expensive, and the enormous fees paid by funds for shelf space in mutual fund supermarkets add even more to the marketing budget. It should not strain credulity to suggest that fund managers may be spending as much as $10 billion per year on marketing their wares—a huge chunk of the $50 billion that investors paid for their mutual funds in 1998, and much larger even than the $3 to $4 billion paid for the investment services that are the ostensible *raison d'être* for owning fund shares in the first place. *It is the "management" fees paid by the fund shareholders that are being poured into these marketing efforts.*

Much of the troublesome rise in fund distribution costs comes from the institution of a novel form of mutual fund fee: the "12b-1 fee" (so named because the fee was permitted under SEC Rule 270.12b-1). Until October 1980, the SEC took the position that fund managers could not spend fund assets on distribution. Before then, the industry distribution effort was largely funded by sales loads (commissions paid by buyers of fund shares to stock brokerage firms). The typical maximum load was 8 percent of the total dollar value of the transaction (8.7 percent of the value of the fund shares acquired). That traditional structure had been in place since the first U.S. mutual fund began operations in 1924. But it had become increasingly difficult to sustain after the terrible 1973–1974 bear market, and at a time when no-load funds, available without sales commissions, began to penetrate the fund marketplace. As a result of this new competition, the typical maximum load has gradually diminished to 6 percent.

Eager to earn the same amount of revenues so that the resources available to pay for the distribution effort would remain undiminished—and equally eager to make it appear that load funds were actually no-load funds—the fund industry, and the stockbrokers who sold fund shares, developed an imaginative plan that would enable them to have their cake and eat it too. They proposed an option under which a crystal-clear front-end load of, say, 6 percent, would be replaced with two decidedly blurry fees: an annual distribution fee (say, 1 percent per year) charged against fund assets; and a descending one-time redemption fee (a so-called "back-end" load) that would make up the difference if the investor withdrew from the fund before all of those annual 1 percent fees totaled 6 percent. For example, if an investor redeemed after having made two payments of 1 percent each over 2 years, the redemption fee would be 4 percent, and after 6 years it would normally (but not always) vanish. The math didn't quite add up. (The shareholder's total costs were actually *increased*, as a fund's assets grew in value in the soaring stock market.) But it came close to simply replacing a one-time front-end fee with an equivalent cumulative annual fee.

Pandora's Box Is Opened

With this seemingly harmless change, however, came a much more ominous turn of events. When the SEC ruled that, subject to meeting the detailed requirements for the imposition of a 12b-1 fee by a fund (including approval by a majority of its independent directors), fund assets could be made available for distribution expenses, it also allowed the imposition of 12b-1 fees to be used as a simple add-on to fund expenses, whether the fund changed its sales charge structure or not. Indeed, it even allowed no-load funds to charge these fees. In a way that even Pandora could not have imagined, a modern-day Pandora's Box was opened, and almost infinite resources became available to accomplish the industry's shift to a marketing focus.

During the waning months of the 1970s, in the aftermath of a market crash, the industry was fighting a plague of net redemptions and shrinking assets for equity mutual funds. Fund managers advanced the argument that if the industry was to build economies of scale for shareholders, it needed these resources to stem redemptions and encourage growth. Alas, the cure was far worse than the disease. Even a 12b-1 fee assessed as low as 0.25 percent of fund assets (the maximum level at which a fund could carry the "no-load" appellation) proved too much to be overcome by any remotely conceivable economies of scale.

For example, if a fund succeeded in building its assets from, say, $500 million to $5 billion, its previous expense ratio *might* have fallen from 1.10 percent to 1.00 percent. But with the addition of a 12b-1 fee of 0.25 percent, the new expense ratio became 1.25 percent, a net increase of 0.15 percentage points over the original fee. Total annual expenses of $5.5 million, paid by a fund when it was small, would rise to $62.5 million at its larger size. At that point, the manager would be receiving fully $12.5 million per year in 12b-1 fees for marketing expenditures, and the income earned by the fund's shareholders would be reduced commensurately.

As the 1990s draw to a close, 12b-1 fees are rife. Some 7,000 of 13,000 mutual funds—including 60 percent of all equity funds, 67 percent of all bond funds, and 35 percent of all money market funds—are charging these onerous fees.* As industry assets have risen, so has the general level of

---

*Although the number of stock and bond funds currently exceeds 13,000, many of these funds represent different share classes of the same underlying portfolio. A single portfolio may feature as many as three or four different share classes—Class A, Class B, Class C, and so on—each with a different fee structure. If we count only the underlying portfolios, there are approximately 8,000 distinct stock, bond, and money market funds.

12b-1 fees. Since 1980, fund assets have risen 35-fold to some $5 trillion. The 12b-1 fee, nonexistent when 1980 began and consuming only 0.08 percent of the assets of funds charging these fees in 1984, averages a full 0.40 percent of the assets of the two-thirds of the funds in this industry that impose 12b-1 fees in 1998. Total 12b-1 fees amount to more than $6 billion annually. Since 1980, the number of funds has multiplied tenfold and fund assets have multiplied twentyfold. But the percentage of funds using 12b-1 fees has multiplied thirtyfold, and the percentage level of 12b-1 fees has soared. Table 16.1 shows the rising rate of 12b-1 fees as a percentage of fund assets, and the amounts of fund shareholder dollars paid to the funds for marketing.

Say what you will about the justification for these fees, $6.5 billion is a huge sum and a staggering burden on fund shareholder returns. It brings with it consequences that are at best otherwise neutral, and at worst nega- tive. The fund shareholder pays the bills, but the fund manager benefits by using these fees to garner more assets under management, higher manage- ment fees, and even higher profit margins. Curiously, there is no indica- tion whatsoever that funds that charge 12b-1 fees are succeeding in their goal of building market share at the expense of funds that do not add these fees. The fees do not appear to be accomplishing their ostensible purpose: building market share in pursuit of economies of scale.

Sadly, even the staggering $6-plus billion of 12b-1 fees paid by share- holders in 1998 does not nearly capture the totality of fund expenditures for distribution and marketing. Some fund advisers make such large prof- its on investment advisory services that, rather than reduce fees to benefit fund shareholders, they spend some portion of them on fund distribution

TABLE 16.1

The Rise of the 12b-1 Fee

	1980	1984	1986	1988	1990	1996	1998 (est.)
Year-end fund assets (billions)	$135	$371	$716	$810	$1,067	$3,539	$5,100
12b-1 fee rate*	0	0.08%	0.16%	0.33%	0.36%	0.39%	0.40%
Total annualized distribution fees (billions)	$0	$0.10	$0.37	$0.85	$1.20	$4.4	$6.5

*Percentage of assets of funds charging 12b-1 fees.

without incurring the onus of gathering proxies requesting that shareholders approve a 12b-1 fee; subjecting themselves to monitoring by the
independent directors (for whatever limited value that has had for shareholders); and carrying the opprobrium of the 12b-1 appellation in the
press and statistical services. Indeed, nothing precludes a fund from raising its *advisory* fee by, say, 0.25 percent and spending the entire windfall on
marketing, and many funds seem to do exactly that.

The Croupier's Take

Still more distribution costs are added by the costs of the fund supermarkets, which represent a rapidly growing form of fund distribution. The
going rate for "shelf space" (a term borrowed from grocery stores and
pharmacies) continues to rise. It is now 0.35 percent of the fund assets acquired from supermarket shoppers. At that rate, fund shareholders are
paying nearly $250 million every year for shelf space in the largest super-
market, which has corralled some $70 billion of fund assets in its "no-fee"
marketplace. These fees may be paid directly by the fund; by a 12b-1 fee
imposed on the fund; by directed brokerage of other commission arrange-
ments that may raise the fund's transaction costs; or by the adviser's willingness to accept a lower profit margin on the assets the fund garners
through the supermarket. (In the absence of a supermarket fee, of course,
such a reduced margin could just as easily have been rebated to fund
shareholders.)

   These fees find an analog in the gambling casino. As increasing numbers of mutual fund investors trade fund shares in ever-shorter periods, the
croupiers receive an ever-growing take. Unaware that "no fee" casinos in
fact entail heavy costs for the funds that participate in them, investors
flock to the casinos. The assets in the casinos grow, and the croupiers
pocket a greater take. Fund investors pay, one way or another, as in the
casino, and the croupiers gather their take at the night's end.

   But whatever value—if any—a supermarket brings to the investors
who purchase shares through it, the cost is paid for by both the shareholders who use it and those who don't. For *all* of the fund's shareholders are assessed these marketing fees. But shareholders are rarely, if ever, informed
about the supermarket fees, perhaps on the ground that it is an adviser's
right to spend its fees as it wishes. Be that as it may, an adviser who is willing to spend some one-third of the fees received from the assets of new
shareholders garnered in the supermarket could just as easily reduce the

fees paid by the existing shareholders who do not use the supermarket. But that does not happen.

12b-1 Fees—Full Disclosure

To make matters worse for the fund *investor* (the *manager* is doing just fine), success in the supermarket can bring great challenges to the fund's investment strategies—challenges that might not be able to be overcome by funds with aggressive investment policies. Funds with high portfolio turnover and funds focusing on stocks with small market capitalizations will have their investment activities muddled by frequent inflows and outflows of cash by supermarket investors. For funds with less aggressive strategies or holding larger stocks, the damage may be less, but it will still exist. Fund shareholders have paid to foster the fund's growth, and they have been disadvantaged in return.

A recent Harvard Business School doctoral paper came to this conclusion: "There is no evidence that 12b-1 fees generate benefits which are passed along to fund shareholders who pay these fees."[1] Rather, the study found that considerable harm was visited on fund shareholders. The analysis showed that equity funds *without* 12b-1 fees had outperformed their peer equity funds *with* such fees by a margin of 1.5 percentage points per year, an astonishing and highly significant gap.

Total returns of bond funds that are charging 12b-1 fees were only slightly higher than the returns of funds not charging them, but the funds imposing the fees were significantly more risky than their peers. The study noted that bond funds have found a fairly simple "remedy" for the performance penalty engendered by a fee that could consume up to 25 percent of a bond fund's return: Increase risk. That is not a happy consequence for fund shareholders who are not informed about the trade off. The normal trade off between risk and return is a sort of one-for-one affair. Here, it is a none-for-one trade off, bereft of economic sense except for the manager.

It should be apparent to even the most naïve observer that funds cannot spend themselves into success. A poorly performing fund, for example, could spend million of dollars in vain to overcome the shortcomings of its investment adviser. Funds, like business corporations, should have no guaranteed right to life.

The 12b-1 plan is not necessarily wrong in theory. But it can be justified only when the distribution expenditures paid for by the fund shareholders are recaptured for them in the form of lower future costs, and when full and clear disclosure is provided to investors. But in practice, 12b-1 plans have failed to fulfill their theoretical justification. The truth, as a shareholder proxy should say, but does not, is: "This plan will increase fund expenses and commensurately reduce returns. There is no evidence either that cash inflow will enhance, or that cash outflow will diminish, the fund's performance. An increase in the fund's assets may or may not benefit shareholders, but it is certain to increase advisory fees. These additional revenues may be used to enhance the adviser's profits, to pay for additional research that benefits the fund's investors, or to foster the sale of fund shares, which does not benefit the fund's investors." Perhaps unsurprisingly, this disclosure has simply never taken place.

HAWKING PRODUCTS, HIDING RISK

Not only are the costs of marketing a burden to investors, but the funds' insatiable reach for more assets has another pernicious side effect: the creation and promotion of a myriad of untested new products that are apt to be attractive only for a moment in time. That is not a very credible strategy for an industry that once viewed sound investing as a lifetime task. Yet in recent years, the industry has brought to investors at least three novel types of funds that made marketing sense but only investment nonsense: the Government-Plus Fund, the Short-Term Global Income Fund, and the Adjustable Rate Mortgage Fund.

The government-plus fund, "investing in the safety of U.S. Government Securities and providing a high return," reached its crest in 1987, when aggregate assets of the dozen funds that had emerged during the previous two years totaled some $30 billion. One of them advertised a 12 percent return when U.S. Treasury bonds were yielding less than 8 percent. Only common sense was needed to see that the yield was false, that the net asset value would decline, and that the income could not be sustained. That's just what happened over the following seven years. The decent, unknowing, and generally older shareholders of these funds never recovered their lost capital, and the assets of government-plus funds plummeted. Finally, they abandoned their fruitless strategy, often changing their names. They have not been heard from again.

Next, there was the short-term global income fund. This concept popped up in 1989, a time of 10 percent-plus yields on short-maturity international bonds. This yield quickly attracted investor assets totaling $25 billion, as nearly 40 funds joined the fray. The concept promptly fell on its face; the funds provided average annual returns of only 2 percent in 1992–1996 as net asset values tumbled, nearly offsetting all of the net income. Total assets of short-term global funds were then truly devastated, falling to $2.5 billion in 1996, at which point the category vanished.

Finally, there was the adjustable rate mortgage fund, the best of this sorry lot, but a failure nonetheless. Billed as akin to a money market fund that offered considerable price stability but a higher yield, it quickly became popular. By 1992, 37 funds had attracted $20 billion in assets. Alas, during the next three years, annual returns averaged only 1.5 percent. By this time, assets had fallen below $5 billion, many funds had changed their objectives and their names, and by 1996 this category too had vanished.

These three examples illustrate the problems created when the fads of the day are allowed to dictate the new financial products offered to investors—when the message is allowed to become the medium. In each case, the fund shareholders paid the piper who had called the tune. The industry proved its marketing savvy, but its management prowess failed to measure up to what reasonable investors had a right to expect. Shareholders lost their capital needlessly, without receiving so much as an apology. The past decade may have been a great decade for creative marketing, but it was hardly great for investment integrity.

This litany of complaints springs from my concern that the mutual fund industry, once a trust service that offered prudent management of other people's money, is now just another consumer products business. Elements of both have always existed in this industry, but I believe that, since the 1980s, the balance has shifted. The business aspect—a drive for market share, no matter what the cost—has sharply increased, and the fiduciary aspect—sound investment programs, fairly priced and fully explained—has been reduced commensurately. Investors are no longer fund owners; they have become mere fund customers.

Owners versus Customers?

How far has the acceptance of the modern concept of a fund investor as a customer instead of a shareholder spread? Consider the recent controversy between Don Phillips, president of Morningstar, which publishes the preeminent mutual fund journal, and the mutual fund industry. Mr. Phillips urged that the new profile prospectus, designed to make mutual fund information more accessible and "reader-friendly" for investors, should begin with this paragraph:

When you buy shares in a mutual fund, you become a shareholder in an investment company. As an owner, you have certain rights and protections, chief among them a largely independent board of directors, whose main role is to safeguard your interests.

The opposition was vocal. The president of the Investment Company Institute (ICI), the industry's trade association, rejected the proposal out of hand, saying that Mr. Phillips was "the only person in the entire industry" who took this position. And the SEC backed up the ICI by requiring no reference to the concept of ownership in the new profile prospectus, nor even in the more lengthy statutory prospectus.

For the record, however, I am one person who stands firmly allied with Mr. Phillips' position. The acceptance of a mutual fund as a mere product (or, in ghastly industry parlance, a "packaged product") is just one more step toward having the marketing message overtake the trusteeship responsibilities. Investors are owners, not customers. The mutual funds in which they invest should accord them the same kind of fiduciary responsibility that they would expect from their accountant or attorney.

An Investment Firm or a Marketing Firm?

Why should investors be concerned when marketing muscle replaces fiduciary duty as the driving force in mutual fund operations? Because this outcome directly counters the interests of investors. Respected financial journalist Jason Zweig expressed this dichotomy beautifully, and in considerable depth, at an industry forum in mid-1997:

> Today, the question that you must decide as we face the future is crystal-clear: Are you primarily a marketing firm, or are you primarily an investment firm? You can be mostly one, or you can be mostly the other, but you cannot be both in equal measure.
>
> How do a marketing firm and an investment firm differ? Let us count the ways:
>
> - The marketing firm has a mad scientists' lab to "incubate" new funds and kill them if they don't work. The investment firm does not.
>
> - The marketing firm charges a flat management fee, no matter how large its funds grow, and it keeps its expenses unacceptably high. The investment firm does not.
>
> - The marketing firm refuses to close its funds to new investors no matter how large and unwieldy they get. The investment firm does not.

- The marketing firm hypes the track records of its tiniest funds, even though it knows their returns will shrink as the funds grow. The investment firm does not.

- The marketing firm creates new funds because they will sell, rather than because they are good investments. The investment firm does not.

- The marketing firm promotes its bond funds on their yield, it flashes "NUMBER ONE" for some time period in all its stock fund ads, and it uses mountain charts as steep as the Alps in all its promotional material. The investment firm does none of these things.

- The marketing firm pays its portfolio managers on the basis not just of their investment performance but also the assets and cash flow of the funds. The investment firm does not.

- The marketing firm is eager for its existing customers to pay any price, and bear any burden, so that an infinite number of new customers can be rounded up through the so-called mutual fund supermarkets. The investment firm sets limits.

- The marketing firm does little or nothing to warn its clients that markets do not always go up, that past performance is almost meaningless, and that the markets are riskiest precisely when they seem to be the safest. The investment firm tells its customers these things over and over and over again.

- The marketing firm simply wants to "git while the gittin' is good." The investment firm asks, "What would happen to every aspect of our operations if the markets fell by 67 percent tomorrow, and what would we do about it? What plans do we need in place to survive it?"

Thus, you must choose. You can be mostly a marketing firm, or you can be mostly an investment firm. But you cannot serve both masters at the same time. Whatever you give to the one priority, you must take away from the other.

The fund industry is a fiduciary business; I recognize that that's a two-part term. Yes, you are fiduciaries; and yes, you also are businesses that seek to make and maximize profits. And that's as it should be. In the long run, however, you *cannot* survive as a business unless you are a fiduciary emphatically *first*.

In the short term, it pays off to be primarily a marketing firm, not an investment firm. But in the long term, that's no way to build a great business.[2]

I strongly agree with the thesis expressed by this principled journalist. At the dinner at which he spoke, however, he was vociferously hooted down and challenged by several members of his audience, who took great

THE PRESS GETS THE MESSAGE

The acceptance of the gospel that marketing is the industry's prime driver—and that *product* is what the industry offers—is so rife today as scarcely to require validation. But, to remove any doubt, let me present a series of recent excerpts from a variety of financial publications:

- *Investment News*

  Headline: "What Are Funds to Marketers? Just Another Can of Peas."

  Article: The challenge for fund managers [sic] is how do you stand out in the crowd and get your product off the shelf ... funds are turning to consumer goods marketers—the toothpaste sellers—to gain an edge over competitors. ... Fund performance and investment expertise are difficult areas ... [but] the basic principles of marketing are the same, whether you're trying to sell a can of peas or a mutual fund.

- *Institutional Investor*

  Photo caption quoting the senior executive of a giant fund complex: "Long term, we believe that distribution is king."

- *Fund Marketing Alert*

  Headline: "Branding Seen as Critical to Investors. But they're clueless on fees."

  Article: "70 percent of investors said that a well-known name is important. A majority do not realize they are paying fees— 60 percent don't know whether they pay 12b-1 (distribution) fees and 40 percent said no when asked whether they pay an advisory fee."

- *Wall Street Journal*

  Headline: "Mutual Funds Use a New Spin to Sell Wares."

  Article: "Fund companies have begun to sell their wares the way consumer goods companies market cereal and laundry detergent. . . . The [fund] supermarket shelf is crowded, [so] promotional budgets are at record levels."

Headline: "Now That It's Harder to Simply Do Well, Mutual Fund Companies Plan the Blitz."

Article: "Fund managers are finding it increasingly difficult to beat the market averages, so name recognition serves as another weapon in the battle for customers. . . . Performance is not a variable the funds can control."

- *Mutual Fund Market News*

  Headline: "More Fund Advisers Snare Marketing Pros."

  Article: "Like tangible consumer products, fund manufacturers are hoping for prime shelf space . . . they want investors to love their brand and come back for more . . . asset management expertise is not the determining factor in success, [rather it is] the ability to get the right product in front of the right audience."

- *Financial World*

  Headline: "Brand War on Wall Street. Financial services firms are spending millions on their brand names to control your assets."

  Article: "The branding companies aren't making product pitches based on low fees and high returns . . . they are working toward an image . . . . 'We want our name to appear next to Budweiser, McDonald's, IBM, Microsoft, and the car companies', says one industry leader. . . . It has become crucial for fund distributors to create demand . . . of course, firms will not be able to justify higher commissions or fees unless they can create at least the *impression* of value." (Italics added.)

umbrage at his candid remarks about how investment principles take a back seat when marketing takes precedence over management. As it happened, his audience consisted largely of heavy-spending mutual fund advertisers. But I have absolutely no doubt that, had his forum been populated with mutual fund portfolio managers and research analysts, he would have received a standing ovation.

The True Business—Gathering Assets

Nonetheless, there can be little doubt about where the industry is headed today. A 1995 report by the prestigious investment banking firm of Goldman Sachs & Co., entitled "The Continuing Evolution of the Mutual Fund Industry" said it well: *"Managing money is not the true business of the money management industry. Rather, it is gathering and retaining assets."* An updated report in 1998 reaffirmed the conclusion even more strongly: "The factors crucial to success are shifting from manufacturing to the distribution of asset management product." From the medium to the message, as it were.

The press understands the nature of the business today, although only a rare journalist examines the negative implications of this baneful trend for fund shareholders. What must be clear is this: Having failed to provide market-beating returns—indeed, having trailed in the wake of the returns provided by the great bull market—the mutual fund industry has effectively dropped its traditional watchword, "management," in favor of a new one, "marketing." The art of persuasion has crowded out the art of performance.

Given that such expenditures on marketing cut the returns of the funds that incur them, it seems anomalous and unfair to have the existing fund shareholders bear the burden of the costs entailed in attracting new fund shareholders. As logic might suggest, the new shareholders, attracted by the lure of the supermarket's advertising of the latest "white sale" (the funds with the best recent performance), with the added putative bargain of a "no fee" marketplace, tend to have much shorter time horizons. They are apt to be highly sensitive to short-term returns, and can move their money seemingly for free. So they shift funds frequently, causing existing shareholders to bear the costs of the extra portfolio turnover as the fund buys and sells stocks to accommodate the inflows and outflows of capital. Serving short-term traders, perhaps even gamblers, at the expense of long-term investors may be a successful strategy for a *marketing* firm, but it is hardly a successful strategy for an *investment* firm.

Remedies for the abuses of good management policy that are engendered by the high costs of good distribution policy are not easy to come by. If adequately informed, individual investors can simply turn their backs on funds that charge direct, explicit 12b-1 fees. Fund shareholders can vote against the imposition of such fees, although they have rarely done so in the past and will probably get few opportunities in the future (most fund managers who want them have already imposed them). They could implore the fund's independent directors to reverse their earlier endorsements, although the record of fund directors' taking actions that fund advisers don't recommend suggests that those who hold hope for this process are leaning on a weak reed.

Is there a cure for the 12b-1 disease? The best remedy is sunlight; we must let more of it shine through the windows. Officials of the Securities and Exchange Commission should bring these issues into the glare of public debate, and collect and disseminate detailed industrywide statistical information on advisory and distribution fees; expenditures on portfolio management and investment research services, advertising and marketing services, and fund operations; and profits earned by advisers.

Mutual funds ought to be held to a higher standard. We are not selling skin care lotions or exotic vacations. We ought not to be selling hope, dreams, youth, or fitness. We are not a collection of brand franchises à la Procter and Gamble, Budweiser, or Coca-Cola. We should not be hawking consumer products or imitating their naturally aggressive product marketing programs. Mutual funds are—or at least should be—first and foremost stewards of investors' savings.

What we need in the mutual fund industry is far more focus on the management of shareholder assets and far less on the marketing of fund shares. We need to reorient our thinking about what a fund *is*, and whom it is designed to serve. Regarding investors as shareholders rather than customers would represent a long-overdue return to the ancient principles of fiduciary duty. And thinking about mutual funds as trusts or trusteed assets rather than products would be a huge step toward improving the lot of today's fund shareholders. Making whatever sells—never mind whether it will stand the test of time—effectively ignores the welfare of our clients. Making something good and selling what we make would illustrate our desire to place our clients' interests first.

Our responsibility of trusteeship for the assets of investors who need our help goes far beyond charging what the traffic will bear for our funds. It goes to giving our owners a fair shake. We'll get there, but only if *management* replaces *marketing* in the mutual fund driver's seat. As I write these words, I'm struck by their similarity to the bedrock principle of the mutual fund industry, explored in the previous chapter, but cited almost 50 years ago in my senior thesis at Princeton: "The principal function of investment companies is the management of their portfolios. Everything else is incidental to the performance of this function."

It is high time we renewed that mission.

CHAPTER

ON TECHNOLOGY
To What Avail?

*L*et's begin with a mutual fund fable based on fact. On May 23, 1996, an increasingly typical sort of mutual fund investor completed his daily review of his 15-fund, $150,000 mutual fund portfolio on his Quicken computer program. Our investor was sure that he was missing out on too much of the action in the stock market. Over America Online, he learned that "The Motley Fool" crowd thought that hot stocks were the way to go, and he decided to switch his money market fund investment of $10,000 into a hot new "momentum" emerging growth fund.

He noted as he browsed the Website of the no-transaction-fee mutual fund marketplace he used for trading his funds, this hot fund was up 60 percent in its first year. Its portfolio manager had run another fund with great success, and, by spending some of the advisory fees the shareholders of his new fund had anted up to be listed in the marketplace, had already attracted more than 100,000 investors and nearly $1 billion of assets. The manager was lionized in the press and on television, and would soon be the star of the Morningstar annual conference in June. A quick check of the Morningstar Website enveloped our investor with all the data he could imagine about the portfolio manager's earlier strategies, including his 10 favorite stocks, the key components of a portfolio with a price–earnings ratio of 45, a median market capitalization of $700 million,

349

a concentration of 53 percent of assets in technology and health care stocks, 500 percent portfolio turnover, and so on.

The investor revisited his marketplace on the Web, hit a few keys on his computer, and immediately transferred his money market fund into the emerging growth fund. Both sides of the trade would be executed—without visible commissions or costs—at the market's close, only a half hour away. Satisfied with his day's labors, the investor shut down his computer.

After two months, late in July, the investor was worried. The market had declined, and the fund was dropping even faster. It was off 22 percent since his purchase. Still, a national mutual fund magazine had heralded it as a leading candidate to be "the next Magellan Fund." The investor decided to hang on for the recovery that would surely come.

Months later, reviewing his portfolio in detail on Quicken at year-end 1996, our investor was very troubled. He had guessed right: the bull market had resumed. The S&P 500 Index was up 11 percent since May 23, but, according to his computer data, his new fund was still down more than 20 percent. He made a note to keep a watchful eye on the fund. By mid-March, 1997, the market continued its roll—up yet another 6 percent—but his fund *lost* another 18 percent and was now down 35 percent, despite an 18 percent market advance. His investment now had a 53 percentage point shortfall to the return of the S&P 500 Index.

He acted swiftly. Dialing up his marketplace at its Website, he switched out of the once-hot fund and into a new one. Index funds hadn't appealed to him (all that tiresome stuff about passive management, owning the market, cost advantage, large-cap stocks, long-term time horizon), but he knew from his weekly review of the top-performing funds that the S&P 500 Index funds were hot and were beating more than 90 percent of all managed funds. In his marketplace, he couldn't buy the S&P Index Fund he wanted, the one called the "industry darling" in *The Wall Street Journal.* (It apparently couldn't afford the cost of joining the marketplace.) But he found another one that was *almost* as good, and made the exchange—again, merely by hitting a few keys on his computer. He'd try that one for a while. If he guessed wrong again, well, he could change his mind with a click on the mouse . . . .

What I have described in microcosm is what the mutual fund industry is becoming in the blossoming of the age of computer technology. The funds in this brief example are factual, but the investor is fictional . . . or is he? I present this example only to introduce you to the miracles technology has brought to the mutual fund industry:

- A financial system that has enabled the professional money managers of funds to offer a whole new variety of investment products, to provide remarkable liquidity for transactions, and to transact business around the globe with the speed of light.

- An up-to-date information network that provides data about mutual fund portfolios and performance so vast as to be beyond the ability of the human mind to absorb.

- A communications network so efficient that any fund investor can place transaction orders instantaneously (albeit so far with the transactions executed no more frequently than hourly), without moving from a desktop computer.

But, with all of this extraordinary technology available to investors, I ask: To what avail?

I freely concede that computer technology has played a major role in the growth of the mutual fund industry. The incredible, virtually uninterrupted, 16-year bull market has been the primary driver of the industry's success and acceptance. But the computer has added a whole new order of magnitude to this growth, and indeed has in some measure created a new industry that is distinctly different from its staid, largely conservative ancestor—in variety, in concept, in investor participation, in service quality, and in pricing.

Most obviously, the number of mutual funds has exploded, providing investors with an enormous panoply of choices in fund objectives, strategies, and managers. The old industry, just 20 years ago, was composed of 300 equity funds—the embattled survivors of the great 1973–1974 bear market, who were licking their wounds. The new industry comprises 3,300 equity funds, half of which have been formed in the past five years. The number of equity funds now exceeds the total of 2,900 individual common stocks of U.S. corporations listed on the New York Stock Exchange.

Today, it is fair to say that, to a surprisingly large extent, stocks are "out" and mutual funds are "in." That is all right, I guess, as far as it goes. But it doesn't go far enough. The reality is that mutual funds are evaluated as stocks, purchased as stocks, traded as stocks, and discussed as stocks in the corridors of commerce and at cocktail parties. For millions of investors, funds *are* stocks.

Consider this very recent example. An article in *Morningstar Investor*[1] presented, deadpan, recommendations by an investment adviser for a married couple investing $350,000, with retirement only five years away. He recommended a portfolio, almost entirely in equities, of 17 mostly small-cap and international funds. We can predict, I think, a high likelihood that the total of 2,000 individual stocks in the 17-fund portfolio will produce at best a market return before expenses. After fund expenses averaging a rather robust 1.6 percent of assets, the trading costs of funds with a 92 percent average annual portolio turnover, and the adviser's fee of 1 percent—let's call it an all-in cost of 3.5 percent, or $12,250 *per year*—it would seem *inconceivable* that the couple will be very happy with the outcome when their retirement comes. They will have paid a significant percentage of their returns to both the adviser and the mutual fund management companies for their putative investment expertise. In return, they will receive, at best, a market return—*before* costs. Does there really seem to be much chance of outperforming the market with a 2,000-stock portfolio that, for all intents and purposes, *is* the market?

The trend that is turning funds into stocks has been gradual, but I like to mark a particular date when the conversion became clear to me: March 19, 1995. This date, if it hardly will live in infamy, serves as my landmark. On that Sunday, the editors of *The New York Times* moved the mutual fund price and performance listings *ahead* of the New York Stock Exchange price quotations. New York Stock Exchange prices had been first in line for the attention of *Times* readers since time immemorial—certainly for more than a century—but, from that day on, the Big Board would play second fiddle to the upstart *nouveau riche* mutual fund colossus.

INVESTMENT TECHNOLOGY—BIGGER, QUICKER, AND MORE COMPLEX

How did this transition come to pass? Let's begin with investment technology and the financial market system. Consider some of the instruments we have today that would have barely been conceivable—and certainly would not have reached the breadth of their usage and the depth of their liquidity—without the computer:

- Something like $20 *trillion* in notional value of derivatives outstanding.
- An estimated $1.5 trillion traded each day in world currency markets.

- A vibrant market in financial futures, including a notional value of nearly $200 billion in futures for the Standard & Poor's 500 Index, updated in real time.

- Market indexes (of which we recently counted more than 3,000!), and, thus, index funds.

- Enormous market volumes, with, on busy days, some 1 billion shares of stock trading on the New York Stock Exchange, and another 1 billion shares on the NASDAQ. In all, $30 billion worth of shares changing hands each day.

Amid this feverish trading, the mutual fund industry has developed sophisticated investment techniques that are aggressive beyond anything we might have imagined 15 years ago. We have micro-cap funds; quantitatively managed funds; funds based on theories of price momentum, earnings expectations, technical readings of the market, and multiple regressions that, dare I say, boggle the mind; funds based on adjustable-rate mortgages, covered call options, and foreign currencies; and funds for stocks in Vietnam and Indonesia and the Czech Republic—not hitherto known as bastions of capitalism. Many old-line funds follow strategies that only yesterday would have been deemed outrageous. On average, mutual fund managers turned over their portfolios at a 15 percent rate in the 1950s and 1960s. Even in the "Go-Go Years" of 1965–68, the rate rose "only" to 40 percent. But in 1997, the average turnover rate was 85 percent, suggesting that the average holding period for a given stock is now but a hair over one year. What ever happened to long-term investing by professional managers? By anyone?

As professional and individual investors alike have become aggressive traders who vigorously use today's computer-driven financial system and the liquidity it has created, mutual funds—once considered long-term investments—have become, to an important degree, short-term speculative vehicles. Many of the former shepherds of the flock have become the sheep of the pasture: a roaming, inconsistent, wild lot, given to impulsive—if sometimes precisely quantified—decisions that frustrate the very purpose of investing on the basis of traditional standards of corporate valuation. We have investment technology to thank for enabling us to engage in all of this feverish activity. But technology has given us the tools without giving us the wisdom to handle them constructively.

Information Technology—Information versus Wisdom

The computer and the Internet have given us nonstop access to data that allow us to analyze and evaluate mutual funds beyond our wildest dreams, and to make fund selections with unimaginably vast information literally at our fingertips. Never again will mutual fund investors lack the ability to make fully informed investment decisions. Mutual fund investors should be among the greatest beneficiaries of the computer revolution.

Perhaps so, but they are also among its greatest victims. Every day, as in the example of investment behavior described at the outset, mutual fund investors are proving (as we must have known all along) that, in investing, information is all too often mistaken for knowledge, and knowledge is all too seldom translated into wisdom. But, wisdom, far more than mountains of detailed data, and common sense, far more than opportunism, are ever destined to be the prime ingredients of long-term investment success.

Communications technology has given us immediate access to abundant information when we are considering our fund decisions—to buy, to hold, to add or subtract, to withdraw entirely. How much information? Even today's garden-variety computer and communications technology takes you to Morningstar's Website or puts its Principia database on your computer in just seconds. Open the Principia program, for example, click on the name of one particularly large, established balanced fund, and then click on "print." Out will come 37 (count 'em) pages of statistics and charts:

- The stock portfolio: ratios of price to earnings and book value, earnings growth, market capitalization, industry diversification.
- The bond portfolio: maturity, credit quality, coupon.
- The whole portfolio: turnover, top 25 holdings, and total issues.
- Risk: R-squares, Betas, Alphas, standard deviations, Sharpe Ratios.
- Return: performance over 25 years, monthly and rolling three months, rankings vs. index and vs. objective group, tax-adjusted returns.
- Investment style (for each year!): nine boxes for stocks, nine for bonds.
- Cost: sales charges, 12b-1 fees, expense ratio comparisons. (Don't ignore costs!)

- The concluding *summum bonum:* the number of stars earned. (Happily, our subject balanced fund rates "four stars.")

It is no exaggeration to say that the superb Morningstar service provides all the information an investor could possibly need to evaluate a fund's characteristics, to understand a fund's *persona,* and to make informed decisions. Indeed, I think it is fair to say that the portfolio managers of many funds could not score more than a "gentleman's C" on a test given by an investor holding the Principia printout, presumably there to give the investor an edge in making investment choices.

Investors who rely on this information, I fear, rarely use it for much knowledge beyond the fund's performance and star rating. Rather, trust is placed "in our stars, not in ourselves" (the opposite of what Cassius told Brutus). Some 85 percent of the $160 billion that flowed into equity mutual funds in 1997 went into funds with five-star or four-star ratings, and only 15 percent to the one-, two-, or three-star funds. (Perhaps ominously, another $60 billion flowed into untested funds, often with hot records, that had not yet received ratings. They had not reached the ancient vintage that is used to establish a manager's *bona fides:* just three years—and during a booming time period at that.)

Knowledge, provided it is translated into wisdom, is indeed power. But information and trusting in the "stars" will not give investors the power to enhance their returns unless they use that information wisely. In short, although the Morningstar Website and software are *priceless* for understanding a fund's investment style, past returns, and present portfolio, the evidence strongly suggests that it is virtually *worthless* in enabling investors to pick the future top performers. Technology has made information accessible without providing knowledge and without engendering wisdom. Perhaps a rereading of Proverbs would remind us of what is really important: "Get Wisdom, Get Insight."

TRANSACTION TECHNOLOGY—SWITCH WHEN THE IRON IS HOT

Transaction technology has given us the ability to trade funds beyond our wildest imagination, as unambiguously unhelpful as it is to fund investors and to the portfolio managers of the funds whose shares they trade. And investors do use that ability. Turnover of equity fund shares by mutual fund investors has soared. In the 1960s and 1970s, redemptions (and their twin, exchanges out) of equity fund shares averaged 9 percent of assets per year; in the 1990s, the rate has more than tripled, to 31 percent. Fund investors appear to change their investment managers and their holdings of individual stocks with almost equal rapidity.

Using the reciprocal of these numbers as a proxy for the average number of years that equity fund shares are held (and it is a pretty good proxy), the holding period has tumbled from eleven years in the 1960s and 1970s, to slightly more than three years in the 1990s. *Just three years.** This trend, in my view, has emasculated the purpose of the best long-term investment medium ever devised: the broadly diversified, soundly managed, efficiently operated mutual fund. Whatever happened to long-term investing by mutual fund shareholders? The greatest investor of our time, Warren Buffett, buys and holds, and describes his strategy to the world in his annual reports. Yet we ignore his sage advice.

Perhaps the apotheosis of the confluence of investment technology, information technology, and transaction technology is found in the great fund casino—the no-transaction-fee mutual fund marketplace in which funds can buy a computer billboard that enables shareholders to turn their shares over rapidly and without apparent commissions. The costs of the system are hidden from view. First, *all* of the shareholders pay for access that is used, in most cases, by a *small minority* of them. An annual fee of about 35 basis points is paid by the funds to the casino that holds the assets of the funds. Second, *all* of the shareholders are burdened by the costs the fund incurs when portfolio transactions are necessitated by the inflows and outflows of capital engendered by the minority. Sensitivity to fluctuations in the stock market is substantially higher among fund shareholders playing in the casino than among other shareholders (although, as my earlier turnover figures suggest, that is quite high enough).

At least a few others share my concern about the role of technology in the world of investing, and about the accelerating pace of investors' turnover of fund shares. A recent *New Yorker* article described it in harsh terms: ". . . giddy money managers [including, I would add, investors who actively manage their own fund portfolios] are enthralled by the new gadgetry—the technology now sits at the center of a speculative frenzy of religious intensity, a financial mania, a bubble."[2]

---

*And three fine market years at that. In the tough climate of 1987, the redemption/ exchange rate took a quantum leap to an astonishing 62 percent of assets, a worrisome omen of what we might face in the next sharp market decline.

That may seem a strong condemnation, but there is some truth in it. Nonetheless, I freely concede that technology has served fund shareholders extremely well in one sense: The unit costs of fund share transactions and fund portfolio transactions have sharply declined. Indeed, their decline has already helped to reduce the costs of operating mutual funds. Computer costs have plummeted by almost 99 percent, from $150,000 per million instructions per second (MIPS) in 1985 to less than $2,000 per MIPS in 1998. The cost of a personal telephone response was $10 in 1985; today, it is only $2 for an automated telephone response (a bit discomforting for many investors). When a printed fund prospectus is delivered, the cost is $8; when the same prospectus is delivered over the Internet, it costs less than $1. Fund transactions can be electronically implemented and processed by pushing just a few keys on a personal computer—a further huge savings.

It was recently estimated that some 20 million of 50 million fund investors have home computers, with 10 million using them in investing. (Another estimate suggests that 30 percent of the shareholders in the largest casino already handle their transactions on its Website.) Today's 10 million users will soon become 15 million and then 20 million, and they will all have the ability to redeem their shares at a moment's notice. It takes only a moment's contemplation to imagine what might happen in the financial markets if, say, half of that number responded to a major earth-shaking (literally or figuratively) news event. The industry's old gate-keeper—a busy signal on the telephone—is retiring, for better or worse. Perhaps busy Internet service provider numbers, or even an Internet crash, will "protect" us. Honestly, it's sort of scary.

As useful and cost-efficient as most of the investor services provided by mutual funds are, the savings engendered by the declining cost of technology have largely benefited fund *managers*, and, only rarely, fund *shareholders*. Indeed, the industry alleges that new services have *increased* costs rather than reduced them. But the new services are often *marketing services* that are designed to attract investors and their dollars, increase advisory fees and record-keeping fees, and escalate the profits earned by the fund's management company.

Little solid information is available on the extent of the decline in the cost of communication and transaction services because fund managers rarely disclose how they spend the fees they receive. But one very large mutual fund firm, operating on an "at-cost" basis—has reduced its aggregate unit expenditures on shareholder services by more than 50 percent—from nearly 20 basis points of assets 15 years ago to less than 10 basis points in 1998—a current *annual* saving of $400 million for its shareholders. In fairness, the fund assets the firm manages have grown some twentyfold, and these economies of scale were passed along to its fund shareholders. A $100 billion fund complex that accomplished a similar feat might have reduced a $200 million cost to $100 million—but does not pass those savings on to shareholders.

With respect to fund portfolio turnover, technology has also reduced costs—but likely only *unit* costs. If the cost of trading stocks drops by 50 percent, for example, and the rate of turnover triples (as it has), the *total* costs borne by fund shareholders will have increased by 50 percent. But again, the fund shareholders, not the managers, are paying the freight—without any evidence whatsoever that all of this feverish activity enhances the net returns they receive.

THE REPORT CARD

Let's grade each aspect of the technologies currently used in mutual fund investing:

- **Investment technology:** Innovative financial instruments, A+; liquidity, A+; cornucopia of funds, A+; soundness of new funds, C; investment behavior of managers, D.

- **Information technology:** Availability of data to investors, A+; completeness and scope, A+; availability of meaningful knowledge, A; effective use of that knowledge, D; intelligent selection of funds for future performance, D; investment behavior of shareholders, E.

- **Transaction technology:** Ease and facility, A+; implicit encouragement to trade funds, A+; efficiency and expense savings, A+; flow-through of lowered costs to fund shareholders, F; facilitation of enhanced shareholder returns, F.

Our report card would rate the contribution of technology to information as A+; to knowledge, C; and to wisdom, D or perhaps even E. In all, good grades go to the technology, bad grades to the users.

What does the technology revolution portend for tomorrow? More Websites, more bulletin boards. More information, more transactions, still more facilitation and speed, and more cost savings (though probably not to the benefit of shareholders). And, I must add, more risk. Most of the new financial instruments made possible by the computer power of technology have never been tested in the crucible of a bear market. Nor have most fund shareholders, who are now able to trade without restraint. And, given the Internet, they can do so without even the intercession that used to be represented—for better or worse—by the inability of funds to staff enough telephone lines. Anyone who is not cognizant of these risks is making, in my view, a serious mistake.

But I am not an aging Luddite who is renouncing the future and calling for a return to the past. We can't go home again, but I do hope we will soon return to the fundamental principle that mutual funds are best used as long-term investments. I'm enough of an idealist to be confident that the kind of casino capitalism that is in the air today will not be a permanent fixture in the mutual fund industry. For trading in fund shares not only places roadblocks in the way of the implementation of fund strategy, but also engenders additional costs to all of the shareholders in the fund. What is more, it is also a loser's game for fund shareholders who elect to follow active trading strategies. Technology, for all its gee-whiz wonder, is both a bane and a blessing.

THE PERVASIVE IMPACT OF TECHNOLOGY

This dichotomy is found in other fields as well. Consider medicine: Dr. Bernard Lown, the brilliant cardiologist whose healing powers helped to keep me alive from 1967 until I received a heart transplant in 1996 (now *there* is a miracle of medical science) recently observed: "Medicine depends profoundly on science, but it is not a science"; the medical establishment "has made a Faustian bargain with technology. What is lubricating it is greed. We have created a system that is bizarre." Ditto for the mutual fund industry.

Best-selling author Michael Crichton has tackled the information technology revolution in the gamut of fields from A to Z—from air transportation to zoology. In *Airframe*, veteran reporter John Lawton, 68, observes, "the irony of the Information Age is that it has given new respectability to uninformed opinion. These days, everybody seems to believe in Santa Claus, in something for nothing." In *The Lost World*, Sarah Harding, a glamorous young biologist, tells her protégé, "Before he goes into the field, the zoologist reads everything that's ever been written about the animal he's going to study. Popular books, newspaper accounts, scientific papers, everything. Then he goes out and observes the animal for himself. And you know what he usually finds? That nearly everything that's been written or said is wrong . . . exaggerated, or misunderstood, or just plain fantasy." The fund industry can only hope that Mr. Crichton doesn't next turn his critical gaze to mutual funds, where the idea of something for nothing is rife, and plain fantasy about future returns abounds.

My asking earlier, "To what avail?" regarding the remarkable advances in the application of technology, was not intended to demean them. I only ask that investors give far more thoughtful consideration to curbing the powerful monster we have created and to figuring out how to make it bow to *our* will, *not us* to its will. We must begin by obliterating the notion that funds should be treated as individual stocks—actively traded, sometimes in exotic forms, by managements that can create miracles. Abandoning the massive advertising of funds as though they were beer or toothpaste or perfume would be a step in the right direction. And we ought to give serious consideration to appropriate limitations on frequency of exchanges, restrictions on telephone exchanges (though that won't help much as the Internet becomes our transaction mode of preference), and fee penalties paid by investors when they redeem shares after short holding periods. All of these steps would be met with horror, not only by short-term investors who are using funds as stocks, but by the fund managers who seek additional assets without concern for their durability. But each of these steps would help the long-term investors we are sworn to serve.

Consider the words of Benjamin Franklin at the close of the Constitutional Convention in 1787. Speaking of the new republic that had just been created, he pointed to General Washington's chair, on which a sun was painted in gold leaf. He observed: "I have in the course of the Session, and the vicissitude of my hopes and fears, looked at that sun without being able to tell whether it was rising or setting. But now I have the happiness to know that it is a rising and not a setting sun."

Similarly, I would express my own hopes and fears about the impact of computer technology on the new mutual fund industry we have created. Whether it is a rising sun or a setting sun is up to mutual fund investors.

ON DIRECTORS
SERVING TWO MASTERS

"No man can serve two masters." Almost 2,000 years ago, the Gospel of Matthew recorded those profound words of the Lord. As U.S. securities law developed, that principle was fully honored. The fundamental role of corporate directors is to serve only one master—the shareholders of the corporation. The operative words are: *with an eye single to their interests.* Directors have willingly accepted this standard of fiduciary duty, exemplified in this excerpt from the board of directors' mission statement of a Fortune 500 corporation:

> The mission of the Board is to achieve long-term economic value for the shareholders. The Board believes that the Corporation should rank in the top third of peer companies in the creation of economic value, as reflected in total return to shareholders. Board members should think of themselves as owners of the business representing other owners.

I am confident that the principles—if not the words—articulated in that statement are observed today by nearly every major publicly held enterprise in the United States.

Except for those corporations known as mutual funds.

Most fund directors seem to operate under a distinctly different mission statement. The gospel that they follow says, in effect, that directors of mutual funds, alone among all corporations, can serve two masters. While fund mission statements are conspicuous by their absence, were the gospel derived from the actions of fund directors, the statement might read something like this:

> The mission of the Board is to serve as a watchdog over the management company that controls and operates every aspect of the Fund's affairs, and to approve a contract with the management company that provides fees sufficient to ensure the company's growth and profitability. The Board may consider the economic value of the returns achieved for the Fund's shareholders relative to its peers and to unmanaged market indexes, but may accept a level of long-term value that fails to meet either standard, even over the long term.

Consider the contrast. The *corporate* mission statement expresses the way things work in America today. The creation of shareholder value has become at once a slogan, a truism, and a mandate. Earning the "cost of capital"—essentially, the return on comparable investments otherwise available in the financial markets—has become the rallying cry. Managers who fail to earn the cost of capital lose either their jobs or their corporations.

The *fund* mission statement, on the other hand, is a pallid imitation of "shareholders first." It suggests that fund directors should do their best to serve the economic interests of the fund shareholders, but they may also serve the economic interests of the fund's management company. As a result, whether fund shareholders are well served or poorly served, fund managers, without significant exception, lose neither their jobs nor their contracts. The balance of interests today is clearly tilted in favor of the management company.

THE LEVERS OF CONTROL

Why? For starters, consider the levers that control a fund's governance. The fund's chairman of the board is typically also the chairman and chief executive of the management company. One of every three or four fund directors is usually an affiliated director—a senior officer, and/or a principal owner of the management company. Typically, the affiliated directors are full-time employees of the company, which provides their entire compensation package. The fund directors usually meet only four times each year. Routinely, most, if not all, of the fund's "independent" directors have been initially selected or approved by the manager (and have had prior personal associations with the chief executive before becoming directors). It would defy credulity to argue that these practices, in their entirety, do not compromise the directors' independence and, to some degree at least, intimidate the fulfillment of their mission.

Further, fees paid to directors who are supposed to be independent ("disinterested" is the legal term) are often set at levels so far above corporate norms that serious questions have been raised about the existence of some subtle quid pro quo between the independent directors and the management company. The average director's fee paid by the 10 highest-paying fund complexes is $150,000 per year—nearly double the $77,000 paid by the 10 highest-paying U.S. Fortune 500 companies. Table 18.1 lists the average fees paid by the five fund firms paying the highest fees to their directors.

Wherever high directors' fees are paid, high management fees are likely to be found, according to a 1996 study by Morningstar.[1] "The more money the trustees get, the more shareholders pay in expenses," the study states. Reasonable people may disagree as to whether this correlation is sufficient to make the case that a quid pro quo exists ("If you want higher management fees, just pay the directors higher fees"), but the facts are hardly reassuring.

Finally, most fund directors are hardly in a position to think of themselves as "owners of the business representing other owners." Their shareholdings, rarely made public and even more rarely reported in the press, ordinarily range from nominal to nonexistent. The recent proxy statements for the funds in one large fund complex, although anecdotal, are hardly

TABLE 18.1

Fees Paid to Highest-Paid Fund Directors

Rank	Annual Fee per Director*
1	$240,986
2	184,750
3**	172,532
4	145,629
5	141,683
Average	$177,116

* 1996 data. New data not yet available.
** The Chairman of the Board of this fund firm, who was considered "independent" (unaffiliated with the manager), received $431,000 for his labors.

unusual. The typical independent director owned shares in 10 of the 24 funds in the complex; the aggregate amount was 1,900 shares, or 190 shares per fund with a market value averaging about $3,000. The total: $30,000 invested in the shares of all of the funds he serves. That financial interest, one might say, is modest to a fault. Given the pervasive nature of minimal personal financial commitments by directors, exemplified in this instance, there is clearly no *necessary* alignment of the interest of the directors with the interest of shareholders.

In all, mutual fund governance is riddled with conflicts—in the composition of the board, in the nature and frequency of the meetings, and in the level of directors' fees—and the situation is exacerbated by the rarity of significant ownership of fund shares by independent directors. If this situation were not sufficient to give the management company *de facto* control over the fund, surely the fact that the company also typically provides virtually every service necessary to the fund—administration, portfolio management, and distribution, under what amounts to a single "bundled" contract—would be the icing on the cake in establishing that the management company, not the fund shareholder, is the master who will be served.

THE CONSEQUENCES OF CONTROL

The results of this structure are clear. First, returns earned for mutual fund shareholders have been lackluster compared to market returns. Over the past 16 years, only 42 of 258 professionally managed equity funds outpaced the unmanaged all-market Wilshire 5000 Equity Index. In bond funds, the picture was even darker relative to appropriate unmanaged bond indexes. And in money market funds, outpacing an unmanaged index of short-term rates proved simply out of the question. No fund did so.

The principal reason for these consistent shortfalls is the drag of fund expenses. Let me apply a legal analogy to the field of financial services. I'll call the equation, Gross Return − Expenses = Net Return, the constitutional principle, and the tenet, "in efficient markets, mediocrity is the norm," the statutory law. But in the financial services arena, the constitutional principle cannot be amended, nor can the statute be repealed. They represent the immutable facts of financial life.

Despite the astonishing growth of fund assets, fee rates continue to rise at an accelerating rate. This pattern of rising fees is not a new phenomenon; indeed, it almost seems eternal. Since the inception of the U.S. fund industry in 1924, *minimum* fee rates on new funds have edged persistently higher; they rose from 0.38 percent to 0.58 percent during the first six decades. (These are minimum fee rates, the lowest rates in the fee schedule, and are usually reached only at very substantial levels of future fund assets that may never be attained. Average rates are inevitably higher, usually substantially so.) During the 1980s and 1990s, however, the rate of increase tripled: the minimum fee rose from 0.58 percent to 0.72 percent—or almost 25 percent. And this increase came hand in hand with a 37-fold increase in fund assets, resulting in a far larger increase in fees. Figure 18.1 shows the near-doubling of minimum fee rates paid by the average fund over the industry's history.

What is more, new types of expenses—added to the management fees paid by the funds—have entered the fee structure. Fees are now paid to advisers who then select subadvisers, who get paid for doing the actual portfolio management, a fairly recent phenomenon. Since 1980, distribution fees charged directly to fund assets have become pervasive. These so-called 12b-1 fees, used solely to foster sales of new fund shares, are now imposed by 60 percent of all funds.

Rising advisory fee rates and new distribution fees, along with higher fund operating expenses, have combined to sharply raise fund expense ratios. During the past 15 years, for example, the expense ratio of the average equity fund has risen from 1.04 percent to 1.55 percent. During the same period, equity fund assets have risen 35-fold, from $80 billion to

FIGURE 18.1

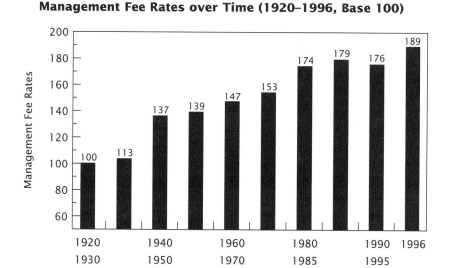

Management Fee Rates over Time (1920–1996, Base 100)

$2.8 trillion. Estimated expenses borne by equity funds have grown from $600 million to $34 *billion*—roughly a sixtyfold increase.

Managers' profits have grown even faster. Despite their widespread failure to outmanage yardsticks that are unmanaged, fund managers are now typically booking pretax profit margins in the range of 40 percent or more. And 50 percent to 70 percent margins doubtless exist before taking into account marketing expenditures—costs that benefit fund *managers* by increasing assets, but are borne by the fund *shareholders*. If these margins seem high, recognize that there are now thriving financial corporations that pay huge prices to buy investment advisory firms, simply for the right to receive 50 percent of their revenues. The advisory firms themselves continue to operate, making good money even after relinquishing fully one-half of their revenues.

Management companies are also being sold in the marketplace to financial services conglomerates at values that assume these remarkable margins will continue. These firms, anxious to make "one-stop shopping" available for their services, typically pay prices for fund managers' firms equal to 3 percent to 5 percent of fund assets managed. For example, a manager of a $10 billion fund complex would be paid $300 million to $500 million, not a penny of which would go to the shareholders of the fund who created the value of the enterprise in the first place.

The clear conflict of interest in the division of rewards between management company owners and fund owners when companies are sold—and, far more fundamentally, in the setting of advisory fee rates that determine what share of a fund's returns will go to each party—is the central issue facing the mutual fund industry, and it is the responsibility of fund directors to resolve it. I do not believe they can resolve it fairly if they attempt to serve two masters.

WHAT THE LAW SAYS

> The national public interest and the interest of investors are adversely affected . . . when investment companies are organized, operated and managed in the interest of investment advisers, rather than in the interest of shareholders . . . or when investment companies are not subjected to adequate independent scrutiny.

These words are the law, as articulated in the preamble of the Investment Company Act of 1940. The spirit of the law clearly says, "Shareholders must come first." Conspicuous by its absence from the statement is any suggestion that *two* masters—the shareholders, who own the fund, and the investment adviser, who controls it—should both be served. It is impossible to imagine that, in the mutual fund industry, either the letter or the spirit of the law is being observed.

Yet no official voices are raised in protest. The Investment Company Institute's *Introductory Guide for Investment Company Directors* focuses heavily on what are often, in truth, fairly trivial administrative issues, and ignores the major issue of control over the fund. The *Guide* explicitly endorses the concept of an existing external management company and, although it acknowledges the responsibility of directors to make a continuing evaluation of a fund's performance, it makes no reference to comparative performance standards, the impact of fund expenses on fund returns, or readily available alternative governance structures. The Institute's official position is that fund directors are the "watchdogs" of the industry, and that ought to be plenty good enough.

The *Fund Director's Guide Book* of the American Bar Association reaffirms that very theme. The unaffiliated directors of a fund, it states, quoting from a U.S. Supreme Court decision, are placed in the role of "independent watchdogs" vested with "the primary responsibility for looking after the interests of shareholders." That's close to the mark in setting a worthy standard. But the *Guide Book* then delves into a myriad of issues—often technical and detailed—for boards to consider and never gets to the heart of the matter: *de facto* control of a fund by its investment adviser, resulting in shareholder returns that are overburdened by fees; returns to advisers that dwarf those earned by most corporations; the absence of express standards by which to evaluate fund performance; and nary a hint that a fund board could choose to eliminate the external management structure and employ its own staff.

Are the independent directors truly watchdogs, with an eye single to the interest of fund shareholders? That central question must be answered in considering the effectiveness of the governance structure of the mutual fund industry. The record of ever-rising fund costs in the face of market-lagging fund returns, along with an awkward board structure and a near-absence of significant fund ownership by board members, hardly suggests that the watchdogs are very alert. Independent observers are beginning to voice their concerns about the situation. With his usual pungent wit, Warren Buffett expressed his view:

> I think the independent directors have been anything but independent. The Investment Company Act, in 1940, made these provisions for independent

directors on the theory that they would be the watchdogs for all these people pooling their money. The behavior of independent directors in aggregate since 1940 has been to rubber stamp every deal that's come along from management—whether management was good, bad, or indifferent. Not negotiate for fee reductions and so on. A long time ago, an attorney said that in selecting directors, the management companies were looking for Cocker Spaniels and not Dobermans. I'd say they found a lot of Cocker Spaniels out there.[2]

It should go without saying that cocker spaniels are not noted for aggressive, guardian-of-the-home ferocity.

AN ALTERNATIVE STRUCTURE

No one asks *why* today's external management structure, with its languid oversight by the board of directors, serves fund shareholders. Why does a $10 billion fund complex *need* a management company? It would not be atypical at an expense ratio level of 1.2 percent for the funds in the complex to spend $120 million per year: say, $20 million for investment management, $20 million for marketing and advertising, and $30 million for administration—a total of $70 million. The remaining $50 million would constitute the management company's profits before taxes. Why wouldn't it make sense to internalize management, slash marketing costs (which don't benefit fund shareholders) and save, say, $70 million a year? Would it serve the economic interests of the adviser? Hardly. Would it serve the interests of the fund shareholders? Yes.

Today's external management system exists only because it represents the status quo. And it won't soon go away. But if fund directors stop, look, and listen to the clear statistical evidence that a causal link exists between performance and expenses, they will begin to recognize a simple principle: When the spoils of economic value are divided, costs matter.

This much is clear: *The easiest and surest way for a fund to achieve the top quartile in investment performance among peer funds is to achieve the bottom quartile in expenses.* Statistics bear out this principle. It is not very complicated. When fund directors come to grips with this fact, and press for sharp fee reductions and a share of the economies of scale for the funds they serve, fund investors will be well served.

Part of the problem today is that the directors fail to recognize that the inverse relationship between performance and expenses is causal. Instead, directors have become part of a process in which an adviser justifies fee increases by comparisons with the rates charged by advisers to other funds. Ostensibly independent fund consultants come before the fund board with a study of the fee rates paid by other funds with similar investment objectives and asset levels. Particularly if the funds' fees are deemed below average (apparently a heinous sin calling for prompt atonement), they assure the directors that the funds would remain competitive under the new higher structure recommended by the management company. The recommendation is of course heartily endorsed by those fund directors who are employed by that same company; the independent directors rarely rock the boat.

My understanding is that at least one consultant omits from the comparisons the expense ratios of the industry's lowest-cost provider—which happens to operate on an at-cost basis. As a result, the costs of competitive funds are overstated, giving an extra nudge to the justification of the proposed fee increases. Given this omission, the fund directors considering the study are left in the dark about the possibility that there are alternative ways to run a fund. This practice suggests that the consultant knows exactly what his or her job is: to provide fodder that justifies the proposal for a fee hike.

In any event, this ratcheting-up process is almost precisely identical to the process by which executive compensation is set in corporate America. (Has a consultant *ever* recommended that compensation to the CEO be slashed?) It can lead only to an upward spiral in executive salaries, bonuses, and stock options. We observe that same phenomenon in mutual fund expense ratios in today's exuberant and unfettered financial environment. What is more, these rising fee *rates* are being hugely leveraged by soaring fund assets, driving the *total dollars* of fees to staggering and ever-ascending levels. A typical reaction among shareholders who become aware of these levels is: "There ought to be a law" against them. There *is* a law—the Investment Company Act, cited earlier—but no one seems to pay much attention to it.

LEGAL ACTION COMING?

Perhaps there *will* be a new law—or, at least, renewed legal recourse under the existing law. Earlier, I noted the correlation showing that shareholders tend to pay more in expenses at funds that pay directors higher fees. Specifically, equity fund families that paid directors at least $100,000 charged fee rates 16 percent higher than funds that paid directors less than

$25,000—especially astonishing because the funds paying large directors' fees have assets many times greater than the others. As a result, the dollar amounts of fees paid by the giant funds are far larger relative to their smaller cousins than the higher fee rates themselves would suggest.

A recent article in the *Columbia Law Review* suggested that the *Morningstar* study could well fit the legal definition of "undue influence."[3] Were undue influence to be the issue before the court, the article pointed out, a plaintiff would need to show that these three standards of evidence could be met in order to make the case for undue influence of a fund board that approved excessive management fees: opportunity, motive, and susceptibility. The article continued: "Since funds are created and managed by the adviser, proving *opportunity* by demonstrating the dependence of outside directors on the adviser . . . should be fairly simple. . . . Because of the percentage nature of management fees, advisers have sufficient *motive* to exert dominating influence over directors so as to cause them to approve advisory contacts that benefit the advisers but hurt fund shareholders. . . . [The results of the Morningstar expense study] show that outside directors are *susceptible* to the adviser because of the position of control the latter possesses over the former."

The article correctly notes that the benefits of mutual funds "do not justify investment advisers taking undeserved windfall gains out of the investment capital of others." That is the crucial issue, no matter how problematic it might be to resolve in a court of law.* So far, the industry has been virtually impregnable in the courts, which have basically found that the approval of management fees by directors should be heavily weighed, provided that the directors: are not dominated by the adviser, have been fully informed that fees could be recaptured by the fund, and have made a reasonable business decision to forgo that recapture. Given this legal background, it would take a long reach indeed to suggest that a novel legal action based on the undue-influence standard would prevail, no matter how clear its merits. But stranger things have happened. More probably, however, long-overdue relief from excessive mutual fund fees will come from a different source—a sort of moral suasion by legislative and regulatory officials.

---

*Depending on the particular circumstances of each case, this type of hitherto-untried litigation may or may not prove successful.

CONGRESS AND THE SEC

In Washington, DC, there are at least faint stirrings that today's comfortable (for advisers) status quo may be changing. The staff of the SEC's Division of Investment Management is "starting to take a hard look . . . at fund groups that enjoy high profitability, but provide shareholders with relatively poor performance and relatively high expenses." Congressmen Gillman (R, Ohio) and Markey (D, Massachusetts) have expressed significant concerns about fund fees and directors' diligence.

More recently, SEC Chairman Arthur Levitt—to my mind, the best champion for the rights of the mutual fund shareholder in the Commission's history—has begun to focus on the issue. At a recent meeting of Investment Company Institute members, Chairman Levitt set forth his views. His first level of concern was the pervasive inadequacy of fund disclosure about the impact of fees and expenses on returns. "I don't have to tell this audience that a 1 percent fee will reduce an ending account balance by 17 percent over 10 years." In fact, the 2-plus percent all-in cost for the average equity fund would reduce the amount of capital accumulated by about 24 percent over 10 years, and 39 percent over 25 years. (The exact figures depend on the actual rate of return.)

In the same talk, Chairman Levitt expressed his concern about the proper role of a fund's board by asking rhetorically, "When is a director independent? What are the respective roles of the board and the shareholders in selecting and terminating the fund's adviser?" After stating that "fees have to be questioned," he added that "no one should 'buy into the myth' that fund directors need not be as strong, vigilant, or independent as corporate directors. Those who do [buy into the myth] are making excuses for the directors who don't have the time or the interest to stand up for shareholders. . . . Funds whose directors forget whom they represent won't be long for the business."[4]

The SEC Chairman also announced that he would soon convene a roundtable "to work toward consensus on whether changes are needed in the current system of [fund] governance." He closed his commentary by saying: "I expect directors to remember whom they serve—fund shareholders—and I expect fund directors to be tireless in the pursuit of shareholders' interests."

Those words may well be the start of some long-overdue improvements in the fund governance system. Chairman Levitt's strongest statements so far from his bully pulpit should help create the initial

Empty Suits?

The financial press has begun, however haltingly, to pay attention to whether mutual fund directors are honoring their responsibilities. In mid-1998, *The New York Times* ran a front-page article headlined: "When Empty Suits Fill the Board Room," featuring a giant photo of empty suits surrounding a boardroom table. The article noted that "to almost any degree that directors hesitate, individual investors stand to lose," and contrasted, in unflattering terms, the duties fulfilled by the boards of publicly held corporations and by the boards of mutual funds. The *Times* went on to describe how "the balance of power has kept shifting from fund directors and toward the companies that conceive, market, and manage mutual funds."

The story closed with two surprises. First, it seemed to view favorably fund structures outside of the United States, under which "fund directors are not responsible for setting a fund's management fee. Free from questions about the economics of a fund's management contracts, directors could spend their time monitoring a manager's business practices [such as] whether investment guidelines are being followed." Ignoring substance and honoring process, however, would seem a peculiar approach to solving the industry's "empty suit" director syndrome in the public interest. The article's second surprise was its abject failure to recognize the entirely different governance structure of the one giant mutual fund complex in which the funds own and control their own management company—and which operates at costs about 75 percent below industry norms, delivering its fund shareholders savings of upward of $3 billion per year. Warren Buffett has said that fund directors could save investors $10 billion annually if they would put into practice some of the policies that follow from this different governance structure. In fact, such savings could easily top $30 billion each year.

momentum needed to broaden public recognition of the negative implications of the industry's intertwined issues of fund costs, directors' duties, and industry structure. Congressional inquiry would provide a further opportunity to consider the preamble of the 1940 Act and its relevance to the industry's embarrassing record on fees. A new federal standard of fiduciary duty for directors would well serve fund shareholder interests. And an activist press, focusing more heavily on the mediocrity of traditional portolio management and on the impact of costs as the enemy of long-term returns would be another major plus. In all, this moral suasion—translated into increased investor awareness and concordant decisions about fund selection—might finally awaken directors to their trustee responsibilities.

SUMMING UP

The focus of corporate directors on shareholder value in the United States has virtually revolutionized the way corporations operate throughout the world. In contrast, the failure of mutual fund directors to observe the primacy of shareholder value has resulted from the limited oversight of boards of directors that serve as timid watchdogs, seemingly ignorant of the principle that *costs matter*.

This difference radiates from the directors' mission statement. For corporate directors, it is: "Do or die." Enhance shareholder value or else. For fund directors, it is: "Accept the status quo." Provide no more than watchdog oversight accompanied by inaction, and accept the creation of shareholder value that is far short of optimal. Or, using Mr. Buffett's formulation: Model yourselves, not on dobermans, but on cocker spaniels.

How can the industry best accomplish an alignment of interest between directors and shareholders? Common sense would dictate an effective and simple start: Have the board of the fund set down in writing—and publish in the fund's annual report—its own mission statement. It would be a good beginning.

Some 50 million faceless and voiceless fund shareholders have been entranced by receiving the magnificent blessings of the long bull market, without realizing that they have received far less than their fair share of these blessings. They deserve better from the directors they have elected to represent them. These directors must serve one master, and only one master: the fund shareholders who trusted them to protect their interests.

The full verse in Matthew's gospel is: "No man can serve two masters, for either he must hate the one and love the other, or else he will hold to the one and despise the other. Ye cannot serve God and mammon." In effect, under the Investment Company Act of 1940, fund shareholders are designated as the gods who are to be served. But the wealth they might otherwise have had has been sharply eroded by excessive fund expenses. But great wealth, surely a proxy for mammon, continues to be reaped by mutual fund managers. Fund directors have a responsibility to serve those who elected them, who trusted them, and who created the fund with their own investments. The shareholders of a fund enterprise must be its master.

ON STRUCTURE
THE STRATEGIC IMPERATIVE

ost mutual fund investors don't understand how their mutual fund company is organized. Actually, very few of us probably give much thought to the structural organization of the companies with which we do business. Why should we care? Does it matter whether our bank is structured as a savings and loan or a commercial bank? In that case, with up to $100,000 per account insured, most of us probably shouldn't care about anything but getting the best service and the highest interest rate.

But in the mutual fund business, we ought to care. A fund's organizational structure can have an enormous impact on our returns. Yet, almost no one pays attention to this issue. The media don't get it, don't care, or have accepted the status quo. But the corporate structure of a mutual fund organization is more than a legal curiosity. It is a fundamental determinant of the relationship between the fund complex and the fund shareholder.

With one significant exception, all mutual fund complexes operate under a single structure: a group of related investment companies (mutual funds), owned by their shareholders (or, less commonly, trusts effectively owned by their beneficiaries), and governed by their directors. Each fund in the group contracts with an external management company to manage its affairs in return for a fee. The management company undertakes to provide substantially all of the activities necessary for the funds' existence: investment advisory services, distribution and marketing services, and operational, legal, and financial services.

Although it has the same basic corporate structure as competing mutual fund organizations, the sole exception marches to a different drummer. Instead of retaining an outside firm to perform the requisite services for a fee, Vanguard Group, the firm that I founded in 1974, manages its own affairs on an at-cost basis. The difference between the two structures is illustrated in Figure 19.1.

Under the Investment Company Act of 1940, both structures are contemplated. The Act treats them objectively and evenhandedly, in effect suggesting that the choice between them is a neutral one. But whichever is the case, the Investment Company Act clearly states that a mutual fund, owned entirely by its shareholders, is to be operated solely in the owners' interest, a principle articulated in the Act's preamble. However, within the existing legal framework, it has proven almost impossible to do justice to this fundamental principle. The industry's conventional structure rests on a profound conflict of interest between the mutual fund shareholders and the owners of the highly profitable management

FIGURE 19.1

Mutual Ownership Structure vs. Traditional Corporate Structure

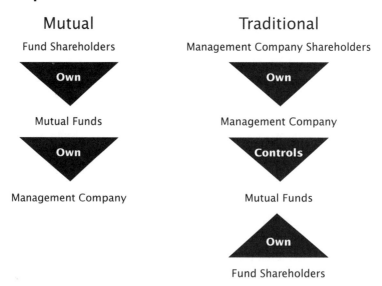

companies that operate the mutual funds. For when investment returns are divided, the more the manager earns, the less the shareholder earns. A dollar in profits for the management company is a dollar less for the mutual fund shareholders. It's as simple as that.

CONTRASTING OWNERSHIP STRUCTURES

In the conventional structure, the fund is merely a corporate shell. Its sole role is to be the legal owner of a portfolio of investment securities. A fund typically exists solely on paper. The shareholders of the funds are its ultimate owners, but, with ownership often spread among hundreds of thousands of investors, it is not these owners who exercise working control. Control is effectively vested in the external management company, which has formed the fund, given (or licensed) it its name, and selected its directors, a majority of whom must be independent of the management company. The company provides the fund's officers and performs all of the services necessary for the fund's existence. In return, the fund pays the company an annual management fee, normally calculated as a percentage of the fund's assets. The company usually performs the same services for perhaps five to fifty, or more, sister funds in the same mutual fund complex. The control of the management company is usually vested in one or two owners, or a small group of partners in its employ, or even a set of outside public stockholders.

As a practical matter, under the industry's existing structure, the fund family is controlled by the adviser; control is completely divorced from ownership. Under a truly mutual structure, on the other hand, the fund is owned and controlled by its shareholders, and operated solely in their interests. Just as does a "normal" corporation, it employs its own officers and staff. The fund family manages its own affairs, but, for the sake of administrative convenience, it does so through a separate management company that is 100 percent owned and controlled by the fund family. The officers and directors, including the independent directors, of both the management company and the fund family are the same. Neither own stock in the management company. Effectively, the mutual structure means that the fund directors provide direction and oversight and take responsibility for the management, not only of the funds themselves, but of the fund "complex"—the business entity that operates the ongoing activities of the funds as a group. With a truly mutual organization, there is only one master to be served—the fund shareholders.

This fundamental difference between the two disparate corporate structures gives rise to very different corporate strategies. With a mutual structure, an organization has no choice but to pursue strategies that serve *solely* the needs of its owners, the mutual fund shareholders. By contrast, with a bifurcated set of masters—the fund shareholders and the management company stockholders—the traditional mutual fund complex pursues a strategy focused on serving both groups, each of which has very different needs. Sheer logic would suggest that these radically different forms of organizational structure would entail remarkably different corporate strategies. And they do. "Function follows form" in the fund industry. This principle is the antithesis of the great Louis Sullivan's principle of architecture: "Form follows function." Actual, if limited, industry experience has confirmed this important linkage. *Strategy follows structure.*

Before we turn to the contrasting strategies that differentiate the two kinds of structure, let's first explore in more detail the issue of ownership and, in particular, the powerful financial incentives that have contributed to the industry's prevailing convention.

HISTORY IN THE MAKING

Imagine our mutual fund industry as seen by an investor newly arrived from another planet. His first reaction would be confusion. Mutual funds operate under an arrangement that would be almost unimaginable in other corners of the capitalist marketplace. The shareholders, who put their capital at risk in the funds, reap their rewards only after the management companies, retained to operate the fund, receive their fees, spend what they must, and reap their own rewards. Without putting significant (if any) capital at risk, these firms enjoy a large share of the rewards. The rewards that accrue to the fund shareholders depend solely on the net returns earned by the fund. Those that accrue to the management company depend largely on the amount of assets managed for the shareholders. The fund's relative return—the extent to which it outpaces or falls short of the return of the market, or even the returns of its peers, over the long term—seems, perhaps surprisingly, to exert little influence on the rewards reaped by the adviser.

To an intergalactic observer who knows nothing of the traditional fund structure, this situation would surely seem odd. Why shouldn't a huge fund complex manage its own affairs? Why doesn't it operate like virtually all other corporations in America, serving the interests of a single shareholder constituency? (While this system hardly functions with perfection, it works fairly well.) Those questions cannot be resolved using logic. History alone offers answers.

Many of the early mutual funds were founded by trustees for the beneficiaries of the trusts they served; they sought merely to pool the capital of smaller individual investment accounts and achieve diversification and efficiency. However, the dominant industry strain that has emerged—and prevails overwhelmingly today—is the fund group that has been organized by entrepreneurs who invest their capital and their reputation in a company whose mission is to develop, market, and manage a group of funds whose assets will grow to substantial levels.

The economic stakes have become huge. Management companies—nearly all of which, at the outset, were wholly owned by their founders—gradually passed into private ownership by partners and executives of the managers. Later, offerings of shares to the public, a trend that accelerated during the 1970s and 1980s, brought in a whole new set of investors, unrelated to the operations of the complex. Their sole interest was sharing in the growing profits of the managers. Now, in the late 1990s, increasing numbers of fund organizations are being sold to other firms. Earlier combinations of private and public ownership are emerging as giant financial conglomerates.

Based on the going rate—the price at which ownership changes hands—management companies are typically (albeit, with some wide variations) worth something in the range of 4 percent of the market value of the fund assets under management. With mutual fund industry assets at more than $5 trillion, the separate management company industry would be worth at least $200 billion—a staggering sum by any measure. To justify this valuation, the acquiring conglomerateurs (or the industry's existing private partners and public owners) must see the prospect of earning a good return on their capital—say, 12 percent per year after taxes, or 17 percent before taxes. For the owners of the management companies to earn a 17 percent pretax return on their $200 billion investment, fund shareholders would have to pay $34 billion annually over and above the actual cost of providing the funds' management, marketing, and administrative services. The questions raised for mutual fund shareholders by this structure include:

- Given this diversion of the investment returns available in the financial markets from fund investors to fund managers, should this traditional fund structure prevail?

- Is the setting of the advisory fees that support this structure appropriate and fair?
- Will fund governance be responsive to the seeming imbalance between the interests of fund shareholders and management company shareholders? Or will some acceptable type of mutual structure finally emerge?

STRATEGY FOLLOWS STRUCTURE

The answers, it seems to me, ought to depend on which corporate strategy best serves the interest of fund shareholders in the long run. Critical contrasts in strategy would be suggested by the differences between, on the one hand, the conventional industry structure, designed to serve the often-conflicting interests of two sets of owners, and, on the other, the mutualized, internally managed structure, designed to serve the interests of the fund owners alone. Many of these differences in strategy, as it turns out, actually exist today in our sole example of the mutualized structure, as illustrated in Figure 19.2. With the sole exception of service strategy, these differences are profound.

Profit Strategy

There is no question that the best externally owned management companies strive to earn the highest possible returns—before the deduction of

FIGURE 19.2

Strategy Follows Structure

Strategy	Mutual Structure	Conventional Structure
1. Profit	High (for shareholders)	Very high (for manager)
2. Pricing	At cost	What traffic will bear
3. Service	Excellence	Excellence
4. Risk management	Risk intolerant	Risk tolerant
5. Product	Sensible	Faddish
6. Indexing	Missionary zeal	Kicking and screaming
7. Marketing	Conservative	Aggressive

their fees—for the fund shareholders. There is also no question that they strive to maximize their own profits as well. That orientation toward maximizing firm profits (as distinct from fund profits) is mandatory. These organizations are under a fiduciary obligation to their own stockholders, who, like the owners of capital in any organization, expect to earn high returns on their investment. These organizations expect to—and do—receive, from the shareholders of their mutual funds, fees that amply cover their expenses. When their fees appear low relative to other comparable funds, they may seek (and usually receive) fee increases from the fund directors, which are duly ratified by shareholders. Even as the soaring stock market has taken management company profits to levels undreamed of even three years ago, serious reductions in fee rates are conspicuous by their absence. There may not be anything wrong, as such, with the fact that the assets entrusted to these fiduciaries by fund shareholders have become the basis for the creation of scores of centimillionaires among management company shareholders. Indeed, that's the accepted way for capitalism—as distinct from trusteeship— to work. But with all due respect, there may be a *better* way.

The mutual organization, too, strives to earn the highest possible return for its fund shareholders. Ideally, it is structured so that its profits are, in substance, rebated to fund shareholders. These so-called profits simply represent the difference between the actual expenses of the mutual organization in operating its funds and the revenues it would have received—at industry norms—if it had been structured as a separate management company. An extra dollar of cost savings for the mutual organization would be an extra dollar in profits for the mutual fund shareholder. It's as simple as that. So, there is a contrast between the mutual organization's *sole* orientation (to enhance the returns of fund shareholders) and the industry's *dual* orientation (to enhance the returns of fund shareholders and management company stockholders alike).

Figure 19.2 differentiated between "high" profit orientation for fund investors and "very high" profit orientation for managers. This simply reflects the hardly counterintuitive notion that the drive to make money for others—the fund shareholders—may not be as powerful as the drive to make money for oneself through ownership participation in the management company. When Adam Smith described the concept of the "invisible hand," he concluded that the individual businessman "generally neither intends to promote public interest, nor knows how much he is promoting it." Hence, Smith argued that "it is not from the benevolence of the butcher, the baker, or the brewer that we expect our dinner, but from their regard to their own interest . . . their self-love." So it is in the traditional mutual fund industry. We cannot expect management companies to operate in the public interest. We must recognize the reality that they are in the business of investing other people's money in order to maximize their own profits, even though those profits come at the expense of their fund shareholders.

Pricing Strategy

The pricing strategy of the conventional (externally managed) fund complex, baldly stated, is to charge what the traffic will bear. Perhaps this strategy arises from the uncritical public acceptance of mutual funds, which have provided remarkably generous absolute returns during the great bull market, even after the deduction of costs. Or perhaps it arises from public ignorance of the role of costs in shaping returns. It may be no coincidence that, in the more sedate investment environment of the 1940s, the traffic could presumably bear an equity fund expense ratio equal to about 0.75 percent of assets per year, for that was the going rate. Today, in an exuberant environment, the traffic bears twice that burden: expense ratios of equity funds average more than 1.50 percent. Industry participants have harnessed their creative energies to justify a whole series of ancillary fees to pay for sales and marketing. The industrywide average expense ratio paid by shareholders of all mutual funds (including bond and money market funds) now approaches 1.2 percent, and continues to rise. In the competition among the externally managed complexes, prices are set by competitors seeking the maximum level that will be perceived as not damaging the returns fund shareholders earn, all the while gaining the managers maximum returns on their own capital. The result: Prices paid by investors are high.

Advisers have long recognized that small increases in fees, often almost invisible to fund shareholders, have an astronomical impact on management company profits. If an adviser to a $25 billion group of equity funds were to raise advisory fees (or add distribution fees) that cause the funds' expense ratio to rise from 0.80 percent to 1.00 percent, most shareholders would hardly notice, and would vote their approval as required by law. These funds' costs would remain in well-below-average territory. But the adviser's fees would rise by 0.20 percentage point, or $50 million. Assuming that the adviser incurs no increase in expenses at the margin, 100 percent of this increase in revenue would filter down to pre-tax profit. There is a lot of profit leverage in raising fees. When the traffic doesn't much care about what cost it bears, this is a logical outcome, although it ill-serves fund shareholders.

As a result of the difference in corporate structure, a firm with a mutual structure offers funds at costs that are far less than what the traffic will bear. On the record, funds managed by the industry's sole mutual organization incur, by far, the lowest costs in the industry. Combined operating, advisory, and distribution costs average less than 0.30 percent of assets annually, or more than 0.90 percentage points below the industry norm of 1.20 percent. Even granting that a smaller mutually structured complex would operate at, say, 50 basis points, the resultant 70-point saving in annual profits—and, therefore, the cost savings to fund shareholders—would be calculated at $70 million for each $10 billion of assets. The mutual fund business is a *very* profitable business . . . for fund managers.

There are widely divergent views about the cost of mutual fund investing. As demonstrated repeatedly in this book, however, *cost matters*. In money market mutual funds, with quality held constant, cost differences account for virtually 100 percent of the differences in net yield to the investor; in bond funds, quality and maturity held constant, cost differences may account for about 80 percent of the differences in returns. Because of the utter clarity of the direct link between cost and return in money market and bond funds, their emergence and rise to prominence over the past 20 years raise profound questions about industry price-setting, and could in time cause investors, fund sellers, and regulators to challenge the threadbare "what the traffic will bear" standard.

In a stock market that delivers more modest returns, investors in equity funds too are apt to demand a more enlightened standard. If we assume a more or less normal 10 percent return on stocks and adjust it for inflation and taxes, the annual return *before fund costs* might amount to just 5 percent. Annual all-in costs of, say, 2.5 percent for an equity fund would consume (believe it or not) 50 percent of the *real after-tax* return. In a low-cost fund, expenses of, say, 0.2 percent per year would consume less than 5 percent of the return. Never forget that while *real* returns (nominal returns less inflation) are what the investor can spend, it is *nominal* costs that must be considered in establishing the penalty investors pay through excessive costs. Whether you garner a 10 percent return on your investment or a 5 percent return, and whether it is measured in nominal or real terms, your costs will be 2.5 percent or 0.20 percent, using the range I have illustrated. Intelligent investors must recognize that the penalties of excessive cost in investing—considering potential future returns and adjusting them, first for taxes, and then for inflation—are apt to be staggering.

Service Strategy

As the mutual fund industry strives not only to meet clients' expectations, but to exceed them, service excellence is becoming a commodity. Are there "better" and "worse" providers of mutual fund investor services? Of course there are. But the gap between the two is narrowing rapidly, and woe to the firm—whatever its organizational form—that does not measure up to high standards.

Here, little contrast exists between the two types of fund organizations. Under the conventional structure, advisers seek to serve shareholders out of an enlightened sense of self-interest. After all, in the short run at least, an individual shareholder is apt to be far more aware of his or her satisfaction (or dissatisfaction) with service than with costs and their impact on returns. Satisfied shareholders don't redeem their shares; indeed, in these days of strong financial markets, satisfied shareholders are likely to increase their investments over time and to invest in other funds offered within the complex. To the manager, a satisfied mutual fund shareholder can be described as money in the bank.

A mutual organization nonetheless enjoys an intrinsic advantage that may enhance its commitment to service excellence. The service is a bit different under a mutual structure, in which the shareholders, through their ownership of fund shares, also own the shares of the management company. Many organizations honor the tenet "Treat your customers as if they were your owners." A mutual organization can, with accuracy, tack on the phrase "because they *are* our owners." It may prove to be a critical difference in a fund's attitude toward serving its clients. What is more, the mutual enterprise is in a position to garner an edge in service because it operates at such low cost. It can easily spend a little more at the margin to go the extra mile for its investors, without impinging significantly on its large cost advantage. The manager of a conventional fund group, on the other hand, may be ambivalent about spending more on service, for expenses reduce the profits of the manager, at least over the short term.

Risk Management Strategy

The risk management strategy of conventionally operated equity funds is best characterized by relative indifference—"relative" because funds in the various categories (large-cap growth, small-cap value, etc.) are expected to carry risks generally appropriate to the classification. In the equity fund arena, risk is, at best, a difficult concept to grasp, and the use of short-term price volatility, although easily quantified, is only a crude proxy. In general, however, investors' expectations regarding risk appear to relate largely to having a fund's price volatility (however measured) fall roughly in the range of peers with comparable investment characteristics, as exemplified by classification according to the Morningstar tick-tack-toe boxes: value, blended, or growth style on the horizontal axis; large, medium, or small size on the vertical axis. Real risk, of course, comes when the stock market takes a sharp tumble, but history suggests that the declines of the funds in these nine boxes are apt to parallel past experience; for example, large value typically suffers the smallest relative decline, and small growth has the largest decline.

When we consider bond and money market funds, however, many conventionally operated funds have demonstrated considerable risk *tolerance*. One of the primary differentiators that affects the choice of an income-oriented fund by investors is *yield*, and a fund's net yield is largely determined by the relationship between its gross yield and its expenses—a direct, dollar-for-dollar yield trade-off. Over time, yield is the overpoweringly predominant component of total return for fixed-income funds. Differences in net yield, then, largely control differences in long-term return. Advisers of funds with very high expenses have to content themselves with noncompetitive yields, and—assuming only that the marketplace is discerning—with modest fund assets on which to earn their higher fees. Alternatively, they could increase risk, accepting some combination of lower portfolio quality or longer portfolio maturity relative to their low-cost peers, and, by so doing, elevating their net yields to marketplace norms.

Portfolio statistics for bond funds show that a good bit of this mongrelizing of quality and maturity is in fact happening. Bond funds with higher costs tend to maintain lower-quality portfolios. (See Chapter 7.) Sometimes, surprising as it may seem, the combination may even enhance returns (in an environment of high prosperity and falling interest rates, for example), but, in the long run, it will almost surely reduce returns. High cost, in and of itself, may confiscate a large portion—even all—of the risk premium accorded by the financial market to lower-grade or longer-maturity bonds.

In the money market arena, however, there is little room to increase risk, given the stringent quality and maturity regulations promulgated by the U.S. Securities and Exchange Commission. Further, management companies must concern themselves with "reputation risk." If a fund's net asset value dropped from the universally expected (if hardly insured or guaranteed) $1.00 per share to $0.99 per share, it would effectively write itself out of the money fund business. A scarlet letter would be associated with the manager, and the reputation of its bond and equity funds would be tarnished as well. For that reason, there are no instances in which the $1.00 share value of a money market fund of a major fund manager has been imperiled. When money funds have reached too far out on the limb of risk (often to compensate for their high fees) and faced this issue as a result, the funds have been bailed out by their management companies, which have bought the questionable money market investments from them at face value.

The risk management strategy for the mutual organization, on the other hand, can be one of risk *intolerance*. What need is there to reach out for a higher yield on a bond or money market fund, if, because of competitively low costs, the fund is already providing a premium yield? If the temptation to climb out to the farthest possible point on the risk limb is virtually irresistible for conventional funds, the temptation can be delightfully resistible for funds operating under the mutual structure, especially for those that maintain quality and constrain variations in maturity. If the yields are equal, as they are apt to be, wouldn't any intelligent investor seek out a well-run, low-cost AAA-rated *intermediate-term* insured municipal bond fund in preference to either an A-rated intermediate-term fund or an AAA-rated insured *long-term* bond fund? Clearly, common sense would dictate such a choice. Contrary to the almost universally accepted maxim that "there is no such thing as a free lunch," there *is* a free lunch in the world of mutual funds. High reward does not necessarily entail higher risk. *Higher* return, where risk is held constant, can be achieved with *lower* cost.

Product Strategy

I abhor the use of the word "product" to describe a mutual fund—which represents, after all, a diversified investment portfolio under prudent trusteeship—but our industry today is fixated on the development of new products designed less for their disciplined investment characteristics than for their perceived attractiveness to the investing public. "Hot new products"—an even more offensive term, if highly popular with fund marketers—are the name of the game today, the better to raise additional assets, and hence additional fees and profits for their sponsors.

In the current environment, a conventional mutual fund management company almost has an obligation to jump on the bandwagon of product development. If emerging markets are hot, quickly establish an emerging market fund product, and so on. When accumulating assets under management is a crucial goal for the owners of investment advisory firms, there is little incentive to hold back from creating funds that the public seems to demand, irrespective of their intrinsic long-term merit.

Hard experience should have taught this industry that the moment of highest public demand for a new concept strongly tends to coincide with the moment when the balloon has been inflated to the maximum possible extent. We have learned that the best time to *sell* a concept may be the worst time to *buy* it. Being *"firstest"* with the mostest" may prove to be *"worstest"* for the mostest." The fund shareholders pay the consequences. Certainly that has not been an infrequent happening, as witnessed by the experience of the government-plus fund, the adjustable rate mortgage fund, and the global short-term income fund, all chronicled in Chapter 16.

The mutual organization, on the other hand, has no particular need to enter the race for so-called new products. It does not need to attract the most dollars. Its business is not to bring in faddish new business that does nothing significant to enhance shareholder returns, but to earn optimal net returns for its owners. If an investment idea is sound and sensible, even if it is momentarily overvalued by the whims of the marketplace, it may ultimately be a useful member of the fund family because it offers an attractive lower-cost option to the shareholders of its other funds who would otherwise have to invest elsewhere. But, in the fullness of time, the mutual fund organization should have the luxury of choosing its entry point based on investment merits, not on marketing opportunities.

If a truly *mutual* fund complex is not maximizing its profits in the conventional sense—that is, not seeking entrepreneurial profits for its manager—it can afford to stand above the fray of the mutual fund marketplace when fads emerge and common sense goes on holiday. Just because "everyone else is doing it" and the industry is making huge profits on new products is no reason for the mutual organization to follow along. Such a structure, given its relative immunity from some of the pressures of the marketplace, should play a major role in a "Just say no" discipline that promotes prudent vigilance in so-called product strategy.

Indexing Strategy

Nearly all mutual funds are actively managed investment portfolios. But passively managed indexed portfolios are now enjoying wide investor acceptance far beyond their limited number (about one fund in every 300).

The secret of the success of the index fund is not alchemy. It is its ability to provide extraordinarily broad diversification at extraordinarily low cost (albeit buttressed by the astonishing performance superiority in recent years of the index funds modeled on the S&P 500 Index). It almost goes without saying that fund management companies, with their very high profit orientation and their high pricing strategies, will fail in their mission to create substantial value for their own stockholders if they sponsor only low-cost index funds. Instead, many companies craft tortuous arguments to dismiss the success of indexing, and struggle to keep the investor focused on high-cost active management.

Nonetheless, the significant growth of the index fund—a distinctively different type of new, if you will, "product," especially in institutional 401(k) savings and retirement plans—has created substantial pressure for conventional managers to enter this arena. Never mind that the offering of low-cost index funds under the same roof as high-cost actively managed funds is a contradiction in terms. But, fearful that their vaunted market share of industry sales volume may drop if they don't provide an index fund for retirement plan clients, conventional managers have reluctantly begun to offer indexed portfolios, temporarily subsidizing expenses to reduce costs to the level of what traffic will bear in this more sophisticated market. These firms almost have to hope that this particular new product will prove to be a short-term fad that is doomed to long-term failure. If not, it will seriously jeopardize the long-term returns earned by their own management company stockholders.

I have both good news and bad news for them. The good news is that the performance of index funds modeled on the Standard & Poor's 500 Index will rarely look as powerful as it has in recent years. Indeed, after such a healthy run in the giant cap stocks that dominate it, the 500 Index may well even lag the total market for a while, as mid- and small-cap stocks finally come to lead the market. The bad news is that index funds are bound to provide long-term returns superior to those of comparable actively managed funds and should outperform about three-quarters of such funds. Elementary mathematics, the industry's current cost structure, and the lessons of history together make this outcome almost inevitable.

The mutual organization is the logical champion for the index fund concept. Such an organization could not avoid offering an index fund even if it wished to. Low cost is its very stock in trade. Indexing may well be a *loss* leader for the industry, but it has clearly been a *gain* leader for investors. While the institutional marketplace is dragging the stockholder organizations kicking and screaming into indexing, the mutual organization approaches the task with something akin to missionary zeal. Indexing is destined to become almost infinitely less profitable for fund management companies as investors not only demand index funds as such—the evidence is compelling—but eventually boycott those index funds with sales loads and with high operating costs. For the investor who decides to go the index route, it should take no more than common sense to select solely no-load index funds offered at minimum cost—funds that are much more likely to be provided by mutual organizations.

Marketing Strategy

If the financial benefits of growth in this industry largely accrue to management companies, not fund shareholders, it follows, then, that stockholder organizations are aggressive asset-gatherers. The industry's largest fund complexes pour up to $100 million annually into media advertising alone. In an earlier era, the industry's bland tombstone ads were virtually obscured by columns of agate type recording the mutual fund returns in the daily business pages. Today, those staid ads have given way to prime-time television spots: rock-music videos hyping past performance, and 20-second theater with melodramatic vignettes. These approaches are likely to cause eventual dissatisfaction born of expectations unrealized by investors.

But, this high-voltage marketing is not only misleading, it can have a pernicious effect on the investment results earned by fund shareholders. Marketing and distribution are highly expensive functions but the burden is borne by the shareholders, not those who promote the fund. "Money is no object" seems to have become the industry mantra in the search for market share and ever-larger management company profits. Why should *management* companies worry about *marketing* budgets? Fees paid by shareholders are the source of the dollars, so marketing costs come right out of the investment profits of the fund shareholders. The investor pays to foster the fund's growth, and suffers in return.

An aggressive marketing strategy is logical and productive for a fund complex that has a conventional structure and is spending a portion of its management fees so as to have larger fees in the future. By the same token, a conservative marketing strategy, with an emphasis not primarily on promotion, but on information, would be a logical and productive strategy for a shareholder-owned complex, operating at cost and so controlling costs

"Simba and the Food Chain"

It is a rare and delightful pleasure to find a kindred spirit in the investment community who shares my views about the structure problems in investment management. Keith Ambachtsheer, a widely respected commentator on pension investment management, recently compared the actual structural of the profession with the ideal structure. These excerpts from his newsletter begin with this dialogue from Disney's "The Lion King," concerning Simba's state of mind:

Q: "What's eating him?"
A: "Nothing, he's on top of the food chain!"

The owners, executives, and professionals of the investment management industry are today's undisputed Simbas of the financial food chain. From a personal wealth creation perspective, they are clearly on top. Yet, something seems to be eating at many of them too. That "something" is the continuing large gap between how the industry should operate if it is to produce "quality products at reasonable prices" for its customers, and how it actually operates. Any narrowing of the "Ideal-Actual" gap will result in more money in the pockets of customers, but less in the pockets of the suppliers.

The Market: How It *Should* Work

The *ideal* investment management industry should have three key attributes: (1) A high proportion of publicly traded financial assets is managed passively at very low fees by a small number of large, global providers, with the large economies of scale inherent in passive management passed on to the customers; (2) A low proportion of publicly traded financial assets is managed actively for *performance-based fees* by a larger number of smaller providers, because true value-adding active management is a scarce resource in both capability and capacity; and (3) Industry investment performance information is expressed as risk-adjusted net performance relative to pre-defined investment benchmark portfolios which reflect the managed portfolios' stated investment policy.

Assessing the "Ideal-Actual" Gap

The *actual* industry characteristics are very different from the ideal: (1) A low proportion of financial assets is passively managed; (2) A high proportion of financial assets is actively managed for largely asset-based fees rather than performance-based fees; and (3) The managing fiduciaries for pension funds are increasingly aware that active management has been destroying pension fund value. *There is little doubt that, were it to be measured properly, value destruction in the mutual fund sector would be greater than in the pension fund sector simply because mutual fund fees are generally higher than the fees pension funds pay.*

The "Ideal-Actual" gap seems to be working in reverse today, with suppliers on top collecting asset-based active management fees, and customers at the bottom paying them without getting sufficient value.

Why Is the Financial Food Chain Working in Reverse?

First, it is counterintuitive to many otherwise perfectly rational people that when you throw tens of thousands of very smart investment professionals controlling billions of dollars at the stock and bond markets, pickings get very small. In their heart of hearts, investment professionals understand this reality. However, it is clearly not in their financial interest to make the customers understand too.

Second, most customers still don't understand the devastating impact high fees have on long-term investment results. *This economic reality has not sufficiently penetrated into the mutual fund arena.*

The fact that the financial food chain is operating in reverse has not been lost on the investment management industry. The dilemma is that a better "value" balance between what the customers get and what the suppliers will take will generally mean more money for the customers, and less for many of the suppliers.

Narrowing the "Ideal-Actual" Gap

Because of the much higher fees, average results (in the mutual fund industry) will be considerably worse than the not very good results in the pension fund sector. The coming single digit return world won't be as kind. In a world of 8 percent stock returns and 6 percent bond returns, high fees simply won't fly. Passive managers will increasingly compete by cutting fees and offering index funds at an extremely low cost. Active managers with enough conviction in their own skill may begin to realize that it is both in their and their clients' interests to implement performance fees. These factors should elevate customers to the top of the financial food chain, where they surely belong.[1]

Enlightened industry professionals, institutional 401(k) thrift plans, average investors, securities regulators, "think tanks," finance professors, and Nobel laureates want to strike a better balance between the interests of clients and of managers. If they speak out like Keith Ambachtsheer, maybe we can make some progress in shaping a better mutual fund industry for the 21st century.

the best it can. Like any business organization, a mutual organization would keep an eye on its market share, but only as a rough measure of its success in meeting the needs of the investing public. The mutual organization has two rules: market share is a measure, not an objective; and market share must be earned, not bought.

Under these two guidelines, a mutual organization can follow a far more conservative marketing strategy. Because the fund shareholder and fund management are united in their war on costs, a mutual structure implicitly calls for a low-budget approach to advertising. Unlike stockholder organizations that rely on aggressive marketing strategies, a mutual organization is likely to understand that "funds" are not "products," to be sold whenever the investing public seems to fancy them. It would embrace a disciplined marketing strategy, refusing to undertake costly promotional campaigns that do nothing to benefit its fund shareholders.

LOOKING TO THE FUTURE

A mutual organization's corporate structure dictates its basic strategy—reliance on the interaction of the four dimensions of investing: risk, return, time, and cost that I described in Chapter 14. Investors, investment advisers, and academics properly accept that risk and return go hand in hand. But as "Amazing Grace" suggests, what investors have lost may soon be found: the element of cost, and how it is magnified by time. And when investors make this discovery, this industry will have to give increased attention to the heavy costs of fund expenses, portfolio turnover, and excessive taxes, and to the inherent advantages of market indexing.

Allow me to offer some futuristic thoughts on the change of course that might follow and the sparks that might eventually ignite an evolution toward more shareholder-focused strategies, if not a revolution. If this industry is to change, the change must come at the fund shareholders' behest, just as the American colonists were required to fight to enforce their rights. The management companies, after all, like the Crown in 1776, reap enormous rewards from the status quo. Without pressure from mutual fund investors, they have no incentive to change.

When investors, as a group, begin to demand a fair shake, the forces of supply and demand will eventually invert the industry, putting fund shareholders on top, where they belong. What might prompt investors to demand a fairer shake? Trial and error is one possibility. Investors who get badly burned by a long period of equity underperformance, or even (and much more memorably!) by a significant plunge in stock prices, will not soon return to the industry's fold. Investors buying hot funds, experimenting with market timing, and shopping and swapping funds with untoward frequency will one day learn, through painful experience, that these short-term approaches have been not only unproductive, but counterproductive.

THE INFORMATION AGE TO THE RESCUE

More optimistically, the promulgation of better investor information may gradually turn the tide. Investors will learn one of the essential principles of investing: *Cost matters.* Fostered by corporate benefits executives who are responsible for selecting funds for tax-deferred employee stock plans with assets now approaching $1 trillion; self-motivated investors with substantial assets; the Securities and Exchange Commission, as it speaks ever more forcefully from the bully pulpit; and the increasingly sophisticated financial media, the mantra that cost matters will finally take hold. But all of that will take time. As long as present excessive costs persist, time does not run in favor of fund shareholders.

If investors vote with their feet—indicating that they favor long-term investing over short-term, and low cost over high cost—fund managers will finally get the message. A focus on long-term portfolio strategy will supplant today's frenetic—and costly—trading of portfolio securities. Funds will more clearly define their investment objectives, describe their performance standards, and report candidly on how their results compare with their expectations. The implicit promise of equity fund managers that, "We can do better than the market," will be supplanted by: "We can approach 100 percent of the market's annual return more closely than others who have similar objectives and strategies." At that point, there would seem to be an obligation to describe to investors how the managers will meet that goal, and then to disclose regularly the extent to which they are meeting it.

Investors must demand that industry creativity turn away from costly marketing efforts and expensive media advertising. What is the point of selling past performance that is almost surely unrepeatable? Or the value of selling hope? (One senior industry marketer approvingly cited perfume as the analogy.) Instead, the industry must focus on better solutions to investors' needs. An investor with minimal curiosity will learn that the shortest and surest route to top-quartile performance is bottom-quartile expenses. And it shouldn't take much more to figure out

A MESSAGE FROM ANOTHER PROFESSION

In Chapter 17, I noted a few comments by my eminent cardiologist, Dr. Bernard Lown, on the subject of the Faustian bargain struck between those who practice medicine and those who provide medical technology. More recently, Dr. Lown has written about the implications of the corporate tidal wave, driven by Health Maintenance Organizations, that is engulfing the medical profession. His concern is that the revered corporate bottom line will destroy the relationship between doctor and patient, that "the gatekeeper serves the owner of the gate, not the people trying to get through the gate."

In this chapter, I have reflected my own concern along these lines, as manifested in the development of the mutual fund industry. The quotations that follow are from Dr. Lown's recent writings, except that I have changed his medical terms into mutual fund terms (i.e., "patient" becomes "client" or "shareholder"; doctor becomes "trustee" or "manager"). The parallels are both disturbing and striking:

> Our profession's fundamental ethics are under assault. Investment mangement is a calling—at its core a moral enterprise grounded in a covenant of trust between managers and shareholders. The primary mission of the manager is to invest wisely, to work for the promotion of the clients' financial well-being. Central to the relationship is the expectation that the manager will put the needs of the shareholder first, over and above the interests of any third party.

In contrast, the fund industry is today organized like any other business, arguably more concerned with the flow of revenue, the market share, and the market value of management company stock than with the wealth of clients. Like doctors, however, fund trustees must not go back on their commitment to serve as honest stewards of the assets of mutual funds and their investor-owners.

that the taxable investors in this industry—more than half of our shareholders—are being ill-served by the baneful tax and trading costs of high portfolio turnover. Lower costs and new approaches to tax sensitivity must be given a higher priority.

REVISION OR RESTRUCTURING?

Once the industry's sole focus turns to serving investors as productively as possible, its further evolution will take one of two critical turns: a revision of the status quo that puts more power in the hands of shareholders or a radical restructuring. The radical restructuring would be the mutualization of at least part of the American mutual fund industry. Funds—or at least large fund families—would run themselves. Funds would no longer contract with external management companies to operate and manage the portfolios. Those functions would be performed in-house. Mutual fund shareholders would, in effect, own the management companies that oversee the fund. They would have their own officers and staff, and the huge profits now earned by external managers would be diverted to the shareholders. They wouldn't waste money on costly marketing campaigns designed to bring in new investors at the expense of existing investors. With lower costs, they would produce higher returns and/or assume lower risks. They would improve their disclosure, and report to their shareholder-owners with greater candor. They might even see the merit of market index funds.

An alternative, and perhaps more likely, turn of events would be the rise of more activist independent mutual fund directors. As noted in Chapter 18, the fund board has so far been a docile body in the industry's conventional structure. Someday, the independent board members may become ferocious advocates for the rights and interests of the mutual fund shareholders they represent. Were they to do so, they would negotiate aggressively with the mutual fund adviser, allowing the management company to earn a fair profit, but recognizing that the interests of the mutual fund shareholders must always come first. These activist directors would parse the management company's fee schedule and financial statements, ensuring that fees paid for advisory services are no longer funneled into the adviser's marketing budget. They would demand performance-related fees that enrich managers only as fund investors are themselves enriched by superior returns. They would challenge the use of 12b-1 distribution fees. Independent directors would also undertake careful analysis of the investment portfolios offered by a fund complex, and would no longer rubber-stamp gimmick funds that have been cooked up by marketing executives to attract attention in an increasingly crowded marketplace. They would approve only portfolios that are based on sound investment principles and meet a reasonable investment need, and the establishment of market index funds would be high on the agenda. In short, the independent directors would become the fiduciaries they are supposed to be under the law, and would aggressively represent the interests of the mutual fund shareholders. It would be quite an imposing bundle of improvements.

If overseen by an activist board, the conventional mutual fund organization would behave much more like a mutually owned complex and recognize that the interests of the mutual fund shareholder must always be paramount. And if the creation and encouragement of activist independent directors is a more practicable solution than the wholesale mutualization of the American mutual fund industry, then perhaps it is an objective deserving our energies and effort. And who knows? As the values of such a refocused organization move toward the values of the mutual organization, full mutualization may be only a step away.

Enhancing Economic Value

Regardless of the exact structure, mutual or conventional, an arrangement in which fund shareholders and their directors are in working control of a fund—as distinct from one in which fund managers are in control—will lead to funds that truly serve the needs of their shareholders. Under either structure, the industry will enhance economic value for fund shareholders. Fund organizations will focus on the seven strategies outlined in this chapter, seeking to provide investors with a higher share of the rewards of investing, reasonable prices, enhanced services, greater risk control, sensible product development, more index funds, and disciplined marketing efforts. Whatever the precise *modus operandi* of the mutual fund industry, strategy will follow structure. Function will follow form. In essence, "The form is the whole, from top to bottom, to the last detail—with the same ideas."[2]

PART V

ON SPIRIT

I have absolutely no doubt that the principles expressed in Part IV will serve the *investment* side of the mutual fund industry, and, in turn, serve mutual fund investors. However, given the way fund management companies currently operate, these principles are unlikely to serve the needs of the *business* side of this industry. Readers may have been surprised to see a discussion of that issue in a book about commonsense principles of investing, but it is of crucial importance for investors.

Part V takes an even more surprising turn. I discuss my own business philosophy as it is reflected in the entrepreneurship, leadership, and human values that I have tried to manifest in the creation of the Vanguard Group, under a structure that is antithetical to the mutual fund industry norm. But while our growth provides evidence that such a structure can function effectively, history tells us that a more enlightened governance structure may not be enough. Life insurance companies, for example, maintained their mutual structure for 100 years or more, but seem to have long since abandoned the principles of mutuality, and are now formally abandoning the structure itself.

Will structure carry the day in the mutual fund industry? No. More than structure will be needed. The business of managing other people's money—no matter how an enterprise is structured—must be focused on the human beings it serves and the human beings who provide those services. A mutual structure may be *necessary* to provide both optimal services and maximum returns to shareholders, but it is not *sufficient*. Mutual funds must also be mutual in spirit. Organizational principles are involved, but so too are human principles.

My discussion of these almost universally overlooked aspects of providing financial services—services of stewardship and trust—requires that I mention Vanguard by name. Until now, I have emphasized the investment principles on which I based Vanguard—commonsense principles such as conservatism, indexing, and low cost, which I regard as the very essence of sound long-term investing. But I have mentioned our corporate name only when it was absolutely necessary to do so. The next three chapters ignore that constraint. Forewarned is forearmed.

ON ENTREPRENEURSHIP

THE JOY OF CREATING

*H*ow did Vanguard even happen? What was the source of its structure? Why did its structure demand its strategy? Or was that sequence reversed? When the path became two roads diverging in the woods, why did I take the road less traveled? I imagine that the fair answer to those questions has something to do with idealism, vision, opportunism, failure, and sheer luck. But I'm certain that the joy of creating was the principal reason Vanguard has been described as a classic case of entrepreneurship. I'm not sure that description fits. Let me tell a bit of the story; then you can decide.

The successful, verdant U.S. economy that we enjoy today has resulted, in important measure, from the imagination and energy of entrepreneurs. From Thomas Paine's pre-Revolution dream of independence for the Colonies—and even earlier—to modern times, most of America's great enterprises began in the dreams of the individuals who founded them. Until a few years ago, I had thought about entrepreneurship in this historical sense, rather than in personal terms. However, in early 1997, my insouciance was shattered when I received in the mail a copy of a 25-page paper by a senior at Yale University. The writer described me as a paradigm of the Schumpeterian entrepreneur.[1]

Joseph A. Schumpeter, a Harvard professor and Austrian economist, in his 1911 work, *The Theory of Economic Development*, first recognized the entrepreneur as the moving force of economic development. His emergence as a pop hero of the so-called "supply side" political movement should not

399

denigrate Schumpeter's seminal approach to economics. Indeed, entrepreneurship, one of the driving forces in the economic boom that has swept the globe in recent years, is most obviously manifested in the flowering of the technological revolution. It is hardly hyperbole to describe the 1990s—the bridge connecting the twentieth and twenty-first centuries—as "The Age of the Entrepreneur."

But few expected it to be that way. Thirty years ago, I began to move—without even realizing it—from a tried-and-true, buttoned-down career of conventional corporate advancement toward the role of the entrepreneur. At the time, many believed that entrepreneurship was dead. In 1967, John Kenneth Galbraith (in *The New Industrial State*) delivered the eulogy. Referring to the entrepreneurial corporation largely in the past tense, the new economy he postulated was characterized by planning, oligopoly, and scale. The (yet-to-be-named) Fortune 500 was in the saddle astride the American economy, and the multi-industry conglomerate was to become the paradigm for the future. Professor Galbraith never envisioned the revolution in corporate America that lay ahead.

I MEET A TRUE ENTREPRENEUR

I suppose it was partly business necessity, partly impetuousness, partly chance, and partly the guiding hand of my mentor, Walter L. Morgan, that led me down an entrepreneurial path. Mr. Morgan was indeed an entrepreneur. A 1920 graduate of Princeton University, a certified public accountant, an investment adviser, and, most of all, a man with a mission, Mr. Morgan had seen firsthand that investors of modest means needed to own not individual securities, as was the fashion of the day, but diversified portfolios of stock and bonds, overseen by professional investment managers. Investors needed diversification, portfolio supervision, and convenience, not complexity. My mentor's investment wisdom and marketing instincts convinced him that mutual funds represented a wonderful business opportunity. In 1928, when he was 31 years of age, this mutual fund pioneer founded Wellington Fund.

In 1947, 27 years after Mr. Morgan's graduation, I too became a Princeton student. In my junior year, I sought, for my senior thesis, a topic that no one had written about in a serious academic paper. In December 1949, I stumbled on an article in *Fortune* magazine entitled "Big Money in Boston," and discovered the mutual fund industry. When I read that "mutual funds may look like pretty small change" but constituted a "rapidly expanding and somewhat contentious industry that could be of great potential significance to U.S. business," I knew immediately that I had found my topic. After a year-plus of intense study, I completed the thesis and sent it to several industry leaders. One recipient was Mr. Morgan. He liked what I had written and was later to write: "A pretty good piece of work for a fellow in college without any practical experience in business life. Largely as a result of this thesis, we have added Mr. Bogle to our Wellington organization." I started my employment right after my graduation in 1951.

During the depression years of the 1930s, few young men had entered the investment field, and far fewer were employed in the tiny mutual fund industry. When I joined Wellington Management Company, which managed Wellington Fund, in 1951, it was a tiny company. I moved up rapidly; in less than a decade, I had become Walter Morgan's heir-apparent. By the early 1960s, I was deeply involved in all aspects of the business, and, in early 1965, when I was just 35 years old, he told me I would be his successor. The company was in troubled straits, and Mr. Morgan told me to "do whatever it takes" to solve our investment management problems. I realized that a great opportunity had been presented to me.

A MERGER, A FIRING, AN IDEA

Headstrong, impulsive, and naïve, I found, in Boston, a merger partner that I hoped would provide the solution. We merged our firm with theirs in 1966. Alas, despite the early glitter, the substance proved illusory. The merger worked beautifully for about five years, but the aggressive investment managers whom I had too opportunistically sought as my new partners let our fund shareholders down. First, our funds lagged as the stock market continued to rise through 1972; then, they led the market downward in the devastating 50 percent drop that followed. The fund assets we managed plunged from $2.5 billion in early 1973 to $1.3 billion in late 1974. Not surprisingly, my new partners and I had a falling out.

My adversaries had more votes at the company than I did, and it was *they* who fired *me* from what I had considered "my" company. The merger—perhaps my first exercise of an entrepreneurial spirit—was a failure. But my failure was not in getting fired, but in jumping on the speculative bandwagon of aggressive investing in the first place. In retrospect, this failing was little short of disgraceful, and I can only be embarrassed about the fact that my determination to move quickly, my naïveté, and my eagerness to ignore the clear lessons of history led me into such an error of judgment. Life was fair: I made a big error and I paid a high price.

After their victory, my former partners intended to move all of Wellington Management to Boston. But I wasn't about to let that happen. I intended to keep Wellington Fund in Philadelphia, where it was formed, where its roots had taken hold, and where it belonged. And I had an idea of how to do just that. When the door slammed, a window opened and gave me my second opportunity to exercise an entrepreneurial spirit. My idea was to parlay a slight difference in the governance structure of the Wellington *funds*, owned by their shareholders, and Wellington *Management Company*, controlled largely by my former partners, into a new career that held the promise of changing the very structure under which mutual funds operated. Pulling off this trick was not easy; doing a deed without precedent never is.

The idea may well have had its genesis in my Princeton senior thesis. I had concluded it with several main themes and had suggested that the industry's future growth could be maximized by a "reduction of sales loads and management fees"; that "fund investment objectives must be stated explicitly"; that mutual funds should avoid creating "the expectations of miracles from management"; and that "the principal function of a mutual fund should be sound management [not peripheral activities]." My idea, simply stated, was that the mutual fund industry would do better for itself if it did better for its shareholders. This simple concept of giving investors a fair shake would be the rock on which the new enterprise was founded.

But how could that goal be accomplished? Again, with the essence of simplicity. Why should our mutual funds retain an *outside company* to manage their affairs—then, and now, the *modus operandi* of our industry—when the funds could manage *themselves* and save a small fortune in fees? Mutual funds would be truly *mutual*. The battle was hard—the Fund Board was almost evenly divided—but this new structure finally carried the day.

STEPS AND STUMBLES

Under the new structure, we needed to form a new company, and I struggled to find just the right name for it. Just as lightning had struck in 1949 in the form of an article in *Fortune*, so it struck again in an antique book, *The Naval Achievements of Great Britain—1789 to 1817*, which fell into my hands quite by accident when I bought some old prints for my office. One of the chapters described the great British victory over Napoleon's fleet at the Battle of the Nile in 1798. There, I read Lord Nelson's congratulatory dispatch to his crew, signed on the deck of his flagship, *HMS Vanguard*, and I knew immediately that I had found my company's name. Under a formal banner inscribed "The Vanguard Group of Investment Companies," the new flagship was launched on September 26, 1974. I hoped that just as Nelson's fleet had come to dominate the seas during the Napoleonic wars, our new flagship would come to dominate the mutual fund seas.

My idea suffered a setback when the Fund directors allowed Vanguard (owned, under our new mutual structure, by the funds themselves) to handle solely the Fund's *administration*, which comprises but one of the three sides of mutual fund operations. Our crew, numbering only 28 members when we began our voyage in May 1975, was responsible only for the Fund's operating, legal, and financial affairs. The more critical sides of the mutual fund triangle—*investment management* and *share distribution*—were to remain with my rivals at Wellington Management.

This setback left me with little room to develop the fully mutualized organization that I had envisioned for the new firm. We could not control our own destiny without controlling our management and distribution activities. The fact that investment management was outside of Vanguard's mandate led me, within months, to an action that, today, seems obvious but was then unprecedented. I brought to fruition an idea I had toyed with for years. Based on evidence that I had ascertained in my Princeton thesis, I had written, that mutual funds should "make no claim for superiority over the market averages." Was this thought the precursor of my later interest in matching the market with an index fund? Honestly, I don't know. Nonetheless, if I had to name the moment when the seed was planted that germinated into the recommendation to the Board of Directors, in September 1975, that Vanguard proceed with the formation of the first market index mutual fund in history, it would be the moment when I wrote those words in 1951.

Before 1975 ended, we had started the index fund. First Index Investment Trust—based on the Standard & Poor's 500 Stock Price Index and now named Vanguard 500 Index Fund—was derided for years and was first copied only after a full decade had passed. But when the new century begins, this index fund, once called "Bogle's Folly," will probably be the largest mutual fund in the world. The trick of the index fund, I argued to the Board in September 1975, was that it didn't *require* "investment management." It would simply own all of the stocks in the Index. This partially disingenuous argument narrowly carried the day, and with this quasi-management step, we had edged into the second side—the investment side—of the fund triangle.

How did we get to the final and third side—share distribution? As we did with our novel corporate structure and our novel index fund, we devised a novel solution to a seemingly complex challenge. The novelty? We eliminated the very *need* for distribution. We did away with the Wellington network of brokers and relied not on sellers to *sell* fund shares, but on buyers to *buy* them. In February 1977, after another divisive battle, we took yet another unprecedented step. We converted overnight from the traditional broker-dealer selling system to a sales-charge-free, no-load marketing system. We've never looked back. We've never had to.

With the extraordinarily low operating expenses that were to become our hallmark—the joint product of our mutual structure and our cost discipline—offering our shares without sales commissions proved a timely step. Developed long before the movie *Field of Dreams* popularized a phrase that inspired the creation of a baseball diamond in Iowa, our fundamental marketing strategy was based on this tenet: "If you build it, they will come." It took years for the investment world to recognize the intrinsic value of the diamond our new structure represented, and of the mutual funds that structure fostered, but the investors finally came. They came by the millions.

The structure we had built during those struggles, however, was still built on sand. In 1977, the Securities and Exchange Commission had given us only a *temporary* order allowing us to take some of the crucial, but unprecedented, steps required to make Vanguard a fully functioning mutual fund enterprise. We endured a two-week regulatory hearing in 1978 and subsequently filed mountains of documents and legal arguments. Astonishing as it may seem today, in 1980, nearly three years after giving us its temporary approval, the SEC reversed its position and ruled that we could *not* continue. Aghast, for I knew we were doing what was right for shareholders, we mounted a vigorous appeal, and we triumphed. The SEC did an about-face, and, in 1981, after a struggle that had lasted *four years*, finally approved our plan. The Commission's opinion concluded with this powerful endorsement:

> The Vanguard plan actually furthers the objectives [of the Investment Company Act of 1940] by ensuring that the Funds' directors . . . are better able to evaluate the quality of services rendered to the Funds. The plan fosters

improved disclosure . . . clearly enhances the Funds' independence . . . and promotes a healthy and viable fund complex.

The Commission's words made the struggle worthwhile. At last, we had our rock foundation.

SCHUMPETER DESCRIBES THE ENTREPRENEUR

I leave it to you to decide whether that brief history of Vanguard qualifies me to be considered an entrepreneur. But allow me to now recount what the Yale senior had to say in his paper, based on Joseph Schumpeter's opinion that a successful entrepreneur had these three personal characteristics: "the dream and the will to found a kingdom, the will to conquer and to succeed, and the joy of creating and exercising one's energy and ingenuity."

"First, the dream and the will to found a kingdom . . . ." Here the Yale senior, using Schumpeter's words, dates my dream as first occurring in my Princeton thesis. He notes, correctly, that "the dream was in and of itself not remarkable, particularly for a young idealist. What was remarkable was that he had the will and the determination to stick with it. He referred back to it, using it to keep the spark of his youthful idealism lit, biding his time until he had created . . . a new sort of investment company 'of, by, and for the investors'—not the investment managers." Here, the author has captured quite accurately what Vanguard is about.

He cites Vanguard for having "a real and tangible sense of purpose," but the author points out (and I can't disagree) that my Princeton thesis provided only a "nucleus of a vision" of a new industry, and "a blurry one at that," and that Vanguard is not as idealistically driven and preordained as the public version of our founding suggests. To this degree, he views Vanguard's creation as a myth—albeit "a good one." But, as to the first test, "Bogle has realized his dream."

"Second, the will to conquer, the impulse to fight, to succeed for the sake, not of the fruits of success, but of success itself." Turning to Schumpeter's next standard, the paper describes how I coped with struggles surrounding Vanguard's foundation and early development by dint of "sheer force of will." But he questions whether, *without* these external circumstances, that internal will would have had the opportunity to function, and he concludes that "were Bogle not forced to act out of the ordinary, he would not have acted out of the ordinary . . . because his conservative nature ensured that his entrepreneurial passions would remain largely checked

until circumstances called for their release." I must concede that these observations seem to me pretty compelling, though, finally, the realities must remain elusive.

Turning to the impulse to fight, he notes that "the fight first to secure Vanguard's independence and then to see it triumph has been the story of Bogle's life since 1974. In fact, Bogle's entire life has been, in a very real way, a series of fights . . . for his world-class education, the creation and growth of his company, and for his life." (The reference here is to my 35-year struggle to conquer a failing heart, capped by the miracle of receiving a brand-new, transplanted heart in 1996.) He describes the rivalry between Vanguard and Fidelity as a "feud," although I really look at it as a fair fight between two firms with approaches toward investing that are polar opposites—philosophically, conceptually, and strategically. In any event, the second chance at life that the transplant gave me has enabled me to continue my fight to make the mutual fund industry a better one for investors. Whether an entrepreneur or not, however, I am hardly unique in having had to stand up for what I believe, and to fight for my life. I'm confident I'm just one person among millions who have done so.

Turning to "the fruits of success," the Yale senior agrees with Schumpeter that material and monetary gain is not the prime mover in the entrepreneurial process. He recognizes that my motivations were "not so purely altruistic as the Vanguard myth would suggest," because my early actions were based importantly on wanting to control my own career. However, he concludes that I've enjoyed success for its own sake, not for its fruits, given that "a man who could have owned a company worth between five and ten billion dollars [in early 1997], but who chose not to, is more interested in creating a thriving enterprise than in its monetary values," even as he notes that I haven't done badly in a financial sense. In a neat turn of phrase, he then says, "Once a man has more than enough for himself, only the fool measures his success in terms of coin and treasure." Entrepreneurs or not, we should all take heed of that thought.

"Third, the joy of creating, getting things done, of simply exercising one's energy and ingenuity." This third standard, the author argues, is at the heart of Schumpeter's understanding of the entrepreneur. His paper cites the joy of creating as most evident in the unique Vanguard structure and in the creation of the first index fund. "While this concept was scorned by the investment community" he points out, "today it is hailed as the hallmark of responsible investing." He adds that "the entrepreneur must be able to give his creations—his gems of vision—the force of hard work so that they

might last and be noticed," and describes me as "a man who does not sit upon his ideas waiting for them to blossom by divine intervention alone. He actively pursues them, forces them to grow, and tells the world they ought to be adopted by everyone."

A Slice of the World in Context

In all, the young author of the Yale paper believes that I qualify as an entrepreneur under Schumpeter's three standards: the dream and will to found a kingdom; the will to conquer and the impulse to fight for success, primarily for its own sake; and the joy of creating and exercising energy and ingenuity. While I candidly admitted to him, "I do not have a great mind," he gives me credit for "the gift of making the obscure seem obvious and the opaque transparent, and the determination and energy to be a tireless crusader for his ideas. The best entrepreneur is an educated man," the paper adds, and describes me as having, if not brilliance, "an uncanny ability to recognize the obvious." And honestly, I think that paradoxical phrase (after all, "the obvious" is what *anyone* can recognize) is a near-perfect metaphor for my career. He credits that gift "as rising from a naturally curious mind combined with a liberal education, facilitating an understanding of the nature and context of a business, and putting his own slice of the world in context."

I'll conclude this chapter by trying to put my own infinitely small slice of the world in context. Times have changed since Vanguard began in 1974. Most obviously, we've grown; our assets have risen from $1.3 billion to more than $450 billion. Our tiny original crew of 28 members now totals more than 8,000, and could constitute a virtual navy. We've served investors well, and our reputation for service, integrity, and investment performance is good. The dream has indeed become the reality.

I don't mind admitting that, if an entrepreneur is defined as a leader who turns an idea into an enterprise, I have succeeded as an entrepreneur. But if, on the other hand, an entrepreneur is one whose ideas are finally accepted in the mainstream, my entrepreneurial success has come hand in hand with this failure: My ideas have not yet been generally emulated in the mutual fund industry. The idea of simple long-term investing in high-quality stocks and bonds remains more the exception than the rule in the mutual fund industry; the index fund is accepted by our peers only as a marketing necessity, not as a mission; disciplined bond and money market portfolios are finding only grudging acceptance; and the drive for lower costs for investors is conspicuous solely by its absence. Rather than representing the leadership exemplified by being "in the vanguard," the one great idea that is central to it all—a corporate structure of a *mutual* mutual fund—has yet to find its first follower. I have not sat on my "gems of vision" (in the paper's phrase). But I might as well have locked them in a safe. Those gems have been recognized to some degree, but only time will tell whether they will endure.

You now know enough about Vanguard, I hope, to decide for yourself whether I'm truly "a classic Schumpeterian entrepreneur" (in the words of the Yale senior) or even an entrepreneur at all. But the creator of Vanguard continues to revel in the joy of creating ideas, retains the entrepreneurial spirit, and remains the missionary. The mission remains unchanged: to provide mutual fund shareholders everywhere with the fair shake they deserve.

CHAPTER

ON LEADERSHIP
A SENSE OF PURPOSE

hether the vision and boldness of the entrepreneur were responsible for the creation of Vanguard, or, far more mundane though it may be, whether the new firm sprang from a mere "uncanny ability to recognize the obvious" does not really matter. Once the struggles of 1974 to 1981 were over and the firm's full scope and structure had been developed, there remained the far more difficult challenge of implementing the strategy entailed by that structure. What attributes of leadership would be required? And what direction would that leadership take?

Creative leadership is often required to give a new venture, above all, *a sense of purpose*. What kind of leadership it should be relates not only to the nature of the enterprise, but to the nature of the leader. What manner of human being *is* the leader? Here, I shall try to speak with special candor. I am, like all human beings, a peculiar balance of contradictions: a large ego and a deep humility; a decent intelligence (no more than that), albeit with periodic blind spots and stupidities; a strong presence along with a profound insecurity; an astonishing confidence, but one that is often punctuated with doubt; an intellectual bent that lacks an academic depth; an aspiring, passionate leader, but without the skills—or, for that matter, the interests—of a manager.

I mention this litany to suggest that I'm no more, nor less, than any other person. I am just another human being. Yet, with some examples based on my experience, perhaps I can tell you a bit about what has

409

brought me through a wonderful life and career. In this chapter, I focus on the direction of leadership at the enterprise I envisioned, founded, and named, and for which, over what will soon be 25 years, I've attempted to develop sound values.

Starting a new firm, with a new name and a clean slate to write on, I had only one ambition. It had nothing whatsoever to do with building a firm with huge assets and dominant market share, nor with getting rich personally, nor with *anything* that can be counted. As I told our Directors at the outset, my goal was straightforward: *To make Vanguard the proudest name in the mutual fund industry.* And I was absolutely determined to lead Vanguard toward that goal.

THE MAJESTY OF SIMPLICITY

The business side of the firm would be based on the majestic, if basic, idea of simplicity. Our funds would have clearly stated investment objectives, explicit investment policies, and precise performance measurement standards. Their portfolios would be broadly diversified, conservatively managed, and invested largely in high-quality securities. We would hold costs to the minimum. (Apparently almost solo, I had discovered the best-kept secret of the investment business: Gross investment return minus the cost of management equals the net return earned by the investor. It's not very complicated.)

With this less-than-remarkable insight, Vanguard could say—though we didn't dare to say it in public for quite a few years—that the central task of investing is to realize the highest possible portion of the annual returns earned in the financial markets by a chosen asset class—stocks, bonds, or money market securities alike—*recognizing and accepting that that portion will be less than 100 percent.** The recognition of this reality finds its apotheosis in our low-cost index funds and our clearly defined fixed-income funds, which provide close to 99 percent of the annual returns in the financial markets in which they invest. For the record, the portion provided by the average actively managed mutual fund—stock, bond, and money market—has been about 85 percent. With the fundamental Vanguard goal of placing the interests of our clients first—via our service orientation,

---

* I first made this simple bold statement in public in mid-1997, in a speech before an audience of 7,000 at *The Los Angeles Times* Investment Strategies Conference. It was presented again as the centerpiece of Chapter 4.

our mutual structure, and our focus on low costs—we have had the best possible opportunity to approach that 100 percent desideratum, a clear manifestation of the value of simplicity.

Once the overarching goal was set, simplicity helped to determine the leadership strategy for our enterprise. I believed that we required not one, but many leaders in order to deal with the growth that I envisioned. Not just the "big shots," but the leaders on the crew—those above and below decks, those who load the cannons and those who fire them; those who let out the sheets and those who man the lines; those who make the ship sail and those who help navigate the course—all must make their own contributions over the years, and all must receive commensurate credit. Nonetheless, the person at the helm—the captain—assumes the ultimate responsibility for the voyage, so I'm going to sketch briefly some of the attributes of leadership that have seemed most important to me. Using some highlights of our history, I'll discuss how leadership depends on opportunity, readiness, foresight, a sense of purpose and a passion, being a servant as well as a leader, failure and determination, patience and courage. To one degree or another, *all* of our leaders at Vanguard—indeed, most human beings—share most of these attributes. Perhaps what matters is only how strong they are, how they are balanced, and whether they can be summoned at the opportune moment.

A FORTUITOUS HISTORY

To begin with the big picture, how did Vanguard grow from a "mom and pop" enterprise managing investor assets of $1 billion when it was founded almost 25 years ago, to the $450 billion mutual fund complex it is today? Let's be fair. We started in 1974 in the worst of times—the bottom of the worst bear market since the Great Depression. Today, we find ourselves in the best of times—at the top of the greatest sustained bull market in U.S. history for stocks and, lest we forget, for bonds too. I've said a thousand times, "Never confuse genius with luck and a bull market." We've surely enjoyed both.

In Chapters 15 and 20, I described how luck brought me into this business and was responsible for many elements of our development: the 1949 *Fortune* article on the then tiny mutual fund industry; my Princeton senior thesis; my mentor, Walter L. Morgan; *The Naval Achievements of Great Britain* and the Vanguard name; the Samuelson–Ellis–Ehrbar articles in 1975 and 1976 that helped inspire the first index fund. When these fortuitous events are strung together, the luck that permeates the Vanguard story takes on almost legendary proportions. But true it is. Luck, which I'll dignify by calling it *opportunity*, is often—perhaps always—a necessary precursor of leadership. (Given the role of luck in our lives, it behooves those who emerge as leaders to have a healthy sense of humility.)

READINESS AND FORESIGHT, PURPOSE AND PASSION

But luck is never enough. The leader needs to be ready when opportunity knocks. It is sad when we don't get any breaks in this life, and sadder still when we don't recognize them when they make their appearance. But the saddest thing of all is not to have readied ourselves to make the most of them. As the brilliant French chemist, Antoine-Laurent Lavoisier, said: "Fortune favors the prepared mind." When opportunity knocked, I was prepared to offer a strategy that would be in tune with the times to come. It didn't take great insight to foresee—accurately, as it turned out—a coming age of rising family incomes and wealth, increasing financial savvy, and pervasive investor education in the United States. The age of the discriminating, intelligent individual investor would ensue. So let's mark *readiness* as the first—or at least the earliest—attribute of leadership.

When all of those earlier breaks came home to roost and Vanguard was created, we set out to provide investors with the very best value that we could. Such a strategy would require sound investment policies, exceptionally low operating costs, and the elimination of sales commissions. Our ideas were poised for acceptance, and Vanguard became the lowest-cost provider of financial services in the world, thereby able to provide commensurately higher returns to our shareholders. That change in the investing environment may seem obvious today; that strategy would surely be the obvious response. Let me add only that they seemed equally obvious to me in 1974. Let's mark *foresight* as a second attribute of leadership.

A third attribute is, as I mentioned at the outset, *a sense of purpose*. In 1974, we made a decision about where we wanted to go, and a commitment to get there ethically. A strong moral compass would be our guide. Our sole purpose was to serve our shareholders—those who would entrust the stewardship of their financial future to us. We created a corporate structure in which our clients literally *became* our owners, a structure that remains unique in the mutual fund industry to this day. As I have noted, the current aphorism, "Treat your customers as your owners," took on real meaning for us. Our corporation turned its ownership over to the shareholders of our mutual funds—not, as in industry practice, to a privately or publicly held profit-seeking corporation. I've been called a fool, a communist, and even a Marxist—and in public, at that—for creating our corporate structure, unique in the fund industry. To me, however, that structure represents the very essence of capitalism: the control of the corporation by its shareholders.

What flowed from our founding purpose was a simple business strategy: Earn the highest possible returns for our shareholders, take care to invest their dollars wisely, and operate at the lowest cost structure in our industry. We have operated a "tight ship," with minimal extravagance. We do not provide our leaders with lavish perquisites, first-class travel, nor executive dining rooms. For our mutual funds in which we retain external investment advisers, we negotiate fees at arm's length, and, as a result, pay fees that are fair to our advisers *and* fair to our shareholders. We don't waste the dollars of our investors on expensive marketing endeavors. Others in this industry don't look at low costs as being very significant. But we are providing, each day, the proof of a logical and unarguable proposition: When other factors are held constant, the lower the costs, the higher the returns earned by the investors. *Cost matters.*

Our sense of purpose called on us not only to prove this proposition and live by it, but also to convey the message to investors. The magnificent English language gives us a marvelous medium in which to convey it, and the flexibility to convey it in a thousand different ways. I wrote all of our fund annual reports for more than 20 years, have given some 50 speeches to the entire crew, have spoken in public all over the United States, and across both the Atlantic and Pacific, and have done my best to drive home to investors the powerful sense of purpose that drives the Vanguard mission.

Purpose without passion, however, rarely does the job. In Hegel's words, "nothing great in the world has been accomplished without passion," and I too have come to regard passion, the fourth trait that I cite, as one of the central characteristics of leadership. A flamboyant display of passion is hardly necessary; a quiet passion that brooks no doubt about its intensity is equally adequate, perhaps even better. Similarly, the enthusiasm and energy that come into the picture may just as easily be contained as kinetic. It all depends on the leader. But whatever the case, passion is essential to the ability to inspire people. Therein lies the difference between management (achieving goals and getting the job done) and leadership (establishing goals, having a vision, enlisting good people to willingly take up the cause). It must be clear that leadership holds sway in taking the dream to reality, and

The Power of Words

In striving to convey purpose and passion, I rely heavily on using the right words. At Vanguard, we have barred the use of *employee*, which suggests a spirit of master versus servant; *customer*, indicating a buyer who does business opportunistically with many different purveyors; and *product*, a synonym for a consumer good such as toothpaste, beer, or canned soup, created to meet the tastes of the day. Instead, we use *crewmember*, part of the team on which any successful voyage depends; *client*, a person with whom we establish a long-term financial relationship; and *mutual fund*, reflecting the fiduciary nature of the services we offer. This choice of words has helped shape the way our investors look at us and the way we look at ourselves.

When I can't find the right words, I'm not above using the words of others, particularly if they turn to the nautical or the inspirational. When I first dedicated Vanguard's headquarters, I recalled a sermon given by the Very Reverend Francis B. Sayre, Jr., Dean of the Washington (DC) Cathedral, when "the tall ships" arrived in Newport, Rhode Island, on July 4, 1976. His words reminded me of Vanguard. In our early years, we faced strong headwinds and high seas. When success seemed impossible, we had to wrest from that opposing wind each yard of progress toward our destiny. But from the time of that 1983 dedication until today, we have experienced affluent and easy times, with tide and breeze at our back. How similar to Dean Sayre's impassioned words about America:

> Sailors know what some citizens have forgot in this latter day; that no purpose is achieved, nor any course made good upon God's ocean, until first you have trimmed your sails and set the helm to fit His winds and the set of His tide upon the deep.
>
> Keen is the mariner's eye to discern those telling signs upon the clouds, at the line 'twixt sky and water, or on the crest of waves where spindrift blows, by which he might foretell the bluster or the calm, the weather God has in store for him.

And if he is so fortunate as to find a wind that blows from Heaven exactly in the direction he would go on earth, then easy and gay the skipper who can barrel down before the wind, all canvas set, rolling upon the bosom of the blast. This has been America in these latter times; affluent and easy, not having to work very hard to run out her log; just cruising wing and wing, tide and breeze at her back, and the men lolling upon the deck.

But more often in this world it is a headwind that we face. Then, though the bearing of your destination be precisely the same, you have to tack—back and forth, back and forth; close-hauled; wind in your face, spray on your legs; fingers white upon the sheet, body tense against the bucking tiller; fine-tuning your lively lade to the majestic forces of splendid Creation; and so wresting from that opposing wind the destiny of your desire.

That's when your boat must be staunch and true, well braced and put together, and lithe like a living thing. And that is when the sailor too is on his mettle, no less in command for all his reverences in the presence of a power mightier than his own.

then to fruition. Management, however, may—perhaps must—finally ride in the saddle when the principles and values of the enterprise have met the test of time, and when growth brings maturity. It is also possible, if not likely, that the years of struggle are more satisfying than the years of forward momentum to the passionate leader. Surely it is those early years that demand the kind of passion evoked by the words of the great sculptor of Mt. Rushmore, Gutzon Borglum: "Life is a kind of campaign. People have no idea what strength comes to one's soul and spirit through a good fight."

SERVANT-LEADERSHIP

A fifth leadership trait may seem paradoxical: the idea of the leader as servant. The concept of servant-leadership did not come to me quickly or easily. Indeed, during at least the first decade of Vanguard's history, when we were a very small organization, I was probably considered an autocrat. But I like to think that I used power, not for its own sake, but to force my novel ideas on a world that looked at them with skepticism, and to develop an organization with a sense of higher values than might be expected from a

During his career, Mr. Greenleaf did an awesome amount of speaking, teaching, and writing about the role he believed his servant-leadership concepts could play in making corporations more humanistic in their focus as well as more successful business enterprises. His ideas rang true to me. In *Servant Leadership*, he wrote: "The very essence of leadership is going out ahead to show the way, an attitude that is derived from more than usual openness to inspiration. Even though he knows the path is uncertain, even dangerous, a leader says: 'I will go; come with me.'" (Here, I am confident that he was referring, not only to a sort of grand idea of corporate leadership, but to the infinite number of tasks where less sweeping forms of leadership are required if an enterprise is to succeed.)[1]

In his focus, business was not peripheral. It was central. He was deeply concerned about creating a superior company with a liberating vision:

> What distinguishes a superior company from its competitors is not the dimensions that usually separate companies, such as superior technology, more astute market analysis, better financial base, etc.; it is *unconventional* thinking about its dream—what this business wants to be, how its priorities are set, and how it organizes to serve. *It has a radical philosophy and self-image.* According to the conventional business wisdom, it ought not to succeed at all. Conspicuously less successful competitors seem to say, "The ideas that the company holds ought not to work, therefore we will learn nothing from it."
>
> In some cases, the company's unconventional thinking about its dream is born of a liberating vision. But in our society liberating visions are rare. Why are liberating visions so rare? They are rare because a stable society requires that *a powerful liberating vision must be difficult to deliver.* Yet to have none is to seal our fate. We cannot turn back to be a wholly traditional society, comforting as it may be to contemplate it. There must be change—sometimes great change.
>
> That difficulty of delivery, however, is only half of the answer. The other half is that so few who have the gift for summarizing a vision, and the power to articulate it persuasively, have the urge and the courage to try. But there must be a place for servant leaders with prophetic voices of great clarity who will produce those liberating visions on which a caring, serving society depends.

I leave to far wiser—and more objective—heads than mine the judgment about whether Vanguard meets the definition of a superior company. But while I believe that it does, I have no hesitancy in saying that it is the product of unconventional thinking about what we want to be, how we set priorities, and how we organize to serve our clients. We have dared to be different, and it seems to be working just fine.

As Vanguard has grown from a small enterprise to a giant one, the challenges of leadership have changed radically. Mr. Greenleaf had some thoughts about that issue too:

> The line that separates a large business from a small one might be drawn at that point where the business can no longer function well under the direction of one individual. If the company has been built largely on one person's drive, imagination, taste, and judgment, it may be difficult to recognize when that point has been reached. The greatest risk may be that the comapny cannot grow and keep its present quality.
>
> At that point, the leader must turn toward building an institution, managing the process that gets that job done, the first step toward the ultimate optimal long-term performance of a large business that is managed by a board of directors who act as trustees. The result would be an institution that would have the best chance of attracting and holding in its service the large number of able people who will be required to give it strength, quality, and continuity if it is to continue to do on a large scale what it was able to do well on a smaller scale.
>
> The successful leader must take on the exciting challenge of transforming a one-person business into an institution that has autonomy and creative drive as a collection of many able people, one that has the capacity for expansion and even enhancing the claim to distinction it has already achieved.

Only time will tell the degree to which we can meet that challenge. But the goal (using Mr. Greenleaf's words) can only be achieved if "the people who staff the institution do the right things at the right time because the goals are clear and comprehensive and they know what ought to be done, and do the right thing without being instructed. It takes a strong leader to put the people who serve first, but that is the way to insure that they will deliver all that people can deliver—and to insure that the business will continue to lead in its field."

typical commercial enterprise. I tried to use whatever intellectual power I had to develop and implement new ways of investing, and whatever moral power I possessed to inculcate ideas such as integrity and fair dealing, candor, and respect for the individual, into a business enterprise that would survive and prosper in a highly competitive world.

For many years, my ideas about running our organization were disorganized, even inchoate. But, as they developed, I articulated them to our crew in frequent all-firm meetings, even setting forth a specific "Vanguard manual of values" in 1987. Around that time, I had begun to read the writings of Robert Greenleaf, a senior executive of American Telephone & Telegraph Corporation, and a visiting lecturer at MIT Sloan School of Management and Harvard Business School. He introduced me to the concept of *servant-leadership* and the development of a model institution in which everyone is part leader, part servant. The goal of these dedicated human beings is to raise to great purpose both those *whom* they serve and those *with whom* they serve.

Mr. Greenleaf articulated the concept of *a distinguished serving institution* in which "all who accept its discipline are lifted up to nobler stature and greater effectiveness than they are likely to achieve on their own." He suggested that *an understanding of leadership and followership* would be required because "everyone in the institution is part leader, part follower." Then he added this vital thought: "If an institution is to achieve as a servant [as was the mission called for by Vanguard's structure and strategy], then only those who are natural servants—those who want to lift others—should be empowered to lead." To this point I would add (and I think Mr. Greenleaf would agree) that even as leaders *give strength* to those who choose to follow, so the best leaders *gather strength* from those who have chosen to follow. In any event, it is hard to know whether the coincidence of this philosophy and my own is merely fortuitous—a happy accident, random molecules bumping together in the night—or powerful evidence of the mysterious universality of a great idea. Perhaps a little of each is present. Nonetheless, it has been an important part of how I've tried to lead Vanguard.

FAILURE AND DETERMINATION

The next trait may surprise you, but I have come to regard *failure* as another essential of leadership. It is often best if things do not come too easily in this life. When I was fired in 1974 from my position as the chief of the mutual fund company I had joined in 1951, I had somehow failed. But out of the ashes of that painful experience arose, like the phoenix, the firm that appears to be "in the vanguard" of the mutual fund field today. Failure, too, seemed to plague our every early step. We experienced net cash outflow from the mutual funds that our new firm administered for eighty consecutive months—think of that!—but in adversity, we gained strength and learned important disciplines. Now, years later, we continue to deal with periodic failures. That they have been overwhelmed by our successes is beside the point. We must still learn from them.

If you must fail, then you must fight. Persistence, the next leadership trait, was essential in our battle, for it was to take time to bring our corporate structure and our business strategy into full flower. The deck was stacked against us at the outset, as our perhaps properly cautious Directors were unwilling to create this mutual structure *de novo*. We had to struggle through those early years and persist in seeking the final fruition of our efforts as we moved from our sole role as fund administrator, to index fund manager, and to fund distributor, but only after overcoming the well-intentioned but misguided opposition of the Securities and Exchange Commission. We took the final step in becoming the full-line mutual fund complex we are today by assuming our first direct responsibilities for traditional active investment management immediately thereafter, in 1981. After seven long years, our structure was at last in place. (The assets we manage internally currently total $260 billion, about 60 percent of our total asset base.) It wasn't easy—nothing worthwhile ever is—but I think we can mark *determination*—call it *persistence* if you will—as a sixth attribute of leadership.

PATIENCE AND COURAGE

Paradoxically, our persistence had to be accompanied by *patience*, another trait of leadership. My favorite example is our pioneering foray into market index funds—today, sadly enough, the "industry darling" or, God forbid, "hot product." Struck by the insight that matching the stock market at minimal costs would, over time, give a low-cost passively managed index fund a near certainty of outpacing the vast majority of high-cost actively managed funds, Vanguard formed the first index fund in 1975. This grand and pioneering idea was scorned by others. But our patience, combined with our persistence, carried the day.

LEADERSHIP FOR THE FUTURE

What are the elements of successful leadership? In *Leadership in Financial Services*, Steven I. Davis[2] surveys the financial services industry around the globe to identify the characteristics of the most successful financial leaders of the twentieth century. His views closely parallel my own, but they carry an objectivity that mine lack. Here are Davis's words about leadership attributes that he identified during his research:

> *Vision.* Successful leaders possess a comprehensive view of the leadership role: a vision or direction of where they want to go, a sense of the processes needed to achieve these goals, and a clear view of what they have to do as individuals within this process.
>
> *Core Values.* Successful leadership demands respect for the individual and personal integrity, which are inextricably linked with providing value for investors. Continuity of leadership over an extended period of time is essential to the development of common values and cultures.
>
> *The Implementation of Leadership.* Having set the direction and the values, the leader's next task is to provide the single-minded determination to make it happen. Leaders spend a vast amount of time communicating at all levels of the organization, from one-on-one dialogues to speeches to hundreds of colleagues. A leader must be there in person, taking direct responsibility for tough decisions, projecting his own personality and character so his followers can see that he is a real person with whom they can identify.
>
> *Resolving Conflict.* Leaders have to make decisions which may go strongly against the views of their colleagues . . . despite his desire to respect others' views and keep the people in the organization aligned, the creator of the firm must take the direction he feels is best.
>
> *Energy.* In the exhausting, perpetual struggle to communicate the leadership message, the leader must, quite simply, do as he is asking others to do. It requires a full-time commitment to the institution and the message, not only a mission, but a high degree of personal energy.

Some attributes of leadership no doubt defy distillation into a simple set of principles. They are the unique products of a single individual's experience, intellect, and character. Davis nonetheless identifies guideposts that can mark the way for the leaders of the future.

The initial offering in 1976—expected to be $150 million—brought in just $11 million. The S&P 500 Index suffered a rare, but substantial, lag in returns relative to most fund managers in 1977–1982, and six years elapsed before our index fund reached the original objective of $150 million. Even in the booming fund industry, that first index fund didn't cross the $1 billion mark until 1990, 15 years after its introduction. But we ran the fund patiently and efficiently, watched it begin to outpace active managers, and then watched its margin of extra return grow steadily. Our confidence that it would work as we had promised has been vindicated—and then some. Indexing has burgeoned, and Vanguard—with indexed assets of $150 billion, spread among 28 funds keyed to various market indexes—is far and away the industry leader. Patience triumphed. (A personal note: I once received a letter from a shareholder who described me as "impatient for action, but patient for results." That seems an accurate enough depiction of my approach to indexing.)

To wrap up this litany, I put before you—both tentatively and humbly—a final attribute of leadership: *courage*. Sometimes, an enterprise has to dig down deep and have the courage of its convictions—to "press on," regardless of adversity or scorn. Vanguard has been a truly contrarian firm in its mutual structure, in its drive for low costs and a fair shake for investors, in its conservative investment philosophy, in market index funds, and in shunning hot products, marketing gimmicks, and the carpet-bombing approach to advertising so abundantly evident elsewhere in this industry today. Sometimes, it takes a lot of courage to stay the course when fickle taste is in the saddle, but we have stood by our conviction: *In the long run, when there is a gap between perception and reality, it is only a matter of time until reality carries the day.*

FATE TAKES A HAND

Readiness, foresight, a sense of purpose, passion, the idea of the leader as servant, failure, determination, patience, and courage. Based on my experience, these are nine of the principal attributes essential to effective leadership. In the waning years of my career, fate was to dictate that I best draw on these attributes in a more personal sphere. To deal with a human failure (of a rather different kind—heart failure), I drew deeply on all of the patience, persistence, and courage that I could muster—as anyone would—when, in 1995–1996, I endured a 128-day hospital wait, on life-sustaining intravenous fluid, before receiving a heart transplant. No one could possibly imagine the renewed strength and the sheer joy that my (new) heart—my miraculous second chance at life—has given me! Part of that joy is in the extra years that miracle has given me to continue to lead—to further my intellectual pursuits in bringing common sense to mutual fund investing and the structure of the mutual fund industry, and my ethical pursuits to bring higher ideals of business management and organization to the corporate world.

CHAPTER

ON HUMAN BEINGS
CLIENTS AND CREW

y account of Vanguard's founding, our persistence through the struggles of 1974–1981, and the qualities of leadership that seem to have been required, is a story that is part tragedy and part triumph. Each crushing disappointment was eventually followed by serendipitous success. Not until 1981, when the modern Vanguard was fully formed, did we begin to sail on an even keel. But even in the rough seas of the early years, when the horizon dissolved in darkness and our very survival was in doubt, I retained my conception of those who would serve within our ranks and those whom we would strive to serve: human beings.

If simplicity was to be the focus of our investment principles, human beings would be the focus of our management principles. Over the years, I have come to love and respect the term *human beings* to describe both our clients and our crewmembers. In December 1997, I gave a talk at Harvard Business School on how our focus on human beings had enabled Vanguard to become what at Harvard is called a "service breakthrough company." I challenged the students to find the term *human beings* in any book they had read on corporate strategy. As far as I know, none could meet the challenge. But "human beingness" has been one of the keys to our development.

How often I have said, over these long years, that those whom we serve must be treated as "honest-to-God, down-to-earth human beings, each with their own individual hopes and fears and financial goals." This credo says nothing about aggregate billions of dollars of assets; nor millions of investors; nor, Lord forbid, market share; nor even about corporate strategy; nor the need for financial controls, technological support, and focused marketing, although all of them are, to one degree or another, necessary. They are secondary to our primary goal: to serve, to the best of our ability, the human beings who are our clients. To serve them with candor, with integrity, and with fair dealing. To be the stewards of the assets they have entrusted to us. To treat them as we would like the stewards of our own assets to treat us. This mission is not very complicated, but anyone who *preaches* it had better *live* it, every single day.

It should go without saying that the concept of human beingness should also apply to those who serve on our Vanguard crew. Those of us who earn our livelihood at Vanguard should treat one another in the way we would like to be treated. The keys are: respect for the individual; recognition that "even one person can make a difference;" and financial incentives to each and every crewmember, based on how the rewards we earn for our fund shareholders compare to those earned by our peers. Our crew has made me look good for almost 25 years, and that is the least that I owe to them.

In this final chapter, I offer some thoughts on what it means to treat those we serve, and those with whom we serve, as honest-to-God, down-to-earth human beings. The idea is not very complicated, but it has a profound impact on the institution's relationship with its investors and with its crew. When you treat the investor as a human being, you must necessarily pursue a fiduciary relationship with a client, as opposed to a business relationship with a customer. And when you treat those who work for the institution as human beings, rather than as soldiers of fortune paid to execute a certain task in a certain period, policies and practices that respect individuals and reward their contributions necessarily follow. In short, a focus on human beings must be manifest in every action of the enterprise.

THE INVESTOR AS HUMAN BEING

When human beings are the focus of an enterprise, certain practices follow naturally. The primary goal is to help clients succeed in the activity of investing, an all too human pursuit in which reaching one's goals seems to depend as much upon emotions as economics. Success in investing in turn allows clients to achieve human goals such as purchasing a home, paying for a child's education, or enjoying a comfortable retirement. Failure means that these basic human goals will not be met. In this long bull market, the mutual fund industry seems to have lost sight of these realities.

Instead of helping people to develop prudent, long-term investment plans, fund firms have mounted aggressive marketing campaigns that suggest that they have found the Holy Grail of investment superiority. Too many funds have followed imprudent policies, and, despite the long bull market, their shareholders have paid a heavy price. When investment returns eventually revert to more normal levels, even more funds will disappoint their shareholders. Firms that focus on human beings, on the other hand, act as fiduciaries, not as aggressive asset gatherers. They strive to uphold fiduciary values: candor, integrity, trust, and fair dealing. Such firms should be far more likely to weather any storms that may come to the financial markets.

How do these values shape Vanguard's dealings with clients? *Candor* means that, in communicating with our shareholders, we must follow a policy of full disclosure: tell the whole truth and nothing but the truth. This policy seems unremarkable. But candor is conspicuous by its absence from the mutual fund industry's promotional materials and shareholder communications. Long-term returns of the stock market are presented without adjustment for the costs of owning stocks through mutual funds. Fund advertisements trumpet past performance that will not be repeated in the future. Fund prospectuses fail to describe the importance of costs. And, too often, mutual fund annual reports neglect to discuss the risks inherent in particular investment strategies. When we see investors as human beings rather than target markets, however, we realize that, if they are to invest successfully, our clients need straight talk and common sense: frank discussions about risk and return; an honest accounting of a fund's success (or failure) in matching its benchmark and its peers; a review of the rudiments of a sensible program of balanced investing; and attention to the critical role that costs play in shaping long-term investment returns.

Candor reinforces a second element in the relationship between fiduciary and client: *integrity*. Integrity comes down to the ability to trust that, when the self-interest of the institution's managers comes in conflict with the interests of the institution's clients, the interests of the clients will be held paramount. Vanguard's unique corporate structure, in which the financial benefits of our success accrue to the fund shareholder rather than to the management company, has eliminated many potential conflicts of interest between a financial institution and its clients. Yet, integrity demands additional practices not necessarily dictated by corporate structure. Integrity means putting the client first in all aspects of the relationship, investing prudently with the sole purpose of meeting a particular investment objective, and operating strictly under generally accepted principles of business conduct. Such practices arise, not from an organizational structure or policy manual, but from a recognition that our clients are human beings who deserve the highest standards of respect.

Closely related to integrity is a third element of the fiduciary relationship, a commitment to *fair dealing*. We pledge to serve all clients to the best of our abilities, making sure that their investment costs remain low, and their investment returns remain as high as possible relative to the asset classes or market segments in which they invest. Not infrequently, conflicts may arise between the business interests and the fiduciary duties of an organization, and the organization that serves human beings must ensure that fiduciary duties remain paramount. Consider this example of a potential conflict. In 1996, an institutional client attempted to invest $40 million in a Vanguard short-term fixed-income fund, a sum that amounted to 10 percent of the fund's assets. To satisfy a prior financial commitment, he intended to redeem his holding within two months. In the client's view, the arrangement would benefit both parties. For Vanguard, we would have a new shareholder with substantial assets. For the client, he would earn an attractive return on a substantial sum of money, and the purchase and liquidation of his investment portfolio would carry no transaction costs whatsoever.

No organization dedicated to the best interests of its clients—rather than to profits, assets, or market share—would be interested in such a transient shareholder. A short-term transaction of that size would have imposed *on the remaining shareholders of the fund* unnecessary transaction costs in purchasing and then selling the portfolio investments. We refused to accept the order. Irate, the investor informed us that he would advise his colleagues "never to do business with Vanguard again." What is more, he took his story to the press, and it wound up on the front page of the Money & Investing section of *The Wall Street Journal*, which duly reported that the client "would no doubt find many eager takers at other mutual fund companies, especially since an investment that size . . . could earn the fund company roughly $30,000 in management fees." To accept the investment and earn the fees, however, would have placed the fund organization's business interests above its fiduciary obligation to the fund's remaining shareholders. In response to the article describing our rejection of this $40 million order, the scores of letters I received from our shareholders, 100 percent of which supported Vanguard's position, were so favorable that I felt obliged to write to the *Journal*'s editor that I was "a bit embarrassed that such favorable public notice arose from the simple act of choosing the path that was honorable and ethical."

SHAREHOLDERS RESPOND

Everyone wants to be treated as a human being. No one wants to be part of a target market. I believe that Vanguard's development in recent years is in part the result of public recognition that Vanguard treats the investor as a valued individual, not a dollar sign. In the many letters I receive from shareholders, a common theme is their appreciation of our efforts to deal with them candidly, fairly, and with integrity, to help them achieve important investment goals. Consider these excerpts from some recent letters. The first is from a shareholder who read *The Wall Street Journal* article just noted:

> I always knew you talked the talk. Now I know you walk the walk, too.

> My wife and I, now in our fifties, find we are now worth better than $1 million, have no debts and paid off the house. Not bad considering that we have never earned much more than $40,000 a year each, that I came to this country at 30 with almost nothing, and spent my first 4 years in college. I hope you know the impact you have on individuals such as us to enable us to reach our own American dream.

> We wish to thank you for your sincere regard for the investor. We like your philosophy—so different from others. Now we want to thank you for making a difference in our lives. There must be many people who can do likewise. . . . Not one of us made our money easy but you helped us to keep more of it.

> One reason why I invest with Vanguard is that it has been guided by Mr. Bogle's Old Testament patriarch image . . . it is not ludicrous to liken old Bogle to Moses bringing the law down off Sinai amidst thunder, lightning, and a thick cloud: simplify, simplify, simplify . . . I would like to see Vanguard stick to its roots. I'm sure Bogle is a hard man to work for. People like that always are. I know. We have one in our family and the fact that he's been dead for 53 years hasn't lessened his influence much. But people like this strike a chord in the public because they stand for something good and pure and true.

> Keep up the good work and high degree of fiduciary responsibility at Vanguard. It is appreciated.

It didn't take long for me to become convinced of the power of what are really some rather simple ideas, and of the wisdom and integrity of the man saying them. Low costs, customer focus, accountability, fund company ownership, full disclosure, tax efficiency, indexing and, in a word, integrity. Simple, yes, but powerful indeed. And truly on target! The shock waves you have unleashed will not soon be quelled by those in the industry who should really be embarrassed by many of their actions, but, instead, will reverberate throughout for a long time to come. I gleefully say "Thank you!"

You "recognize the obvious, follow powerful ideas with prompt action, and press on regardless" . . . words of wisdom for steering a true course regardless of the seas you sail. I am in your debt.

Thank you for all the things that you have done over the years that seem, always, to have the best interests of your shareholders at the top of your priority list. You are a throwback to an age when a businessman's handshake was worth more than a contract. Thank you for resisting many of the current popular trends that focus on high fees rather than quality performance and service. From all the working stiffs of America one more time: Thank you!

You look at households as your clients rather than accounts. This was common sense and brilliant (and something the banks still don't get). I want to express my admiration for the job you have done at Vanguard—not only in building a first class institution but also for your sound and sage advice as spokesman. In style and substance you remind me of my Dad, who also talked often of the wisdom of low costs, mistake avoidance, and a long-term buy and hold philosophy. It rewarded him well. Please continue to spread the message of commonsense investing. You have been an important, clear voice of reason in an industry increasingly dominated by quacks.

THE VANGUARD CREW

These letters are a tribute not only to the fiduciary values of candor, integrity, and fair dealing, but also to the human beings who uphold these values: the Vanguard crew. When we began operations in 1975, the choice of the word *crew* may have seemed a bit trite and corny. But it is well accepted now, suggesting, as it does, the nautical heritage of our *HMS Vanguard* symbol—the crew of a battleship, working together in partnership; fighting for each knot of progress on a sea voyage in which even one member's failure to perform can sink the ship; doing our best to ensure a voyage that is safe and sound; and sailing purposefully and on course through calm and rough waters alike.

It almost goes without saying that any enterprise that aspires to measure up to the symbolism of a fighting ship must rely on the loyalty of its crew. And there are few leaders who do not invoke the need for loyalty—whether through a shared mission, or through compensation programs, or, for that matter, even through a climate of fear. But however loyalty may be built into a firm's values and character, the one message that must come through is: Loyalty is not a one-way street. No enterprise, no matter what endeavor it pursues, has any right to ask for loyalty from those who do the hard work required for its success, without a reciprocal commitment that the enterprise will offer its own loyalty in return. If an institution is to care for its clients, it must care too about the human beings who assume the responsibility for serving them. The members of the crew are the heart and soul of the enterprise; without their care and effort, the enterprise will fail.

In my frequent speeches to our crew, I have, on several occasions, cited this marvelous quotation from Dean Howard M. Johnson, former Chairman of the Massachusetts Institute of Technology, on the need for individual human beings to care for the institutions of which each of us is a part:

> We need people who care about the institution. In an increasingly impersonal world, I have come to believe that a deep sense of caring for the institution is requisite for its success.
>
> The institution must be the object of intense human care and cultivation: even when it errs and stumbles, it must be cared for, by all who own it, all who serve it, all who are served by it, all who govern it.
>
> Caring, we know, is an exacting and demanding business. It requires not only interest and compassion and concern; it demands self-sacrifice, wisdom and tough-mindedness, and discipline. Every responsible person must care, and care deeply, about the institutions that touch his life.

If we ask those who work at Vanguard to treat the institution with care, to ensure that it meets the needs of the human beings we serve as clients, we must in turn care for our crew. We manifest our regard for the human beings who work here by treating each individual, from the highest to the humblest, with respect. We simply won't tolerate a "big shot" demeaning one of the "working stiffs." (If I learn of it, I'm tempted to have the former do the latter's work for a day—if he or she is able to do it!) This policy carries over to a "no perquisite" rule—no leased cars, no reserved parking places, no first-class flying, no officers' dining room. One of the greatest treats of each of my workdays is to have lunch in our "galley" and chat with some of the crewmembers who are doing the work of serving our shareholders. And we trust our crewmembers. For years, I told our crew that we had just one rule of business conduct. "Do what's right. If you're not sure, ask your boss."

In addition to this list of values, we have established formal rituals to celebrate the efforts of our crew. The most important are The Award for Excellence and the Vanguard Partnership Plan. The former recognizes the achievements of a single outstanding individual; the latter rewards the collective efforts of our crew. Together, the Award for Excellence and the Partnership Plan recognize that to provide valuable services for our clients, we need the human beings who serve on our crew to uphold our values, corporate character, and spirit.

The Award for Excellence: Even One Person Can Make a Difference

When I created The Award for Excellence in 1984, my purpose was to honor those crewmembers who embody "The Vanguard Spirit." Since then, more than 350 crewmembers have received the award, which is presented in each quarter of the year to five to ten individuals who demonstrate particular excellence in the performance of their duties. What makes these awards especially meaningful is that the recipients are nominated by their peers. At an award luncheon, we quote from the nominations submitted by fellow crewmembers, commending those who "give 110 percent," demonstrate "speed, determination, energy, and smarts," or are "unflappable, dependable, responsible, and indefatigable" (to cite a representative set of comments). In an organization that serves, and is served by, human beings, the ceremony is an opportunity to reaffirm our core value of respect for the individual.

In this increasingly impersonal era, when bureaucracy and technology threaten to obscure the contributions of individual human beings, the Award for Excellence is a tribute to individual effort. Each winner receives a plaque inscribed with a phrase I have used throughout my career to recognize the potential of a single human being: *"I believe that even one person can make a difference."* And so one person can, and does, at Vanguard. Even as we have grown, we continue to recognize that our crew is a group of individual human beings, and that, no matter the size of our fleet, even one person can make a difference.

PARTNERSHIP: SHARING THE FRUITS OF OUR LABORS

If the Award for Excellence celebrates individual effort, then Vanguard's Partnership Plan recognizes the collective efforts of our crew in creating value for our shareholders. Each Vanguard crewmember is made a partner in Vanguard on the first day on the job, and, without investing one cent of capital in the organization, shares in the Vanguard Group's earnings. Because Vanguard is effectively owned by the shareholders of its mutual funds, rather than third-party stockholders, earnings are defined as a combination of the value added to our shareholders' returns by (1) the difference between Vanguard's expenses and the expenses that would prevail if our average expense ratio equaled those of our largest competitors, and (2) the extra returns (net of any return shortfalls) earned for shareholders by the investment strategies of our funds and the portfolio supervision skills of our managers. In 1998 alone, based on our assets then under management, more than $3 billion of value was added to our clients' returns. I have no doubt that the few percentage points of these annual savings that are shared among the crewmembers, in recognition of their contributions to the value created for our shareholders, are repaid manyfold by our operational effectiveness, efficiency, and productivity.

Since the firm's founding, we have consistently reduced our average expense ratio. That achievement is the result of our unique mutual structure and the energy and initiative of the thousands of crewmembers who work tirelessly to better serve our owners. The crew is continually finding ways to offer enhanced services and to save our shareholders additional millions of dollars: the introduction of cost-saving services on the World Wide Web, the development of more useful account statements, the elimination of duplicate mailings, more informative tax reporting, to name just a few. The Partnership Plan helps to reward these collective efforts.

Each spring, we distribute the partnership checks at the Vanguard Partnership Picnic. The checks can amount to as much as 30 percent of a crewmember's annual compensation, leaving little reason to wonder why thousands of crewmembers seem so enthusiastic about gathering under a huge tent in our Valley Forge parking lot and listening to some informative and hopefully inspirational comments (mine have been called "sermons," but I'm not sure that word is used in a complimentary sense!) about Vanguard's corporate values. Over the years, I have regularly reminded the crew that we're engaged in an important pursuit, serving our shareholder-owners, and that the efforts of each individual human being who serves on the HMS Vanguard crew make a difference. That sense of participating in a worthy human enterprise is evident in these excerpts from letters I have received from current and former crewmembers.*

> I wanted to congratulate you for . . . building something . . . that is a source of pride for all of us who work here. Rarely do companies possess such high standards of ethics and honesty. The best thing about your talks . . . is that you always reminded us of our importance in the lives of others and our great responsibility. We can frequently lose sight of these things in the every day hustle and bustle. . . .

> . . . Having been away from Vanguard for about four months, I have had an opportunity to reflect on the organization and what it meant to serve as an officer and crew member. I have decided that there are three things I miss most: the crew, dedication to the cause, and the presence of a strong and visible leader.

> I feel especially fortunate to have the opportunity to work at Vanguard. Vanguard, as you know, is an organization like no other. An organization with the primary concern of providing reasonable returns for a given level of risk, informing shareholders about their investments in a straightforward manner, and servicing shareholders with unparalleled levels of quality. It certainly does the conscience good at the end of each day knowing that I work for such a company.

> What impresses me about this company is the positive attitude of all the associates . . . the environment here is unique and hard to find in business today. Everyone I come into contact with seems to enjoy their job. I ask myself why are all these people satisfied with Vanguard? Because Vanguard puts a high priority on the well being of its crew—the extensive benefits offered, the opportunity for advancement, the friendly and helpful atmosphere fostered, and management's genuine interest in the welfare of the staff.

> Thank you for the opportunity and honor of serving for a great captain. Your leadership, caring, integrity and indomitable spirit are standards which I strive to emulate. The example you set every day has made a major difference in my life.

> The success of Vanguard is in very large part due to the values you have taught me, and thousands of current and past Vanguard crewmembers. Your values permeate the institution, they truly do! Asking the crew to "do the

---

*Perhaps these words should be taken with a grain of salt, since one cannot be certain of the motivations that underlie a note from a crewmember to his or her captain.

right thing" by clients while at the same time "doing the right thing" by the crew reinforces in us all a simple but powerful life lesson almost daily.

As a leader you have clarified our mission in a manner which draws everyone at all levels of the organization into your vision. This vision, and the clarity with which it is presented, create a willingness among crew members to make personal sacrifices and accomplish extraordinary things for the good of all Vanguard's clients.

THE GOLDEN RULE

The Vanguard story has been a unique combination of the unforeseen circumstances and unusual ideas recounted in Chapters 20 and 21 on entrepreneurship and leadership. As much as any of these odd twists of fate and flashes of inspiration, however, I believe that our decision to put human beings at the center of our enterprise has been key to everything that Vanguard has become. Like much of the wisdom presented in this book, the idea of treating people as human beings is common sense. It is a simplified, if dual, version of the Golden Rule: "Treat those whom you serve as stewards as you would like your stewards to treat you, and treat those with whom you serve as you would like them to treat you." Once a firm puts these ideas at the heart of its organizational values, treating both clients and crewmembers as honest-to-God, down-to-earth human beings with their own hopes, fears, and aspirations, the result shapes everything the firm accomplishes.

Many will regard this vision as utopian. And even I am not foolish enough to think that every firm in the mutual fund industry is prepared to operate as a demanding, disciplined financial service organization that relies largely on simplicity as the cornerstone of its investment strategy and on the Golden Rule as the cornerstone of its service strategy, placing its future in the hands of all too fallible human beings and retaining the good will of its clients through rough and calm seas alike. However, as Christopher Hitchens, columnist for *The Nation*, has recently noted, "Man cannot live on Utopias alone. But as Oscar Wilde so shrewdly remarked, a map of the world that does not include Utopia is not even worth glancing at." Thomas Paine, with his innate common sense, would surely have agreed.

Afterword

We have concluded our commonsense journey through the world of investment strategy, investment choices, and investment performance in establishing a simple, sensible, and effective fund portfolio. Following the investment principles set forth in these pages, I have no doubt, will make you a more successful long-term investor. Similarly, I have no doubt that a prompt return of the mutual fund industry to the traditional principles of prudent, disciplined portfolio management will make mutual funds far more productive investments. This change can best be facilitated under a structure that focuses on the primacy of the interests, not of fund managers, but of fund shareholders—the individual human beings to whom this industry is responsible.

Even as I remind you, for a final time, of the importance of common sense in establishing an investment program, and in industry governance as well, so too I remind you of the importance of "Common Sense" as my inspiration for this book's title. There is more than a passing similarity between the injustices suffered by the American colonies, articulated so powerfully by Thomas Paine, and the insufficient investment returns suffered by mutual fund shareholders. In the context of a mutual fund's relationship to its shareholders, some of Paine's words in "Common Sense" appear almost eerily prescient:

> Paine on the Logic of Representative Government: *". . . As a colony increases the public concerns will increase likewise, and the distance at which the members may be separated will render it too inconvenient for all of them to meet on every occasion. . . . This will point out the convenience of their consenting to leave the legislative part to be managed by a select number chosen from the whole body, who are supposed to have the same concerns at stake which those have who appointed them, and who will act in the same manner as the whole body would act were they present. . . . I draw my idea of this form of government from a principle in nature, which no art can overturn, viz. That the more simple anything is, the less liable it is to be disordered, and the easier repaired when disordered."*

435

The parallel situation in the mutual fund industry is found in a governance structure in which the board of directors—in theory, elected to represent the interests of a large and diffuse body of fund shareholders—has lost sight of its mission. The arrangement is admirably simple, but it has produced a disordered result. The reality is that when a mutual fund delegates all of its operations to an external management enterprise under contract, it is not the fund that controls the manager, but the manager that controls the fund. Experience has shown that neither the managers nor the directors selected by the managers "have the same concerns at stake" as the shareholders. The board too often acts to serve the needs of the mutual fund management company first and those of fund shareholders second.

> Paine on Specious Arguments against Independence: "... *these colonies sustain many material injuries . . . by being connected with and dependent on Great Britain. . . . I have heard it asserted by some, that as America hath flourished under her former connection with Great Britain, that the same connection is necessary towards her future happiness, and will always have the same effect. Nothing can be more fallacious than this kind of argument. We may as well assert, that because a child has thrived upon milk, that it is never to have meat; or that the first twenty years of our lives is to become a precedent for the next twenty.*"

For nearly two decades now, mutual fund shareholders have reaped large rewards from the returns earned by their funds. But because of high costs, they have missed much of the feast available in the much more generous rewards provided in the thriving stock market. In a less bountiful future environment, which we may well face, this substantial opportunity cost will loom even larger in its impact on fund returns. What is more, like a child, the mutual fund industry has grown to adulthood, with assets increasing fully ninety times in the twenty years. Now that they are adults, mutual funds no longer require the oversight of even benign parents, and fund management companies, receiving ever-soaring fees from the funds, have hardly been benign. If it is time for shareholder independence, and I believe that it is, shareholders will be best served if our industry's past is not allowed to be prologue to its future.

> Paine on the Cost of an Ideal Government: "... *I offer the following extracts from that wise observer on governments Dragonetti (On Virtue and Rewards). 'The science says he, of the politician consists in fixing the true point of happiness and freedom. Those men would deserve the gratitude of ages, who should discover a mode of government that contained the greatest sum of individual happiness, with the least national expense.'*"

Mutual fund shareholders are beginning to act on a parallel desire in their investments. Even as governments should provide the greatest sum of individual happiness with the least national expense, so mutual funds should provide the greatest sum of investor returns with the least management expense.

Paine on the Natural Balance of Power between Leader and Subject: *". . . small islands not capable of protecting themselves, are the proper objects for kingdoms to take under their care; but there is something very absurd in supposing a continent to be perpetually governed by an island. In no instance hath nature made the satellite larger than its primary planet."**

So too, in the mutual fund industry, the natural order has been turned on its head. The management company, typically requiring a minuscule amount of capital, is effectively the island, governing the huge continent of capital represented by the enormous assets owned by mutual fund shareholders. In today's mutual fund world, the primary planet is held in the orbit of its satellite. That result not only defies nature, it offends common sense.

In each of these excerpts, Thomas Paine inveighed against a distant, omnipotent leadership that served its own interests at the expense of its far more numerous subjects—the residents of a large and prosperous colony, who were angrily agitating for change. It would be extreme to argue that the mood of mutual fund shareholders today is analogous to that of the American colonists of two centuries ago, but the parallels are surely striking. The best way for fund investors to receive a fair shake is for them to have the funds that they own governed solely in their interest—in terms of management focus, marketing policies, and cost structure alike—with that one aim in mind. In the long run, investment success is most likely to come to fund shareholders who apply common sense to investment strategy, investment choices, and investment performance, and who recognize that common sense demands that funds be governed in the interests of those who own them.

---

* Ironically, I used this same formulation in my Princeton senior thesis in 1951: "Providing advantages to the mutual fund investor . . . is the function around which all others are satellite." More recently, in *Bogle on Mutual Funds*, I noted how amazed Copernicus would have been to observe that, in the mutual fund industry, "the giant sun would revolve around its small satellite."

APPENDIX

Some Thoughts about the Current Stock Market as 1999 Begins

Looking back on the decade of the 1990s holds many lessons for the intelligent investor. But most of us will want to look at the full range of possibilities that may lie ahead. So I have written this appendix to add some further thoughts to those expressed in Chapter 2 on the challenging task of considering stock returns in the years ahead. I also want to contrast the range of stock returns I set forth in that chapter for the coming decade—which might strike some readers as exceedingly modest—with today's prevalent "new-era" thinking about the stock market, which has gained currency as the market has risen even higher.

As the stock market soared through 1998, the ranks of skeptics who declared that the stock market was overvalued continued to dwindle. Equity mutual fund cash positions, for example, were at an all-time low. It is ever thus in the financial markets. When the bull market began in 1982, with stocks priced at eight times earnings, caution was the order of the day. Sixteen years later, with a multiple of 27 times earnings, exuberance calls the tune. With this one change alone, the speculative element of stock prices added eight percentage points per year to the fundamental return of 12.1 percent—the initial dividend yield of 4.5 percent, plus unusually robust earnings growth of 7.6 percent—accounting for fully 40 percent of the market's remarkable 20 percent annual return during the past 16 years.

Fairly Valued at 100 Times Earnings?

Indeed, in the waning days of the twentieth century, observers who believed that the market was in fact *undervalued* were making a strong case.
In an article on the editorial page of *The Wall Street Journal* in March
1998, James K. Glassman and Kevin A. Hassett of the American Enterprise Institute accentuated the positive. A four-column banner headline
asked: "Are Stocks Overvalued?" The answer followed immediately: "Not
a Chance." The writers suggested that stocks (then trading at 25 times
earnings) could safely double in price—to 50 times earnings. "We are not
so foolish as to predict the short-term course of stocks, but we are not re-
luctant to state that, based on modest assumptions about interest rates and
profit levels, current P/E levels give us no great concern—nor would levels
as much as twice as high."

Their analysis depended primarily on two assumptions. The first was
that stocks deserve no risk premium over bonds. Citing research by Wharton Professor Jeremy Siegel, indicating that real long-term stock returns
are less volatile than those from bonds or bills, Glassman and Hassett argued that the historical risk premium of 3.5 percent that stocks com-
manded over bonds could disappear altogether. As the risk premium
declines, stock prices rise.

Their second assumption was that cash flows to the stock investor
would, over the long term, grow at roughly the same rate as the economy.
When both assumptions are plugged into a rudimentary mathematical
model, the result implies that there is almost *no* price–earnings ratio at
which stocks would be overpriced. In their article, the authors report: "We
find the P/E that would equalize the present value of the cash flow from
stocks and bonds is about 100. By this measure, the stock market is undervalued by a factor of about four," indicating that the stock market, then
priced at roughly 25 times earnings, could quadruple. That analysis would
seem to be the strong form of the bullish case.

But the case did not wait long for rebuttal. "Stocks Undervalued? Well
Not Quite" read a smaller (two-column) headline in *The Wall Street Journal*
a few weeks later. The attack came from none other than Professor Siegel,
whose research had undergirded the original article's claims. He noted
that the Glassman–Hassett assumptions about growth in per-share cash
flows were in error. "Although it is reasonable to assume that aggregate
earnings of firms will grow at the rate of growth of the economy, it is totally unrealistic, and contrary to historical data, to assume that per-share

cash flows will grow at this rate without 'borrowing' from either current or prospective investors."[1]

The model in the article, Siegel noted, had failed to observe that continued earnings growth would demand additional investment in new assets such as factories and equipment. To finance that investment, a company must issue new shares, or borrow money, or retain earnings for reinvestment, all of which reduce per-share cash flows. So, Siegel wrote: "[It] is wrong to say that stocks are underpriced at current levels . . . . In no way can the high stock returns of the past five years or even the past 15 years persist."

Glassman–Hassett, Siegel, and Occam

Whichever case prevails, these forecasters are all working in an Occam-like way, relying principally on the long-term fundamentals of dividend yields and earnings growth to make their evaluations. Glassman and Hassett, in their thesis, added a second, deceptively simple variation. With the stroke of a pen, they eliminate what has been an almost infinitely variable risk-premium in favor of a single unvarying standard: a zero premium. Would that investing were that easy! By postulating that stocks have room to rise until expected stock returns equal bond returns, they eliminate the role of speculation. At that point, of course, stocks would be valued to provide future returns equal to the current yield of the U.S. Treasury bond. It's as simple as that.

The Glassman–Hassett argument notwithstanding, I am not willing to concede that stocks deserve no risk premium, nor even the slim premium that would be required based on current fundamental investment values of stocks and bonds. Simple logic says that, over time, a final outcome that is predictable on a straight-line basis (compound interest on a zero-coupon Treasury bond, for example) is more attractive than the same final outcome that is subject to wide fluctuations before the end point (i.e., a stock portfolio with a guaranteed long-term return). Nonetheless, it is possible that we are indeed at the dawn of a new economic era in which stock risk is muted, stock return is more certain, and the risk premium is accordingly more modest.

Rightly or wrongly, many institutional investors seem to be even more strongly concerned about the course of future stock returns than I am. Jeremy Grantham, founding partner of institutional investing powerhouse Grantham, Mayo and Van Otterlo, looks for nominal stock returns of about 3 percent during the coming decade, well below the range of 5 to 8 percent that my analysis, based on good fundamentals and some diminution of the price–earnings ratio suggests. Gary Brinson, head of investment policy for some $1 trillion of assets managed by international banking giant Swiss Bank Corp., is only slightly more optimistic. He looks for future returns on U.S. stocks in the 7 percent range in nominal terms. His version of Occam's Razor is based on, as he puts it, "Simple math. The dividend yield is 1.5 percent. Real growth has historically been 2.8 percent. Let's be heroic and say it'll be 3.5 percent going forward . . . which gets me to 5 percent. Add inflation of 2 percent, and there's my 7 percent. *In the long run, stock prices have to track underlying fundamentals.*"[2]

HISTORIC PARALLELS?

One final thought: There are some remarkable historic parallels between today's investment thinking and the investment thinking that prevailed in 1929. The 1929 mood was well captured by Graham and Dodd in their original (1934) edition of *Security Analysis*—perhaps the most powerful financial textbook of the century. In Chapter XXVII, the authors examined in retrospect the causes of the 1929–1933 market crash. Consider these excerpts (italics added):

The New-Era Theory

During the latter stage of the bull market culminating in 1929, the public acquired a completely different attitude towards the investment merits of common stocks. The new theory may be summed up in the sentence: "The value of a common stock depends entirely upon what it will earn in the future." Hence, the dividend rate and the asset value were entirely devoid of importance. This complete revolution in the philosophy of common-stock investment took place virtually without realization by the stock-buying public.

A new conception was given central importance—that of trend of earnings. The past was important only in so far as it showed the direction in which the future could be expected to move. Along with this idea there emerged a companion theory that common stocks represented the most profitable and therefore the most desirable media for long-term investment. This gospel was based upon research showing that diversified lists of common stocks had regularly increased in value over stated intervals of time for many years past. The combination of these two ideas supplied the "investment theory" upon which the 1927–1929 stock market proceeded. The theory ran as follows:

1. The value of a common stock depends on future earnings.
2. Good common stocks will prove sound and profitable investments.
3. Good common stocks are those with rising past earnings.

These statements sound innocent and plausible. Yet they concealed two theoretical weaknesses which could and did result in untold mischief. The first of these defects was that they abolished the fundamental distinctions between *investment* and *speculation*. The second was that they ignored the *price* of a stock in determining whether it was a desirable purchase.

"New-era investment," as practiced by the representative investment trusts, was almost identical with speculation—buying stocks instead of bonds, emphasizing enhancement of principal instead of income, and stressing the changes of the future instead of the facts of the past. New-era investment was simply old-style speculation confined to common stocks with a satisfactory trend of earnings. The notion that the desirability of a common stock was entirely independent of its price seems incredibly absurd. Yet the new-era theory led directly to this thesis.

An alluring corollary of this principle was that making money in the stock market was now the easiest thing in the world. It was only necessary to buy "good" stocks, regardless of price, and then to let nature take her upward course. The results of such a doctrine could not fail to be tragic. Countless people asked themselves, "Why work for a living when a fortune can be made in Wall Street without working?" *The ensuing migration from business into the financial district resembled the famous gold rush to the Klondike, with the not unimportant difference that there really was gold in the Klondike.*

Investment trusts were formed for the purpose of giving the untrained public the benefit of expert administration of its funds—a plausible idea. The earliest trusts laid considerable emphasis upon time-tried principles of successful investment. But these traditional principles disappeared from investment-trust technique. The investment process consisted merely of buying shares of prominent companies with a rising trend of earnings—a select list of highly popular and exceedingly expensive issues, appropriately known as the "blue chips"—regardless of price.

(Continued)

Investment trusts actually boasted that their portfolios consisted exclusively of the most popular and highest priced common stocks. *With but slight exaggeration, it might be asserted that under this convenient technique of investment, the affairs of a 10-million-dollar investment trust could be administered by the intelligence, the training, and the actual labors of a single thirty-dollar-a-week clerk.* The man in the street, having been urged to entrust his funds to the superior skill of investment experts—for substantial compensation—was soon reassuringly told that the trusts would be careful to buy nothing except what the man in the street was buying himself.

In the new-era bull market, the "rational" basis was the record of long-term improvement shown by diversified common-stock holdings . . . as exemplified by a book entitled *Common Stocks as Long-Term Investments*, by Edgar Lawrence Smith, published in 1924, in which common stocks were shown to have a tendency to increase in value with the years, for the simple reason that they earned more than they paid out in dividends, and thus the reinvested earnings added to their worth. [But there was] a radical fallacy involved in the new-era application of this historical fact.

The attractiveness of common stocks for the long pull thus lay essentially in the fact that they earned more than the bond-interest rate upon their cost, for example, a stock earning $10 and selling at $100. But as soon as the price was advanced to a much higher price in relation to earnings, this advantage disappeared, *and with it disappeared the entire theoretical basis for investment purchases of common stocks.* When investors paid $200 per share for a stock earning $10, they were buying an earning power no greater than the bond-interest rate, without the extra protection. Hence in using the past performances of common stocks as the reason for paying prices 20 to 40 times their earnings, the new-era exponents were starting with a sound premise and twisting it into a woefully unsound conclusion.[3]

If the 1929 investment environment described by Graham and Dodd sounds like today's to you (except that, in today's market, $200 buys less than $8 of earnings), I'm not surprised. Consider the similarity of the ideas expressed by Edgar Lawrence Smith in his 1924 book and by Professor Jeremy Siegel in his 1998 book. Consider today's similar price–earnings ratios. Consider the seemingly parallel roles of the investment trusts of that era and the mutual funds of this era. Consider even whether the 1929 focus on portfolios, consisting of the most popular and highest-priced blue chips in an investment trust "administered by a single clerk," isn't a parallel to today's popularity of index funds modeled on the Standard & Poor's 500 Stock Index, heavily weighted as it is by growth stocks with enormous market valuations.

But things change. Today's interesting historic parallels with the late 1920s may produce similar destructive consequences to those of that earlier era—or they may not. Nonetheless, better to know about the past than to remain ignorant of the lessons it may hold.

* * *

An interesting postscript: Chapter XXVII of the original edition of *Security Analysis* is conspicuous by its absence from the current edition. According to Raymond DeVoe of Legg, Mason & Company ("The Strange Case of the Missing Chapter"[4]), it was gradually abbreviated in subsequent editions, then omitted entirely in the most recent editions. That may be the most ominous sign of all.

Supplemental Data

Supplemental Data

Equity Fund Data

	Number of Funds[a]	Category Average				Low-Cost Quartile versus High-Cost Quartile								Index Data			
		5-Year Return %[b]	5-Year Risk %[c]	Risk-Adjusted Rating[d]	Cost Ratio %[e]	% Return Low Cost	% Return High Cost	% Risk Low Cost	% Risk High Cost	Risk-Adjusted Rating Low Cost	Risk-Adjusted Rating High Cost	Expense Ratio Low Cost	Expense Ratio High Cost	5-Year Return %[b]	5-Year Risk %[c]	Risk-Adjusted Rating[d]	Cost Ratio %[e]
LV	100	13.8	9.8	1.23	1.38	15.5	10.3	9.6	10.3	1.42	0.89	0.56	2.91	16.6	8.9	1.54	0.20
LB	211	13.2	9.9	1.09	1.07	14.2	12.3	9.8	9.9	1.23	0.99	0.53	1.70	15.1	8.6	1.31	0.20
LG	58	11.9	12.0	0.80	1.18	13.5	10.6	12.6	12.1	0.89	0.67	0.77	1.69	13.3	9.5	0.98	0.20
MV	54	14.2	9.9	1.20	1.35	16.4	11.3	9.5	10.8	1.55	0.95	0.79	2.21	17.1	8.6	1.55	0.30
MB	84	14.0	11.3	0.98	1.22	15.2	12.1	12.0	11.7	1.11	0.71	0.76	1.79	15.5	9.3	1.27	0.30
MG	90	13.3	15.8	0.67	1.33	14.3	12.1	14.9	16.0	0.80	0.55	0.84	2.01	12.9	11.3	0.83	0.30
SV	52	15.1	11.6	1.15	1.33	16.4	14.4	12.1	11.2	1.18	1.08	0.84	2.01	18.2	8.8	1.61	0.30
SB	32	15.1	13.9	0.93	1.17	15.1	15.6	13.8	14.0	0.97	1.04	0.62	1.68	15.7	10.7	1.12	0.30
SG	60	15.0	18.7	0.69	1.54	15.0	15.4	17.7	19.5	0.70	0.65	0.90	2.44	12.2	13.9	0.63	0.30
Average[f]	741	13.7	11.9	0.99	1.25	14.9	12.3	11.8	12.2	1.13	0.84	0.69	2.03	15.1	9.7	1.23	0.25

[a] Standard & Poor's indexes for large-cap funds and Frank Russell indexes for medium- and small-cap funds; returns adjusted for estimated expenses.
[b] Annual rate of return (after estimated expenses) 1992–1996.
[c] Standard deviation of returns 1992–1996.
[d] Sharpe ratio.
[e] Expenses as percentage of average assets 1996.
[f] Weighted by number of equity funds.

Data from Morningstar.
Prepared by: The Vanguard Group, Inc., June 1997.

Notes

Chapter 1

1. Jerzy Kosinski, *Being There* (New York: Harcourt Brace Jovanovich, 1970), pp. 54–55.
2. J. J. Siegel, *Stocks for the Long Run*, 2d ed. (New York: McGraw-Hill, 1998), p. 11. Reproduced with permission.
3. *Ibid.*, p. 5.
4. Peter L. Bernstein, "Off the Average, or the Hole in the Doughnut," *Economics and Portfolio Strategy* (September 1, 1997).
5. Kosinski, *Being There*, pp. 66–67.

Chapter 2

1. John C. Bogle, "Investing in the 1990s: Remembrance of Things Past, and Things Yet to Come," *The Journal of Portfolio Management* (Spring 1991), pp. 5–14.
2. John C. Bogle, "Investing in the 1990s; Occam's Razor Revisited," *The Journal of Portfolio Management* (Fall 1991), pp. 88–91.
3. John C. Bogle, "The 1990s at the Halfway Mark," *The Journal of Portfolio Management* (Summer 1995), pp. 21–31.
4. "Look at All Those Beautiful Scantily Clad Girls Out There," *Forbes* (November 1, 1974).
5. Peter L. Bernstein and Robert Arnott, "Bull Market? Bear Market? Should You Really Care?" *The Journal of Portfolio Management* (Fall 1997), pp. 26–29.

Chapter 3

1. Kenneth L. Fisher and Meir Statman, "Investment Advice from Mutual Fund Companies: Closer to the Talmud Than to Markowitz," *The Journal of Portfolio Management* (Fall 1997), pp. 9–24.

2. Gary P. Brinson, L. Randolph Hood, and Gilbert L. Beebower, "Determinants of Portfolio Performance," *Financial Analysts Journal* (July/August 1986), pp. 39–44. Quoted passage is on p. 39.

3. Gary P. Brinson, Brian D. Singer, and Gilbert L. Beebower, "Determinants of Portfolio Performance II: An Update," *Financial Analysts Journal* (May/June 1991), pp. 40–48.

4. William Jahnke, "The Asset Allocation Hoax," *Journal of Financial Planning* (February 1997), pp. 109–113.

5. *Ibid.*, p. 110.

Chapter 4

1. Berkshire Hathaway Inc., Chairman's Letter, 1996.

2. *Ibid.*

Chapter 7

1. Peter Lynch with John Rothchild, *Beating the Street* (New York: Simon & Schuster, 1993), p. 57.

2. *Ibid.*, p. 58.

Chapter 8

1. R. Lowenstein, "'97 Moral: Drop Global Investing Bank," *The Wall Street Journal* (December 18, 1997), p. C1.

Chapter 9

1. William F. Sharpe, "The Styles and Performance of Large Seasoned U.S. Mutual Funds, 1985–1994." Published on the World Wide Web, March 1995.

2. Mark M. Carhart, "On Persistence in Mutual Fund Performance," *The Journal of Finance*, vol. 52 (March 1997), pp. 57–82.

3. Burton G. Malkiel, "Returns from Investing in Equity Mutual Funds, 1971 to 1991," *The Journal of Finance*, vol. 50 (June 1995), pp. 549–571.

4. William N. Goetzmann and Roger G. Ibbotson, "Do Winners Repeat?" *The Journal of Portfolio Management* (Winter 1994), pp. 9–17.

Chapter 10

1. Barton Biggs, "A New, Higher Mean to Revert To?" Morgan Stanley (February 24, 1997).

Chapter 11

1. Carla Fried, "Protect Your Profits," *Money* (November 1997), pp. 91–97.

Chapter 12

1. Peter L. Bernstein, "Where, Oh Where, Are the 400 Hitters of Yesteryear?" *Economics and Portfolio Strategy* (April 15, 1998).

2. Excerpted from Warren E. Buffett's letter to Peter L. Bernstein, *Economics and Portfolio Strategy* (June 1, 1998).

3. Roger Lowenstein, "Why Closing Fidelity's Magellan Isn't Enough," *The Wall Street Journal* (September 4, 1997), p. C1.

Chapter 13

1. A similar study by T. Rowe Price Associates estimated that taxes would have reduced pretax (and publicly reported) returns by an even greater 3.9 percentage points in the 20 years through 1996. Donald J. Peters and Mary J. Miller, "Taxable Investors Need Different Strategies," *The Journal of Investing* (Fall 1998), pp. 37–44.

2. Robert M. Jeffrey and Robert D. Arnott, "Is Your Alpha Big Enough to Cover Its Taxes?" *The Journal of Portfolio Management* (Spring 1993), pp. 15–25.

3. James P. Garland, "The Attraction of Tax-Managed Index Funds," *The Journal of Investing*, vol. 6 (Spring 1997), pp. 13–20.

4. Joel M. Dickson and John B. Shoven, "Mutual Funds and Taxes: An Investor Perspective," James Poterba (ed.), *Tax Policy and the Economy*, vol. 9 (1995).

5. Jeremy J. Siegel, "The Nifty-Fifty Revisited: Do Growth Stocks Ultimately Justify Their Price?" *The Journal of Portfolio Management* (Summer 1995), pp. 8–20.

6. John B. Shoven, "The Location and Allocation of Assets in Pension and Conventional Savings Accounts," working paper (March 1998).

Chapter 14

1. Suzanne McGee, "Money Business in Scotland Under Seige," *The Wall Street Journal* (November 12, 1998), p. C1.

Chapter 15

1. Michael Kelly, "Cranks for Veep," *The New Yorker*, 72(29) (September 30, 1996), p. 40.

Chapter 16

1. Nicolaj Siggelkow, "Soft Dollars and 12b-1 Fees: Agency Issues in the Mutual Fund Industry," paper submitted to the Harvard University Department of Economics and Graduate School of Business Administration (March 9, 1998).
2. Jason Zweig, unpublished speech, 1997. Reprinted with permission.

Chapter 17

1. Pat Regnier, "Trouble in Paradise," *Morningstar Investor* (February 1997), pp. 14–16.
2. Kurt Andersen, "The Digital Bubble," *The New Yorker* (January 19, 1998), p. 30.

Chapter 18

1. Michael Mulvihill, "A Question of Trust," *Morningstar Mutual Funds* (August 30, 1996), pp. S1–S2.
2. "A Quick Q&A with Warren Buffett," Morningstar Website (www.morningstar.net), May 6, 1998.
3. Samuel S. Kim, "Mutual Funds: Solving the Shortcomings of the Independent Director Response to Advisory Self-Dealing through Use of the Undue Influence Standard," *Columbia Law Review* (March 1998).
4. "Remarks by Chairman Arthur Levitt, U.S. Securities and Exchange Commission," Investment Company Institute, Washington, DC, May 15, 1998.

Chapter 19

1. Keith Ambachtscheer, "Today's Financial Food Chain: Getting the Customers on Top," *The Ambachtscheer Letter*, no. 150 (June 30, 1998). Reprinted with permission.
2. Ludwig Mies van der Rohe.

Chapter 20

1. Gearhart Thatcher Lane, "The Entrepreneur in American Economic History," Yale University (Spring 1997).

Chapter 21

1. Robert K. Greenleaf, *Servant Leadership: A Journey into the Nature of Legitimate Power and Greatness* (Mahwah, NJ: Paulist Press, 1991). Reprinted with permission.
2. Steven I. Davis, *Leadership in Financial Services: Lessons for the Future* (London: Macmillan Press, 1997). Quotations excerpted from pp. 127–151. Reprinted with permission.

Appendix I

1. J. J. Siegel, "Stocks Underpriced? Well, Not Quite," *The Wall Street Journal* (April 14, 1998), p. A23.
2. Bruce Upbin, "Unrealistic Expectations," *Forbes* (July 6, 1998), pp. 266–268.
3. Graham and Dodd, *Security Analysis* (1997) by The McGraw-Hill Companies. Reproduced with permission of The McGraw-Hill Companies.
4. Raymond DeVoe, "The Strange Case of the Missing Chapter," *The DeVoe Report*, vol. 20 (June 4, 1998).

Index